Security Issues in Communication Devices, Networks and Computing Models

The importance of addressing security issues in communication devices, networks, and computing models in Industry 5.0 cannot be overstated. Industry 5.0 represents the next phase in the evolution of manufacturing and industrial processes, characterized by increased connectivity, automation, and integration of smart technologies. Industry 5.0 involves the convergence of information technology (IT) and operational technology (OT), making industrial control systems susceptible to cyber threats. A breach in security could compromise critical infrastructure, such as power grids, transportation systems, and water treatment plants. Securing computing models and networks is vital for protecting critical infrastructure and ensuring the safety and stability of essential services.

Industry 5.0 encourages the use of advanced technologies like the Industrial Internet of Things (IIoT) and edge computing, leading to increased data exchange and collaboration. Security issues could result in the theft or manipulation of intellectual property, proprietary designs, and sensitive business information. Robust security measures are necessary to safeguard intellectual property, maintain a competitive edge, and foster innovation within Industry 5.0 ecosystems. Communication devices and networks in Industry 5.0 transmit vast amounts of sensitive data, including production data, supply chain information, and operational metrics. Ensuring the integrity and confidentiality of this data is crucial for informed decision-making and maintaining a competitive advantage. Security breaches could lead to data manipulation, unauthorized access, and exposure of sensitive information, jeopardizing the trust of stakeholders and partners. Industry 5.0 involves interconnected supply chains, where multiple entities collaborate and share data. Weaknesses in communication devices and networks can be exploited to compromise the integrity of the entire supply chain, impacting product quality and safety. Securing communication channels and computing models is vital for maintaining the trustworthiness of the supply chain, ensuring product quality, and minimizing the risk of counterfeit components.

In summary, addressing security issues in communication devices, networks, and computing models is fundamental to the successful implementation of Industry 5.0. It not only protects the assets and operations of organizations but also contributes to the overall safety, reliability, and sustainability of advanced industrial systems.

Security Issues in Communication Devices, Networks and Computing Models

Volume 2

Edited by

Budati Anil Kumar
Akella Ramakrishna
Goutham Makkena
Gheorghita Ghinea

CRC Press
Taylor & Francis Group
Boca Raton London New York

CRC Press is an imprint of the
Taylor & Francis Group, an **informa** business

Designed cover image: © Shutterstock

First edition published 2025
by CRC Press
2385 NW Executive Center Drive, Suite 320, Boca Raton FL 33431

and by CRC Press
4 Park Square, Milton Park, Abingdon, Oxon, OX14 4RN

CRC Press is an imprint of Taylor & Francis Group, LLC

ISBN: 978-1-032-97027-1 (hbk)
ISBN: 978-1-032-97031-8 (pbk)
ISBN: 978-1-003-59178-8 (ebk)

DOI: 10.1201/9781003591788

Typeset in Sabon
by SPi Technologies India Pvt Ltd (Straive)

Contents

About the Editors

Dr. Budati Anil Kumar received a PhD. Degree in Electronics and Communication Engineering from GITAM Deemed to be University, Hyderabad, India, in 2019, and MTech. Degree from JNTU Kakinada, Andhra Pradesh India, in 2010, and BTech degree from JNTU Hyderabad, India, in 2007. He completed his PDF from the Institute of Computer Science & Digital Innovation, UCSI University, Kuala Lumpur, Malaysia, in 2024. He is currently working as an Associate Professor & RPAC Chair in the ECE Department, Koneru Lakshmaiah Education Foundation (Deemed University), Aziz Nagar Campus, Hyderabad and Adjunct Professor at Institute of Computer Science & Digital Innovation, UCSI University, Kuala Lumpur, Malaysia. He has more than 14 years of experience in teaching and six years of experience in research. Besides, he has published 70 research articles in highly reputed publisher journals and conferences whose indexing is in SCIE, SCOPUS, etc. He acts as Guest Editor for various reputed publisher journals like Springer, IET, Inderscience, bentham Science and Emerald publishers etc. He has authored six textbooks published by Taylor & Francis, UK, and Wiley, UK. He has been a senior member of IEEE, IEI, and IAENG since 2019 and has served as a reviewer for various international journals and conferences. He has conducted various Faculty Development Programs as a coordinator, which are funded by AICTE, DST New Delhi, India. He has organized and attended various FDPs and conferences/workshops in India and abroad and has also acted as speaker/session chair in various FDPs and conferences. His current research interests include Cognitive Radio Networks, Software Defined Radio Networks, Artificial Intelligence, 6G emerging Technologies, Mulsemedia Computing, and UAVs in 5G and 6G.

Dr. Akella Ramakrishna, currently working as the Professor and Principal of KL University, Hyderabad, India, is an accomplished Electronics and Communications Engineer with a wealth of experience in academia, research, and industry. He holds a Doctorate in Wireless Communications and a Masters in Telecommunications & Electronics Engineering from Sheffield Hallam University, UK. He started his career as a Design Engineer at Sheffield Centre for Robotics and later in CPI Electronics Ltd. and worked in an Engineering sales role at British Telecom. He has published papers in reputed journals. Dr. Ramakrishna has contributed to the development of 5G Technology. With his expertise in wireless communications, research, and industry–academia partnerships, he can help drive innovation in this field and shape the future of communication technology while continuing to guide and support the next generation of engineers and researchers. Currently, he is guiding eight research scholars. He is also associated with several professional bodies such as ISTE (Indian Society for Technical Education), CSI (Computer Society of India), IEEE (Institution of Electrical and Electronics Engineers), and IET (Institution of Engineering & Technology). Dr. Ramakrishna has fulfilled his administrative and managerial roles with dedication and creativity. He has demonstrated vision and outstanding commitment to excellence in undergraduate & and postgraduate education in engineering, management, and arts. Dr. Ramakrishna has joined KL University as a faculty member in different roles in the areas of teaching, placements, internships, research, academics, administration, and the Internal Quality Assessment Cell (IQAC). He was the Founder-Director of KLH Global Business School, Kondapur, India, and is one of the key people for the establishment of the KL University campus in Hyderabad. Dr. Ramakrishna, during his tenure as Director (Placements & Internships), has worked in different capacities and also achieved bridging the gap between the industry and academia by placing more than 20,000 students for internships in different companies in the last 10 years. He is the key person in getting several research and consultancy projects to the University. He has conducted various international conferences, workshops, and programs in imparting good knowledge to the students. He has established KL Placements and Industry Interaction offices in Chennai, Bangalore, and Pune (India) with the objective of recruiting students to premier companies in South India. He has established the PEGA UAP & Centre of Excellence in Automation Anywhere, a tool for Robotic Process Automation. He is credited for placing more than 10,000 students into many top MNCs. He has connections with more than 500 recruiters across both IT & Core areas. He has received awards from various corporate companies and from the Confederation of Indian Industry for conducting the best campus drives during the past 10 years. Dr. Ramakrishna has been honored with the Best Academic Leadership Award at the IKON – Talent Acquisition Conclave held at T-Hub, Madhapur, India, on 16 December 2022.

Dr. Goutham Makkena is an Associate Professor in the Department of Electronics and Communication Engineering (ECE) at KL University, Hyderabad, where he has made significant strides in both teaching and research. Holding a Master's degree and a PhD. in Microelectronics from the Birla Institute of Technology and Science, Pilani, Hyderabad, his academic journey is marked by a deep-rooted passion for advancing Microelectronics. Before embarking on his academic career, he gained valuable industry experience as a Software Engineer at Infosys Technologies Pvt. Ltd. for two years and as a Field Engineer at Microsemi SOC division for six months, laying a solid foundation for his research endeavors. His research interests are focused on the design and implementation of pulse-shaping filters and the innovative use of Carbon Nanotube Field-Effect Transistors (CNTFETs) for developing ternary logic circuits. A contributor to GSOC2022, he is deeply committed to the open-source community, with a keen interest in open-source FPGA and Open Lane, aiming to further the development of open-source hardware. Additionally, his expertise in creating interactive H5P content demonstrates his dedication to enhancing learning through interaction. At KL University, he has also established a drone lab, furthering practical learning and research in drone technology, highlighting his commitment to integrating hands-on experience with academic rigor.

Prof. Gheorghita Ghinea is working as a Professor in the Department of Computer Science at Brunel University of London, UK. He obtained his BSc. Degree with Computer Science and Mathematics majors from the University of the Witwatersrand, South Africa. Later, he went on to obtain his BSc. (Hons.) and MSc. Degrees, both in Computer Science, from the same university. He was awarded a PhD. – *Quality of Perception: An Essential Facet of Multimedia Communications* – from the University of Reading, UK, in 2000. His research activities lie at the confluence of Computer Science, Media, and Psychology. In particular, his work focuses on the area of perceptual multimedia quality and how one builds end-to-end communication systems incorporating user perceptual requirements. He was particularly interested in building human-centered e-systems, particularly, integrating human perceptual requirements.

His research work has been funded by both national and international funding bodies – all of it being collaborative work with other teams and stakeholders whom he had the privilege to be involved with. He has also been honored to supervise 33 PhD. students to completion and to have published over 350 high-quality Research articles with them and other research collaborators. Currently, his research pursuits are centered on extending the notion of multimedia with that of mulsemedia – a term which has been put forward to denote multiple sensorial media, i.e., media applications that go beyond engaging the by-now traditional auditory and visual senses, engaging three of our other human in a realistic manner akin to our experiences of everyday life.

Contributors

Prasanna Lakshmi Akella
National Institute of Technology
Nagaland, India

Ramakrishna Akella
Koneru Lakshmaiah Education Foundation
Deemed to be University
Hyderabad, Telangana, India

Patil Ambika
Koneru Lakshmaiah Education
Foundation
Hyderabad, Telangana, India

S. Sai Anuraghav
San Jose State University
San Jose, California

Gagandeep Arora
Vardhaman College of Engineering
Hyderabad, India

K. Bhuvaneswari
Sathyabama Institute of Science and
Technology
Chennai, India

E. Hima Bindu
Geethanjali College of Engineering and
Technology
Keesara, India

Ravi Boda
Koneru Lakshmaiah Education Foundation
Deemed to be University
Hyderabad, Telangana, India

Priyanka Chawla
National Institute of Technology
Warangal, India

Sridhar Chintala
SR University
Hyderabad, India

Pandi Chiranjeevi
ACE Engineering College
Hyderabad, India

Subrangeeni Das
Koneru Lakshmaiah Education Foundation
Hyderabad, Telangana, India

Rajib Debnath
Koneru Lakshmaiah Education Foundation
Deemed to be University
Hyderabad, Telangana, India

P. S. Devi
Kuppam Engineering College
Kuppam, India

M. Dharani
Mohan Babu University
Tirupathi, India

S. B. Goyal
City University
Petaling Jaya, Malaysia

K. Hemakumari
Sasi Institute of Technology & Engineering
Tadepalligudem, India

Irene Lee Joseph
Adi Shankara Institute of Engineering and Technology
Kalady, India

C. Joshitha
Koneru Lakshmaiah Education Foundation
Hyderabad, Telangana, India

Veera Venkata Raghunath Indugu
Mutual of Omaha
Exton, Pennsylvania

Arun Kumar Katkoori
CVR College of Engineering
Hyderabad, India

Harmandar Kaur
Guru Nanak Dev University
Regional Campus
Jalandhar, India

C. Kavitha
Vardhaman College of Engineering
Hyderabad, India

C. V. Kavya
Adi Shankara Institute of Engineering and Technology
Kalady, India

G. N. Kodandaramaiah
Kuppam Engineering College
Kuppam, India

Satveer Kour
Guru Nanak Dev University
Amritsar, India

Budati Anil Kumar
Koneru Lakshmaiah Education Foundation
Hyderabad, Telangana, India

P. Ashok Kumar
ACE Engineering College
Hyderabad, India

Kotha Ajay Kumar
Koneru Lakshmaiah Education Foundation
Hyderabad, Telangana, India

R. Kumar
Koneru Lakshmaiah Education Foundation Deemed to be University
Hyderabad, Telangana, India

Ch. Vijaya Lakshmi
Sasi Institute of Technology & Engineering
Tadepalligudem, India

Y. Sai Madhuri
Koneru Lakshmaiah Education Foundation
Hyderabad, Telangana, India

Shanthi Makka
Vardhaman College of Engineering
Hyderabad, India

Chinthakindi Nandini
Koneru Lakshmaiah Education Foundation
Hyderabad, Telangana, India

T. P. Nimmy
Adi Shankara Institute of Engineering and Technology
Kalady, Telangana, India

Rithika Pagadala
Koneru Lakshmaiah Education Foundation
Hyderabad, Telangana, India

Keerthi Pendam
Vardhaman College of Engineering
Hyderabad, India

V. K. Pooja
Adi Shankara Institute of Engineering and Technology
Kalady, India

P. Poojitha
Mohan Babu University
Tirupati, India

J. V. Preethi
Kuppam Engineering College
Kuppam, India

Thatikonda Radhika
SR University
Hyderabad, India

Shaik Mohammad Rafee
Sasi Institute of Technology Engineering
Tadepalligudem, India

Prerana Rangdal
Vignana Bharathi Insitute of Technology
Hyderabad, India

B. Mohan Rao
Koneru Lakshmaiah Education Foundation
Hyderabad, Telangana, India

K. Rasadurai
Kuppam Engineering College
Kuppam, India

S. Bharath Reddy
KG Reddy College of Engineering and Technology
Moinabad, India

M. Gopinath Reddy
Sasi Institute of Technology & Engineering
Tadepalligudem, India

K. Revathi
Kuppam Engineering College
Kuppam, India

Dedeepya Sai
Simplyturn Technologies
Princeton, New Jersey

Himali Sarangal
Guru Nanak Dev University
Regional Campus
Jalandhar, India

Bommidi Sathvik
Koneru Lakshmaiah Education Foundation
Hyderabad, Telangana, India

Bukka Sathyanarayana
Koneru Lakshmaiah Education Foundation
Hyderabad, Telangana, India

Abhishek Kumar Shrivastava
Koneru Lakshmaiah Education Foundation
Hyderabad, Telangana, India

Butta Singh
Guru Nanak Dev University
Regional Campus
Jalandhar, India

Manjit Singh
Guru Nanak Dev University
Regional Campus
Jalandhar, India

Vikramjeet Singh
IK Gujral Punjab Technical University
Amritsar, India

A. Sowmya
Vardhaman College of Engineering
Hyderabad, India

Sreedhar
Kuppam Engineering College
Kuppam, India

Gudi Srikanth
Koneru Lakshmaiah Education Foundation
Hyderabad, Telangana, India

Kurma Srujan
Koneru Lakshmaiah Education Foundation
Hyderabad, Telangana, India

M. V. Sruthi
Mohan Babu University
Tirupathi, India

Nattala Subbarayudu
Sasi Institute of Technology & Engineering
Tadepalligudem, India

G. Krishna Subramanyam
Koneru Lakshmaiah Education Foundation
Hyderabad, Telangana, India

Thatikonda Supraja
CVR College of Engineering
Hyderabad, India

D. Kavitha Thenmozhi
Lincoln University College
Malaysia

Winnie Ann Thomas
Adi Shankara Institute of Engineering and Technology
Kalady, India

Chilakalapudi Naga Venkata Tirumala
Sasi Institute of Technology & Engineering
Tadepalligudem, India

T. Venkatakrishnamoorthy
Sasi Institute of Technology & Engineering
Tadepalligudem, India

B. Vivekanandam
Lincoln University College
Malaysia

Sridhar Reddy Vulapula
Vignana Bharathi Insitute of Technology
Hyderabad, India

S. Yazhini
Velalar College of Engineering and Technology
Erode, India

Chapter 1

Effect of different vehicles' speed on QoS performance metrics and WAVE metrics on OLSR VANET routing protocol

Satveer Kour, Manjit Singh, Himali Sarangal, Butta Singh, Vikramjeet Singh, and Harmandar Kaur

1.1 INTRODUCTION

Wireless ad hoc networks are categorized into two types of user-based application domains, namely mobile ad hoc networks (MANETs), and vehicular ad hoc networks (VANETs), which are the two popular wireless ad hoc networks used in day-to-day human activities. MANET is the most dynamic and efficient wireless communication network in the modern era of information communication technology [1]. MANETs play a crucial role in enabling various end-user applications [2]. MANET is a self-configuring, self-organizing, infrastructure-less network consisting of mobile wireless devices [3, 4]. VANET is controlled by a sequence of distributed RSUs to monitor, guide, and track the vehicle movements from one moment in time to the next [5]. The infrastructure in every region holds a set of subunits such as field supporters, survey trackers, and search and rescue for emergency vehicles. The existing VANET system is infrastructure based, where vehicular nodes (i.e., vehicles) connect to an intermittent series of wireless communication infrastructure units along the urban/highway roads [6]. Unique on-board units (OBUs), which contain processors capable of handling the majority of smartphone functions and infotainments, are embedded into or fitted with the vehicle nodes. While in transit, OBUs periodically transmit a beacon message indicating their current state, including position, velocity, and other details, to the closest communication facility and other continuing or approaching vehicular nodes [7]. In order to communicate with the appropriate vehicular nodes, the request/response data packets carrying the message flow to provide service from the source—that is, either the base control station or nearby infrastructure—are forwarded through a series of wireless communication infrastructure units [8]. The infrastructure takes the liberty to process data packets periodically in the event of risks, warnings, or emergency notifications. It then notifies the closest subunits to watch, follow, and instruct the vehicle nodes to safety. The VANET architecture is presented in Figure 1.1. The communication in VANET architecture can be of two categories: communication between vehicles (V2V) or communication between vehicle and infrastructure (V2I) [9].

1.2 REVIEW LITERATURE AND PROBLEM DEFINITION

In the last few decades, routing in VANETs has been the subject of extensive analysis. The primary distinction between MANETs and VANETs, which are specialized forms of ad hoc networks, is the mobility pattern and abrupt topology changes [10]. Unsurprisingly, different ad hoc routing protocols are first created on MANETs, tested in various scenarios, and then determined to be suitable for usage in a VANET environment. As a result, in a highly VANET environment, various addressing techniques now in use in MANETs are rarely appropriate [11]. According to their role claim and route update process, routing protocols for VANETs

DOI: 10.1201/9781003591788-1

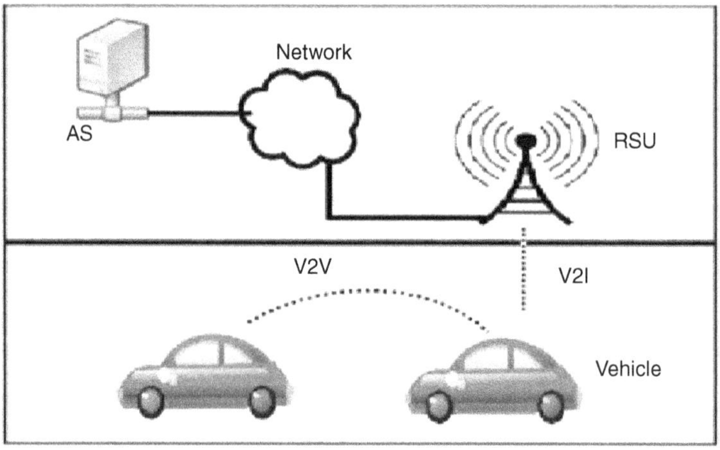

Figure 1.1 VANET architecture.

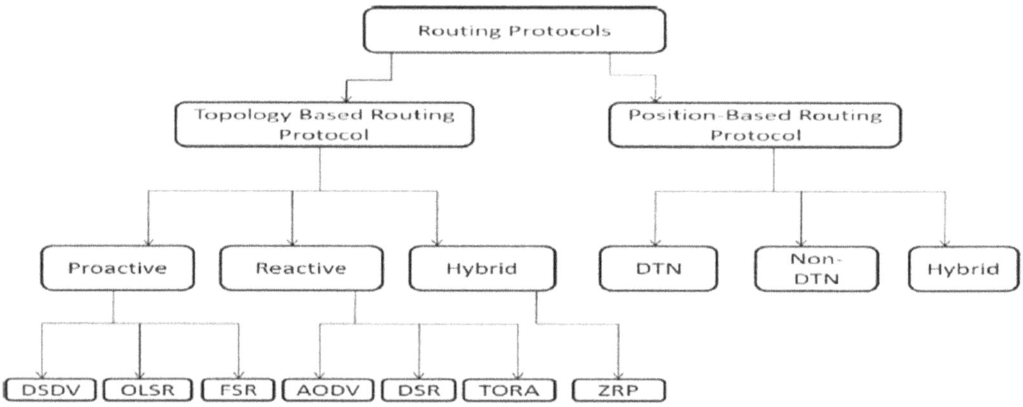

Figure 1.2 VANET routing protocols.

are specifically divided into position, topology, broadcast, cluster, and geo-cast based routing protocols [12]. In position-based routing protocol, whenever a source node communicates with the destination node, it uses its geographical position in addition to the address of its network. In topology-based routing protocol, to forward the packet from the source node to the destination node, it uses the available connection information that exists on the network. These can be categorized into three major classifications: proactive, reactive, and hybrid routing. In proactive routing, the route path that normally relies on the shortest path algorithms is chosen by the protocol. Standard distance–vector routing protocols (e.g., DSDV) or link state routing approaches (e.g., OLSR) are used. Reactive routing protocols define the appropriate routing path and retain only the routing paths currently in use until only a number of available routing paths are currently in use at any time, thus minimizing overhead on the network (e.g., dynamic source routing [DSR], temporarily ordered routing algorithm [TORA], ad hoc on-demand distance vector [AODV]). In hybrid routing, the network is split by this protocol into two regions: local and worldwide (e.g., ZRP). The types of VANET routing protocols are shown in Figure 1.2 [13].

One proactive routing technique, optimized link state routing (OLSR), takes the following processes to determine the path: (1) it sends a HELLO message to its neighbors on

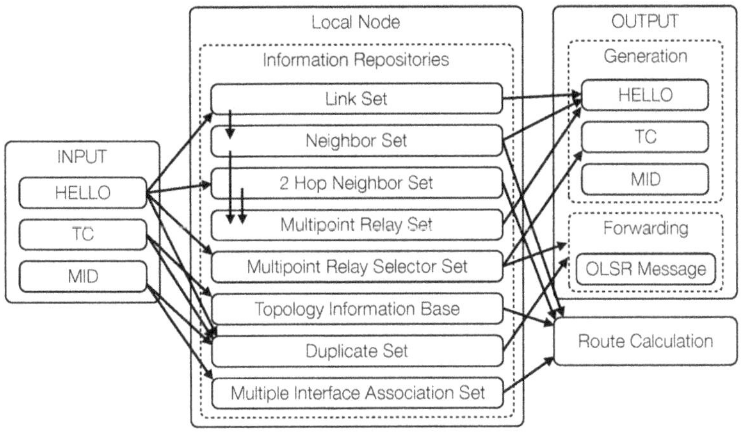

Figure 1.3 Finding optimized route in OLSR.

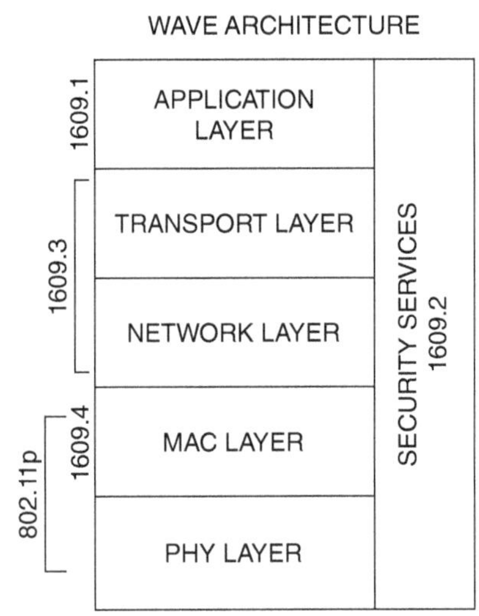

Figure 1.4 WAVE architecture in VANET.

a regular basis to gather information; (2) it uses relays to flood control packets at many points; and (3) it uses the shortest-path algorithm to choose the way. Every node is reachable along with its two-step neighbors. Messages are sent via multipoint relay (MPR) nodes and then rebroadcast by the nodes. It manages the packet overhead automatically. A partial topological graph is used by each node [14]. Relay selectors can verify a relay node's existence by receiving control topology packets from it. The origin usually uses the shortest path first algorithm to select the best route. The route finding procedure in OLSR is shown in Figure 1.3 [15].

Wireless access vehicular environment (WAVE) is the most recent version of intelligent transportation system (ITS) standards derived from IEEE organization [16]. The IEEE 1609 WAVE outlines the architecture, process, protocol set, and interface utilized to construct V2V and V2I communications [17]. The WAVE architecture is shown in Figure 1.4.

In order to examine how speed impacts protocol performance, Sami et al. [18] replicated the AODV protocol in a city setting with changes in vehicle speed. Three measures were

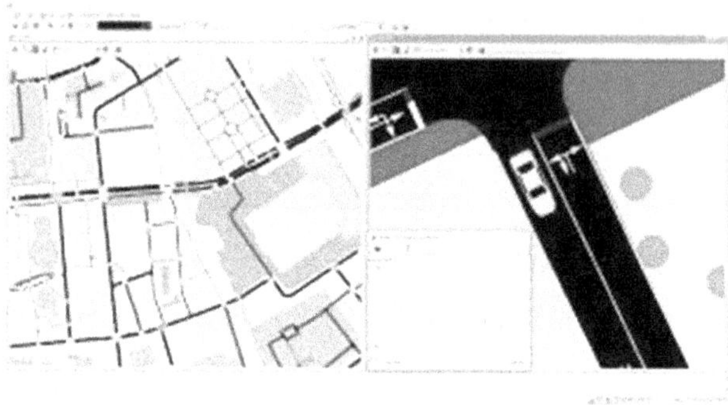

Figure 1.5 SUMO-3.0.1 tool.

used to assess the performance: packet delivery ratio (PDR), overhead, and end-to-end delay (E2ED). A speed and position aware dynamic routing (SPDR) protocol was introduced by Han et al. [19] for the distribution of emergency messages in VANETs. NS-2 and VanetMobiSim simulations in a realistic highway situation demonstrate that SPDR performs better than the current protocols in terms of average dissemination delay, network performance, and message delivery ratio. Popescu et al. [20] have discussed that more than 1.2 million people die due to dilemma zones, i.e., vehicles may decide to proceed or stop at the onset. Qi et al. [21] have done a detailed study about the dilemma zones where most of the countries find nearly 30% to 60% of all road accidents occur at the intersection points. Therefore, for designing next-generation communication infrastructures, Tahmasebi et al. [22] have discussed the use of vehicular cloud computing capabilities where, most of the time, vehicular nodes functionalities are not periodically used and maintained correctly. Thus, the utilization of resource management is kept off-grid with the appropriate nearby data centers nearby. Amina et al. [23] investigated the impact of vehicle density on the working of well-known routing protocols. The network scenario has been designed by NS-3, and Simulation of Urban MObility (SUMO) tools and various metrics are tested.

On the basis of review study of VANET, the following objectives are defined:

1. Study the basic concepts of VANET and its routing mechanisms.
2. Design a VANET scenario with movement of vehicles using NS-3.31 and SUMO tools.
3. Run the designed scenarios for OLSR VANET routing protocol for five different speeds.
4. Analyze the generated results.

1.3 PERFORMANCE METRICS

The experiment is performed on network simulator NS-3.31 [24]. Movements of vehicles are generated by random waypoint (RWP) mobility model [25] and implemented by SUMO-3.0.1 tool. One of the execution scenarios of SUMO is shown in Figure 1.5. The experiment is executed for OLSR routing protocol for five different speeds which varies from 20 mps to 100 mps in increments of 20 mps in every experiment. The list of network parameters is given in Table 1.1.

Performance metrics are analyzed over the designed scenario. They are grouped into two categories: quality-of-service (QoS) metrics (packets received, receive rate, basic safety messages packet delivery ratio (BSM PDR), MAC/PHY overhead) and WAVE metrics [26, 27, 28].

Table 1.1 Network parameters

Parameter	*Value*
NS-3 Version	NS3.31
Experiment time	50 seconds
Map Area	X = 2,000 m, Y = 1,500 m
Vehicle speed	20–100 mps (20 mps increment in every experiment)
Number of vehicles	50
Routing Protocol	OLSR

Packet Received refers to the successful reception of data packets by a vehicle or a node in the network.

Receive Rate in VANETs is typically expressed as the proportion of packets successfully received by a node to total packets delivered, expressed as a percentage.

MAC/PHY Overhead in VANETs refers to the additional information and processes required at these layers, which can impact the overall efficiency and performance of the network. The MAC layer is responsible for managing access to the shared wireless channel. The PHY layer is in charge of physically transmitting data across the wireless channel.

Average Routing Goodput is determined as the ratio of useful data of file size to transfer time. It is demonstrated as application layer throughput. The outcome of this metric is in bits per second (bps), kilobytes per second (kbps), or megabytes per second (Mbps).

BSM PDR is fundamental components of VANETs, providing information about a vehicle's status, speed, and other safety-related data. PDR is a key metric used to evaluate the reliability of communication in a network. It is the ratio of the number of successfully received packets to the total number of packets transmitted.

WAVE Packets Sent is the exact number of WAVE packets transmitted and varies depending on the application context and network conditions. It also depends on factors such as the density of vehicles, the frequency of message generation, the type of messages being transmitted, and the communication protocols in use.

WAVE Packets Received is the number of WAVE packets received in a VANET and is an important indicator for assessing the communication system's efficiency and dependability.

WAVE Packets Proportion is the proportion of WAVE packets refers to the ratio of WAVE packets to total packets transmitted or received in the network.

Expected WAVE Packets Received is the number of WAVE packets expected to be received in a VANET and is determined by a number of factors, including the programs deployed, communication patterns, and the individual use case.

Expected Wave Packets in Coverage Received refers to the number of WAVE packets that a vehicle or infrastructure node is likely to receive within its communication range or coverage region.

1.4 RESULT AND DISCUSSION

The analysis of QoS performance metrics of different mobility speeds of moving vehicles is shown in Figure 1.6. In receive rate, OLSR performed well with value 1.02 in all categories of mobility speeds. It is due to the link on which packets are sent being reliable. The packet received is also achieved better in all categories of speeds in OLSR routing protocol. It is due to the user-friendly nature of OLSR protocol. Due to the flat routing nature of OLSR routing protocol, the better performance metric MAC/PHY overhead was achieved at all

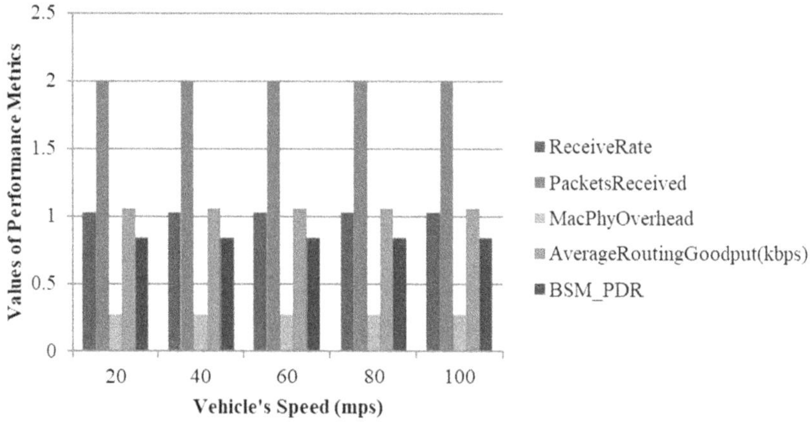

Figure 1.6 QoS performance metrics.

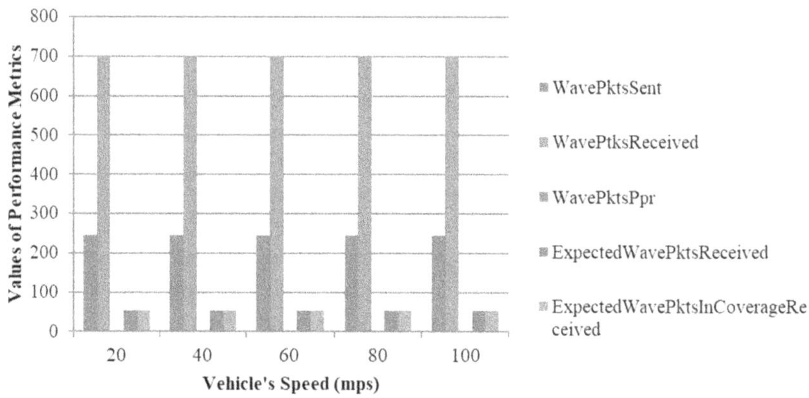

Figure 1.7 WAVE performance metrics.

mobility speeds. The metric average routing goodput also received better value with OLSR routing protocol because OLSR protocol increases the protocol's acceptance with the frequent changes of the origin and destination pairs. The achieved BSM PDR ratio is 84% in all mobility speeds of vehicles of OLSR protocol. It is due to the delivery of packets over the reliable links, and the delivery does not have to be sequential.

The analysis of WAVE performance metrics at different speeds of moving vehicles is shown in Figure 1.7. The WAVE packets sent metric showed its good performance with OLSR routing protocol in all categories of mobility speeds. It is due to its proactive routing property, and it does not allow multiple routes of travel. The WAVE packets received also performed well at all speeds due to medium congestion occurrence in the designed network scenario. The WAVE packets proportion also received better value in all speed categories because it allows a lesser number of hop counts to send packets if the target is not in the range of the source. The expected WAVE packets received showed better results because OLSR allows the shortest path route metric for all pairs of nodes. Similarly, the expected WAVE packet in coverage received also performed well at all speeds of moving vehicles due to less routing overhead created by OLSR.

The quantitative analysis of QoS metrics and WAVE metrics is presented in Tables 1.2 and 1.3 respectively.

Table 1.2. QoS performance metrics

Vehicle speed (mps)	*Receive rate*	*Packets received*	*Macphy overhead*	*Average routing goodput (kbps)*	*BSM_PDR*
20	1.024	2	0.2743	1.0577	0.84259
40	1.024	2	0.2743	1.0577	0.84259
60	1.024	2	0.2743	1.0577	0.84259
80	1.024	2	0.2743	1.0577	0.84259
100	1.024	2	0.2743	1.0577	0.84259

Table 1.3. WAVE performance metrics

Vehicle speed (mps)	*Wave packets sent*	*Wave packets received*	*Wave packets Ppr*	*Expected wave packets received*	*Expected wave packets in coverage received*
20	245.16	700.645	2.642	53.419	53.419
40	245.16	700.645	2.642	53.419	53.419
60	245.16	700.645	2.642	53.419	53.419
80	245.16	700.645	2.642	53.419	53.419
100	245.16	700.645	2.642	53.419	53.419

1.5 CONCLUSIONS AND FUTURE SCOPE

VANET is a wireless communication system among many vehicles. Its main goal is to provide safety, secure communication, and intelligent service for transportation. The primary purpose of this research is to analyze the impact of varying vehicle speed over VANET environment to improve the user's privacy and quality-based transmission as well as the usability of VANET applications. The different categories of vehicle speed were analyzed over OLSR VANET routing protocol and investigated two groups of performance metrics: QoS and WAVE. In almost all categories of speed, the OLSR routing protocol has provided significant results. Further research has been conducted for the inserting of user interface to deliver the best answer for the VANET framework. Although the majority of the characteristics needed to make VANET a practical technology depend on the use of multicast communication paradigms, this research focuses on unicast VANET routing protocols. Multicast, geocast, and any cast communication in VANET have been the subject of extensive investigation. Additional investigations should focus on average delay metrics from designed applications in order to make the OLSR protocol suitable for delay-critical safety applications.

REFERENCES

1. Islam M. and Jin S.: An overview research on wireless communication network, *Adv. Wireless Commun. Networks* 5, 19–28 (2019).
2. Raza N., Aftab M.U., Akbar M., Ashraf O. and Irfan M.: Mobile ad-hoc networks applications and its challenges, *Comm and Netw* 8, 131–136 (2016).
3. Bhatt D., Agrawal B.: Major challenges of Mobile Adhoc Networks, *Orient J Comp Sci and Tech* 10, (2017).
4. Vignesh S.: Mobile Ad-Hoc Networks: Applications, advantages & disadvantages, *Study.com*, 20 December 2018.

5. Ghori M.R., Zamli K.Z., Quosthoni N., Hisyam M. and Montaser M.: Vehicular ad-hoc network (VANET): Review, *IEEE International Conference on Innovative Research and Development (ICIRD)*, Bangkok, Thailand, 1–6, 2018.
6. Deshmukh M. A. and Dinesh D.: Challenges in vehicle ad-hoc network (VANET), *Int J of Engg Tech, Manag and App Sci* 2, 76–88 (2014).
7. Sharma B., Sharma M.S.P. and Tomar R.S.: A survey: Issues and challenges of vehicular Ad Hoc networks (VANETs), *Proceedings of International Conference on Sustainable Computing in Science, Technology and Management (SUSCOM)*, Jaipur, India, 2491–2503 (2019).
8. Cavalcanti E.R., Souza J.A.R., Spohn M.A., Gomes R.C.M. and Costa A.F.B.F.: VANETs' research over the past decade: Overview, credibility, and trends, *ACM SIGCOMM Comp Comm* Rev 48, 31–39 (2018).
9. Kugali S.N., Kadadevar S.: Vehicular ADHOC network (VANET):- A brief knowledge, *Int J of Engg Resh & Tech* 9, 1026–1029 (2010).
10. Yasser A., Zorkany M. and Kader N.A.: VANET routing protocol for V2V implementation: A suitable solution for developing countries, *Cogent Engg* 4 1–26 (2017).
11. Brendha R. and Prakash V.S.J.: A survey on routing protocols for vehicular Ad Hoc networks, *4th International Conference on Advanced Computing and Communication Systems (ICACCS)*, Coimbatore, India, 1–7 (2017).
12. Kumar R. and Dave M.: A comparative study of various routing protocols in VANET, *Int J of Comp Sci Iss* 8, 643–648 (2011).
13. Abdeen, M.A.R., Beg A., Mostafa S.M., Abdul Ghaffar, A., Sheltami T.R. and Yasar A.: Performance evaluation of VANET routing protocols in Madinah City, *Electronics* 11, 777 (2022).
14. Gaikwad, D.S. and Zaveri M.: VANET routing protocols and mobility models: A survey, *Trends in Netw and Comm* 197, 334–342 (2011).
15. Gadkari M.Y., Sambre N.B.: VANET: Routing protocols, security issues and simulation tools, *IOSR J of Comp Engg* 3, 28–38 (2012).
16. Kenney J.B.: Dedicated short-range communications (DSRC) standards in the United States, *Proc of the IEEE* 99, 1162–1182 (2011).
17. IEEE Draft Trial-Use Standard for Wireless Access in Vehicular Environments (WAVE) - Resource Manager, *IEEE Std P1609.1/D17*, (2019)1–66.
18. Sami M., Qasim O. and Mohammed E.: Effect of speed on the performance of VANET routing protocol, *Int. J. Mech. Eng.* 7(1), (2022).
19. Ruiyan H., Jinglun S., Quansheng G., Farhad B., Weiqiang S.: Speed and position aware dynamic routing for emergency message dissemination in VANETs, *IEEE Access* 10, 1376–1385 (2022)
20. Jacquet P., Popescu, D. and Mans B.: Information dissemination in vehicular networks in an urban hyperfractal topology, arxiv (2017).
21. Qi L., Zhou M.C., Luan W.J.: Emergency traffic-light control system design for intersections subject to accidents, *IEEE Trans. Intell. Transp. Syst.* 17(1), 170–183 (2016).
22. Tahmasebi M., Khayyambhashi M.R.: An efficient model for vehicular cloud computing resources, *Peer-to-Peer Networking and Applications* 12(5), 1–10 (2018).
23. Amina B., Mohamed E.: Performance evaluation of VANETs routing protocols using SUMO and NS3, *IEEE International Conference on Information Science and Technology*, Marrakech, Morocco, 525–530 (2018).
24. Kaur R., Singh G., Kumar A., and Kour S.: A review study of VANET, mobility models and traffic generator tools, *Proceedings of 5th International Conference on Contemporary Computing and Informatics*, Uttar Pradesh, India, 1055–1060 (2022).
25. Kour S. and Singh J.: Performance evaluation of enhanced manhattan mobility model over GM, RWP, Manhattan grid, SLAW, and TLW mobility models in MANETs, *Rec Adv in Comp Sci and Comm* 15, 992–1000 (2022).
26. Kour S. and Singh J.S.: A novel approach to predict mobility pattern of mobile nodes in mobile Ad-hoc networks, *J Sci & Indu Res* 77, 629–632 (2018).
27. Kour S. and Singh J.S., Singh M.: QoS improvement using enhanced manhattan mobility model on proposed ant colony optimization technique in MANETs, *J Sci & Indu Res* 82, 616–628 (2023).
28. Kour S., Singh M., Sarangal H. and Singh B.: Terrain dimensions and node density analysis of MANET using NS2 and BonnMotion, *Lect. Notes Data Eng. Commun. Technol.*, 171, 163–175 (2023).

Chapter 2

Equitable edge coloring of unionized triangular patterns in graphs

D. Kavitha Thenmozhi, B. Vivekanandam, and K. Bhuvaneswari

2.1 INTRODUCTION

Equitable edge coloring is a widely practiced and extensively researched method of edge coloring in addition to acyclic edge coloring. In addition to having numerous fascinating applications, equitable edge coloring of graphs is related to several intriguing research issues, including transmit assignments in networks of computers, scheduling issues, and route-planning challenges. For instance, equitable edge coloring can be used to arrange the bare minimum of rooms required at any given time when dealing with the scheduling problem. A graph G = (V, E) can be edge-colored using an edge-coloring mapping, which also ensures that the number of edges in each of the two color classes varies by no more than one. It possesses an edge family E = E(G) and a vertex family V = V (G).

The term "equitable coloring" was initially coined by Mayer [1]. It refers to the process of assigning colors to a graph's vertices so that no two neighboring vertices share identical color and there is a maximum variation of one in the quantity of vertices within each color class. Following that, Hilton and D. de Werra [2] presented a proposal of equitable border coloring in 1994 as a further development of equitable coloring. Doro [3] has discussed equitable coloring of a multipartite graph on its whole. Prism equitable coloring has been addressed by Sudha et al. [4]. The equitable edge chromatic count of the partition of the Helm and Sunlet graphs was demonstrated by Veninstine Vivik et al. [5], who additionally provided the algorithm. It was proven by K. Kaliraj [6] that some joined graphs have equitable edge coloring. In 2020, Bryson Stemock [7] introduced a new coloring patterns for the bird's nest graph and the Petersen graph, demonstrating that both have a total chromatic number of 4. Stemock's work also explored total (k + 1) colorings for k regular graphs. More recently, in 2023 [8], various studies have focused on equitable edge coloring on specific graph families, including sunlet graphs, wheel graphs, helm graphs, fan graphs, gear graphs, and double star graphs, formed by a union of line segments.

This chapter's primary aim is to use the idea of equitable edge coloring to combine multiple simple undirected triangular graphs to generate patterns. Regardless of whether the number of edges and vertices is even or uneven, we show that the union of numerous triangular patterns may be equitably colored with the minimal Δ colors. We also established the minimum chromatic number for the networks like V-shaped graphs, bridge graphs, and cone graphs.

2.2 PRELIMINARIES

Definition 2.1. Proper edge coloring

A graph's edges are colored by assigning the fewest possible colors to each edge so that none of the neighboring edges have an identical color.

DOI: 10.1201/9781003591788-2

Definition 2.2. Color classes

In edge coloring of a graph, edges that share the identical color are grouped into the identical color class. In k-edge coloring of a graph, there are k-color classes. If 1,2,...k are colors, then $C_1, C_2, \ldots C_k$, represents the color classes [9–12].

Definition 2.3. Path

A route with no repeating edges or vertices is called a Path P_n.

Definition 2.4. Cycle

If all of the vertices in a cycle C_n have the same degree, then the cycle C_n, $n \geq 3$, is a simple regular network of degree 2. C_n is the quantity of edges in a cycle, which in turn is its length.

Definition 2.5 Equitable edge coloring

Equitable edge coloring is a kind of edge labeling that satisfies the subsequent requirements:

1. No consequent edge in any vertex has two identical colors.
2. There is a maximum of one edge difference between any two color classes.

An equitable edge coloring of a graph H is defined as follows: for any s, t $\in \{1, 2, 3,\ldots, \Delta\}$, $|E(s) - E(t)| \leq 1$; here, Δ denotes the highest degree of the graph H, and E(s) and E(t) stand for the number of edges in the s and t color classes, respectively.

Definition 2.6 Equitable Chromatic count

For a graph H, the equitable chromatic count is $\chi_e(H)$ denotes the minimal number k of colors required for achieving an equitable coloring of H.

Lemma 1:
Using a maximum of Δ+1 colors, one can edge color any basic undirected graph H, where Δ is the graph's highest degree.

1. Equitable Edge Coloring: Where E(s) and E(t) represent the number of edges in color classes s and t, respectively, an Appropriate Edge Coloring of H is said to be Equitable if $|E(s) - E(t)| \leq 1$.
2. Nearly Equitable Edge Coloring: An appropriately colored H is said to be Nearly Equitable if $|E(s) - E(t)| \leq 2$, where E(s) and E(t) stand for the number of edges in the corresponding color classes, s and t.

Conjecture 1: If $\Delta(H) + 1 \leq k$, then graph H is equitable k-colorable.

Conjecture 2: H is equitable Δ-colorable if it is a connected graph with a highest degree of $\Delta \geq 3$, provided it is a complete graph or $K_{2m+1,2m+1}$ for $m \geq 1$.

Conjecture 3: An equitable three-edge coloring can be found where each color class is of equal size, accommodating any polychromatic of k_3.

2.3 BASIC NOTATIONS

Let's look at a graph T, which has a collection of edges represented by E(T) and a collection of vertices represented by V(T). In this case, $\chi_e(T)$ stands for the equitable chromatic number of T, and Δ(T) for the highest degree of T. The graph $T_1 \cup T_2$ has an edge set made up of a combination of $E(T_1)$ and $E(T_2)[E(T_1) \cup E(T_2)]$, and a vertex set made up of the combination of $V(T_1)$ and $V(T_2)[V(T_1) \cup V(T_2)]$, if T_1 and T_2 are graphs.

2.4 MAIN RESULT

2.4.1 Equitable edge-coloring in a triangular graph

In a equilateral triangular network T = (V, E), the edges are 1-2, 2-3, and 3-1, and the vertices are 1, 2, and 3, which are considered successive if they form a path or a cycle of length 3. An equitable three-edge coloring of G involves coloring the consecutive edges with color classes of similar dimensions, For three successive edges 1-2, 2-3, and 3-1 each edge receives a color denoted by C_1, C_2, and C_3, respectively.

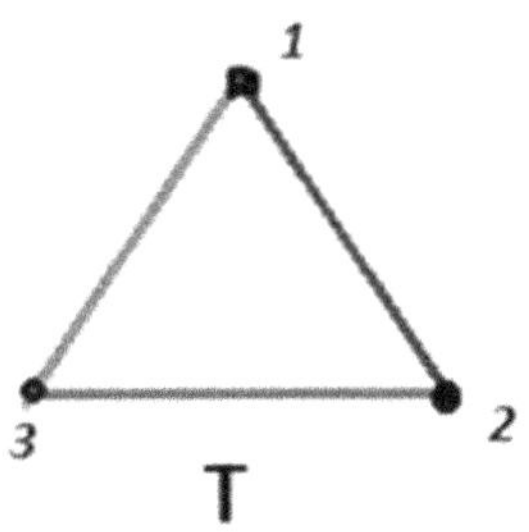

$E(C_1) = \{1\text{-}2\}$

$E(C_2) = \{2\text{-}3\}$

$E(C_3) = \{3\text{-}1\}$

Figure 2.1 (T) Equilateral triangular network.

From Figure 2.1, this is the entire graph colored in an equitable three-edge manner k_3. We define a vertex set of k_3 as {1, 2, 3} and designate the colors as follows: C_1 for red, C_2 for green, and C_3 for blue. The graph T exhibits $\Delta(T) < \chi(T)$. Hence, Δ(G) is even and T is equitably $\Delta(T) + 1$ colorable.

2.4.2 Triangular graph pasting

The union of two equilateral triangular graphs involves unifying them along a whole edge so that their interiors do not intersect, forming a new figure.

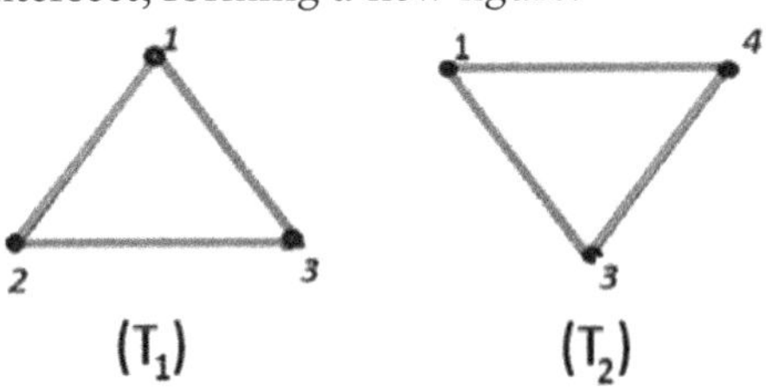

There are possibilities to unite another graph H to G at the top side of G. The second possibility is to unite another graph H to G at the right side of G. An equitable three-edge coloring k_3 can be found. It is evident that only one possibility from each set can be applied at the same time in order to generate a picture tiled by equilateral triangular graphs.

Theorem 1: Each STS allows a three-edge coloring that is equitable (relative to the vertices) and polychromatic (relative to the triples). Next $T_1 + T_2$ (Figure 2.2) is equitably k-colorable if two graphs, G and H, with disjoint vertex sets, are both equitably k-colorable.

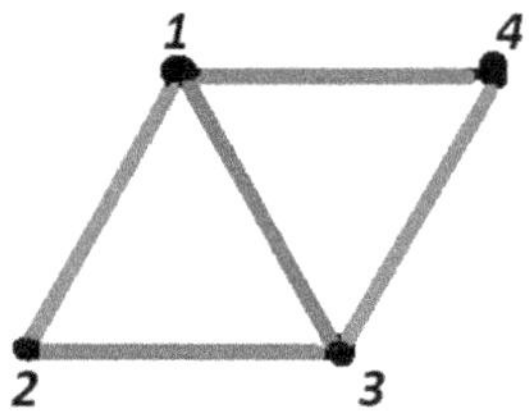

Figure 2.2 Illustration of Theorem 1.

In $(T_1 + T_2)$, C_1 for red, C_2 for green, and C_3 for blue.

$E(C_1) = \{1-4, 2-3\}\ E(C_2) = \{1-3\}\ E(C_3) = \{1-2, 4-3\}$

Theorem 2: Two graphs G and H. Let n = max $(\chi'(G), \chi'(H))$. Then GUH is equitably n-colorable

Proof: Given two graphs, G and H, each having v_1 and v_2 vertices, respectively, then $v_1 = v_2$. Let max $(\chi'(G), \chi'(H)) = n$, without loss of generality, let $v_1 \geq n$. $\chi'(G) \leq n \leq v_1$. Since G is equitably n-colorable, let $\delta_1 = \{c_1, c_2, c_3 \ldots\}$, be an equitable color partition of G such that $|c_{i+1}| \geq |c_i|$ and i is equal to 1, 2, 3...n-1.

Similarly, let $v_2 \geq n$. $\chi'(H) \leq n \leq v_2$. Since H is equitably n-colorable, let $\delta_2 = \{w_1, w_2, w_3 \ldots\}$ be an equitable color partition of H such that $|w_i| \leq |w_{i+1}|$ and i is equal to 1, 2, 3...n-1.

Assume that in G and H, the first x color classes in δ_1 and δ_2 has ℓ elements and the remaining n-x color classes have $\ell + 1$ elements, where $0 \leq x \leq n$, $\chi'(G) \leq n$ and $\chi'(H) \leq n$

Therefore, max $(\chi'(G), \chi'(H)) = n$, then GUH is equitably n-colorable.

The validity of Theorem 2 has been established for networks having a highest degree (Δ) not exceeding 3.

Lemma 2: It is possible to color G + H with an equitable three-edge coloring of five edges. Two edges that are identical in color, except the shared vertex, meeting the requirements. Every incident edge at every vertex receives a different color, and there is no more than one difference in the number of edges between any two color classes.

$|E(C_1) - E(C_2)| \leq 1, |E(C_2) - E(C_3)| \leq 1, |E(C_3) - E(C_1)| \leq 1$

Example 1: Consider the extended triangular graph formed by the union of four equilateral triangular graphs (Figure 2.3). These triangles are arranged in an alternating pattern, with edges of the same color joined together. The resulting configuration forms a larger triangle.

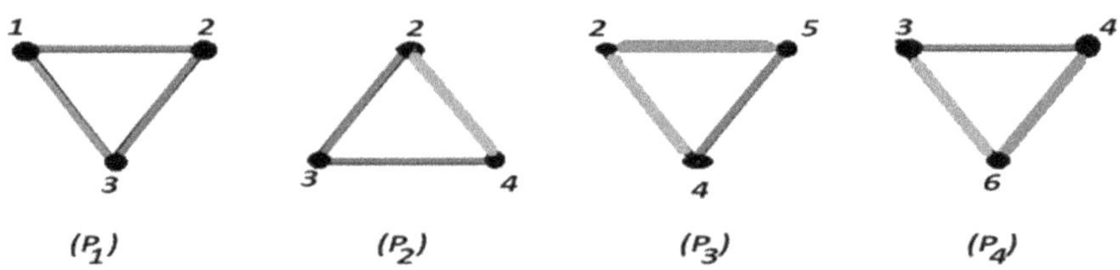

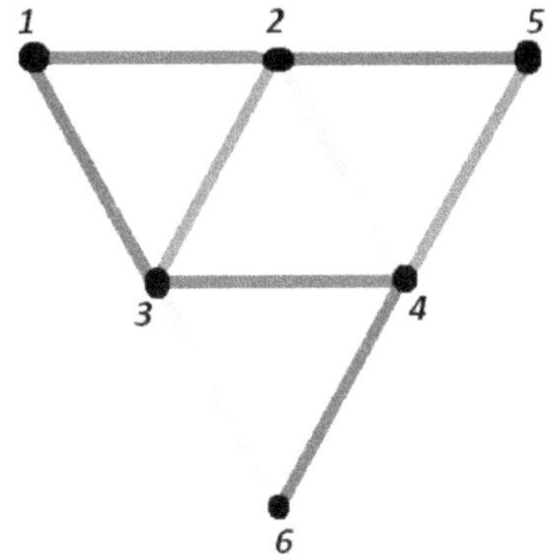

Minimum degree = 2
Maximum degree = Δ = 4
No of vertex = 6
No of edges = 9
No of colours = χ = 4
Clearly. χ (P) = Δ (P) = 4

Figure 2.3 (P) Extended triangular cone graph.

In $\mathrm{P} = (P_1 \mathrm{U} P_2 \mathrm{U} P_3 \mathrm{U} P_4)$, red, green, blue, yellow, and black are represented by $C_1, C_2, C_3, C_4,$ and C_5, respectively.

$$\mathrm{E}(\mathrm{C}_1) = \{1-2, 3-4\},\ \mathrm{E}(\mathrm{C}_2) = (5-4, 2-3\},$$

$$\mathrm{E}(\mathrm{C}_3) = \{\ 1-3, 2-5, 4-6\}\ \mathrm{E}(\mathrm{C}_4) = \{\ 2-4, 3-6\}$$

All four colors are evenly distributed among nine edges, except for the red edges, which are one fewer in number compared to the others. The occurrences are as follows: C_1 appears two times, C_2 appears two times, C_3 appears three times, and C_4 appears two times.

Example 2: Consider the extended undirected triangular graph (Figure 2.4) composed of the union of seven equilateral triangular graphs $H_1, H_2, \ldots, H_7$. These triangular graphs are arranged in an alternating pattern, with edges of the same color joined together. The resulting structure forms a bridge pattern, which is the strongest configuration.

In $\mathrm{H} = (H_1 \mathrm{U} H_2 \mathrm{U} \ldots H_7)$, red, green, blue, and yellow are represented, respectively, by $C_1, C_2,$ C_3, and C_4.

$$\mathrm{E}(\mathrm{C}_1) = \{1-2,\ 3-4,\ 6-7,\ 8-9\},\ \mathrm{E}(\mathrm{C}_2) = \{2-6,\ 3-7,\ 4-8,\ 5-9\},$$

$$\mathrm{E}(\mathrm{C}_3) = \{1-6,\ 2-7,\ 3-8,\ 4-9\},\ \mathrm{E}(\mathrm{C}_4) = \{2-3,\ 4-5,\ 8-9\}$$

The occurrences are as follows: C_1 appcars four times, C_2 appears four times, C_3 appears four times, and C_4 appears three times

Example 3: Consider an extended triangular graph (Figure 2.5) constructed from the union of 13 right-angled isosceles triangles, each having two sides of equal length and a third side of varying length. These triangles are arranged in an appealing sequence, with the differing third sides joined together and edges of the same color connected. This arrangement spans three dimensions, culminating in a distinctive V-shaped formation.

In Graph V, red, green, blue, and yellow are represented, respectively, by C_1, C_2, C_3, and C_4.

$$E(C_1) = \{1-6, 2-7, 3-8, 4-9, 10-15, 11-14, 12-13\},$$

$$E(C_2) = \{5-6, 2-3, 7-8, 4-15, 9-10, 13-14, 11-12\},$$

$$E(C_3) = \{1-5, 2-6, 3-7, 4-8, 9-15, 10-14, 11-13\},$$

$$E(C_4) = \{1-2, 3-4, 6-7, 8-9, 10-11, 14-15\}$$

The occurrences are as follows: C_1 appears seven times, C_2 appears seven times, C_3 appears seven times, and C_4 appears six times

Theorem 3: Let there be several triangular networks $G_1, G_2, \ldots,$ and G_x. Let n + 1 be the highest degree of $G_1 \cup G_2 \cup \ldots \cup G_x$. Then $G_1 \cup G_2 \cup \ldots \cup G_x$ is equitably (n+1)-colorable.

Theorem 4: Let graph G be the union of multiple triangular graphs. The distribution of each color is between $\frac{E}{\chi}$ and $\frac{E}{\chi}$ + 1 times of colors.

Proof: Let χ be the graph's greatest degree and let E be the total number of edges in the graph. Let K denote this composite graph's greatest degree. For edge coloring this graph, K is the number of colors needed so that none of the two consequent edges in any vertex has the identical colors. This ensures the edge coloring property is satisfied, which requires that each color class be used equitably.

The number of colors used in each coloring cycle is equal to $\frac{E}{\chi}$. In cases where E is not exactly divisible by χ, the remainder of this division is always less than E. The remaining colors are then distributed equally among the given colors.

Therefore, the minimum number of times a color is used is $\frac{E}{\chi}$, and the maximum number of times a color is used is $\frac{E}{\chi}+1$. This approach ensures that the edge-coloring property is maintained, meaning that none of the two consequent edges in any vertex share the identical color, and the number of edges in any two color classes differs by at most one.

In summary, to satisfy the edge0coloring property of the network G, the count of colors used will be similar to the maximum degree K, and the distribution of colors will ensure that each color is used between $\frac{E}{\chi}$ and $\frac{E}{\chi}+1$ times, achieving a balanced and efficient edge coloring.

2.5 CONCLUSION

Equitable edge coloring focuses on distributing colors as evenly as possible across the edges of the graph. In equitable edge coloring, each color class (set of edges with the same color) should ideally contain roughly the same number of edges. This property is advantageous in situations where balance or fairness is important, such as in load balancing in computer networks or resource allocation problems. Conversely, if achieving a balanced distribution of colors is the primary goal, equitable edge coloring might be more suitable. Real-world applications or scenarios where these coloring patterns are utilized. Determine which coloring pattern aligns better with the requirements and constraints of the application domain. For example, in scheduling problems or network design, equitable edge coloring could be more suitable for resource allocation or load balancing.

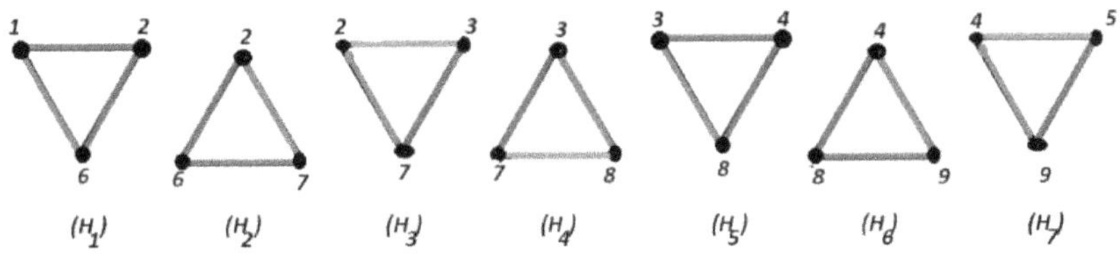

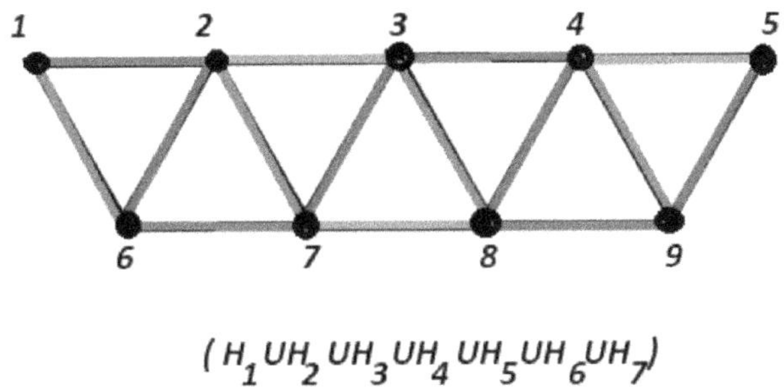

Minimum degree = 2
Maximum degree = Δ = 4
No of vertex = 9
No of edges = 15
No of colours = χ = 4
Clearly. χ (H) = Δ (H) = 4

Figure 2.4 (H) Extended triangular bridge graph.

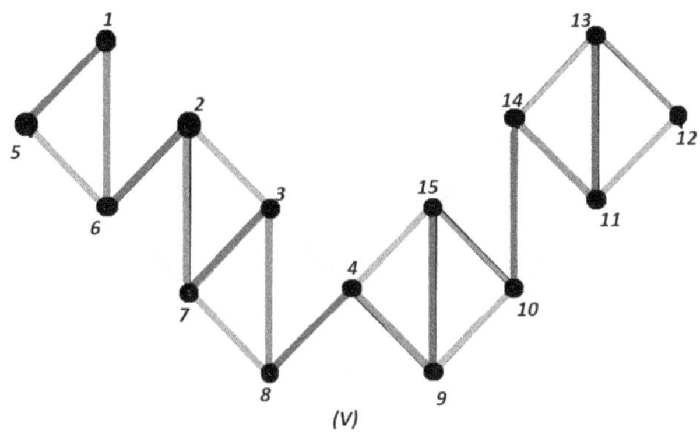

Minimum degree = 2
Maximum degree = Δ = 4
No of vertex = 15
No of edges = 27
No of colours = χ = 4
Clearly. χ (H) = Δ (H) = 4

Figure 2.5 (V) Illustration of Theorem 3, extended triangular V-shape graph.

REFERENCES

1. Mayer, W., Equitable coloring, *American Mathematical Monthly* 80, 143, 1973.
2. Hilton, A.J.W.D., De Werra, A sufficient condition for equitable edge-colorings of simple graphs, *Discrete Mathematics*,128, 179–201, 1994.
3. Doro Thee Blum, *Equitable chromatic number of complete multipartite graphs*, Millersville University, Millersville, PA 175513.
4. Sudha, S., Raja, G.M., Equitable Coloring of Prisms and the Generalized Petersen Graphs, *International Journal of Research in Engineering and Technology* Vol. 2, 105–112, 2014.
5. Veninstinevivik, J., John, Catherine Grace, Merlin, Sheeba, Determination of equitable edge chromatic number for the splitting of helm and sunlet graphs, *International Journal of Mechanical Engineering and Technology*, 9(10), 820, 2018.
6. Kaliraj, K., Equitable edge coloring of some join graphs, *International Journal of Mathematics and its Applications*, 5(4-F), 971–975, 2017.
7. Stemock, B., On the Equitable Total (k + 1)-Coloring of k-Regular Graphs, *Rose-Hulman Undergraduate Mathematics Journal*, 21, 2020.
8. Suresh, T., Srinivasu, G., *On equitable edge coloring of different types of graphs*, MUK Publications, 2023.

9. Manikandan, K., Moidhen Aliyar, S., Manimaran, S., An equitable edge coloring of some classes of product graphs, *Malaya Journal of matematik*, 8(4), 1354, 2022.
10. Hajnal, A., Szemerédi, E., Proof of a conjecture of Erdős, in: A. Rényi, V.T. Sós (Eds.), *Combinatorial Theory and Its Applications. Vol. II*, in: Colloq. Math. Soc. János Bolyai, vol. 4, North-Holland, Amsterdam, 601, 1970
11. Pelsmajer, M.J., Equitable list-coloring for graphs of maximum degree 3, *Journal of Graph Theory* 47, 1, 2004.
12. Kostochka, A.V., Pelsmajer, M.J., West, D.B., A list analogue of equitable coloring, *Journal of Graph Theory* 44, 66, 2003.

Chapter 3

IoT-based development of smart building applications

P. S. Devi and K. Rasadurai

3.1 INTRODUCTION

The world of modern human interaction shows a clear propensity for automation. As human activities of daily living continue to become more complex, there is a sense of urgency for making circuits that would support this complexity. Whereas a building benefit design and a planner are sufficient for a conventional building, a smart building requires a building benefit build, a planner, and a planner & equipment build. Residential buildings that offer comfortable, adaptable, and vitality-promoting living environment at affordable costs have been the desire of building owners, managers, and residents for quite some time. To accomplish this objective, a variety of innovations have been attempted in the past two decades, pointing to a continuous progress toward fulfilling and supporting various human needs. Modern computerization systems are smart frameworks that incorporate a combination of necessary computer program and equipment utilized in their automation. These frameworks ease the implementation of vital capacities such as door opening, entryway opening, lighting, fire suppression, and security. Some building automation frameworks can also offer better alarm notification for various crisis situations.

Be that as it may, current building applications have quite a few things in common, such as comprehensive capacities within a small space, that cannot be overseen in general design regardless of the extent of potential for future applications. European Union–backed Building as a Benefit (BaaS) deals with this and other issues that offer comprehensive programmatic ways of future commercial building administration and advancement, with adaptable and cost-efficient integration of specific administrations. In the modern urban framework, the advancement of innovation has compelled the concept of smart buildings, revolutionizing the way we see, connected with, and manage our built environments. At the heart of this change lies the amalgamation of Internet of Things (IoT) capabilities with building administration frameworks, displaying a worldwide move toward smart, connected, responsive architectures. This chapter delves into the execution of an IoT door for a comprehensive smart building management system (SBMS). Our focus is on the consistent integration of four crucial applications: the smart door, smart light, smart plug, and smart energy meter. Each of these applications includes a set of components and functionalities to optimize different features of building operations.

The smart lighting framework leverages node MCU, light-dependent resistor (LDR), LED driver, and LEDs to offer energy-efficient lighting arrangements. The smart plug, utilizing node MCU, Blink app, relay module, and fundamental electrical components, promotes expanded control and monitoring of electrical appliances, improving client comfort and energy savings. The smart door, consisting of a node MCU, servo engine, and smart door components, allows secure automated entry and exit. Complementing these functionalities,

DOI: 10.1201/9781003591788-3

the smart energy meter, comprising sensors, an energy meter, and a comprehensive interface, enables clients to view energy utilization in real time, cultivating educated decision-making for assets optimization.

Central to the operation and administration of these applications is the IoT Blink app, acting as a fully connected control interface for clients to direct and screen these frameworks remotely. Moreover, the utilization of IoT UBIDOTS empowers comprehensive information visualization for the smart energy meter, giving noteworthy analytics to upgrade energy efficiency and supportability inside the building.

This chapter traces the engineering system, detailed components, functionalities, and the interconnected nature of these applications inside the IoT-driven SBMS. It aims to explain the transformative potential of such a framework in optimizing building operations, improving client involvement, and cultivating maintainability for present-day urban living.

Section 3.2 presents the review of literature pertaining to the subject. Section 3.3 presents the concept of SBMS, and Section 3.4 details the implementation strategy. Section 3.5 proposes the testing approach for the new system. Section 3.6 concludes with the suggestions for and scope of future applications.

3.2 LITERATURE REVIEW

Kamble et al. [1] present an automatic gate control system using Arduino and Bluetooth technology. It emphasizes the ease of access and automation provided by Bluetooth communication for gate control in smart buildings. Asha et al. [2] introduce an RFID-based system for automated gate control, highlighting its advantages in enhancing security and efficiency in managing access to buildings. Bhutada et al. [3] discuss a gate sensor detection system using the ESP8266 Wi-Fi module, illustrating its application in smart building systems for real-time monitoring and control. Oh and Yim [4] explore the use of the ESP8266 Wi-Fi module in developing monitoring systems, highlighting its potential for various IoT applications in smart buildings. Xiao and Xu [5] present a web-based interface for robot control, demonstrating the integration of web technologies with IoT devices for smart building automation. Hamidi and Effendi [6] describe a heart rate monitoring system that uses web-based technologies, illustrating the application of IoT in health monitoring within smart buildings. Győrödi et al. [7] evaluate MySQL and MongoDB databases for their capabilities in supporting online platforms, crucial for data management in IoT applications for smart buildings. Asiminidis and Kokkonis [8] evaluate the performance of various database systems in IoT applications, focusing on their suitability for smart building applications. Marhoon and Mahdi [9] discuss the design and implementation of smart home appliances, emphasizing the integration of IoT technologies to enhance home automation. Dwarakanath and Sanjay [10] describe an Arduino-based system for automatic railway gate control and obstacle detection, applicable to smart building security and automation. Wicaksono and Rahmatya [11] explore the implementation of Arduino and ESP32 CAM for smart home applications, focusing on the integration of IoT devices for home automation. Hazhari and Azizi [12] present a smart delivery agent system that uses IoT technologies to automate delivery processes within smart buildings. Azad [13] focuses on IoT-based home automation using Bluetooth, highlighting the security enhancements made to protect smart building systems. Omijeh and Ajabuego [14] introduce a metal detection system using microcontrollers and GSM technology, applicable to security in smart buildings. Bhattacharyya [15] discusses a Bluetooth-controlled metal detector robot, showcasing its application in enhancing security within smart buildings.

3.3 BASIC FUNCTIONS OF SBMS

To improve human comfort when it comes to dwelling living, numerous building frameworks have been automated, with the goal of networking every detail of residential life while decreasing costs. The building superstructure is constructed with electronic circuits, controllers, sensors (and their supporting equipment), and current generators. Further automation for the office building environment is also made possible by the incorporation of smart circuits and appliances. The full picture of SBMS functions is given in Figure 3.1.

3.3.1 Problem statement

The chapter for the most part examines building automation frameworks and building management systems (BMS) for the administration of various building parameters. Most of the arrangements in the existing BMS do not support automation, but a few of the papers examine automation with limited objectives or as future work. The proposed arrangements take decision-making out of the hands of the human end-user, which is an essential difference from the existing BMS with its limited energy efficiency and security automation, i.e., turning the lights on or off as the system detects a person walking by, activation of sprinklers upon detection of fire by smoke detectors, etc. Current BMS also does not improve office administration or interior comfort. Additionally, commercially accessible BMS frameworks have very particular sets of capacities chosen by the builder. If additional capacities, such as increased automation, are required, the supplier will provide them only at an additional (universally considerable) cost. As an alternative, we propose a comprehensive BMS that covers what the current BMS lacks, based on a greatly compatible/scalable framework due to quick information collection and programmed control.

3.3.2 Solution

Progress in innovation is a live of illustration of this concept. It is difficult for a person to imagine – and may even appear concerning to some – that all or nearly all functions in a single building can be done without manual input from a human being. Individuals, for the most part, still have to came out of their vehicles to physically open doors to their dwellings, which, in the long run, is wasteful of both time and effort. The concept of smart building applications utilizing IoT comes in mind as a viable solution to a problem like this. Security is another vital issue when it comes to dwelling entryways – and which can also be solved by a device like a smart door. This would allow not only to lock and unlock doors from a considerable distance (not even requiring a line of sight) but also to monitor visitors and other residents for the purpose of allowing (or not allowing) them access to the dwelling.

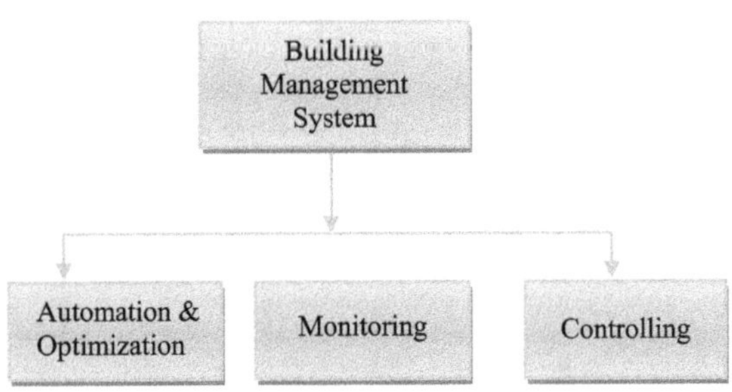

Figure 3.1 Basic function of SBMS.

3.4 PROPOSED METHOD

The most fundamental requirements for building automation are to guarantee comfort and security for clients by controlling the building's mechanicals while minimizing energy expenditure. Ensuring comfort implies creating ideal conditions in terms of lighting and temperature and integrated control of energy outlets. Ensuring security implies monitoring various parts of the interior and nearby exterior and controlling who has access to automatically secured regions of the building. Numerous computerized building energy management applications are commercially available to screen and control energy utilization. These rely on the physical equipment inside the building, which limits their scope of operation. Cloud computing and cloud-based access address these limitations by equipping the controlling applications with adaptable assets and removing them from the immediate vicinity of the building they control. Applications such as smart lighting system, smart plug, smart door, and smart energy meter represent an essential part of such new and improved systems.

3.4.1 Architectures

i. Smart Lighting System, Smart Plug, and Smart Gate
ii. Smart Power Meter

Figures 3.2 and 3.3 shows the block diagram of the proposed system. It contains different sensors and functions.

3.4.2 Working

3.4.2.1 *Smart lighting system*

A smart lighting system consolidates networked clusters of house lights. It permits office managers to remotely control house lights while keeping track of energy utilization. The proposed IoT-based framework allows for considerable energy savings. The proposed system utilizes light-dependent resistors (LDRs) and node MCU (ESP8266) for smart network

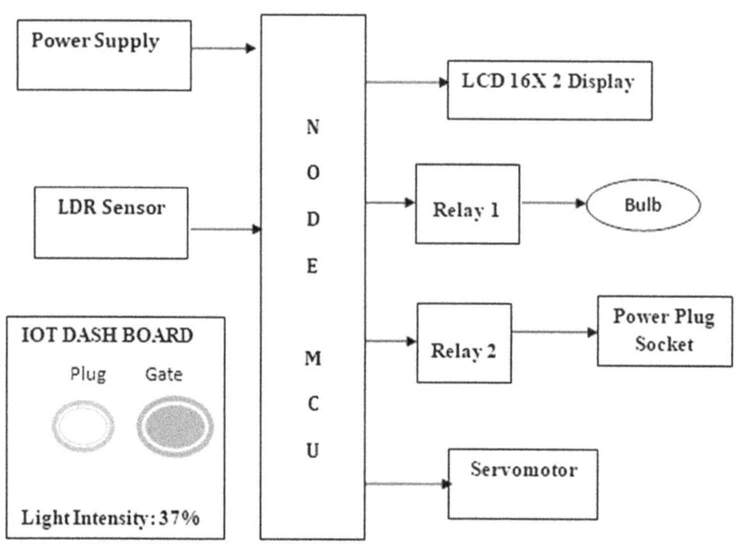

Figure 3.2 Proposed architecture for smart lighting, smart plug, and smart gate system.

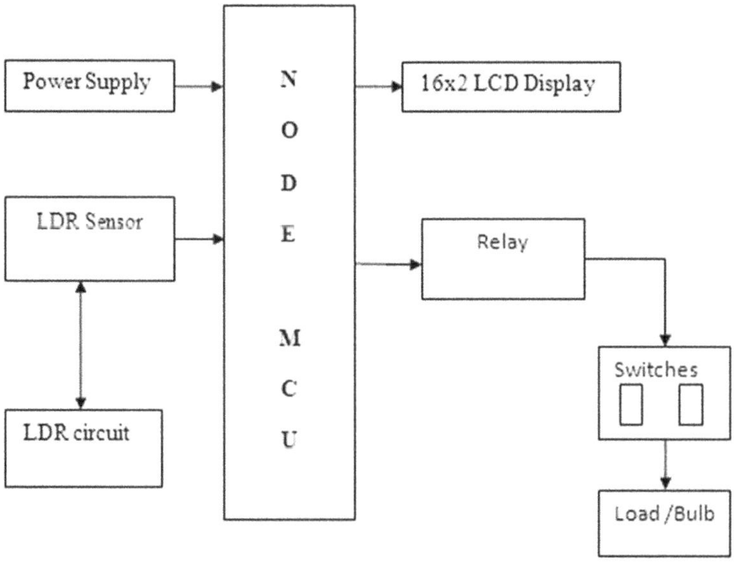

Figure 3.3 Proposed architecture for smart power.

creation. The role of the LDR is to recognize changes in lighting levels at different times of day and to both adjust brightness and utilize the ON/OFF function as necessary.

3.4.2.2 *Smart plug*

A smart plug is a control device that plugs into a conventional electrical outlet and turns it into a smart home space organizer, permitting a user to control anything plugged into it using a smartphone app or via voice through a virtual partner. In a way, a smart plug allows the user to give other home appliances a "smart" upgrade without actually buying things like a smart coffeemaker or a table lamp. For the most improvement and consistency, smart plugs should interface through the house Wi-Fi either directly or through an extender.

3.4.2.3 *Smart door*

A programmed entryway is one of the most ideal household gadgets, expected to streamline access to a dwelling. A system like a smart door reduces the need for direct physical control, resulting in considerable time savings through functions like remote access and facial recognition. One way to control a smart door is through a smartphone app. The smartphone is integrated with node MCU while node MCU is interfaced with a microcontroller. Microcontrollers are, in turn, connected to locks and servo motors necessary to operate the physical door.

3.4.3 Hardware requirements

1. Node MCU(ESP8266)
2. Relay
3. LCD display
4. Power meter
5. LDR sensor
6. Servo motor

3.4.4 Software requirements

3.4.4.1 *Arduino IDE*

Arduino IDE is an open-source program that simplifies coding by transferring any typed code into the Arduino board; the transferred code contains the program that depicts the working of the handle. The primary advantage is the computer program can be utilized in any Arduino board. The Arduino can be integrated with a wide assortment of sensors like temperature, accelerometer, and heartbeat monitor.

3.4.4.2 *UBIDOTS*

The essentials components of any IoT application are UBIDOTS. which are gadgets, factors, manufactured factors motor, dashboards, and occurrences.

3.4.4.3 *Blink app*

The Blink app serves as an interface, enabling clients to consistently control, monitor, and activate their smart domestic or building appliances and gadgets, promoting comfort, security, and efficiency in the associated environment.

3.5 EXPERIMENTAL RESULTS

The hardware setup is designed using different sensors. The LDR sensor is used to measure light intensity. The parameters are measured and transferred to a smartphone via IoT. The hardware design is shown in Figure 3.4.

Figure 3.4 shows the hardware setup of IoT-based smart lighting, smart plug and smart door systems. Data from input sensors are transmitted to the node MCU controller. LCD display shows the displayed output of different applications.

Figure 3.5 shows that when no light is detected in the interior, the system automatically turns them on. The corresponding data are sent to a cloud. These applications of data are communicated via IoT as shown in Figure 3.6.

Figure 3.7 shows the light intensity value in cloud (UBIDOTS) when lights are on in the building.

Figure 3.8 shows that the switch available in cloud to control the ON and OFF functions for the smart plug. Smart plug application condition is displayed in LCD as shown in Figure 3.9.

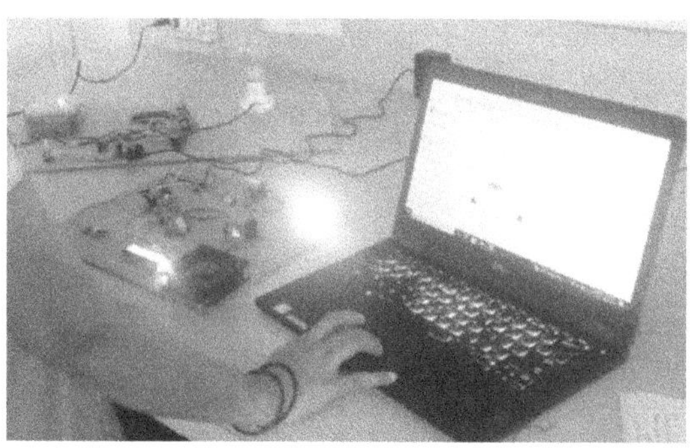

Figure 3.4 Hardware setup.

Figure 3.5 LCD indicates lights ON when no light is detected.

Figure 3.6 LCD shows data being sent via IoT.

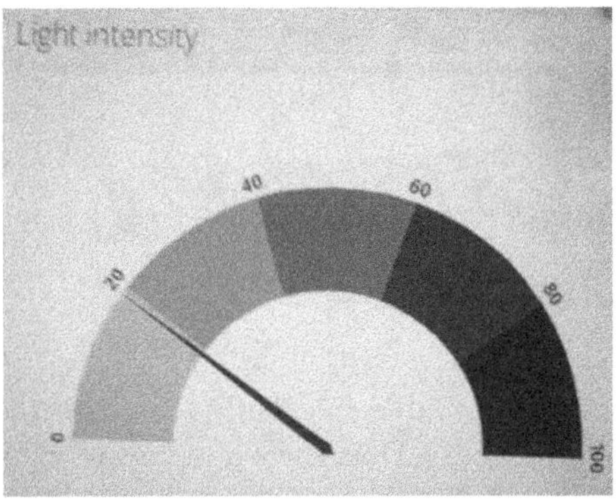

Figure 3.7 Light intensity value in cloud (UBIDOTS).

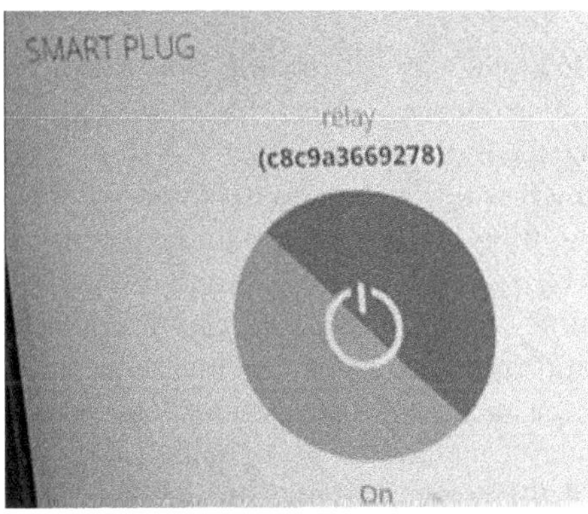

Figure 3.8 Smart plug switch in cloud.

Figure 3.9 LCD shows the condition when the smart plug is on.

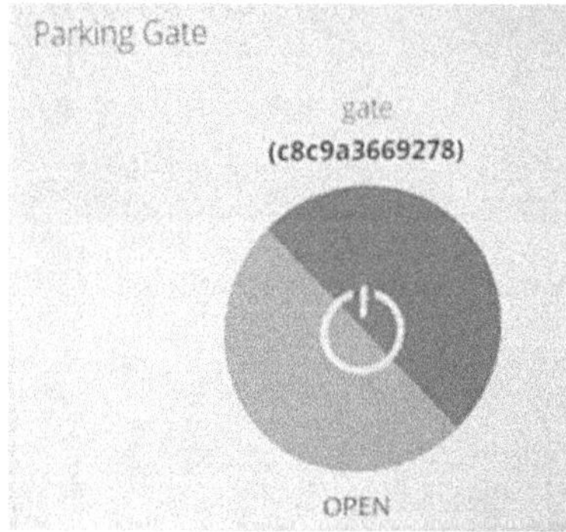

Figure 3.10 Smart gate switch in cloud.

Figure 3.11 LCD shows the smart gate condition.

Figure 3.10 shows the switch available in cloud to control the smart door. Smart door application condition is displayed in LCD as shown in Figure 3.11.

3.6 CONCLUSION

The implementation of an IoT gateway integrating four distinct applications – smart door, smart light, smart plug, and smart energy meter – has demonstrated the potential for creating a cohesive and efficient smart building management system. Each application, comprising specific components and functionalities, has contributed to enhancing different aspects of building operations: smart lighting offers adaptive and energy-efficient illumination through node MCU, LDR, LED driver, and LED bulbs. Smart plug facilitates remote control and monitoring of devices via node MCU, Blink app, relay modules, and AC plugs. Smart door ensures secure access and automated entry/exit points using node MCU, servo motor, and gate mechanisms. Smart energy meter provides comprehensive insights into energy consumption through sensors, an energy meter, and IoT-enabled data visualization via UBIDOTS. Control and management of these applications through the Blink app and UBIDOTS have brought forth convenience, remote accessibility, and data-driven insights into building operations, contributing to enhanced efficiency and user experience.

3.6.1 Future scope

Further development of automation features is essential for scheduling, adaptive controls, and machine learning algorithms to optimize energy usage and user convenience. Strengthening security measures in the smart gate system shows potential for incorporating facial recognition or advanced authentication methods.

REFERENCES

[1] Kamble, V., Taralekar, S.S., Kharat, A.P.., and Shinde, P.P., Arduino Based Automatic Gate Control Using Bluetooth, *International Journal of Research in Engineering and Technology*, vol.6, pp. 62–63, e ISSN: 2319-1163 pISSN: 2321-7308, January 2017.

[2] Asha, N., Navaz, A. S. S., Jayashree, J., Vijayashree, J.., RFID Based Automated Gate System, *ARPN Journal of Engineering and Applied Sciences*, vol.*13*, pp. 8901–8906, ISSN 1819-6608, November 2018.

[3] Bhutada, S., Tharuni, M.K., Kumar, B.V., Ragadeepthi, T., Gate Sensor Detection System Using ESP8266, *International Research Journal of Engineering and Technology*, vol.5 Issue:04, pp. 2037–2039, eISSN: 2395-0056 p-ISSN: 2395-0072, April 2018.

[4] Oh, T.G., Yim, C.H., Kim, G.S., ESP8266 Wi-Fi Module for Monitoring System Application, *Global Journal Of Engineering Science And Researches*, vol.4, pp. 1–6, ISSN 2348-8034, January 2017.

[5] Xiao, Z., Xu, Y., Web-Based Robot Control Interface, *IOP Conference Series: Earth and Environmental Science*, vol. 252, no. 04, pp. 2–9, ISSN: 1755-1315, April 2019.

[6] Hamidi, E.A.Z., Effendi, M.R., Ramdani, F., Heart Rate Monitoring System Based on Website. *Journal of Physics: Conference Series*, vol.1402 Issue:04, pp. 1–6, e-ISSN: 17426588 p-ISSN:17426596, December 2019.

[7] Gyorodi, C., Olah, I.A., Bandici, L., A Comparative Study Between the Capabilities of MySQl Vs. MongoDB as a Back-End for an Online Platform, *International Journal of Advanced Computer Science and Applications*, vol. 7, Issue:1, pp. 73–78, e-ISSN: 2156-5570 p-ISSN: 2158-107X, 2016.

[8] Asiminidis, C., Kokkonis, G., Kontogiannis, S., Database Systems Performance Evaluation for IoT Applications, *International Journal of Database Management Systems*, vol. 10 Issue: 6, pp. 1–14, e-ISSN - 2394-4196 pISSN - 2350-0921, December 2018.

[9] Marhoon, H.M., Mahdi, M.I., Hussein, E.D., Ibrahim, A.R., Designing and Implementing Applications of Smart Home Appliances, *Modern Applied Science*, vol. 12, Issue:12, e-ISSN 1913-1852 p-ISSN 1913-1844, November 2018.

[10] Dwarakanath, S.K., Sanjay, S.B., Soumya, G.B., Arjun, V., Vivek, R., Arduino Based Automatic Railway Gate Control and Obstacle Detection System, *International Journal of Advanced Research in Electrical, Electronics and Instrumentation Engineering*, Vol. 5, Issue:5, pp. 4335–4341, e-ISSN: 2278 – 8875 p-ISSN: 2320 – 3765, May 2016.

[11] Wicaksono, M.F., Rahmatya, M.D., Implementasi Arduino dan ESP32 CAM untuk Smart Home, *Journal Teknologi dan Informasi (JATI)*, vol.10 Issue:1, pp. 40–51, e-ISSN 2655-6839 p-ISSN 2088-2270, March 2020.

[12] Hazhari, M.H.B., Azizi, M.A.B., Zariman, A.B., Smart Delivery Agent, *International Journal of Recent Technology and Applied Science*, vol.12, Issue:01, pp. 36–47, e-ISSN: 2721-7280 p-ISSN: 2721-2017, March 2020.

[13] Azad, A.K. IoT Based Home Automation Using Bluetooth with Security Enhancement, *International Journal of Innovative Science and Research Technology*, vol.4, Issue: 12, pp. 1179–1182, ISSN: 2456-2165, December 2019.

[14] Omijeh, B.O., Ajabuego, G.O., Osikibo, L.T., Microcontroller-Based Metal Detection System with GSM Technology, *IOSR Journal of Electrical and Electronics Engineering*, vol.10, Issue:01, pp. 80–87, e-ISSN: 2278-1676 p-ISSN: 2320-3331, January-February 2015.

[15] Bhattacharyya, A., Bluetooth Controlled Metal Detector Robot, *ADBU Journal of Electrical and Electronics Engineering (AJEEE)*, vol.1, Issue:01, pp. 1–5, ISSN: 2582-0257, May 2017.

Chapter 4

Secure biometric authentication of E-Passport system

Nattala Subbarayudu, M. Gopinath Reddy, M.V. Sruthi, Chilakalapudi Naga Venkata Tirumala, M. Dharani, and T. Venkatakrishnamoorthy

4.1 INTRODUCTION

An e-passport works on the potential of the embedded rectangular antenna type electronic chip of 64-kilobyte storage. An e-passport in India with an electronic data chip gives an added layer of security compared to a regular one. It better links a passport to its original owner and prevents counterfeiting. Generally, a regular passport, or machine-readable passport (MRP), has data pages with printed information about the owner that an optical reader can scan. Biometric authentication uses physical characteristics, such as fingerprints, iris scans, or retina scans, to verify identity. Depending on the security requirements, one or multiple characteristics can be used. Typically, these physical traits are linked to a username, which is then used for decision-making post-authentication. Sometimes users must enter their username during authentication, while other times the system determines the username by examining the biometric sample. Devices employing biometric authentication compare the provided sample to a stored biometric template or identifier, which must be stored in a database. This method is increasingly popular for purposes such as network logins and is often combined with smart cards in high-security environments.

4.2 PERIPHERALS

Radiofrequency identification (RFID) technology is increasingly being utilized across various sectors for a range of applications. RFID facilitates wireless data collection by allowing readers to interact with electronic tags attached to objects, enabling identification and other functions. This chapter presents a do-it-yourself project for developing an Arduino RFID access control system. By using an Arduino UNO and an EM-18 RFID reader module, this system can control a light-emitting diode (LED) and a relay. The project includes a circuit schematic and an Arduino sketch for guidance. RFID readers come in two types: fixed and mobile. These network-connected devices can be portable or permanently installed. They use radio waves to transmit signals that activate the tag, which then sends a signal back to the reader's antenna, translating it into data. A buzzer is an electronic device used to produce sound, with the piezo buzzer operating on the inverse piezoelectric principle discovered by Jacques and Pierre Curie in 1880. This principle involves generating electricity when mechanical pressure is applied to certain materials, known as piezoelectric materials, and vice versa. Organic light-emitting diodes (OLED) represent a relatively new and rapidly advancing display technology. While many flexible OLED panels are already in use, next-generation displays are under development, promising innovations such as foldable, rollable, and stretchable displays. The next wave of OLED displays is expected to focus on foldable panels, potentially

 DOI: 10.1201/9781003591788-4

transforming mobile devices with phones that unfold into tablets and smartwatches that expand into smartphone-sized displays. An LED emits light when an electric current passes through it, which act as input.

4.3 LITERATURE SURVEY

Vandana et al. [1] focuses on biometric identification and verification system to secure privacy of travelers' information stored in e-passports. It ensures that biometric data, such as fingerprints and iris scans, are accessed only by authorized passport inspection systems. The study presents four schemes for verifying inspection systems at border control to enhance information privacy. Raghavendra [2] discusses a new finger vein sensor that captures patterns from multiple fingers in a single attempt. This low-cost sensor uses a single camera and a physical structure to guide illumination across multiple fingers. Honade et al. [3] developed an electronic passport using RFID, which describes programming techniques for creating valid electronic identification documents. The system attaches an electronic signature to the document, encrypting the data to ensure security. This electronic passport serves as a legal form of identification. Hamad et al. [4] developed a secure authentication system for e-passport detection and verification, which proposes the RFID-based location authentication protocol (RFIDLAP) for e-passport detection and verification. RFIDLAP aims to reduce passenger lead time at border control and enhance processing efficiency without increasing human resources. It establishes ultra-secure access control between RFID tags and readers. Ioana et al. [5] suggested future schemes for stronger verification of the access rights of border control inspection systems by analyzing the security mechanisms of integrated e-passports, focusing on threats, security, and privacy issues. The study discusses the design and development of e-passports with biometric access control systems and the use of unique cryptographic keys during validation to secure passport data. Kundra et al. [6] analyze the recent technologies used in e-passport systems, specificlly in response to increased terrorist and illegal attacks. This paper highlights the importance of stringent passport verification processes to enhance security and prevent fraudulent activities. Rana et al. [7] suggested many sensors using IOT applications for waste management. Jeng et al. [8] suggested a secure e-passport system using advanced sensors to avoid from theft using biometric information.

4.3.1 Proposed method

Biometric passports aim to prevent illegal entry into a country and reduce the use of counterfeit documents by providing more accurate identification of individuals [9]. Porwik [10] explores the requirements, national regulations, and application procedures for introducing a new biometric passport in the European Union (EU), with a particular focus on the Republic of Poland. An e passport contains a microprocessor chip that stores biometric data to verify the identity of the passport holder [11]. An algorithm has been developed to securely link and retrieve a digital key through the use of a biometric image, such as a fingerprint [12]. The IoT developed many industrial and household devices, such as the smart cradle, which also work with various types of sensors to control the cradle and feeding application using advanced sensors [13]. Various types of sensors are implemented for a passport verification system with advanced sensor input and database [14, 15].

The output of the completed project is observed through the developed prototype. A e-passport holds a magnetic stripe card. The card contains three tracks of information that hold a reference code. The code is retrieved from the database when the card is swiped across the magnetic stripe reader. Passport holder's information is displayed on the monitor and then verified with the fingerprint given. The prototype of the project consists of an OLED display, buzzer, fingerprint sensor, and EM-18 RFID reader. The output of the project is verified with remote monitoring and controlling applications.

Figure 4.1 shows the working procedure of the biometric authentication of an e-passport system. The necessary information collected and the database search is initiated. The RFID acts as an information-collecting system. The database information retrieved is repeatedly compared with the RFID information until a match is achieved. The fingerprint is used for further authentication. If authentication fails, a buzzer sounds.

Figure 4.2 shows the interfacing of EM-18 reader, which is connected to proposed passport verification system. After RFID verification, the corresponding results of checking the fingerprint and output of RFID are shown in Figures 4.3 and 4.4.

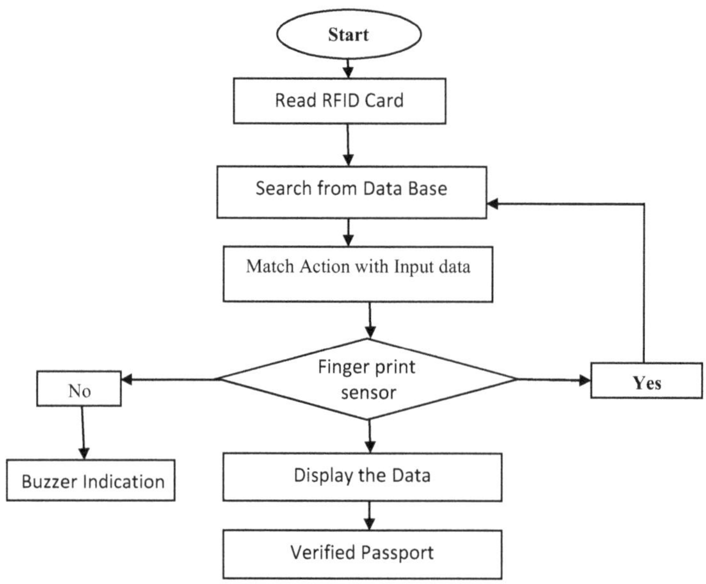

Figure 4.1 Flow chart for proposed method.

Figure 4.2 Interfacing EM-18 reader.

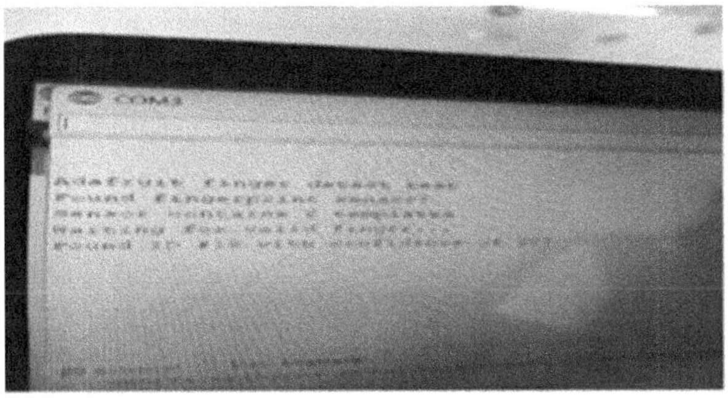

Figure 4.3 Output of fingerprint.

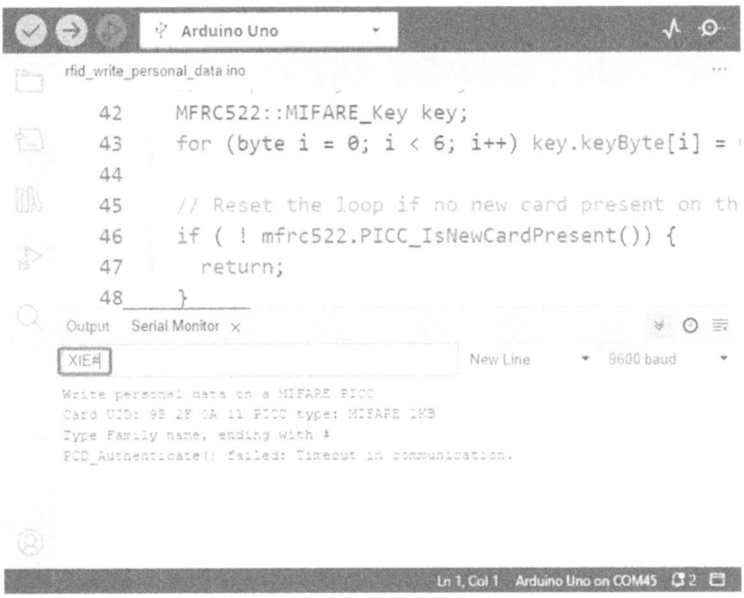

Figure 4.4 Output of RFID reader.

4.4 CONCLUSION

This project is fully verified by using the industrial-standard sensors like fingerprint sensor and smart card for real-time applications. By integrating system boards, the project can be extended to multiple finger vein identification to tighten the security to improve the smart card technology and reduce human error. By creating our own cloud platform and smartphone application, the sensor output parameters are monitored and the security environment is controlled.

BIBLIOGRAPHY

[1] Navdeep Kaur, Vandana, "*A Study of Biometric Identification and verification system*" 978-1-7281-7741-0/21/2021 IEEE

[2] R. Raghavendra, Sushma Venkatesh, Kiran Raja, Christoph Busch, Norwegian Biometrics Laboratory, NTNU - Gjøvik, Norway, "*A low-cost Multi-Fingervein Verification System*" 978-1-5386-6628-9/18 2018 IEEE

[3] Snehal Honade, Ayesha Sarwar, Suyog Kanawade, Akshay Hawl " Electronic Passport using RFID" ISSN No: 2456-2165 2018
[4] Fadi Hamad, Jamal Zraqou, Adi Maiita, Anas Abu Taleb Isra University, Amman, Jordan "*A Secure Authentication System for ePassport Detection and Verification*" 9978-1-4799-8657-6/15 2015 IEEE DOI 10.1109/EISIC.2015.21
[5] Ioana Rodhe, Johan Bengtsson, Amund Hunstad and Henrik Karlzén "*Future Schemes for Stronger Verification of the Access Rights of Border Control Inspection Systems*" 978-1-4799-8657-6/15 2015 IEEE
[6] Shivani Kundra, Aman Dureja, Riya Bhatnagar, "*The study of recent technologies used in E-passport system*" 978-1-4799-4097-4/14 2014 IEEE
[7] K. S. Rana, S. M. Rafee, K. Rajesh,T. V. K. Moorthy, M. Dharani "Arduino Based Automatic Waste Segregation and Composite System "*international Review of Electrical Engineering (IREE)*, 2024, 19 (1), pp. 1–9.
[8] Albert B. Jeng, Lo-Yi Chen, "*How to enhance the security of e-passport*" 978-1-42443703-0/09/2009 IEEE
[9] V.K. Narendira Kumar, B. Srinivasan. "Design and Development of E-Passports Using Biometric Access Control System" *I. J. Computer Network and Information Security*, 2013, Vol. 12, pp. 80–90.
[10] P. Porwik, "The Biometric Passport: The Technical Requirements and Possibilities of Using," *2009 International Conference on Biometrics and Kansei Engineering*, Cieszyn, Poland, 2009, pp. 65–69, doi: 10.1109/ICBAKE.2009.14
[11] P. Punithavathi, S. Geetha. "Cancelable Biometric Transformations for E-Passport Security" *International Journal of Engineering and Advanced Technology (IJEAT)*, 2019, Vol.9 (1S3), pp. 346–349.
[12] C. Soutar, A. Roberge and B. Vijaya Kumar, " *Biometric Encryption using Image Processing*," SPIE,1998, pp. 17–188.
[13] M. Bharathi, M. Dharani, T. Venkata Krishnamoorthy, D. Prasad, "IoT-Based Infant Cradle Monitoring System", *Blockchain Technology for IoT and Wireless Communications*, CRC Press, 2023, pp. 133–143.
[14] T. Vignesh, K. K. Thyagharajan, R. Beaulah Jeyavathana, R. Prasanna Kumar, "An Improved E-Passport System with Secured IOT and Wireless Communication Technology", *AIP Conference Proceeding*, 2022, pp. 060001-1–060001-9.
[15] S. Sharma and H. Zodpe, "Implementation of cryptography algorithm for E-passport security," *2016 International Conference on Inventive Computation Technologies (ICICT)*, 2016, pp. 1–3.

Chapter 5

Efficient scalable binary counter using low-complexity sorting networks for VLSI applications

K. Hemakumari, Shaik Mohammad Rafee, Ch. Vijaya Lakshmi, M. Dharani, T. Venkatakrishnamoorthy, and E. Hima Bindu

5.1 INTRODUCTION

Parallel counters in VLSI design enable high-speed counting of '1' bits by processing input bits simultaneously, offering significant performance advantages over sequential counters. They are crucial in applications like digital signal processing, error detection, and network processing. Despite their higher area and power consumption, their speed benefits make them indispensable in high-performance circuits. Balancing speed, area, and power efficiency is key in their design. Energy efficiency is a fundamental need for nearly all electronic devices, particularly portable ones like smartphones, tablets, and other devices. Achieving this minimization with the least amount of performance (speed) penalty is highly sought [1]. For the realization of diverse multimedia applications, transportable components with digital signal processing (DSP) blocks are highly desired. The ALU, which performs most of the work in these blocks, is their computational core [2]. The primary operation in the processing elements that can result in excessive energy and power consumption is multiplication. A large number of DSP cores carry out algorithms for processing photos and movies, with the end product being either an image or a video that is ready for human consumption.

It makes it easier to use approximations to increase the energy and speed of arithmetic circuits. This stems from humans' restricted perceptual capacities when viewing an image or a video. Apart from the domains of image and video processing, there exist other applications where the precision of arithmetic operations is not crucial for the operation of the system (refer to [3, 4]). Precise computation offers precision, velocity, and energy/power usage. The benefit of an approximation multiplier is that it increases speed and lowers error rates. The entire multiplication procedure takes longer to complete because each operand needs to have a memory lookup and compare operation performed in order to fix the division error [5]. The approximation is handled at many levels of abstraction, such as circuit, logic, and architecture levels [6].

A variety of approximating arithmetic building blocks, such as multipliers and adders, at different design levels have been proposed in various structures under the category for approximation approaches in functions [2, 7, 8]. The broken array multiplier was created to implement VLSI more effectively [9]. In comparison to the accurate WPA, the imprecise model's mean and variance errors rise by just 0.63% and 0.86%, respectively, while the maximum error rises by 4%. Approximate adders are used in low-power DSP and are used in many signal processing methods and designs. As opposed to a regular multiplier, the ETM's dissipated power decreased from 75% to 90%.

In order to achieve high-speed realization and reduce implementation complexity, several additional RB multipliers have also been designed [10, 11, 12, 13]. Public key cryptosystems, computer algebra systems, coding theory, and other topics all depend on efficient computations in finite fields and associated structures. Despite the isomorphism of all

DOI: 10.1201/9781003591788-5

finite fields with the same cardinality, the choice of bases for field element representations has a significant impact on the arithmetic efficiency of these fields. Polynomial bases (PB) and normal bases (NB) are the most often utilized bases; dual bases (DB) are occasionally combined with them [14]. One of the main advantages of normal bases in characteristic two fields is that they can be used to compute huge exponentiations and multiplicative inverses because the squaring operation in NB is just a cyclic shift of the element coordinates [1, 12, 15]. Furthermore, a normal basis's multiplication table is symmetric, making hardware implementation possible.

On a general-purpose computer, multiplication over can be implemented; however, using a general-purpose computer to implement cryptographic systems in consumer products that are cost sensitive is inefficient. Furthermore, because the word-length of low-end microprocessors is too short in relation to the order of typical finite fields used in cryptography systems, these processors cannot satisfy the real-time requirements of many applications. Finite field arithmetic operations must consequently be implemented on hardware in the majority of real-time applications in order to reap the benefits of low cost and high throughput rate. The polynomial, normal, triangular, and redundant bases (RB) are the four that can be used to represent field elements. These bases have a significant effect on how well arithmetic circuits function [8, 16]. Due to their many benefits, the multipliers based on RB [2, 17] have attracted a lot of interest recently. Like normal basis, they can be implemented in highly regular computing structures and incur less computational cost in addition to providing free squaring.

5.1.1 Literature survey

In [18], a short path activation function technique was put forth in an effort to enhance the variable-latency circuit's performance and hold logic's accuracy. In order to increase the performance of Very Long Instruction Word processors and plan operations on nonuniform latency functional units, an instruction scheduling technique was presented in [19]. A Booth algorithm-based variable-latency pipelined multiplier architecture was presented in [20]. The effect of process variation is taken into consideration to boost the circuit yield in [21], where process-variation-tolerant architecture for arithmetic units was presented. Furthermore, the clock cycle is set to the delay of the longer path, and the critical paths are split into two shorter paths that may not be equal. Although these research designs were able to increase performance by reducing the timing waste of conventional circuits, they were unable to self-adjust during runtime and failed to take the aging impact into account. In [20, 21], a variable-latency adder design taking the aging effect into account was presented. By employing the radix-4 Booth algorithm to reduce the switching activity of partial products, at low-power 2's complement multipliers.

5.2 COMPRESSOR USING SORTING ALGORITHM

Compared to traditional adders that use full and half adders, a compressor adder offers less delay. N-r, where N is the number of bits and r is the total count of 1s in N bits, is how it is represented. It is called a compressor because, in comparison to other adder circuits, it has fewer gates and a lower latency. Research is being done to enhance lower-order compressor circuits [3]. The following provides an explanation of the compressor circuits that can be utilized for multiplication processes, including 5-3, 10-4, 15-4, and 20-5. a diagram showing the 5-3 compressor adder. A maximum of five bits can be added to this compressor adder, yielding a result of three bits. Decimal 5's three-bit binary value, 101, is the highest value that may be obtained. Figures N2, N3, and N4 show 4:1 multiplexers, which reduce delay and power consumption by allowing just one output to be high at a time. Figure 5.2 displays a schematic view of a 10-4 compressor adder that was created in cadence using an incisive simulator. A maximum of ten bits can be added to this compressor adder, yielding a result of four bits. The four-bit binary equivalent of decimal 10 (11010) is the maximum value that may be produced. A group of interconnected compare-and-exchange (CAE) blocks is called a sorting network. Comparators, which are essentially hardware versions of the CE operation, make up sorting networks. Two inputs and two outputs make up a comparator. As seen in Figure 5.1(a), there are two types of comparators based on the sense of ordering.

An algorithm that arranges items in a list in a specific order is called a sorting algorithm. The two most popular orders are lexicographical and numerical. Effective sorting is crucial for maximizing the application of other algorithms (like merge and search algorithms), which need sorted lists of input data. It is also frequently helpful for canonicalizing data and generating output that is legible for humans. Formally speaking, the result needs to meet two requirements: The output is a permutation (reordering) of the input and is in non-decreasing order (none of the elements are smaller than the preceding element in the required total order). Furthermore, while though algorithms may frequently be applied to either type of data with the appropriate modification, it is typically assumed that the data is in an array, which permits random access, rather than a list, which only allows sequential access. The two most basic sorts are selection and insertion, which are both effective on tiny data because of their minimal overhead but ineffective on big data. Because it requires fewer comparisons and performs well on nearly sorted data, insertion sort is typically faster than selection sort. Selection sort, on the other hand, requires fewer writes and is therefore employed when write speed is a constraint.

5.3 SORTING NETWORKS

Comparators and wires are the two sorts of components that make up a sorting network. It is conceived of the wires as running from left to right, each carrying a single value that travels the network simultaneously. Two wires are connected by each comparator. A comparator exchanges values when two values passing via two wires come into contact with it if and only if the value on the top wire is higher than the value on the bottom wire. A mathematical representation of a network of wires and comparator modules used to order a series of numbers is called a sorting network. By connecting two wires, each comparator sorts the values by sending the larger value to one wire and the smaller value to the other. Sorting networks and comparison sorting algorithms differ primarily in that a sorting network sets the sequence of comparisons ahead of time, independent of the results of earlier comparisons. The independence of the comparison sequences helps the algorithms run in parallel. Sorting network theory is surprisingly deep and sophisticated, despite the model's simplicity.

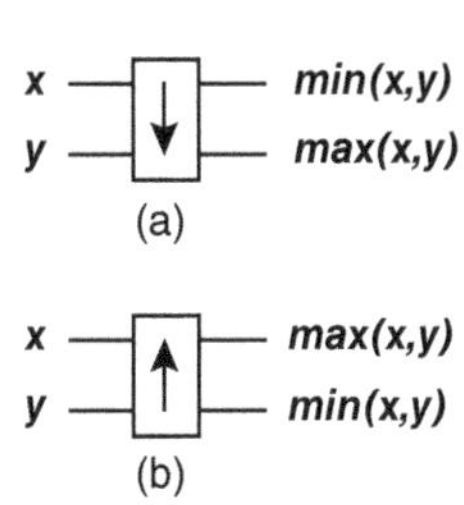

Figure 5.1 Comparator diagrams.

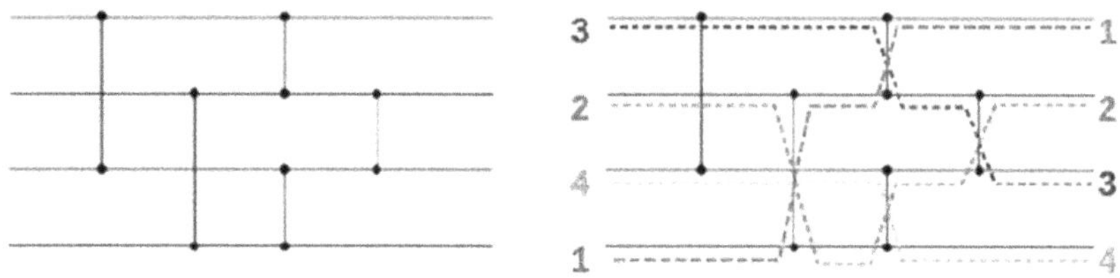

Figure 5.2 Simple sorting network.

Figure 5.2 presents a diagram that illustrates a basic sorting network in action. Given that the first four comparators will "float" the smallest value to the top and "sink" the largest value to the bottom, it is simple to understand why this sorting network will appropriately sort the inputs. The middle two wires are simply sorted by the final comparator.

5.4 BITONIC SORTING

Bitonic sort is a comparison-based parallel sorting algorithm that has performed more comparisons than other widely used sorting algorithms. It is more suitable for parallel implementation, since the user compares the items in a predetermined order every time, and this order is independent of the data. Thus, in essence, hardware implementations are appropriate for this bitonic sort. Prior to comprehending bitonic sort, it is necessary to grasp the bitonic sequence and the process by which a sequence becomes bitonic. A sorting network is a unique type of sorting algorithm and speed in which the order of comparisons is independent of the data. Because of this, sorting networks can be implemented in parallel processing arrays or hardware. Bitonic sorting networks use comparators of size $O(n \bullet \log(n)^2)$ to do sorting. Asymptotically, it is as complex as shellsort and odd-even mergesort. While it is known that a sorting network with just $(n \bullet \log(n))$ comparators exists, for all practical issue sizes it is slower than bitonic sort because of its huge constant.

5.4.1 Bitonic sort algorithm

Bitonic sorting involves the following steps:

- Use the provided random sequence array to perform the bitonic sequence.
- Compare each element in the first and second halves, starting with the first element and ending with the second. This process is repeated until the final element in the first half and the final element in the second half are compared.
- If an element in the second half is significantly smaller than one in the first, swap them.
- Every element in the first half will now be smaller than every element in the second half. This comparison and swap function use two sequences of length "n/2." Until there is a single sorted series of length n, repeat step 2 recursively for each sequence.

5.5 RESULT AND DISCUSSION

Bitonic sort is one of the fastest sorting networks. A sorting network is a special kind of sorting algorithm in which the sequence of comparisons is not data dependent (Figure 5.3).

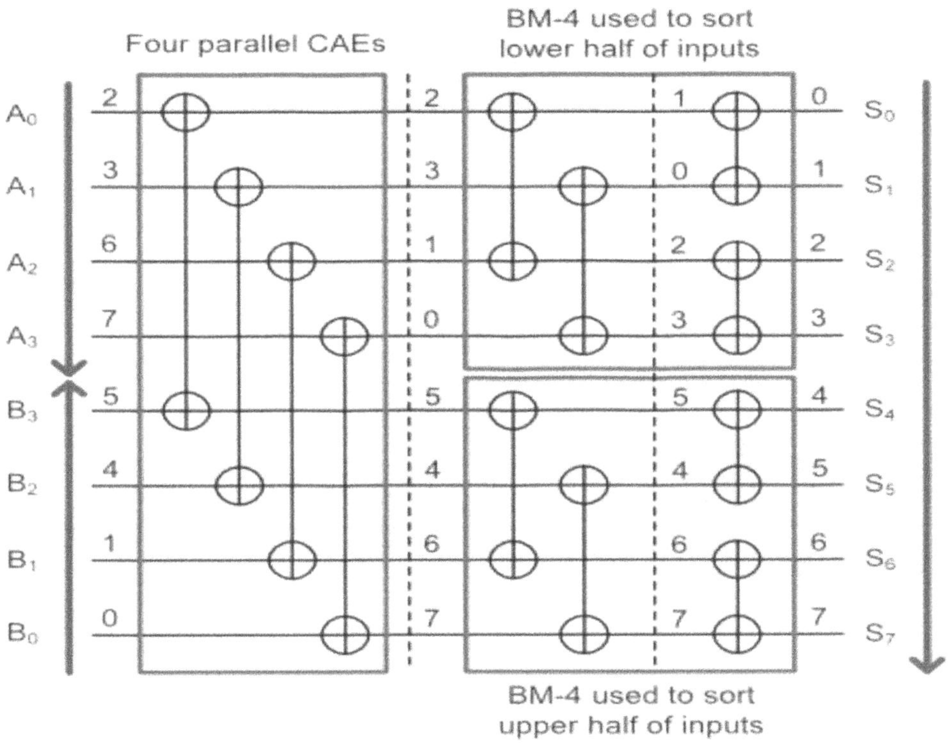

Figure 5.3 An increasing 8-input bitonic merging unit.

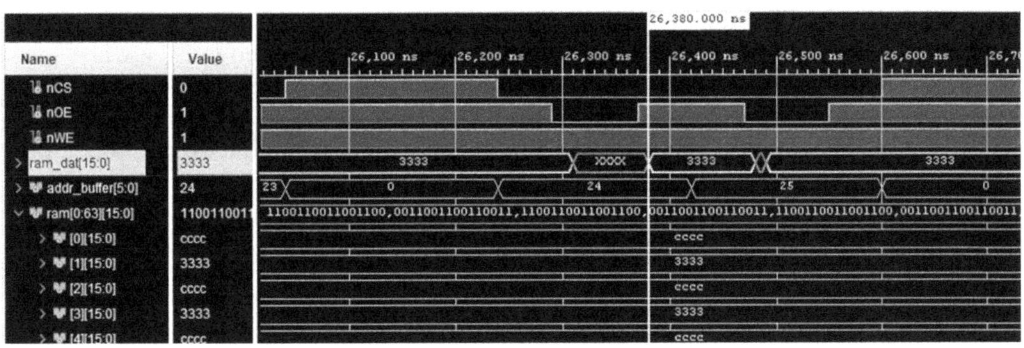

Figure 5.4 Existing simulation output.

Every box works in the same way as a blue box, but the sort is done in the opposite manner. Hence, each green box might be swapped out for a blue box, and then there would be a crossover where all the wires would go to the opposite location. This would keep the horizontal lines from being straight but allow all arrows to point in the same direction. But since a bitonic sequence's reverse is also bitonic, a comparable crossover might be positioned to the right of the bottom half of any red block's outputs, and the sort would still function as intended. If a red box has crossovers before and after it, it can be internally modified so that the two crossovers cancel and the wires straighten out once more. As a result, the diagram presented in Figures 5.4 and 5.5 is equal to the one before in that each orange box represents a red box that has absorbed two crossings, and each green box has become a blue plus a crossover.

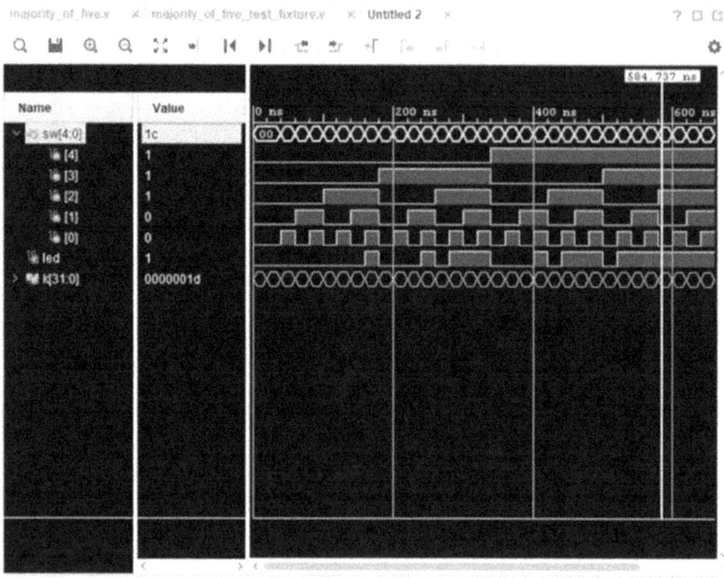

Figure 5.5 Proposed simulation output.

5.6 CONCLUSION AND FUTURE SCOPE

This study plans and reproduces a strategy for a counter that is both speed effective and practical in the region. A dual counter with regard to a new symmetric component A computation strategy called "aggregate and convey" is suggested. We create the (7,3), (15,4) counters based on this biotonic sorting technique, which is a novel counter design method based on a sorting network. Because the proposed counters accomplish reduced latency when speed is crucial and perform better in automated data processing, they are more adaptable than present designs. Approximative multipliers can be used to examine images, videos, and video sharpness. We can utilize the Brent Kung Adder to decrease area and the Kogge Stone Adder to boost speed for faster multiplication.

REFERENCES

[1] Wen-Chang Yeh and Chein-Wei Jen, "High-speed Booth encoded parallel multiplier design," *IEEE Trans. on Computers*, 2000. Vol. 49(7), pp. 692–701.

[2] S. Hus, V. Venkatraman, S. Mathew, H. Kaul, M. Anders, S. Dighe, W. Burleson and R. Krishnamurthy, "A 2GHZ 13.6mW 12x9b mutiplier for energy efficient FFT accelerators," *Proc. of IEEE ESSCIRC*, pp. 199–202, Sept. 2005.

[3] Jung-Yup Kang and Jean-Luc Gaudiot, "A simple high-speed multiplier design," *IEEE Trans. On Computers*, 2006. Vol. 55(10), pp. 1253–1258.

[4] Shiann-Rong Kuang, Jiun-Ping Wang and Cang-Yuan Guo, "Modified Booth multipliers with a regular partial product array", *IEEE Trans. on Circuit and Systems*, 2009. Vol.56(5), pp. 404–408.

[5] Li-rong Wang, Shyh-Jye Jou and Chung-Len Lee, "A well-structured modified Booth multiplier design," *Proc. of IEEE VLSI-DAT*, pp. 85–88, April 2008.

[6] A. A. Khatibzadeh, K. Raahemifar and M. Ahmadi, "A 1.8V 1.1GHz Novel Digital Multiplier," *Proc. of IEEE CCECE*, pp. 686–689, May 2005. Journal of Interdisciplinary Cycle Research, Volume XIV, Issue V, May/2022, Page No: 1316

[7] Hwang-Cherng Chow and I-Chyn Wey, "A 3.3V 1GHz high speed pipelined Booth multiplier," *Proc. of IEEE ISCAS*, vol. 1, pp. 457–460, May 2002.
[8] M. Aguirre-Hernandez and M. Linarse-Aranda, "Energy-efficient high-speed CMOS pipelined multiplier," *Proc. of IEEE CCE*, pp. 460–464, Nov. 2008.
[9] Yung-chin Liang, Ching-ji Huang and Wei-bin Yang, "A 320-MHz 8bit x 8bit pipelined multiplier in ultra-low supply voltage," *Proc. of IEEE A-SSCC*, pp. 73–76, Nov. 2008.
[10] C. S. Wallace, "A suggestion for a fast multiplier," *IEEE Trans. On Computers*, vol. BC13, pp. 14–17, Feb. 1964.
[11] M.D. Ercegovac et al., [a]Fast Multiplication without Carry- Propagate Addition, *IEEE Trans. Computers*, vol. 39, no. 11, Nov. 1990.
[12] R.K. Kolagotla et al., [a]VLSI Implementation of a 200-Mhz 16 _ 16 Left-to-Right Carry-Free Multiplier in 0.35_m CMOS Technology for Next-Generation DSPs, *Proc. IEEE 1997 Custom Integrated Circuits Conf.*, pp. 469–472, 1997.
[13] P.F. Stelling and V.G. Oklobdzija, [a]*Optimal Designs for Multipliers and Multiply-Accumulators,*° *Proc. 15th IMACS WorldCongress Scientific Computation, Modeling, and Applied Math.*, A. Sydow, ed., pp. 739–744, Aug. 1997.
[14] Passport 0.35 micron, 3.3 volt, Optimum Silicon SC Library, CB35OS142, Avant! *Corporation*, Mar. 1998.
[15] M. D. Ercegovac and T. Lang, *Digital Arithmetic*, Morgan Kaufmann Publishers,Los Altos, CA 94022, USA, 2003.
[16] S. B. Tatapudi and J. G. Delgado-Frias, "Designing pipelined systems with a clock period approaching pipeline register delay," *Proc. of IEEE MWSCAS*, vol. 1, pp. 871–874, Aug. 2005.
[17] A. D. Booth, "A signed binary multiplication technique," *Quarterly J. Mechanical and Applied Math*, vol. 4, pp.236–240, 1951.
[18] G. Goto et al., [a]A 4.1ns compact 54 _ 54-b Multiplier UtilizingSign-Select Booth Encoders,° *IEEE J. Solid-State Circuits*, vol. 32, no. 11, pp. 1,676–1,682, Nov. 1997.
[19] G. Goto et al., [a]A 54 _ 54-b Regularly Structured Tree Multiplier, *IEEE J. Solid-State Circuits*, vol. 27, no. 9, Sept. 1992.
[20] R. Fried, [a]Minimizing Energy Dissipation in High-Speed Multipliers, *Proc. 19r97 Int'l Symp. Low Power Electronics and Design*, pp. 214–219, 1997.
[21] N.H.E. Weste and K. Eshraghian, *Principles of CMOS VLSI Design: A Systems Perspective*, second ed., chapter 8, p. 520. Addison Wesley, 1993.

Chapter 6

Convolutional neural networks

Based EEG signal fervor identification

P. Poojitha and M. Dharani

6.1 INTRODUCTION

Emotion recognition is a critical area of research in affective computing, human–computer interaction, and neuropsychology [1]. It aims to understand and interpret human emotions through various signals, one of which is the electroencephalogram (EEG) [2]. All the electrical activities in the human brain responsible for emotional states and cognition are measured by EEG. Deep convolutional neural networks (CNNs) in particular have been successful in various domains due to their ability to automatically learn hierarchical feature representations from raw data [3]. CNNs have been applied in image and speech recognition with outstanding results, suggesting their potential utility in EEG-based emotion recognition [4]. Despite potential of EEG for emotion recognition, existing methods face several challenges:

1. **Noise and Artifacts:** Artifacts and noise are often contaminated by EEG signals from muscle movements, eye blinks, and other sources, making accurate analysis difficult.
2. **Feature Extraction:** Traditional approaches rely heavily on handcrafted features, which will not grasp the full severity of EEG signal data.
3. **Classification Accuracy:** Previous studies have used classifiers such as support vector machines (SVMs), which, while effective, may not fully leverage the depth of information available in EEG signals.

These challenges necessitate expansion of more accurate methods for emotion recognition using EEG data [5, 6]. This signal-based fervor identification by this study is to monitor the limitations by leveraging the capabilities in deep learning. By automating feature extraction and focusing on the intricate patterns in the EEG data, CNNs offer a promising alternative to conventional methods.

The remaining part of this context is framed as follows. The relevant research review on EEG-based fervor identification is presented in Section 6.2 while Section 6.3 deals with the current system methodology, describing the signal-processing methods and the deep CNN classifier's design. The experimental results and setup of this research are presented in Section 6.4. The concluding Section 6.5 delivers a review of research findings and suggestions for future investigations.

6.2 RELATED WORK

Because affective computing is so important to comprehending and connecting with humans, the topic has attracted a lot of attention [7]. The capacity to identify emotions using EEG data is one of the key elements that has aided in the development of this technology. Numerous

 DOI: 10.1201/9781003591788-6

strategies and tactics have been created over time to increase the reliability and precision of EEG type–based methods for fervor identification [8, 9]. A major goal of this evaluation is to give a thorough rundown of the most recent advancements in this field. He and colleagues presented a temporal adversarial network [10]. They then presented a learning approach that tackles the problem of emotion recognition domain shift. Their findings demonstrate that their strategy can produce encouraging outcomes [11]. In order to continuously detect emotions, the focus needs to be on the relationship between facial expressions and EEG waves. Subsequently, they propose an approach that combines these two elements to raise the accuracy of the system.

6.3 PROPOSED METHOD

In order to categorize emotions from EEG signals, this research presents a novel method that makes use of deep CNNs. These perform exceptionally well at automatically extracting informative features from the raw EEG data, in contrast to SVMs, which rely on predefined features. CNNs can recognize the most discriminative patterns within the EEG signals that are most pertinent for emotion categorization by directly learning features from the input. This lessens the burden and gets rid of any biases that could be brought in by selecting features by hand. This method's architecture is shown in Figure 6.1.

This is especially crucial for real-world scenarios when the system may come across EEG data that differ somewhat from the training set. Enhanced generalizability guarantees the system's efficacy in wider settings and augments its overall dependability. The proposed block diagram is shown in Figure 6.2.

6.3.1 Data Acquisition and preprocessing

- **EEG Data Acquisition:** A standardized EEG dataset comprising recordings from people in a range of emotional states (excitement, happiness, and depression) will be used in this investigation.

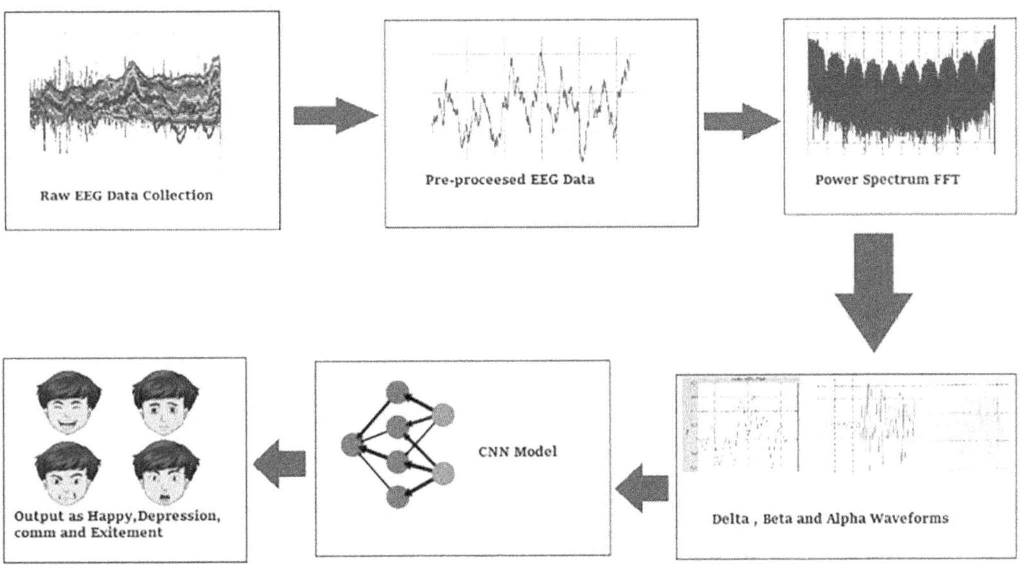

Figure 6.1 System architecture.

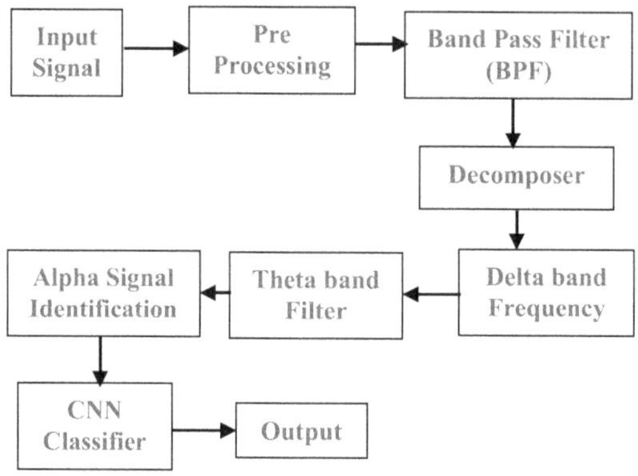

Figure 6.2 Proposed method block diagram.

- **Preprocessing:** To eliminate noise and artifacts that could skew the emotional data, the raw EEG data will be cleaned. Filtering and baseline correction are two methods that may be used to guarantee a high-quality signal for additional processing.

6.3.2 Feature extraction using band-pass filtering

Using band-pass filters, the preprocessed EEG signal will be divided into several bands of frequency. Theta band (4–8 Hz), alpha band (8–13 Hz), and delta band (1–4 Hz) are the most probable frequency bands to be targeted because studies have linked these bands to various emotional states.

6.3.3 Training and evaluation

To train the CNN model, preprocessed EEG data with matching emotional labels will be utilized. In order to reduce the classification error, the weights of the data models were iteratively adjusted in the phase of training on the trained datasets.

6.3.4 Comparison with existing method (SVM)

The suggested CNN-based method's efficiency will be contrasted with a cutting-edge technique for classifying emotions that makes use of SVMs. Both models will be trained and evaluated using the same EEG dataset

6.3.5 Measures of performance

- **Accuracy:** Calculates the percentage of photos that are correctly identified overall. It represents the proportion of photos that your model accurately classifies as either having disasters or not. Accuracy is calculated based on Eq. (6.1)

$$(\text{TP} + \text{TN}) / \text{Total Images} \tag{6.1}$$

- **Specificity:** It shows how effectively the model handles non-disaster photos without raising false warnings, it can be calculated by shown in Eq. (6.2).

$$\text{TN} / (\text{TN} + \text{FP}) \tag{6.2}$$

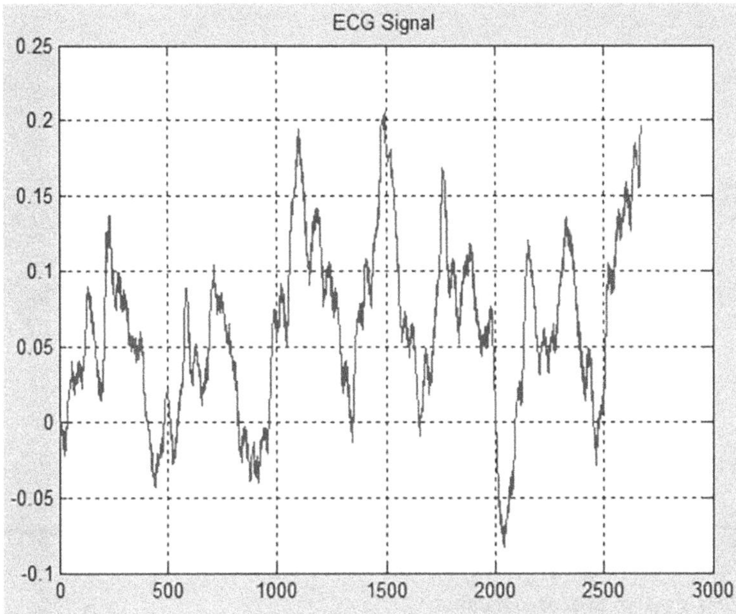

Figure 6.3 Input EEG signal.

- **Sensitivity (Recall):** This can be calculated by Eq. (6.3). It shows how accurately the model detects real-world disasters.

$$TP/(TP+FN) \tag{6.3}$$

- **Precision:** It indicates the accuracy of the model's positive predictions. This can be calculated as shown in Eq. (6.4).

$$\text{Precision} = TP/(TP+FP) \tag{6.4}$$

6.4 RESULTS AND DISCUSSIONS

6.4.1 Existing method

Figure 6.3 displays the raw EEG signal acquired from the subject. It serves as the initial input to the emotion recognition system.

6.4.2 Proposed method

Similar to the existing method, Figure 6.4 shows the raw EEG signal that serves as the input to the proposed emotion recognition system.

Similar to the existing method, the proposed method outputs the detected emotional state based on the processed EEG signal. Figure 6.5 reveals the recognized emotion, demonstrating the effectiveness of the proposed method in identifying the subject's emotional state as "excited."

6.4.3 Comparison table

Table 6.1 provides a concise overview of the performance metrics of two different models used for EEG-based emotion recognition: (SVM) and (CNN).

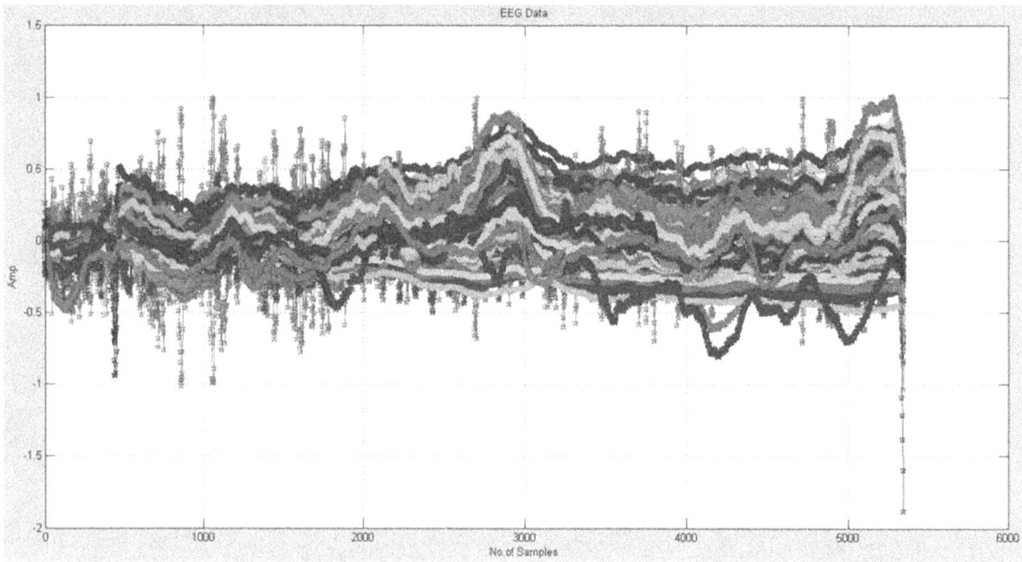

Figure 6.4 Input EEG signal to proposed method.

Figure 6.5 Shown excited emotion in proposed method.

Table 6.1 Comparison of performance metrics with existing methods and proposed methods

S. No	*Model*	*SVM*	*CNN*
1	Accuracy	90.12	95.08
2	Sensitivity	91.02	92.18
3	Specificity	85.15	89.28
4	Precision	89.16	90.73

6.5 CONCLUSION

The potential of CNNs for fervor classification from EEG signals was examined in this domain. In an effort to get around the drawbacks of conventional techniques, we put forth a novel strategy that takes advantage of deep learning's advantages for feature extraction and classification. The deep CNN architecture outperformed previous SVM-based techniques in identifying emotions from EEG data with substantial accuracy.

6.5.1 Future scope

Most of the current studies are concentrating on the very basic fervor identification. Future research can expand the spectrum of identified emotion spectrum, which in turn leads to improvement in accuracy of identification. In order to perform this, most typical datasets should be incorporated, including deep emotions.

REFERENCES

[1] "Review and classification of emotion recognition based on EEG brain-computer interface system research: A systematic review," Appl. Sci., vol. 7, no. 12, 2017, A. Al-Nafjan, M. Hosny, Y. Al-Ohali, and A. Al-Wabil.

[2] "A review of channel selection algorithms for EEG signal processing," T. Alotaiby, F. E. A. El-Samie, S. A. Alshebeili, and I. Ahmad, EURASIP J. Adv. Signal Process., vol. 2015, no. 1, 2015.

[3] The paper "Emotion recognition and classification using EEG: A review" by N. K. Bhandari and M. Jain was published in the International Journal of Scientific and Technological Research in 2020.

[4] "Deep learning for electroencephalogram (EEG) classification tasks: A review," by A. Craik, Y. He, and J. L. Contreras-Vidal Journal of Neural Engineering, 16(3), 2019.

[5] "EEG-based emotion recognition: Review of commercial EEG devices and machine learning techniques," by D. Dadebayev, W. W. Goh, and E. X. Tan J. King Saud Univ. - Comput. Inf. Sci., vol. 34, no. 7, pp. 4385–4401, 2022.

[6] "A Systematic Review for Human EEG Brain Signals Based Emotion Classification, Feature Extraction, Brain Condition, Group Comparison," by M. Hamada, B. B. Zaidan, and A. A. Zaidan 2018, vol. 42, no. 9, J. Med. Syst.

[7] "Emotion recognition techniques using EEG data: a survey by C. Yu and M. Wang," Cogn. Robot., vol. 2, no. June, pp. 132–146, 2022.

[8] In Sensors (Switzerland), vol. 20, no. 8, pp. 1–21, 2020, J. Z. Lim, J. Mountstephens, and J. Teo, "Emotion recognition using eye-tracking: Taxonomy, review, and current challenges".

[9] A review of computational approaches for estimating emotional state from human EEG is presented by M. K. Kim, M. Kim, E. Oh, and S. P. Kim in Comput. Math. approaches Med., vol. 2013.

[10] Multimodal system for emotion recognition utilizing eeg and customer review, vol. 1112, D. Panda, D. Das Chakladar, and T. Dasgupta springer 2020 in Singapore. Comput. Biol. Med., vol. 141, p. 105048, 2022.

[11] Z. He, Y. Zhong, and J. Pan, "An adversarial discriminative temporal convolutional network for EEG-based cross domain emotion recognition".

Chapter 7

LSTM-based cloud workload prediction using PSO-GA hybrid algorithm

Thatikonda Supraja, Priyanka Chawla, Pandi Chiranjeevi, and P. Ashok Kumar

7.1 INTRODUCTION

Cloud computing has a huge demand association with what users and applications make on cloud infrastructures for computing resources such as processing power, storage, and network bandwidth. It includes the changing levels of system activity and resource usage that cloud service contributors encounter over time. Dynamic variations in workload patterns can be attributed to various reasons, including user activity, application behavior, seasonal variations, and the latest trends [1]. Accurate workload prediction is essential for effective resource provisioning and performance optimization in cloud systems. Thus, to guarantee scalability, cost effectiveness, and high-quality service delivery in cloud computing systems, reliable workload prediction models are crucial.

The resource management structure in these large data centers is made up of servers, virtual machines (VMs), and various management issues. Cloud computing infrastructures are built on virtual computers, which provide effective resource allocation and management and improve service delivery reliability [1].

Servers, VMs, and assorted management concerns collectively establish the resource management framework within these expansive data centers. Virtual machines serve as the foundation for cloud computing infrastructures, enabling efficient resource allocation and management while enhancing service delivery reliability [2].

Recurrent neural network (RNN) [3] with LSTM [4] architecture plays a crucial role in cloud workload prediction by effectively identifying temporal dependencies and patterns from the historical workload data. As an enhanced version of RNNs, LSTMs are excellent at representing sequential data and maintaining long-term dependencies, which makes them a good fit for workload prediction problems involving time-series forecasting. Cloud service providers can benefit from proactive resource allocation and optimization by using RNN LSTM models, which can accurately anticipate future workload behavior by learning from past workload data. On the other hand, problems like overfitting, vanishing gradients, and choosing the right hyperparameters make it difficult to train and adjust these models efficiently. Furthermore, a major obstacle that will require continued study and innovation to overcome is guaranteeing the scalability and efficiency of LSTM-based models to handle large-scale cloud workload datasets.

Characteristics of a time sequence work that are demonstrated earlier exhibit workload [5], implying that each workload instance at a given time interval is closely linked to its provisional workloads. Traditional statistical techniques used for analyzing time series data, such as auto-regressive models (AR) [6], moving average models (MA), and auto-regressive integrated moving average models [7], have been used to predict workload. While these models offer reasonable accuracy, they rely heavily on the static form of collected data. Moreover, the outcome of these models can vary significantly depending on the chosen model parameters,

 DOI: 10.1201/9781003591788-7

necessitating considerable manual intervention or the expertise of experienced practitioners to fine-tune the parameters to suit the relevant characteristics of the data [8].

In this chapter, our proposed model initially predicts the workload on cloud servers with LSTM. Secondly, to optimize performance and speed up the optimization process, we are using a hybrid approach that is a combination of PSO and GA to fine-tune the parameters. For the practical implementation, we are considering a dataset of Azure cluster traces. We also adopt root mean square error (RMSE) used mainly to calculate the prediction performance as well as accuracy [9].

The chapter is structured as follows. Section 7.2 provides a comprehensive literature review encompassing cloud computing, workload prediction, deep learning, optimization methods, and associated challenges. Section 7.3 outlines the proposed working model, including its design and procedural aspects. In Section 7.4, experimental results are presented, along with a comparative analysis between the proposed model and existing solutions. Finally, Section 7.5 offers conclusions drawn from the research findings and discusses potential future directions for further exploration.

7.2 RELATED WORKS

We referred to multiple research articles on cloud workload prediction with various deep learning techniques. Virtualization contributes to resource optimization by enabling workload consolidation, where multiple VMs or containers can coexist [10] on the same physical server, leading to improved resource utilization and cost efficiency. We also reviewed the role of LSTM in collaboration with various machine learning and artificial intelligence techniques [11]. Various comparative analyses were employed to evaluate research gaps in prior studies.

7.2.1 LSTM-based workload prediction

Yonghua Zhu et al. [8] introduced an approach using the LSTM encoder-decoder network with an attention mechanism that is used to increase workload prediction accuracy in cloud-end clusters. Challenges identified include the tangled execution [12] of running applications and batching, which significantly reduce server efficiency. Peyman Yazdanian et al. utilized a fusion of 1D Convolutional Neural Networks (ConvNets) and a series of LSTM blocks to analyze extensive sequences of Google traces data [13]. Peyman Yazdanian et al. [14] proposed GAN/LSTM [15] deep learning architecture to forecast workload time series for each sub-band individually, considering their distinct levels of complexity and volatility.

7.2.2 Machine learning–based cloud workload prediction

Minxian Xu et al. [16] suggested the effective supervised learning-based cloud workload prediction approach named deep neural network (esDNN), aimed at addressing issues in resource provisioning for dynamic workloads in cloud computing. By translating multidimensional data into a supervised learning data time series [16] using a sliding window, the method enables deep learning processing. Additionally, esDNN is applied for machine autoscaling, optimizing service provider costs by efficiently reducing the number of active hosts.

7.2.3 Heuristic-based cloud workload prediction

Jitendra Kumar et al. [17] projected meta-heuristic algorithms for cloud workload prediction and the system performance measured using RMSE and mean absolute error (MAE).

Masoud Barati et al. [18] proposed a tuned support vector regression (TSVR) [6] scheme by hybrid GA and PSO techniques to prove prediction accuracy.

7.3 BACKGROUND CONCEPTS

7.3.1 Partial swarm optimization

Partial swarm optimization (PSO) can significantly enhance cloud workload prediction by optimizing various aspects of the prediction process [19]. PSO optimizes cloud workload prediction by selecting the best parameters. PSO supports looking for the proper combination of input attributes as well as system parameters for predicting workload in clouds, which would produce minimum forecast errors thus bringing about more accurate forecasts of workloads. It can also assist in feature selection by identifying the most relevant variables, optimizing hyperparameters to fine-tune model performance [12, 20], facilitating model selection by exploring different algorithms, improving ensemble models by optimizing individual model weights, and enabling dynamic adjustment of parameters based on real-time workload data. By leveraging PSO, cloud workload prediction models can achieve higher accuracy, efficiency, and adaptability to evolving workload patterns in cloud environments.

Additionally, for large-scale applications, PSO offers the advantage of being computationally efficient and easily parallelizable cloud environment with vast amounts of data and computational resources. Moreover, this meta-heuristic approach can be employed for dynamic adjustment of prediction models using real-time workloads on the basis of which allows adaptive and responsive forecasting in dynamic cloud environments [21]. Its ability to explore dense search spaces effectively and find near-optimal solutions makes it as valuable tool for fine-tuning and optimizing cloud workload prediction models, ultimately leading to more reliable and scalable cloud services.

7.3.2 Genetic algorithm

Genetic algorithm (GA) is a robust approach for optimizing cloud workload prediction models [22] by mimicking the process of natural selection and evolution. In real-time scenarios of cloud computing resource utilization patterns can be complex and more dynamic, GA provides a powerful tool for fine-tuning model parameters and feature selection. By representing potential solutions as individuals in a population and iteratively evolving realms over generations, GA can effectively search through the vast space of possible model configurations to identify those that best fit the underlying workload data. This evolutionary process allows GAs to adaptively adjust model parameters and feature labels, optimizing the prediction accuracy while mitigating issues such as overfitting. Moreover, GAs can able to handle high-dimensional and nonlinear datasets [23], especially in cloud workload prediction, as they can explore input features of diverse combinations and model architectures to capture the intricate relationships between workload characteristics and resource utilization Figure 7.1.

Further, features of GA such as scalability and parallelizability [24] make them well suited for cloud workload prediction tasks in large-scale domains. GAs can efficiently handle the computational complexity associated with optimizing prediction models over extensive datasets by distributing the optimization process across multiple processors or nodes. In cloud computing scenarios, this scalability measure is particularly advantageous when the volume of historical workload data is massive, as GAs can leverage parallel processing to expedite the search for optimal model configurations. Additionally, GAs enable evolving workload patterns by continuously evolving the population of candidate solutions based on real-time

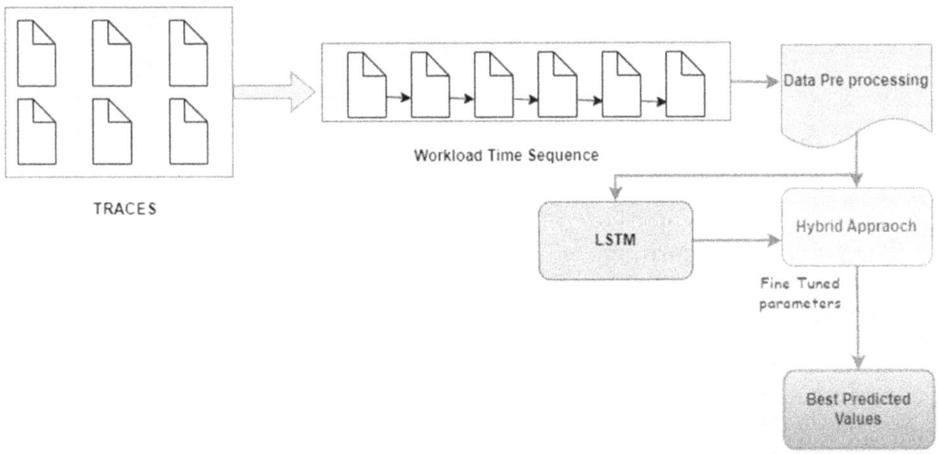

Figure 7.1 Proposed architecture.

data inputs [25]. This adaptability ensures that cloud workload prediction models remain robust and effective in capturing changes in resource demands and workload dynamics over time, ultimately enhancing the performance and efficiency of cloud services.

7.4 WORKLOAD PREDICTION MODEL

7.4.1 Problem statement

The forecasting of cloud workloads can be framed as a time series regression task, given that resource usage is recorded over time. Various metrics can measure cloud workload, with CPU utilization typically considered paramount. Consequently, this chapter focuses on using CPU utilization to forecast container workloads. Data preprocessing is essential for time series analysis. This chapter presents the structure of the data for time series regression post-processing. Earlier approaches are taking a longer time to predict cloud workload with existing machine learning algorithms.

7.4.2 Proposed method

LSTM [26] represents an RNN designed to undertake the challenges of gradient vanishing inherent in RNNs, achieved through the insertion of gated units. Primarily utilized for portraying long-term dependencies that describe the long-term relationship in data [27], LSTM proves ideal for predicting CPU utilization in containers due to the strong correlation between successive time series data points.

The proposed method uses LSTM-based cloud workload prediction using PSO and GA combined hybrid algorithm to predict workload on the cloud even more accurately and quickly. In cloud layer environments, the hybrid GA-PSO algorithm tries to balance the load of dependent activities across heterogeneous resources while minimizing make span and costs. A hybrid GA-PSO technique is presented to efficiently assign tasks to the resources. By distributing the burden of dependent jobs among heterogeneous resources in the cloud computing environment, data can be processed in parallel and quickly. The genetic-based algorithms provide better outcomes than other algorithms and approaches when the number of iterations is large. The step-by-step data flow is explained as follows. First, consider the time series data from the dataset and preprocessing the data. Second, apply LSTM for predicting workload on the cloud. Thirdly, employing a hybrid approach combining PSO and GA to fine-tune parameters enhances the models' adaptability, enabling them to better associate with the specific traits of the new data.

7.4.2.1 PSO GA hybrid algorithm

The hybrid approach utilizing the combined benefits of PSO [28] and GA in cloud workload prediction offers significant advantages. By integrating the strengths of both optimization techniques, this hybrid approach optimizes model parameters and feature selection to adapt to the dynamic behavior of cloud workloads. PSO excels in efficiently exploring the search space and identifying promising regions [28], while GA leverages evolutionary principles to iteratively refine solutions and handle high-dimensional datasets. Together, they provide a comprehensive optimization framework that not only fine-tunes model parameters but also selects the most relevant features, resulting in improved prediction accuracy and robustness.

Algorithm 1: Hybrid PSO-GA Algorithm

```
Initialize
Initialize initial population and velocity
pBest as initial population
Initialize random number r=0
Initialize pBest=0, x=0
Initialize inertia, C1,C2
for t = 1 to max iters do
for each particle in population do
  Evaluate the current population
 end for
end for
for b = 0 to populationSize-1 do
pBest[b] ← getParticle(population[b])
 update gBest and gWorst
end for
for each particle in population do
 for i = 0 to population-1 do
  for j = 0 to dim-1 do
  velocity[i][j] ← (int)(r.nextDouble() + C1 * r1 *
    (pBest[i][j] - x[i][j])+
    C2 * r2 * (gBest[j] - x[i][j]))
  update particleposition and velocity
  end for
 end for
end for
for each particle in population do
select two particles
if random < mutation then
  Perform crossover
 end if
Perform mutation
end for
return gBest
```

Moreover, our hybrid approach can effectively handle large-scale datasets and offers scalability and adaptability even with dynamic workload patterns commonly encountered in cloud environments. By leveraging the complementary strengths of PSO and GA, this hybrid approach enhances the efficiency and performance of cloud workload prediction systems, ultimately leading to more reliable and efficient cloud services.

Our proposed PSO-GA hybrid algorithm works by initializing the population values with random solutions constrained with bounds. Also, initialize velocity with zero. pbest and best values are initialized to zero as well. Next, iterate through the loop to evaluate the best possible population values. At each iteration, the best possible values are identified and considered further. We consider the best values for further iterations. In a sequence, find the velocity by using PSO approach and clip the particle position bounds. To perform crossover, mutate the best particles for further position extraction. This process will identify the new solutions. Finally, this process concludes by extracting the best possible solutions for cloud workload prediction. The number of populations and iterations are customized by the user. This process predicts the best possible outcomes to help predict possible workload values for customized period.

7.5 EVALUATION ENVIRONMENT

Experiments conducted on Azure workload trace datasets validate the efficacy of our method, showcasing state-of-the-art performance in predicting mixed workloads within cloud computing environments. The workload traces datasets are collections of real-world workload data captured from cloud computing environments. These datasets serve as valuable resources for researchers and practitioners in the field of cloud computing, providing insights into the patterns and characteristics of workloads experienced by cloud services.

Here in this proposed work, we are using cloud trace. The cluster trace dataset provides detailed records of GPU usage within a cluster computing environment. The dataset offers insights into the complexities of managing GPU resources in cluster environments.

7.5.1 Experimental results

Experiments are conducted by using a Python programming environment. Parameters considered for this experiment are defined in Table 7.1. Population size represents the count of particles defined for the optimization process. Cognitive constants define the parameter setting to influence the position of the particle. Inertia weight is one of the important parameters that govern the relation between exploration and exploitation. The mutation is the parameter that identifies the best-rated particles or genes out of all possible particles. The provided experimental results detail the predicted workload for the next 24 hours, showcasing fluctuating demands over the time period. These predictions, ranging from 7.923 to 12.173, offer valuable insights for efficient resource allocation. Python is a convenient programming platform to perform simulations to predict the workloads of cloud. We conducted various experiments to identify variations in predicted workloads with different approaches

Table 7.1 Parameter setting for proposed approach

Population size	*Inertia weight*	*Cognitive component 1*	*Cognitive component 2*	*Mutation rate*
30	0.5	0.5	0.5	0.1

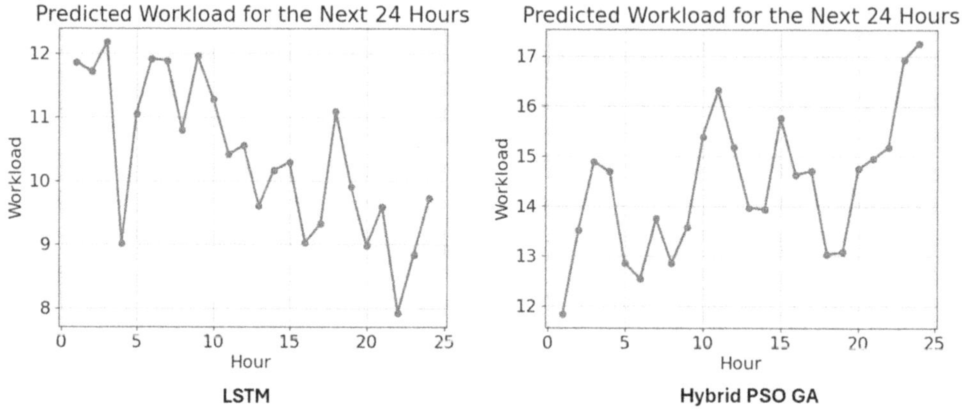

Figure 7.2 LSTM model predicted workload vs proposed model predicted workload.

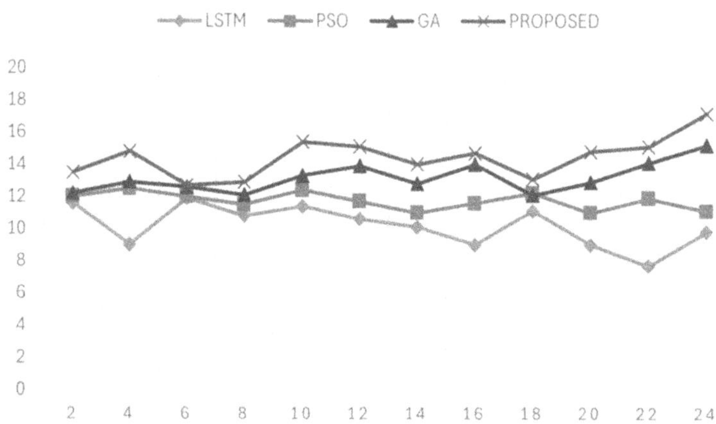

Figure 7.3 Workload comparison with other approaches.

like LSTM, PSO, GA, and our proposed approach. In Figure 7.2 predicted workloads are compared with LSTM and our proposed hybrid PSO-GA approach.

Our experimental results are analyzed and compared with other approaches to verify the accuracy of our predicted model. Workload predictions of specified time intervals of LSTM, PSO, GA, and our proposed approach are depicted in Figure 7.3.

In comparison, we find that our approach outperformed predicting cloud workload in a specified period. Heuristic and meta-heuristic approach inclusion in cloud workload prediction increases accuracy, but hybridization of meta-heuristic approaches outperforms and increases the prediction accuracy.

7.6 CONCLUSION AND FUTURE SCOPE

This study introduces a hybrid approach for cloud workload prediction, amalgamating LSTM with PSO and GA. By combining LSTM's capacity to capture temporal dependencies with PSO and GA optimization techniques, the proposed method offers a robust solution to the challenge of accurate workload forecasting in cloud computing environments.

Through experiments on real-world datasets from Azure Cloud, the hybrid PSO-GA algorithm demonstrates superior performance in predicting cloud workloads, enhancing prediction accuracy and scalability for efficient resource allocation and service optimization. This research contributes to advancing cloud workload prediction methodologies, offering insights for future exploration into hybrid optimization techniques and tailored application scenarios, ultimately fostering more effective resource management and service delivery in cloud computing.

This project entails further advancing the hybrid approach for cloud workload prediction by refining optimization techniques, tailoring the model to diverse application scenarios, and addressing scalability challenges. This involves exploring variations and enhancements to the hybrid PSO-GA algorithm. Additionally, if the predicted workload is high, then apply federated learning techniques to share the cloud workload evenly. There is scope in federated learning.

REFERENCES

[1] F. Kluge, S. Uhrig, J. Mische, B. Satzger, and T. Ungerer, "Dynamic workload prediction for soft real-time applications," in *2010 10th IEEE International Conference on Computer and Information Technology*, pp. 1841–1848, IEEE, 2010.

[2] R. Bianchini, M. Fontoura, E. Cortez, A. Bonde, A. Muzio, A.-M. Constantin, T. Moscibroda, G. Magalhaes, G. Bablani, and M. Russinovich, "Toward ml-centric cloud platforms," *Communications of the ACM*, vol. 63, no. 2, pp. 50–59, 2020.

[3] L. R. Medsker, L. Jain, *et al.*, "Recurrent neural networks," *Design and Applications*, vol. 5, no. 64–67, p. 2, 2001.

[4] A. Sherstinsky, "Fundamentals of recurrent neural network (RNN) and long short-term memory (LSTM) network," *Physica D: Nonlinear Phenomena*, vol. 404, p. 132306, 2020.

[5] P. Grassberger, T. Schreiber, and C. Schaffrath, "Nonlinear time sequence analysis," *International Journal of Bifurcation and Chaos*, vol. 1, no. 03, pp. 521–547, 1991.

[6] J. Durbin, "Efficient estimation of parameters in moving-average models," *Biometrika*, vol. 46, no. 3/4, pp. 306–316, 1959.

[7] M. Louzazni and H. Mosalam, "Dailly forecasting of photovoltaic power using non-linear autoregressive exogenous method," *in 2020 International Conference on Decision Aid Sciences and Application (DASA)*, pp. 1016–1020, IEEE, 2020.

[8] Y. Zhu, W. Zhang, Y. Chen, and H. Gao, "A novel approach to workload prediction using attention-based lstm encoder-decoder network in cloud environment," *EURASIP Journal on Wireless Communications and Networking*, vol. 2019, pp. 1–18, 2019.

[9] C. J. Willmott and K. Matsuura, "Advantages of the mean absolute error (MAE) over the root mean square error (RMSE) in assessing average model performance," *Climate research*, vol. 30, no. 1, pp. 79–82, 2005.

[10] I. Mavridis and H. Karatza, "Combining containers and virtual machines to enhance isolation and extend functionality on cloud computing," *Future Generation Computer Systems*, vol. 94, pp. 674–696, 2019.

[11] A. Sircar, K. Yadav, K. Rayavarapu, N. Bist, and H. Oza, "Application of machine learning and artificial intelligence in oil and gas industry," *Petroleum Research*, vol. 6, no. 4, pp. 379–391, 2021.

[12] Y. Wang, H. Zhang, and G. Zhang, "cpso-cnn: An efficient pso-based algorithm for fine-tuning hyper-parameters of convolutional neural networks," *Swarm and Evolutionary Computation*, vol. 49, pp. 114–123, 2019.

[13] P. Yazdanian and S. Sharifian, "Cloud workload prediction using convnet and stacked LSTM," in *2018 4th Iranian Conference on Signal Processing and Intelligent Systems (ICSPIS)*, pp. 83–87, IEEE, 2018.

[14] P. Yazdanian and S. Sharifian, "E2lg: a multiscale ensemble of LSTM/GAN deep learning architecture for multistep-ahead cloud workload prediction," *The Journal of Supercomputing*, vol. 77, pp. 11052–11082, 2021.
[15] X. Liang, Z. Hu, H. Zhang, C. Gan, and E. P. Xing, "Recurrent topic-transition gan for visual paragraph generation," in *Proceedings of the IEEE international conference on computer vision*, pp. 3362–3371, 2017.
[16] M. Xu, C. Song, H. Wu, S. S. Gill, K. Ye, and C. Xu, "esdnn: deep neural network based multivariate workload prediction in cloud computing environments," *ACM Transactions on Internet Technology (TOIT)*, vol. 22, no. 3, pp. 1–24, 2022.
[17] J. Kumar and A. K. Singh, "Performance evaluation of metaheuristics algorithms for workload prediction in cloud environment," *Applied Soft Computing*, vol. 113, p. 107895, 2021.
[18] M. Barati and S. Sharifian, "A hybrid heuristic-based tuned support vector regression model for cloud load prediction," *The Journal of Supercomputing*, vol. 71, pp. 4235–4259, 2015.
[19] Z. Chen, L. Yang, Y. Huang, X. Chen, X. Zheng, and C. Rong, "Pso-ga-based resource allocation strategy for cloud-based software services with workload-time windows," *IEEE Access*, vol. 8, pp. 151500–151510, 2020.
[20] T. Y. Tan, L. Zhang, and C. P. Lim, "Intelligent skin cancer diagnosis using improved particle swarm optimization and deep learning models," *Applied Soft Computing*, vol. 84, p. 105725, 2019.
[21] H. A. Kholidy, "An intelligent swarm based prediction approach for predicting cloud computing user resource needs," *Computer Communications*, vol. 151, pp. 133–144, 2020.
[22] V. R. Messias, J. C. Estrella, R. Ehlers, M. J. Santana, R. C. Santana, and S. Reiff-Marganiec, "Combining time series prediction models using genetic algorithm to autoscaling web applications hosted in the cloud infrastructure," *Neural Computing and Applications*, vol. 27, pp. 2383–2406, 2016.
[23] G. K. Walia, M. Kumar, and S. S. Gill, "Ai-empowered fog/edge resource management for iot applications: A comprehensive review, research challenges and future perspectives," *IEEE Communications Surveys & Tutorials*, vol. 26, issue 1, pp. 619–699, 2023.
[24] R. Arora, R. Tulshyan, and K. Deb, "Parallelization of binary and real-coded genetic algorithms on gpu using cuda," in *IEEE Congress on Evolutionary Computation*, pp. 1–8, IEEE, 2010.
[25] H. Ding, L. Benyoucef, and X. Xie, "A simulation-based multi-objective genetic algorithm approach for networked enterprises optimization," *Engineering Applications of Artificial Intelligence*, vol. 19, no. 6, pp. 609–623, 2006.
[26] A. Graves and A. Graves, "Long short-term memory," in *Supervised sequence labelling with recurrent neural networks*, Studies in Computational Intelligence vol. 385. Berlin: Springer, pp. 37–45, 2012.
[27] C. Pandi, T. S. Dandibhotla, and V. V. Bulusu, "Corpus linguistic rules based review sentence selection for opinion targets extraction and opinion orientation: A distant supervision approach," *International Journal of Intelligent Engineering & Systems*, vol. 11, no. 5, pp. 114–124, 2018.
[28] L. Chen and W. Zhang, "A deep learning-based approach with pso for workload prediction of containers in the cloud," in *2021 13th International Conference on Advanced Infocomm Technology (ICAIT)*, pp. 204–208, IEEE, 2021.

Chapter 8

An improved noise filter design for Canny edge detection with pipeline architecture

K. Revathi and K. Rasadurai

8.1 INTRODUCTION

Detecting edges in images serves critical purposes across diverse fields including imaging in medical sciences, finding mineral resources in less time and at lowest cost, and remote sensing in satellites. Canny algorithm has been the preferred choice for detecting edges due to its exceptional performance over the years. However, its complexity and time-consuming nature, coupled with the reliance on fixed values of threshold for input images, pose significant challenges. Fluctuations in external conditions, such as lighting changes, necessitate adaptive threshold adjustments. These constraints significantly undermine the system's real-time performance, adaptability, and flexibility.

Hence, implementing the Canny algorithm directly is not feasible for actual implementation. Various methods have been explored by researchers to overcome these challenges, such as utilizing field programmable gate arrays (FPGAs) to implement Canny algorithm on hardware. Numerous studies have focused on implementing the Canny algorithm on FPGAs for real-time applications. Each of these approaches reduces the complexity to some extent. For instance, constant low and high threshold values are employed for hysteresis thresholding to simplify the algorithm, albeit at the cost of performance degradation. In contrast, Khidhir and Abdullah [1] compute the threshold using gradient magnitude histogram data. Additionally, Elham et al. [2] and Brown et al. [3] utilize block classification techniques to determine threshold.

In this chapter we discuss a refined Canny algorithm for detecting edges, offering improved precision, decreased complexity of computation, and automatic calculation of threshold. Threshold is calculated by using Otsu's algorithm, leveraging existing FPGA-based implementations of Otsu's algorithm [4, 5]. To streamline computation complexity, we introduced approximation method and logarithmic operations.

Below are the details of our input toward the suggested design approach:

1. Utilizing approximate method to compute gradient magnitude and orientation.
2. Calculating the adaptive threshold using Otsu's algorithm.
3. Introducing a 32-bit logarithmic arithmetic unit to simplify Otsu's algorithm.

The structural framework of this study categorizes the research into distinct sections. Literature review is presented in Section 8.2. Section 8.3 presents the concept of the existing method. Section 8.4 discusses the proposed method. Section 8.5 presents the simulation results of the existing and proposed methods. Section 8.6 summarizes the results, and Section 8.7 offers some forward-looking ideas.

DOI: 10.1201/9781003591788-8

8.2 LITERATURE REVIEW

Abbasi et al. [4] proposed an efficient way to implement the Canny algorithm to detect edges on hardware tailored for FPGA devices. They discussed techniques to reduce latency and improve throughput for real-time applications.

Gonzales et al. [5] explored parallel processing methodologies to enhance the Canny edge detection algorithm's performance on FPGA. They investigated strategies to exploit FPGA parallelism effectively.

Anusha et al. [6] focused on deploying the Canny algorithm for edge detecting on FPGA using pipeline architecture. They explore optimizations to improve edge detection performance while considering FPGA resource utilization.

Gonzales [7] explored an energy-efficient implementation of the Canny algorithm for detecting edges on FPGA. They emphasized techniques to minimize power consumption without compromising edge detection accuracy.

RangacharKasturi and Schunck [8] explored hardware acceleration of the Canny algorithm for edge detecting on FPGA utilizing OpenCL. They explored the benefits of using OpenCL for FPGA-based acceleration and its impact on performance. A novel design to detect edges by using the Canny algorithm optimized for real-time applications on FPGA. They focused on achieving low latency and high throughput.

Groups of researchers [9–10] explored hardware acceleration of the Canny algorithm for edge detecting on FPGA utilizing OpenCL. They explored the benefits of using OpenCL for FPGA-based acceleration and its impact on performance. Authors presented an FPGA-based Canny algorithm for edge detecting that is implemented on hardware suitable for embedded systems. They discussed optimizations for resource-constrained environments. Authors proposed a hybrid FPGA-CPU implementation of the Canny algorithm for real-time processing. They explored the synergy between FPGA and CPU to optimize performance. Authors introduced an adaptive method to implement the Canny algorithm to detect edges on FPGA as an algorithm capable of handling variable image sizes efficiently. They addressed scalability concerns for different image resolutions.

8.3 EXISTING METHOD

The conventional method for detecting Canny edges involves Canny's approach to identifying the optimal edge detector for handling all edges affected by white Gaussian noise. The original Canny edge detection algorithm [11] for an input image of size $M \times M$ with n bits per bit is outlined in Figure 8.1. It encompasses the following steps:

1. Use gradient masks to determine the vertical gradient Gy and horizontal gradient Gx at each pixel point.
2. Determine the gradient's direction (ϸG) and magnitude (G) at every pixel position.
3. Non-maximum suppression: Suppress minima in a gradient image while maintaining local maxima and transform the image's fuzzy edges into crisp ones.
4. Calculation of threshold: The magnitude of gradient histogram of the complete image serves as the basis for the computation of the high and low thresholds, which identify potential edges.
5. Hysteresis thresholding: This method compares each pixel's gradient magnitude values with low and high threshold values to produce a continuous edge map. This eliminates edge pixels brought on by noise and changes in lighting.

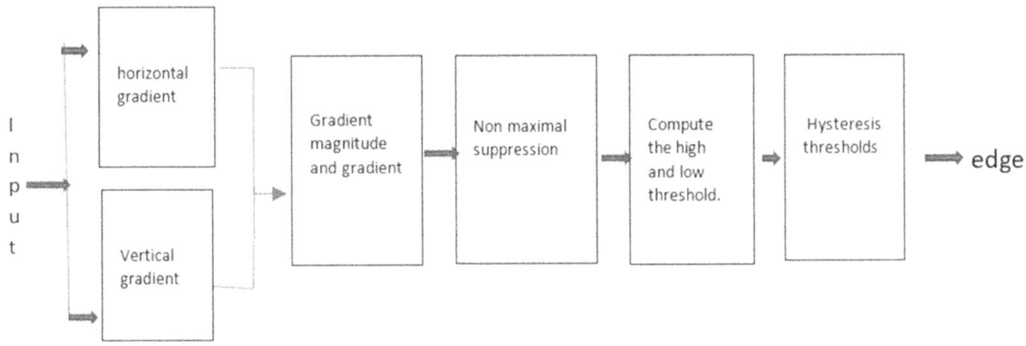

Figure 8.1 Diagrammatic representation of the Canny algorithm.

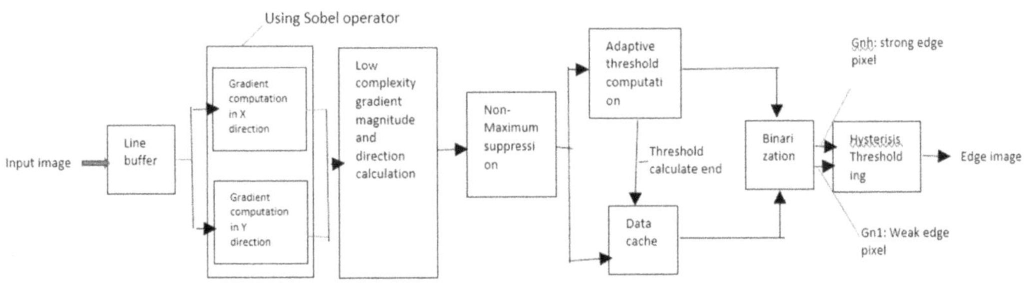

Figure 8.2 Architecture of the enhanced Canny edge detection method.

8.4 PROPOSED METHOD

8.4.1 Enhanced Canny edge detection algorithm

Threshold selection process typically falls into two main categories: fixed thresholds and adjustable thresholds. Opting for a fixed threshold undoubtedly reduces hardware resource usage and algorithm complexity. However, the drawback is that the threshold must be readjusted whenever there are changes in the object being detected or its external conditions, such as variations in lighting. This adjustment doesn't align well with real-time performance requirements. Conversely, employing an adaptive threshold effectively addresses these challenges.

In this section, we introduce three methods for improving the hardware implementation of the Canny algorithm for detecting edges. These methods include logarithmic approximation to simplify Otsu's algorithm, a method for calculating gradient magnitude and direction with low complexity, and the use of Otsu's algorithm for automatic threshold selection. Figure 8.2 presents an enhanced design technique for Canny edge detection.

8.4.2 Gradient computation based on sobel operator

Here, a gradient mask is created using a Sobel operator. The Sobel operator's combination of differentiation and Gaussian smoothing provides a compelling reason to utilize it instead of other operators in this context. Pixel intensities near edges are given more weight. The 3 × 3 sub-window of a picture and horizontal (x) and vertical (y) Sobel operator kernels are displayed in Figure 8.3.

P0	P1	P2
P3	P4	P5
P6	P7	P8

(a)

-1	0	1
-2	0	2
-1	0	1

(b)

-1	-2	-1
0	0	0
1	2	1

(c)

(a) A 3*3 sub window of an image

(b) Sobel operator Kernel in x direction

(c) Sobel operator Kernel in y direction

Figure 8.3 Subsection of an image and the Sobel operator kernel.

Eqs. (8.1) and (8.2) are employed to compute gradients in the direction of x and y.

$$f_x(x,y) = (p_2 - p_0) + 2(p_5 - p_3) + (p_8 - p_6) \tag{8.1}$$

$$fy(x,y) = (p_6 - p_0) + 2(p_7 - p_1) + (p_8 - p_2) \tag{8.2}$$

Prior to calculating Eqs. (8.1) and (8.2), we must acquire the matching pixels. A line buffer oversees this Figure 8.4.

Once matching pixels are obtained, we can start calculating $Zx\ (x,\ y)$ and $fy\ (x,\ y)$. The architecture for calculating $Zx\ (x,\ y)$ is illustrated in Figure 8.5. The calculation of $fy\ (x,\ y)$ involves only those pixel values that are part of the same architecture but differ in their computations. The signed values of fx and fy in this section are determined by their MSBs.

8.4.3 Simplified calculation of gradient magnitude and direction

Edge strength at a certain pixel is determined by the pixel magnitude. Edge direction at a certain pixel is determined by its orientation. Eqs. (8.3) and (8.4) provide gradient magnitude and direction computations for one pixel.

$$\text{mag}(x,y) = \sqrt{fx(x,y)^2 + fy(x,y)^2} \tag{8.3}$$

$$\theta(x,y) = \arctan\left(\frac{fy(x,y)}{fx(x,y)}\right) \tag{8.4}$$

Expensive hardware is required to implement the two equations above. To obtain the gradient magnitude mag (x, y) for Eq. (8.3), we sum the modulus of fx(x, y) and fy(x, y). The CORDIC module proposed in Eq. (8.4) is utilized to determine θ(x,y). Drawback of the CORDIC module is that it takes a lot of iterations to get a satisfactory level of precision, which means more hardware is used.

The shift-based orienting approach is used in this section. As seen in Figure 8.6, orientations are evenly divided and separated into eight zones. According to the tabulated value, the first quadrant has the orientations from 0° to 90° of tan, while second quadrant contains the remaining orientations up to tan180°.

The first and second quadrants' tan values are the same, but their polarity is different. The quadrant flag is used to locate the quadrant. The calculations of the quadrant flag and gradient magnitude are displayed in below diagram.

To simplify, Eq. (8.4) can be expressed as

$$\tan\theta(x,y) = fy(x,y)/fx(x,y) \tag{8.5}$$

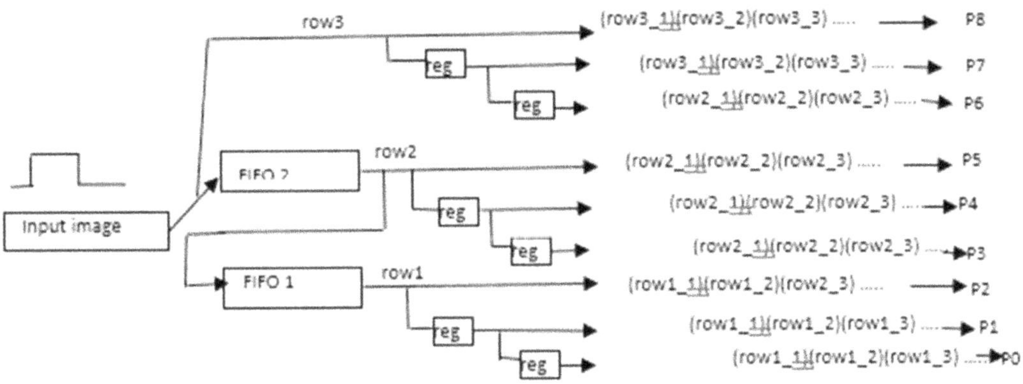

Figure 8.4 Design of the line buffer architecture.

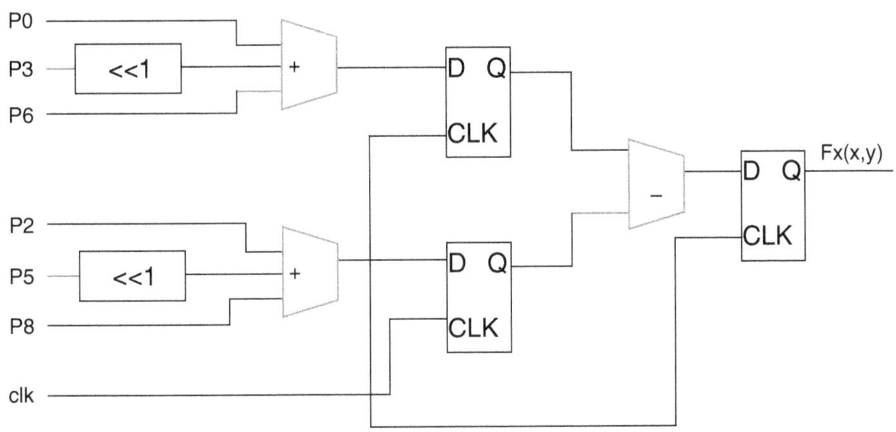

Figure 8.5 Architecture of fx(x, y).

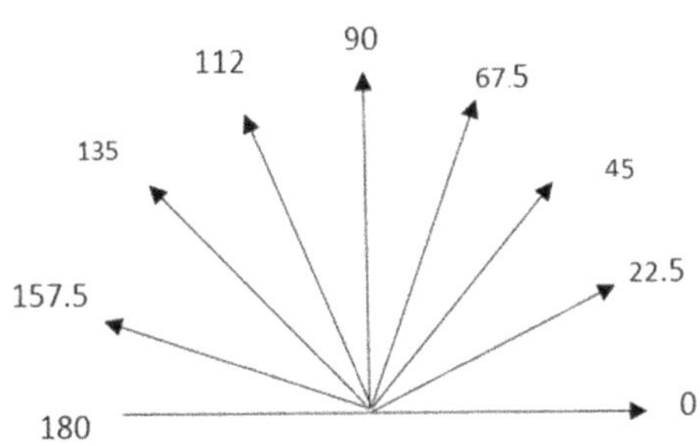

Figure 8.6 Eight sectors of gradient orientation.

Eq. (8.6) defines value of tan θ(x,y):

$$\tan \theta j(x,y) \le \tan \theta(x,y) < \tan \theta j+1(x,y) \tag{8.6}$$

Eq. (8.7) is derived by rewriting Eq. (8.6):

$$\tan \theta_j(x,y) \le \frac{fy(x,y)}{fx(x,y)} < \tan \theta_{j+1}(x,y) \tag{8.7}$$

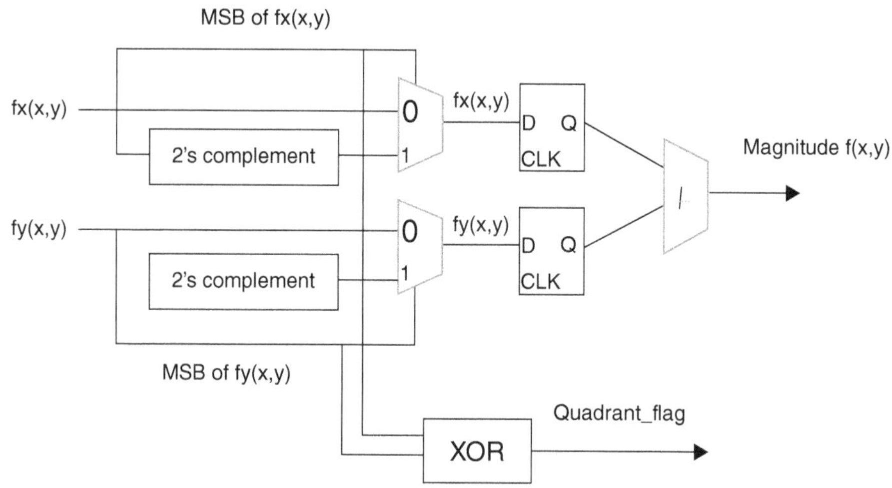

Figure 8.7 Design of the module for calculating gradient magnitude and computing quadrant flags.

Eq. (8.8) represents the condition derived from Eq. (8.7):

$$f_x(x,y)^* \tan\theta_j(x,y) \le f_y(x,y) < f_x(x,y)^* \tan\theta_{j+1}(x,y) \tag{8.8}$$

See Figure 8.7 and Figure 8.8.

8.4.4 Non-maximum suppression

A technique for edge thinning that preserves local maxima along the gradient direction of a picture is called non-maximum suppression (NMS). The a and b pixels in Figure 8.9 represent the current pixel, and the selection is utilized to locate pixels in a direction similar to that of the current pixel.

The values of a and b are g3 and g5 for directions 1 or 8; g0 and g8 for directions 2 or 3; g5, and g6 for directions 4 or 5; and g1 and g7 values for directions 6 or 7. To find out if maxima are present, the comparator (CMP) compares the current pixel (g4) with a and b. It is preserved if the current pixel contains the maxima. It is suppressed as 0 otherwise. We restrict the value range to 8 bits because g4 requires maximum value of 10 bits, which saves hardware requirement for further statistics.

8.4.5 Adaptive threshold computation

One of the most crucial components of the suggested clever edge detector system is the adaptive threshold computation. We determined necessary threshold adaptively using Otsu's technique after NMS. It is necessary to cache the NMS data beforehand, and the SDRAM controller does this. Histogram data were used to determine the pertinent Otsu's algorithm parameters, after which the threshold was computed. Simultaneously, SDRAM signal reading was enabled when threshold calculation was finished. After that, the NMS data was compared to binarization threshold value, and lastly, the hysteresis was performed.

8.4.6 32-bit logarithmic arithmetic

To reduce difficulty in calculation, LNS has been investigated for arithmetic calculations. It is made up of a fractional part generation block (FPGen), a barrel shifter, a characteristic

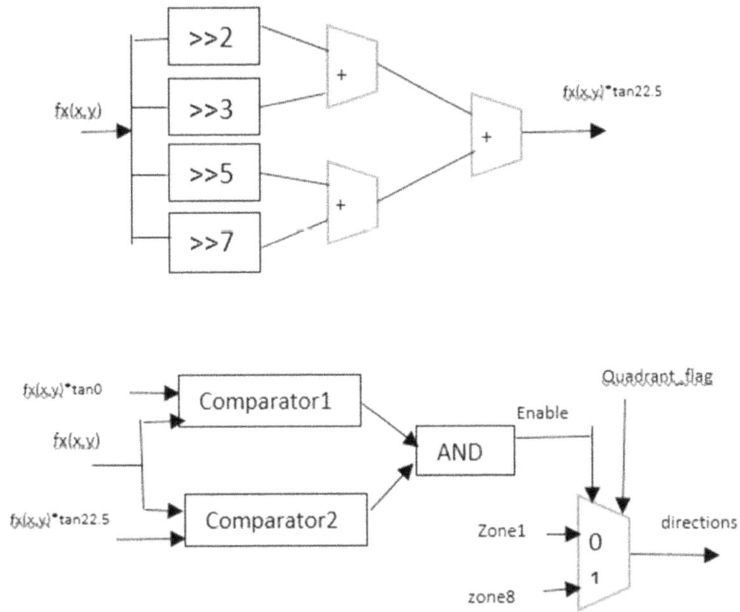

Figure 8.8 Design for determining direction.

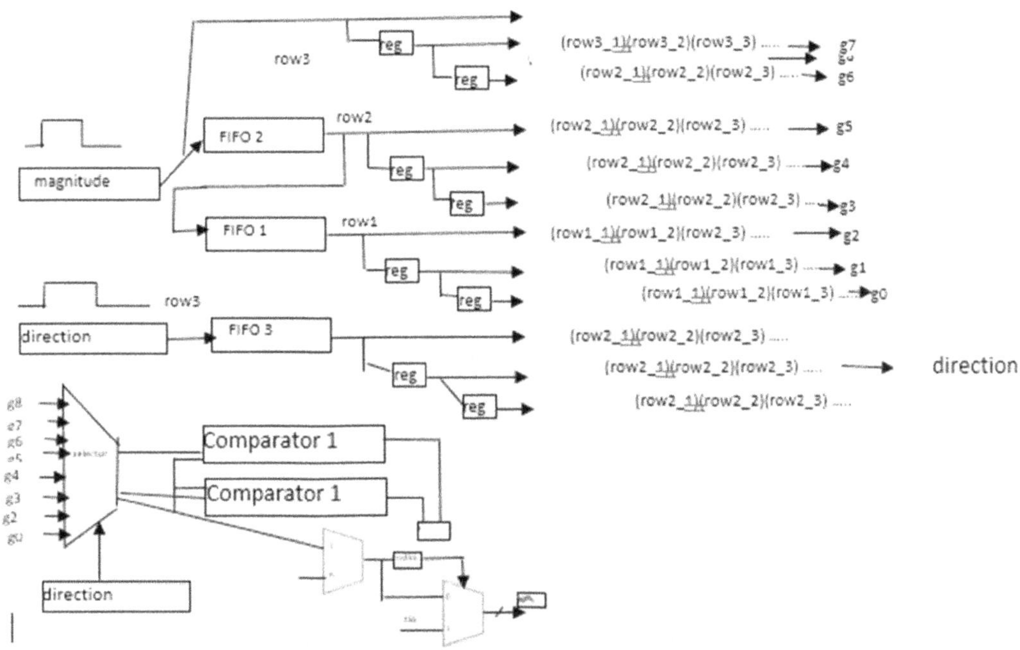

Figure 8.9 Architecture of NMS.

generator, and a 32-bit count leading zero. At the conclusion of the logarithmic converter, the variable input number range Qm.n. is changed Q6.26, which is a fixed number range. The number of leading zero bits in the input is determined by the CLZ. The characteristic value and amount of shift value of the BSH are determined by five bits of the CLZ block output. The input number range of Qm.n. is converted to Q6.26 by BSH. Following the shifting

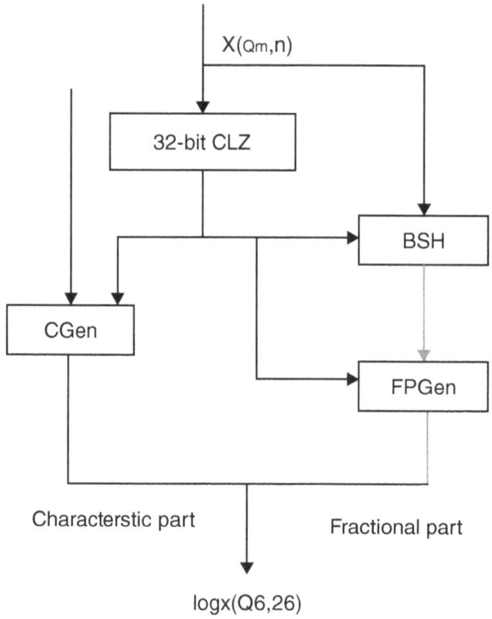

Figure 8.10 Architecture of logarithmic converter.

operation, FPGen block generates the fractional portion and the CGen block generates the characteristic part. The logarithmic conversion result is obtained by combining the two values mentioned above Figure 8.10.

8.5 SIMULATION RESULTS

8.5.1 Existing system

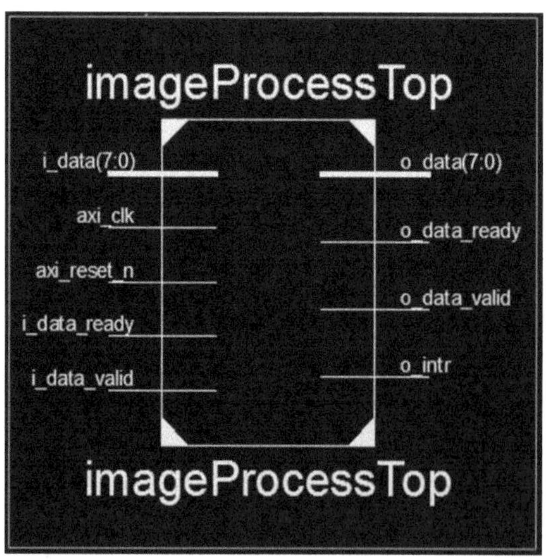

Figure 8.11 Schematic diagram of existing Canny edge RTL design.

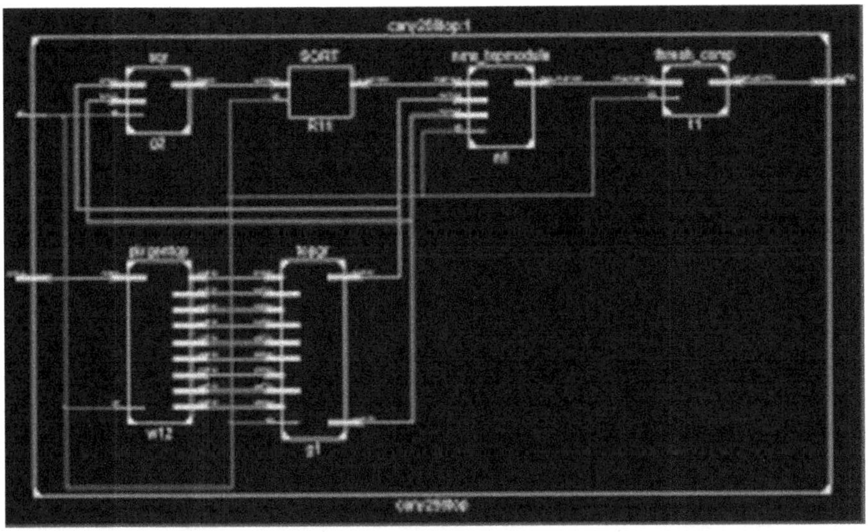

Figure 8.12 Schematic diagram of existing Canny edge RTL design.

```
Device utilization summary:
---------------------------

Selected Device : 7vx485tffg1157-3


Slice Logic Utilization:
 Number of Slice Registers:              219  out of  607200     0%
 Number of Slice LUTs:                  1854  out of  303600     0%
    Number used as Logic:                702  out of  303600     0%
    Number used as Memory:              1152  out of  130800     0%
       Number used as RAM:              1152

Slice Logic Distribution:
 Number of LUT Flip Flop pairs used:    1858
   Number with an unused Flip Flop:     1639  out of    1858    88%
   Number with an unused LUT:              4  out of    1858     0%
   Number of fully used LUT-FF pairs:    215  out of    1858    11%
   Number of unique control sets:         18

IO Utilization:
 Number of IOs:                           23
 Number of bonded IOBs:                   23  out of     600     3%

Specific Feature Utilization:
 Number of BUFG/BUFGCTRLs:                 1  out of      32     3%
 Number of DSP48E1s:                       2  out of    2800     0%

---------------------------
```

Figure 8.13 Area utilization of existing Canny edge RTL design.

```
Timing Summary:
---------------
Speed Grade: -3

   Minimum period: 3.471ns (Maximum Frequency: 288.085MHz)
   Minimum input arrival time before clock: 1.212ns
   Maximum output required time after clock: 0.543ns
   Maximum combinational path delay: No path found
```

Figure 8.14 Delay of existing Canny edge RTL design.

```
2.3.  Power Supply Summary
-------------------------------------------------------------
|                     Power Supply Summary                  |
-------------------------------------------------------------
|                        | Total  | Dynamic | Static Power |
-------------------------------------------------------------
| Supply Power (mW)      | 284.36 | 43.06   | 241.30       |
-------------------------------------------------------------
```

Figure 8.15 Power consumption of existing Canny edge RTL design.

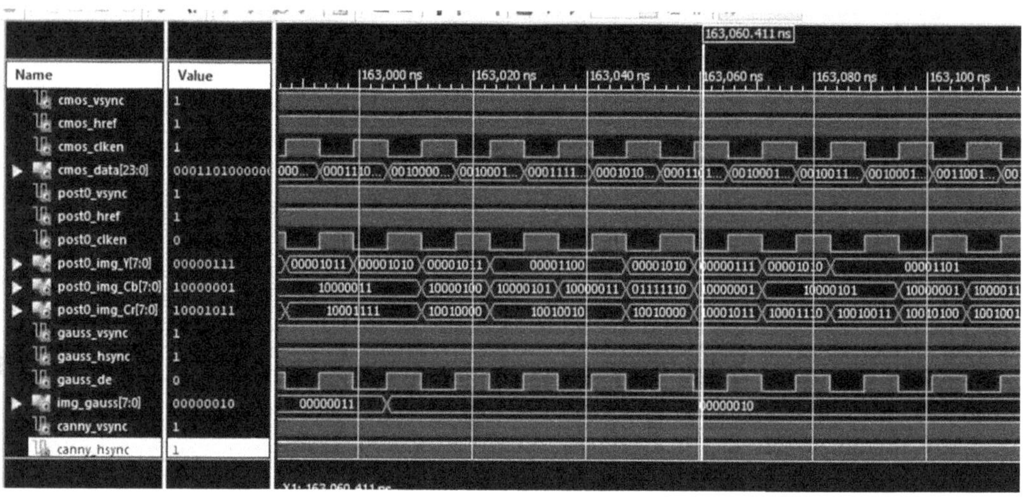

Figure 8.16 Output wave form for existing Canny edge RTL design.

8.5.2 Proposed method

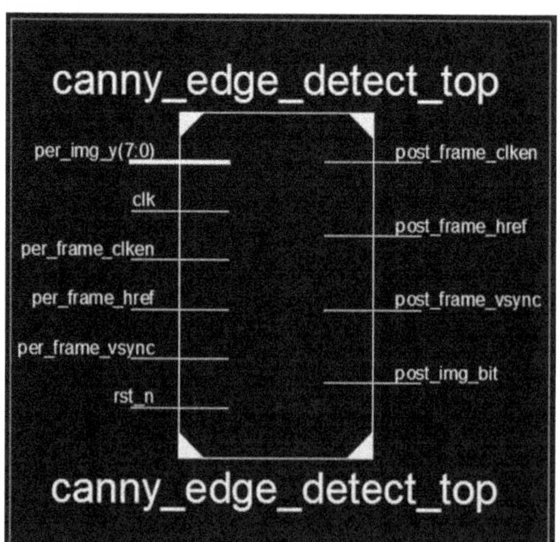

Figure 8.17 Schematic diagram of proposed Canny edge RTL design.

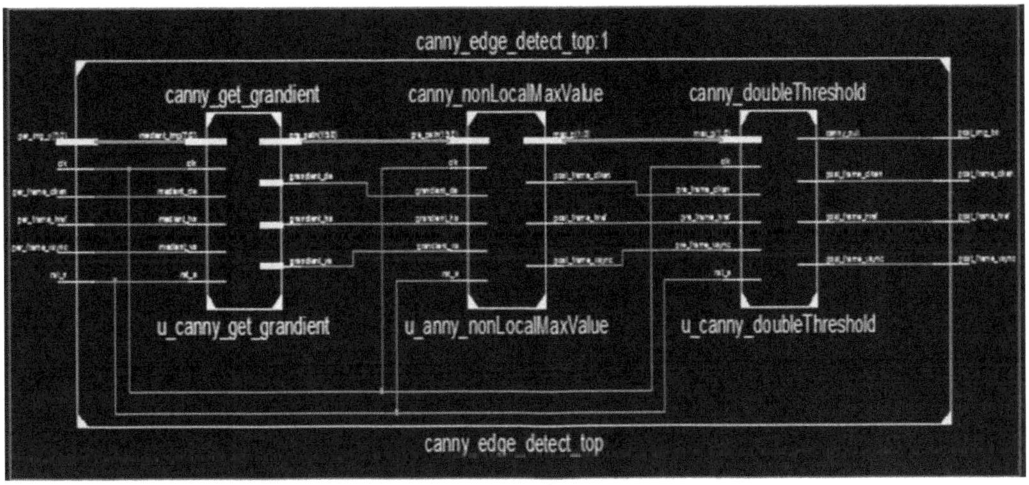

Figure 8.18 Schematic diagram of proposed Canny edge RTL design.

```
Device utilization summary:
---------------------------

Selected Device : 7vx485tffg1157-3


Slice Logic Utilization:
 Number of Slice Registers:              729  out of  607200     0%
 Number of Slice LUTs:                   889  out of  303600     0%
    Number used as Logic:                875  out of  303600     0%
    Number used as Memory:                14  out of  130800     0%
       Number used as SRL:                14

Slice Logic Distribution:
 Number of LUT Flip Flop pairs used:     976
   Number with an unused Flip Flop:      247  out of     976    25%
   Number with an unused LUT:             87  out of     976     8%
   Number of fully used LUT-FF pairs:    642  out of     976    65%
   Number of unique control sets:         14

IO Utilization:
 Number of IOs:                           17
 Number of bonded IOBs:                   17  out of     600     2%

Specific Feature Utilization:
 Number of Block RAM/FIFO:                 3  out of    1030     0%
    Number using Block RAM only:           3
 Number of BUFG/BUFGCTRLs:                 1  out of      32     3%
 Number of DSP48E1s:                       1  out of    2800     0%

---------------------------
```

Figure 8.19 Area utilization of proposed Canny edge RTL design.

```
Timing Summary:
---------------
Speed Grade: -3

   Minimum period: 3.897ns (Maximum Frequency: 256.614MHz)
   Minimum input arrival time before clock: 1.300ns
   Maximum output required time after clock: 0.511ns
   Maximum combinational path delay: No path found
```

Figure 8.20 Delay of proposed Canny edge RTL design.

```
2.3.  Power Supply Summary
-----------------------------------------------------------
|                  Power Supply Summary                    |
-----------------------------------------------------------
|                      | Total  | Dynamic | Static Power |
-----------------------------------------------------------
| Supply Power (mW)    | 277.61 | 36.31   | 241.30       |
-----------------------------------------------------------
```

Figure 8.21 Power consumption of proposed Canny edge RTL design.

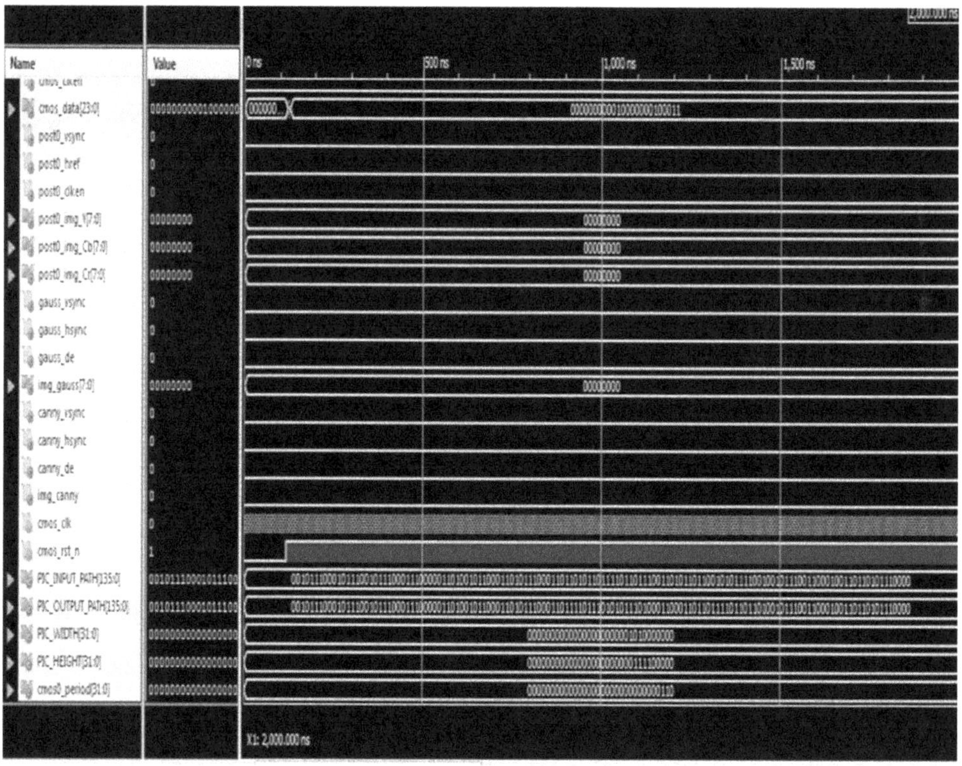

Figure 8.22 Output Wave form for proposed Canny edge RTL design.

Table 8.1 Results comparison

S. No	*Parameter*	*Existing method*	*Proposed method*
1.	Area in LUT's	1,854	889
2.	Delay in ns	3.741	3.897
3.	Max. Frequency in MHz	288.085	256.614
4.	Power Delay Product (PDP) in W/sec	1,063.790	1,081.846
5.	Power in MilliWatts	284.36	277.61

8.5.3 Results of discussions

A comparison is made between the exercise outlines of each design after they have been synthesized on the Vertex7 – 7vx485tfgg1157 board and the results are shown in Table 8.1. Verilog HDL is used in the implementation of the suggested architectures. After simulation, the Xilinx Vertex7 – 7vx485tfgg1157 FPGA board is used for synthesis. Using various-sized grayscale images as a preset threshold, the simulation is finished.

In all cases, a threshold of 27 intensity levels was applied. The planning can operate at a frequency of 100 MHz. Tables that compare the current style with the planning are made to highlight the architectures' execution times. The results of the synthesis indicate that 889 cells were employed, occupying an area of around 1.951.288 μm^2. It used roughly 277.61 mW of power and delayed by 9.599 ns.

8.5.4 Performance comparison

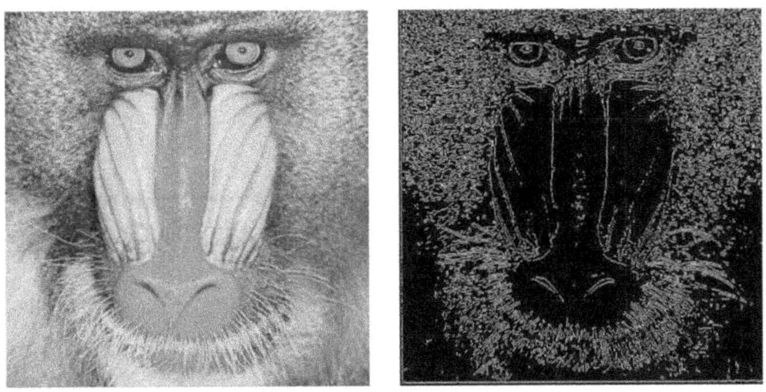

Figure 8.23 Corresponding edge images by hardware and software package implementation.

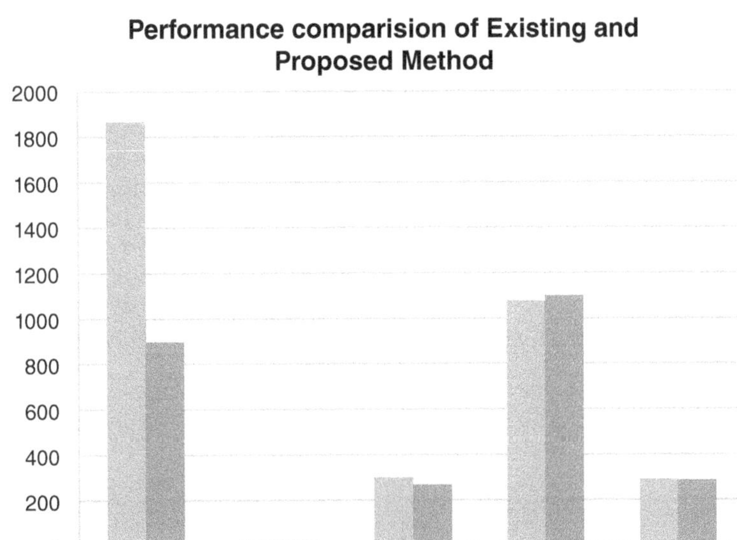

	Area in LUT's	Delay (ns)	Max. Frequency (MHz)	Power Delay Product (PDP) (W/sec)	Power (mW)
Existing Method (Canny Edge Detection)	1854	6,061	288,085	1063,79	284,36
Proposed Method (Improved Canny Edge Detection)	889	3.897	256,614	1081,846	277.61

Figure 8.24 Performance of existing and proposed methods.

8.6 CONCLUSION

This chapter included a thorough investigation of the application of pipeline architecture on FPGA for the Canny edge detection algorithm. It was shown through comparative analysis that the suggested approach significantly decreased latency, leveraging 889 Slice LUTs on the FPGA device 7vx485tffg1157-3 to achieve a minimum period of 3.897 ns (maximum frequency: 256.614MHz). This represents a significant improvement over the current procedure, which used 1,908 Slice LUTs on the same FPGA and produced a delay of 6.061 ns (maximum frequency: 165.003 MHz). The efficiency and effectiveness of the suggested solution in real-time edge detection applications are highlighted by the improvements made in delay reduction while optimizing FPGA resources. The results indicate that edge detection procedures on FPGA platforms are accelerated greatly by the improved pipeline architecture.

8.7 FUTURE SCOPE

Further optimizations within the Canny edge detection algorithm can be explored to leverage FPGA architecture more efficiently. This involves refining edge detection stages or exploring alternative algorithms that might offer better performance.

REFERENCES

1. A.M. Khidhir Dr., N.Y. Abdullah, "FPGA based edge detection using Sobel filte", *Int. J. Res. Dev. Engineer.* 2(1), June-July 2022, 22–32.
2. J.M. Elham, J.M. Ahmed, J.M. Zainab, et al., Design study Sobel edge detection, *Int. J. Appl. Innov. Eng. Manage.* 2 (12) (December 2022), 248–253 ISSN 2319-4847.
3. S.D. Brown, R.J. Francis, J. Rose, Z.G. Vranesic, *Field-Programmable Gate Arrays*, 180, Springer Science & Business Media, 2022.
4. T.A. Abbasi, et al., A proposed FPGA based architecture for sobel edge detection operator, *J. Act. Passive Electron. Devices* 2 (2019), pp. 271–280.
5. R.C. Gonzalez, R.E. Woods, S.L. Eddins, Digital image processing using Matlab (2015).*University of Tartu Image Processing Textbook* 1, 1. "Introduction to Image Processing"
6. G Anusha, T. JayaChandra Prasad, D. SatyaNarayana, Implementation of Sobel edge detection on FPGA, *Int. J. Comput. Trends Technol.* 3(3) (2012). R. Muthukrishnan, M. Radha, Edge detection techniques for image segmentation", *Int. J. Comput. Sci. Inf. Technol. (IJCSIT)* 3 (6) (Dec 2021), pp. 259–269.
7. Rafael C. Gonzales, "*Digital Image Processing*", 3rd edition, Pearson, 2009
8. Ramesh Jain RangacharKasturi, Brian G. Schunck, *Machine Vision*, New York: McGraw-Hill, 1995.
9. "*Xilinx Products*" https://www.xilinx.com/products/silicon-devices/fpga/what-is-an-fpga.html
10. "DigilentZybo Z-10 Product Information" https://www.xilinx.com/products/boards-and-kits/1-pukimv.html
11. Y. Kashyap, A. Vyas, R. Raghuwanshi, R. Sharma, "Edge detection using sobel method with median filter", 2(5), May 2020

Chapter 9

FPGA implementation of 256-bit Key AES algorithm using a modified S-box sharing algorithm

J. V. Preethi, G. N. Kodandaramaiah, and K. Rasadurai

9.1 INTRODUCTION

In a number of ways, internet communication helps convey a massive amount of data and information. A portion of the data may be sent from the sender to the recipient across the open channel. There are various approaches to safeguarding the information from intermediaries. We can keep confidential information safe from prying eyes by utilizing the principles of cryptography. By using techniques like encryption and decryption, we can keep the information safe from prying eyes. Data is transformed via encryption such that the recipient shouldn't be able to decipher it. Both the transmitter and the recipient will already be aware of the original data or information. This is possible in the AES by using the block cipher technique. The block cipher will only work with those specific blocks or groups with unaltered key lengths. Encryption and decryption processes both make use of the four transformations. It goes through a series of processes for the encryption that are dependent on the key. The architecture of the 256-bit advance encryption standard (AES) is depicted in Figure 9.1. Symmetric key cryptography, which uses comparable keys for the two processes of encryption and decryption, is the foundation of this architecture. In an encryption procedure, plain text input is converted to cipher text output, and vice versa, in a decryption procedure. A cipher key of roughly 128 bits is also utilized, while the input for AES encryption is 128 bits of plain text. It first executes an add round key operation. This involves the use of an XOR operation. Modern cryptographic techniques are built around the AES, which ensures safe data storage and transmission for a variety of purposes. The improvement of AES implementations on FPGAs continues to be an important field of research due to the constantly changing cybersecurity concerns. This chapter investigates the Vertex 7 FPGA platform's implementation of the 256-bit key AES algorithm, with a focus on examining the effects of using a modified S-Box technique in contrast to the traditional S-Box method.

The U.S. government selected the symmetric encryption algorithm AES, which has since spread throughout the world as a standard for protecting sensitive data. It has established itself as a key cryptographic tool thanks to its resilience to brute-force attacks and its effective data encryption and decryption capabilities. However, the computational demands of AES, especially when operating with large key sizes, pose challenges in terms of resource utilization, speed, and power consumption when implemented on hardware platforms like FPGAs. AES's key component, the S-Box, adds a great deal of security to the encryption process by substituting bytes. Standardized S-Box architectures are the foundation of traditional implementations [9–12]. Nevertheless, more recent studies have looked into modified S-Box variants that may be able to enhance performance parameters including power consumption, latency, and space utilization.

DOI: 10.1201/9781003591788-9

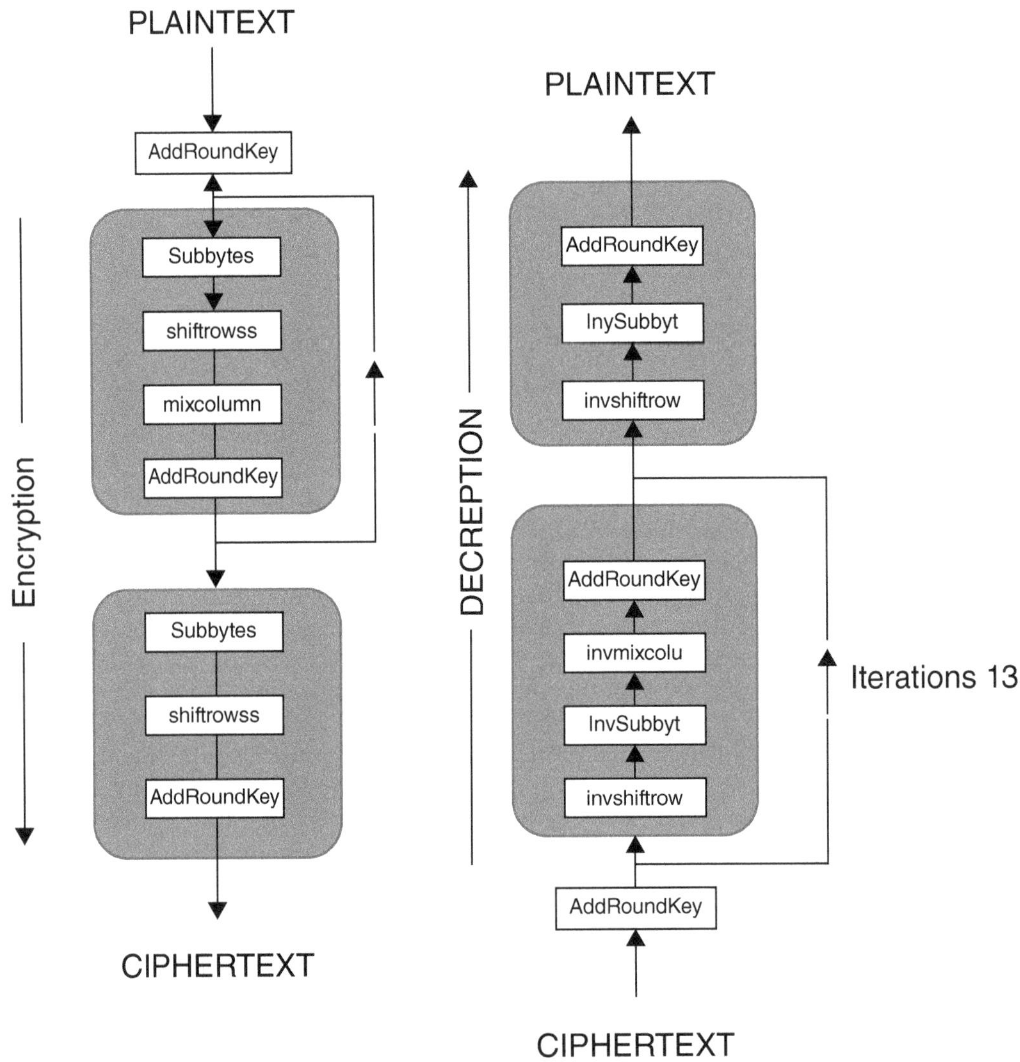

Figure 9.1 Architecture of 256 AES algorithm.

The aim of this study is to analyze and compare two distinct approaches to the S-Box: the traditional S-Box and a suggested modified S-Box approach [13]. Evaluation criteria such as power consumption in milliwatts, delay in nanoseconds, and area usage measured in Look-Up Tables (LUTs) will be thoroughly investigated to determine the effectiveness of the modified S-Box technique in maximizing AES implementation on the Virtex 7 FPGA [14, 15].

By using modified S-Box approaches, this study seeks to provide important insights into improving the effectiveness and performance of AES encryption on FPGAs, potentially opening the door to more secure and resource-efficient cryptographic implementations. This study's organizational framework separates the research into several areas. Section 9.2 provides literature review. Section 9.3 demonstrates the concept of the current method. Section 9.4 introduces the concept of the proposed method. The simulation results of both methods are presented in Section 9.5. Section 9.6 offers conclusions.

9.2 LITERATURE REVIEW

In their study, Michael et al. [1] examined the application of cloud-based side-channel prevention techniques in contrast to more conventional side-channel attacks. They outlined the prerequisites for addressing such challenges and emphasized the need for new techniques to defend against these types of attacks in cloud systems. A helpful PRIME+PROBE side-channel attack against the last level cache was presented by Fangfei et al. [2]. They successfully executed a cross-core, cross-VM attack on various versions of GnuPG and evaluated the bandwidth of the covert channel created by the attack. This method attains a high attack resolution without depending on memory sharing between the attacker and the victim or on flaws in the operating system or virtual machine monitor.

By applying the notion of fault sensitivity, Yang Li et al. [3] have discovered a novel fault-based side-channel attack. The FSA attack has a strong emphasis on fault sensitivity, testing the leakage of critical information through fault novel attacks on reduced round AES with very little data complexity and, consequently, identify enhanced AES attacks has been shown by Charles et al. [4]. According to Chari et al. [5], AES can be easily broken with a single sample by template attacks, and it cannot be adjusted to techniques like SPA and DPA. The user is required to deal with the noises that emerge in each sample in order to accomplish these attacks in realistic situations.

The concept of leakage attacks was devised by Itai Dinur and Adi Shamir [6] against iterated block ciphers, where the attacker can find side channels through physical searching, power measurement, or any other method. While side channel attacks provide noisy data, the unique cube assault requires especially clean data. According to Zhao et al.'s research [7], algebraic side-channel assaults are a potent cryptanalysis technique that is unique when compared to traditional side-channel attacks. They have suggested many deductions-based ASCAs to improve ASCA and handle the many deductions caused by inaccurate measurements or invasions. Shaheb et al. [8] have found that the SCCA on the block can be advanced by iterating selected plaintexts and cube iteration after the quadratic equations are removed.

9.3 EXISTING METHOD

9.3.1 Architecture of AES algorithm

There are four operations in the AES algorithm: Sub-bytes, Shift Rows, Mix Columns, and Add Round Key as shown in Figure 9.1. There are a total of 14 rounds for both encryption and decryption operations. Once encrypted, the ciphertext will be transmitted through the channel. The same key that is used for encryption will be utilized by the recipient side to decrypt the communication. In AES-256, the key size is 256 bits, and the data block size is 128 bits. Data includes the encrypted data, the plaintext message, and the ciphertext. Figure 9.1: 256 AES Algorithm Architecture.

Figure 9.2 depicts the internal data structure of a 128-bit data block. It shows a 4 x 4 matrix where each element is 8 bits, derived from the original 128-bit data. The transformation

A_0	A_4	A_8	A_{12}
A_1	A_5	A_9	A_{13}
A_2	A_6	A_{10}	A_{14}
A_3	A_7	A_{11}	A_{15}

Figure 9.2 Data structure of 128-bit message.

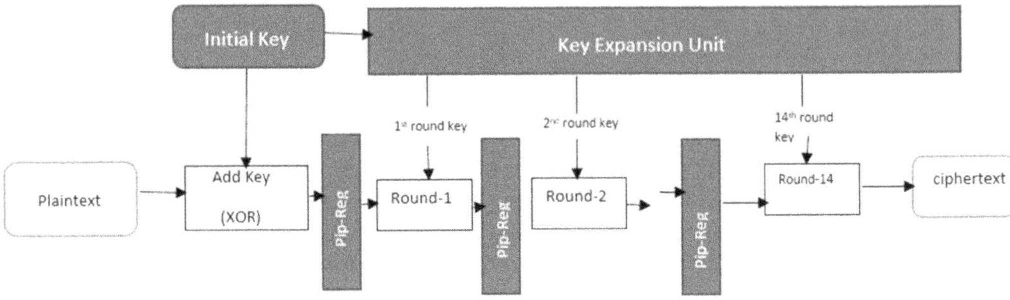

Figure 9.3 The diagram illustrating the loop-unrolled and pipelined implementation of AES-256.

involves executing four operations column-wise, resulting in a 4 x 4 matrix where each element consists of eight bits.

9.4 PROPOSED METHOD

This chapter describes how the 256 AES algorithm is implemented using both the suggested and standard architectures. Additionally, this article examines the FPGA implementation's power, performance, and area number.

9.4.1 High throughput implementation for AES-256

Initially, AES-256 was selected due to its larger key size and greater number of rounds, which enhance its security compared to AES-128 and AES-192. As a result, we made an effort to suggest a productive implementation. Loop-unrolling techniques are employed in our AES-256 implementation to remove all necessary loops from the algorithm, hence altering the critical path. This critical path adjustment makes it possible to insert a few pipelining registers, which increases the operational frequency, accelerates the algorithm, and improves the quality of service for AES-256 applications. We use both full-pipelining and sub-pipelining methods.

Effective strategies are implemented to manage complex AES-256 operations. The following sections will delve into these techniques in detail (see Figure 9.3).

9.4.2 Efficient mix-columns transformation

To calculate the Mix-Columns transformation, use Eq. (9.4). The only numbers in the Mix-Columns matrix are 00, 01, 02, and 3. The computation of multiplication between 00 and 01 doesn't take long. Eq. (9.1), where an is a GF (28) element, can be used to carry out the multiplication with element 3.

$$3 \times a = 2 \times a + a \ldots \quad (9.1)$$

$2 \times a$ can be written as shown below:

$$\times a = (a_7 a_6 a_5 a_4 a_3 a_2 a_1 a_0) \times (00000010)(X^8 + X^4 + X^3 + X + 1) \quad (9.2)$$

Consequently, we have:

$$2 \times a = (a_7X^8 + a_6X^7 + a_5X^6 + a_4X^5 + a_3\ X^4 + a_2X^3 + a_1X^2 + a_0X)$$
$$(X^8 + X^4 + X^3 + X + 1) \tag{9.3}$$

Substitute Eq. (9.8) in Eq. (9.7):

$$(a7X8 + a6X7 + a5X6 + a4X5 + a3X4 + a2X3 + a1X2 + a0X)$$
$$= a_7 \times (X^8 + X^4 + X^3 + X + 1) + a_6X^7 + a_5X^6 + a_4X^5 + (a_3{+}a_7)^4 + (a_2{+}a_7)^3 \tag{9.4}$$
$$+ a_1X^2 + (a_0 + a_7)\,X + a_7$$

9.4.3 Efficient S-box method using logic optimization based on the truth table

We utilize an optimized pipelined S-Box implementation to resolve the unavoidable delay caused by the lookup table, utilizing combinational logic. Additionally, it reduces the complex field arithmetic's critical path delay. The S-Box transformation features a table with 16 × 16 bytes. Its truth table therefore comprises 128 rows. An 8-bit output is produced by this truth table. As a result, it is exceedingly difficult to shrink this intricate table. The primary truth table of the S-Box can be divided into smaller 16 sub-truth tables based on which 4 bits of the main truth table are the least (or most) significant.

As depicted in Figure 9.5, these 4 bits serve as inputs to the logic functions of 16 modules (from M1 to M16). The Karnaugh map, implemented using fundamental gates and the Sum of Products technique, minimizes these functions. After reducing the sub-truth tables, sixteen 8-bit logic output functions are generated. Additionally, four least significant bits of data are chosen to supply a 16:1 multiplexer, which produces the final S-Box output. Figure 9.4 illustrates the use of five smaller (4:1) multiplexers to efficiently achieve the 16:1 multiplexing. This approach allows for the insertion of pipelining registers between these multiplexers, facilitating sub-pipelining. This reduces critical delay paths, enhances S-Box speed, and ultimately boosts the overall performance of the AES-256 algorithm.

Because cryptography offers security services including secrecy, data integrity, authentication, access control, and non-repudiation, it is an important part of safe communication and information transmission. Sensitive data undergoes transformation into an unreadable format, accessible only to authorized individuals who can revert it to its original text. There are two primary forms of cryptography: symmetric and asymmetric key systems. In symmetric systems, the same private keys are used for both encryption and decryption. In asymmetric systems, encryption and decryption utilize distinct keys. One well-known and often used symmetric key cryptography algorithm is AES.

Because AES has so many uses in the military, IoT, electronic banking, communication, and other fields, it has drawn a lot of interest from researchers lately. AES can be included into a hardware or software architecture. Reconfigurable devices, like FPGAs, can be used to design hardware structures with high performance requirements. In hardware implementations, loop unrolling and partial rolling techniques can reduce area costs and improve throughput-to-area ratio. This chapter introduces an FPGA implementation of AES-256, leveraging loop unrolling, full pipelining, and sub-pipelining strategies. Additionally, various effective techniques, including Mix-columns and S-Boxes, are used to the most complicated portions of AES-256.

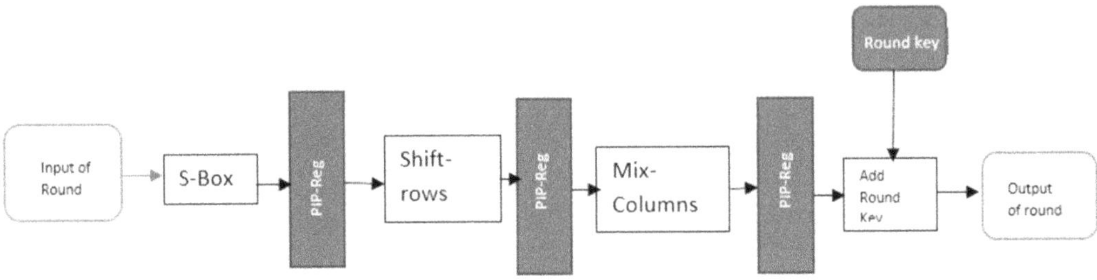

Figure 9.4 The block diagram of the sub-pipelined round of AES-256.

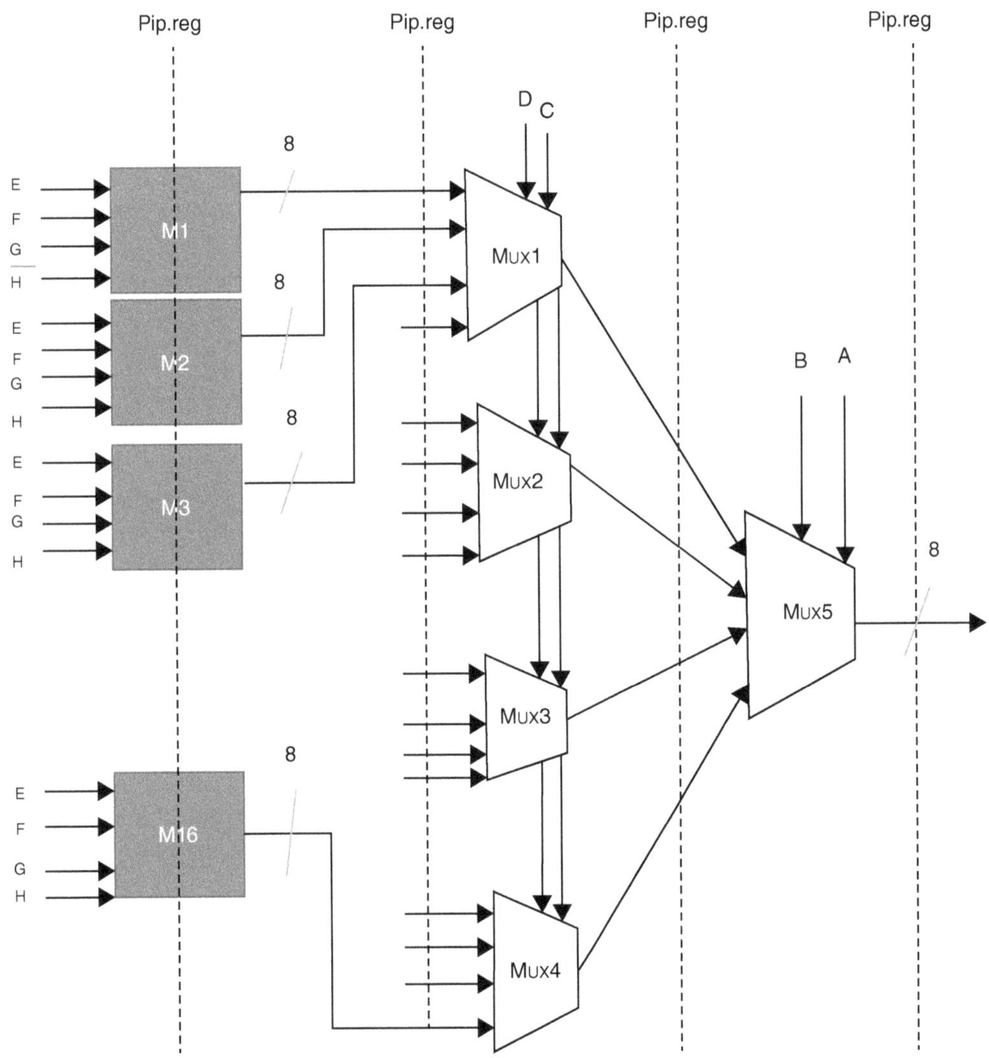

Figure 9.5 The architecture of the S-Box using logic circuits.

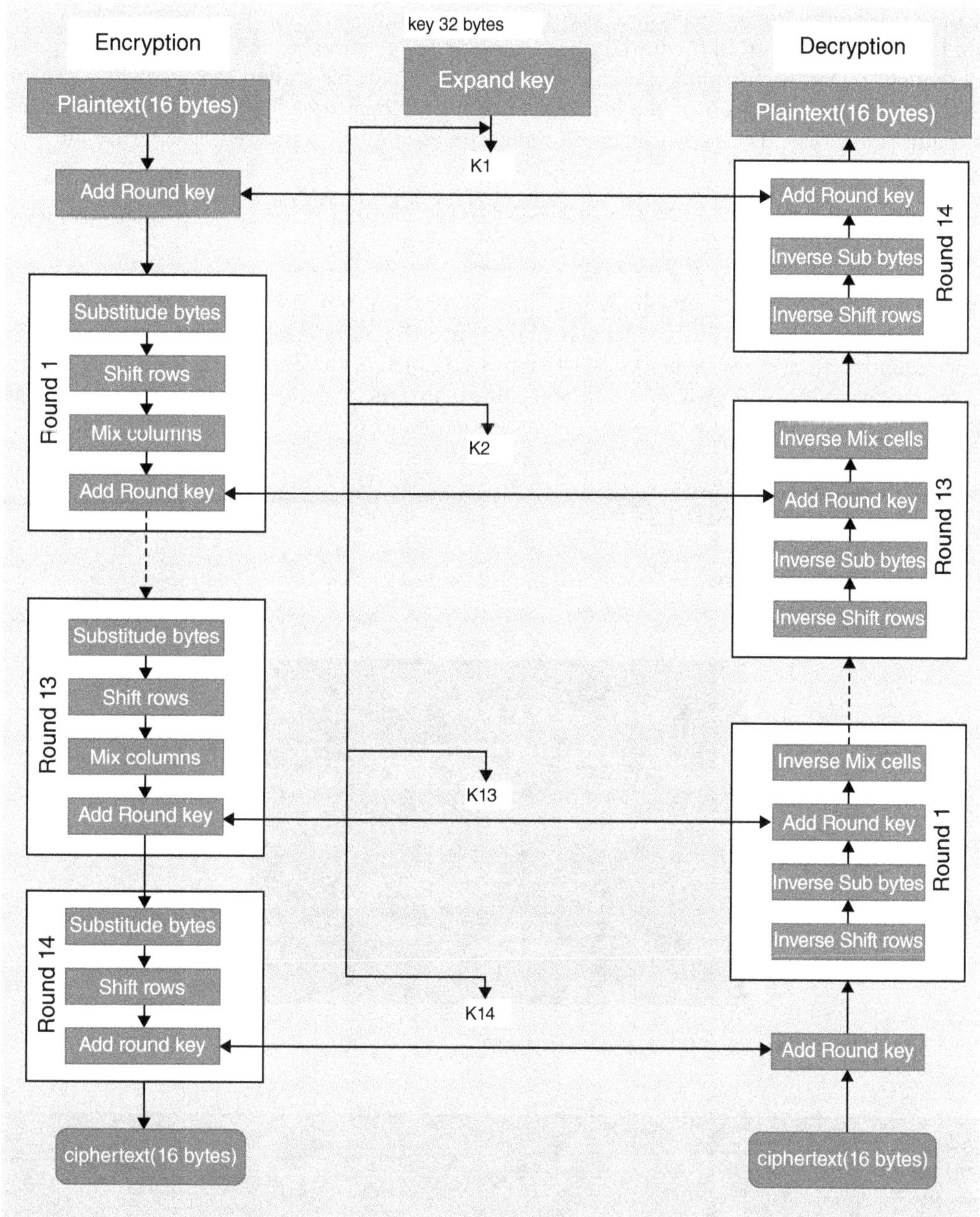

Figure 9.6 The proposed architecture of AES-256.

AES is the most powerful and authorized standard for various applications, replacing the previous data encryption standard (DES) and 3DES. Since AES is not based on the Feistel Structure like DES and 3DES, it can process an entire data block as an array during each round. As seen in Figure 9.6, AES is a symmetric block cipher that generates a ciphertext message based on two inputs: the plaintext message and encryption key.

Depending on the key length, the technique is referred to as AES-128, AES-192, or AES-256. Three basic steps make up the AES encryption/decryption process: adding the initial key at the Add-Round key stage, where the number of rounds is determined by size of the key and key expansion unit. In the initial phase, the first key is added to the plaintext. During the subsequent phase, each round consists of four transformations (called replacement bytes, or S-Box), with the exception of the last one, which only has three: shift-rows, mix-columns, and add-round key. The polynomial described in Eq. (9.10) is utilized to execute all AES operations over 8-bit values.

$$(X) = X^8 + X^4 + X^3 + X + 1 \tag{9.5}$$

Processing occurs one 128-bit block at a time. State array, a 4 x 4 square array of bytes, is how block is arranged. 128-bit block is placed into the State array. Every step of the AES process updates the array. When the last step is completed, the State array is transferred to an output array. We will provide a summary of each round's changes in the subsections that follow.

9.5 SIMULATION RESULTS

9.5.1 Existing system

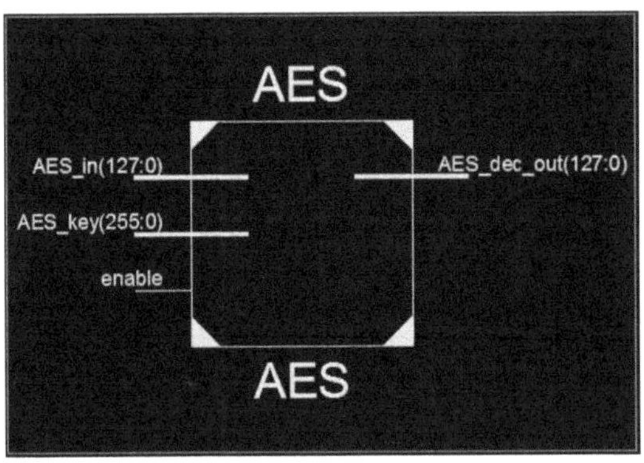

Figure 9.7 Schematic diagram of existing AES RTL design.

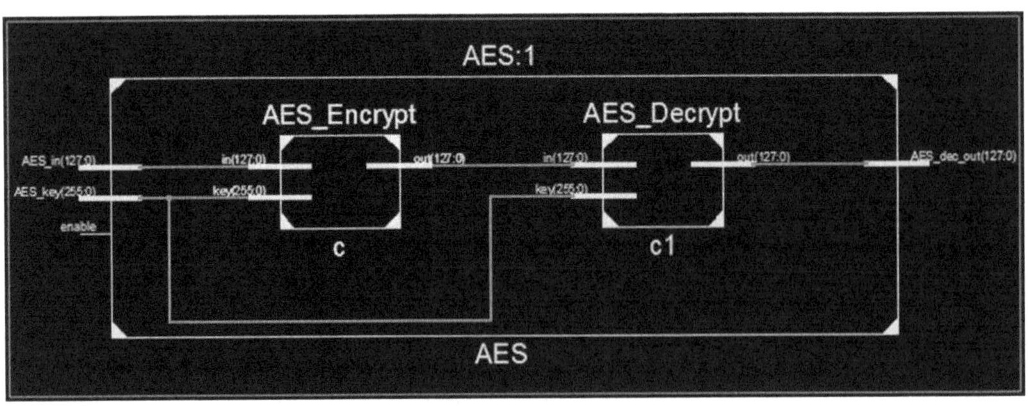

Figure 9.8 Schematic diagram of existing AES RTL design.

```
Device utilization summary:
---------------------------

Selected Device : 7vx485tffg1157-3


Slice Logic Utilization:
 Number of Slice LUTs:                  29175  out of  303600     9%
    Number used as Logic:               29175  out of  303600     9%

Slice Logic Distribution:
 Number of LUT Flip Flop pairs used:   29175
   Number with an unused Flip Flop:    29175  out of   29175   100%
   Number with an unused LUT:              0  out of   29175     0%
   Number of fully used LUT-FF pairs:      0  out of   29175     0%
   Number of unique control sets:          0

IO Utilization:
 Number of IOs:                          513
 Number of bonded IOBs:                  512  out of     600    85%

Specific Feature Utilization:

---------------------------
Partition Resource Summary:
---------------------------

  No Partitions were found in this design.

---------------------------
```

Figure 9.9 Area utilization of existing AES RTL design.

```
Timing Summary:
---------------
Speed Grade: -3

   Minimum period: No path found
   Minimum input arrival time before clock: No path found
   Maximum output required time after clock: No path found
   Maximum combinational path delay: 66.579ns
```

Figure 9.10 Delay of existing AES RTL design.

```
2.3.  Power Supply Summary
-----------------------------------------------------
|                 Power Supply Summary              |
-----------------------------------------------------
|                     | Total  | Dynamic | Quiescent |
-----------------------------------------------------
| Supply Power (mW)   | 206.42 | 0.00    | 206.42    |
-----------------------------------------------------
```

Figure 9.11 Power consumption of existing AES RTL design.

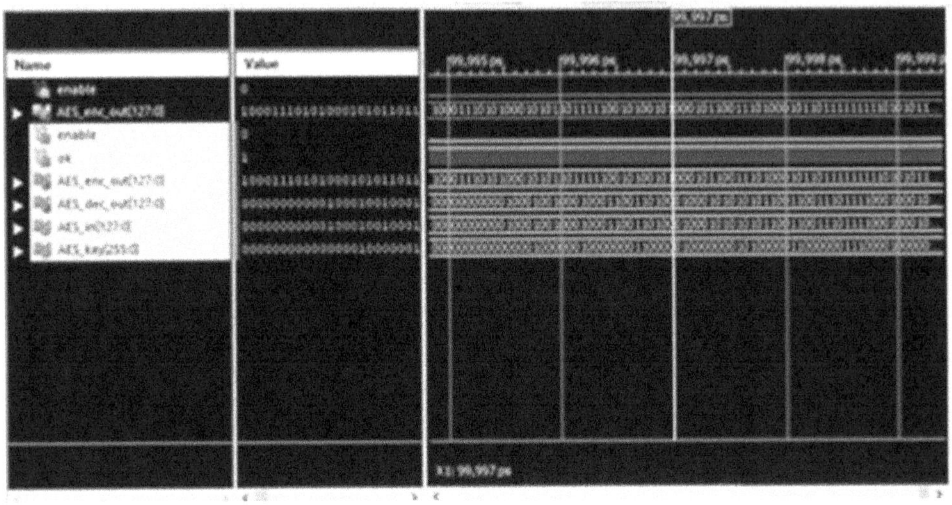

Figure 9.12 Output wave form for existing AES RTL design.

9.5.1.1 Proposed method

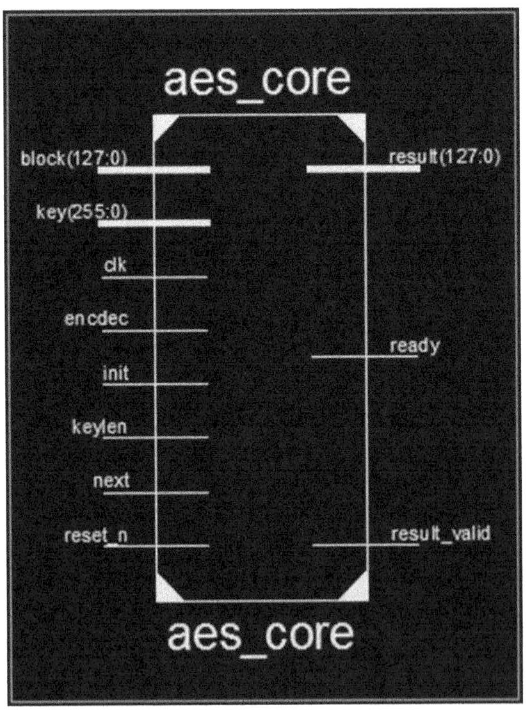

Figure 9.13 Schematic diagram of proposed AES RTL design.

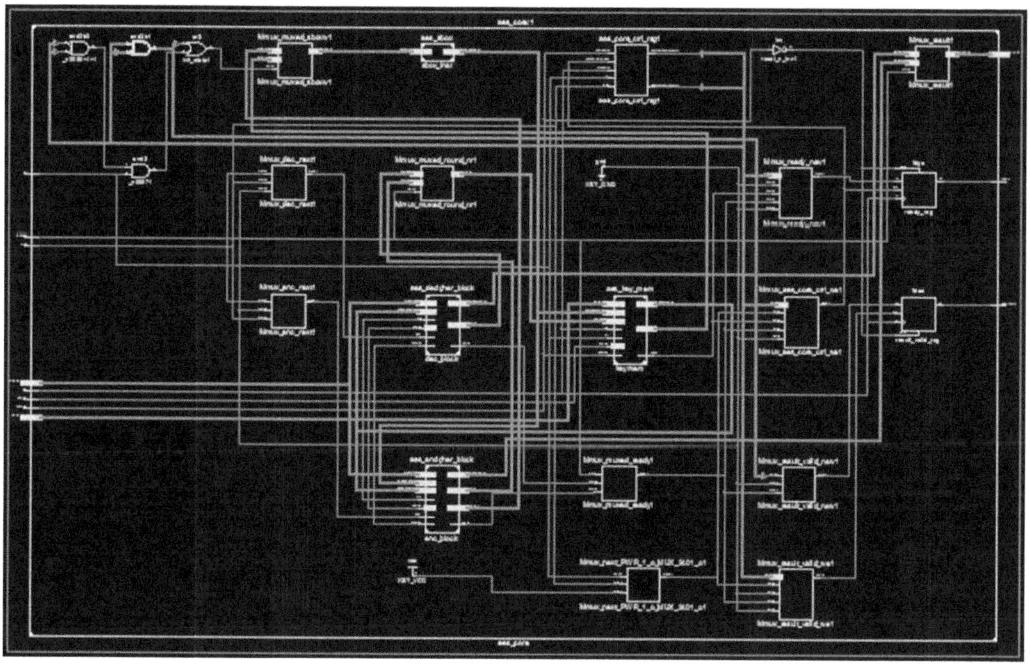

Figure 9.14 Schematic diagram of proposed AES RTL design.

```
Device utilization summary:
---------------------------

Selected Device : 7vx485tffg1157-3


Slice Logic Utilization:
 Number of Slice Registers:           2471  out of  607200     0%
 Number of Slice LUTs:                7347  out of  303600     2%
    Number used as Logic:             7347  out of  303600     2%

Slice Logic Distribution:
 Number of LUT Flip Flop pairs used:  7349
   Number with an unused Flip Flop:   4878  out of    7349    66%
   Number with an unused LUT:            2  out of    7349     0%
   Number of fully used LUT-FF pairs: 2469  out of    7349    33%
   Number of unique control sets:       23

IO Utilization:
 Number of IOs:                        520
 Number of bonded IOBs:                520  out of     600    86%

Specific Feature Utilization:
 Number of BUFG/BUFGCTRLs:               1  out of      32     3%
```

Figure 9.15 Area utilization of proposed AES RTL design.

```
Timing Summary:
---------------
Speed Grade: -3

   Minimum period: 3.463ns (Maximum Frequency: 288.778MHz)
   Minimum input arrival time before clock: 3.155ns
   Maximum output required time after clock: 0.962ns
   Maximum combinational path delay: 0.874ns
```

Figure 9.16 Delay of Proposed AES RTL design.

```
2.3.  Power Supply Summary
-------------------------------------------------------
|                  Power Supply Summary                 |
-------------------------------------------------------
|                      | Total   | Dynamic | Quiescent  |
-------------------------------------------------------
| Supply Power (mW)    | 206.42  | 0.00    | 206.42     |
-------------------------------------------------------
```

Figure 9.17 Power consumption of Proposed AES RTL design.

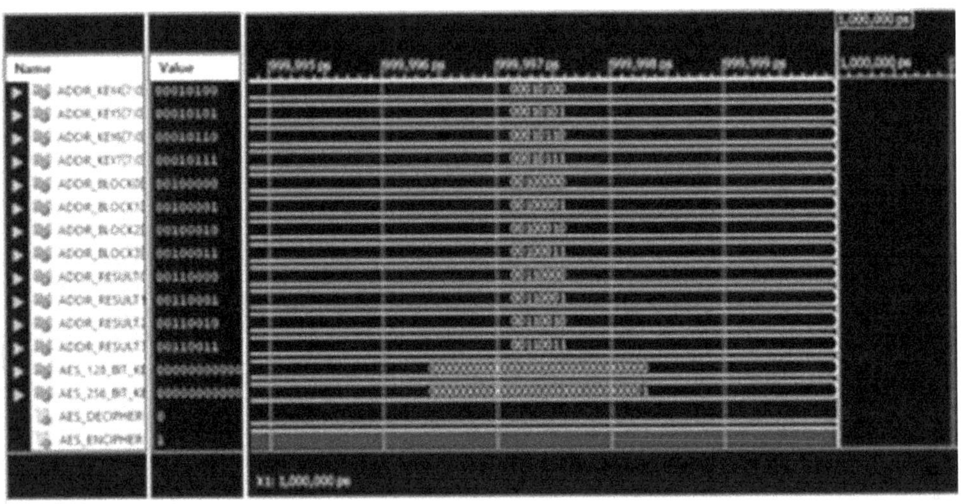

Figure 9.18 Output wave form for proposed AES RTL design.

9.5.2 Results of discussions

Table 9.1 presents a comparative analysis of device performance for both designs after synthesis on the Vertex7 – 7vx485tfgg1157 board. The proposed architectures were developed using Verilog HDL, followed by simulation and synthesis on the Xilinx Vertex7 – 7vx485t-fgg1157 FPGA board.

1. **Area in LUTs:** The existing method utilizes 513 LUTs, while the proposed method requires a slightly higher number, standing at 520 LUTs. This indicates a marginal increase in resource utilization with the proposed method. While this increment is

Table 9.1 Results comparison

S. No	*Parameter*	*Existing method*	*Proposed method*
1.	Area in LUTs	513	520
2.	Delay in ns	66.579	0.874
3.	Power in milli watts	206.42	206.42

present, it might not be substantial enough to hinder the overall implementation considering the capabilities of the Vertex 7 FPGA.

2. **Delay in nanoseconds:** This metric showcases a significant improvement in the proposed method. The delay with the existing method is measured at 66.579 nanoseconds, whereas the proposed method remarkably reduces this delay to just 0.874 nanoseconds. This reduction signifies a substantial enhancement in processing speed, indicating that the proposed method performs AES encryption and decryption operations much faster compared to the existing method.
3. **Power consumption in milliwatts:** Both methods demonstrate identical power consumption values, both registering at 206.42 milliwatts. This suggests that despite the efficiency improvements in the proposed method in terms of delay, there's no significant impact on power consumption. It implies that the faster processing speed achieved in the proposed method doesn't come at the expense of increased power usage, which is crucial in power-sensitive applications.

In summary, while the proposed method marginally increases resource utilization (LUTs) compared to the existing method, it offers a substantial improvement in processing speed (delay) without impacting power consumption. This presents a promising advancement in AES algorithm implementation on Vertex 7 FPGA, indicating a trade-off between resource utilization and performance that Favors faster processing without compromising power efficiency.

9.5.2.1 *Performance comparison*

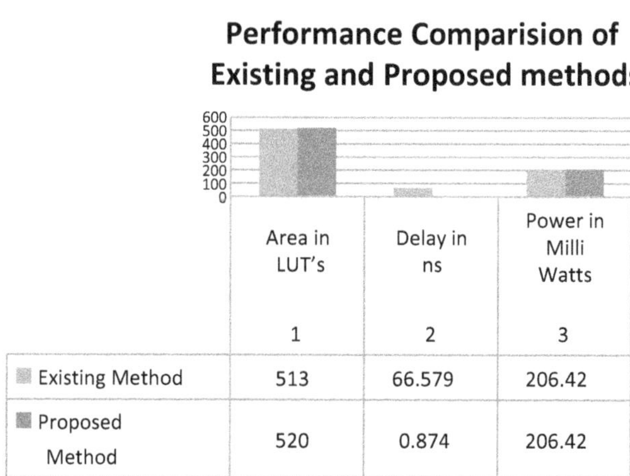

Figure 9.19 Performance of existing and proposed methods.

9.6 CONCLUSION

Important insights have been gained from the study of the 256-bit key AES algorithm implementation on Vertex 7 FPGA using a modified S-Box approach. The suggested approach has demonstrated a notable gain in processing speed with constant power consumption, even with a slight increase in resource use. Key findings show that the improved S-Box methodology reduces the delay in nanoseconds dramatically, with the proposed method obtaining an amazing 0.874 ns, a remarkable decrease from 66.579 ns in the present method. This significant increase in processing performance shows how well the improved S-Box method works to speed up AES encryption and decryption processes on the Vertex 7 FPGA platform. Although the suggested approach uses a little more LUTs than before, the performance improvements show that it has the potential to improve the effectiveness of cryptographic implementations. The suggested methodology's practicality and appeal are further highlighted by the fact that this speed increase doesn't affect power consumption.

9.7 FUTURE SCOPE

Continued exploration into optimizing the resource utilization of the modified S-Box implementation could lead to minimizing LUT usage further, potentially achieving a more balanced trade-off between resource consumption and performance gains.

REFERENCES

1. Fangfei Liu, Yuval Yarom, Qian Ge, Gernot Heiser and Ruby B. Lee, "Last-Level Cache Side-Channel Attacks are Practical", *Proceedings of IEEE Symposium on Security and Privacy*, pp. 605–622, 2015.
2. Yang Li, Kazuo Ohta and Kazuo Sakiyama, "New FaultBased Side-Channel Attack using Fault Sensitivity", *IEEE Transactions on Information Forensics and Security*, Vol. 7, No. 1, pp. 88–97, 2012
3. Charles R Harrell and Ken Tumay, "Promodel Tutorial", *Proceedings of 24th Conference on Winter Simulation*, pp. 405–410, 1992.
4. Suresh Chari, Josyula R. Rao and Pankaj Rohatgi, "Template Attacks", *Proceedings of 4 th International Workshop Cryptographic Hardware and Embedded Systems*, Vol. 2523, pp. 13–28, 2002.
5. Itai Dinur, Orr Dunkelman and Adi Shamir, "Improved attacks on full GOST", *Proceedings of 19th International Workshop Fast Software Encryption*, Vol. 7549, pp. 9–28, 2012.
6. Xinjie Zhao, Fan Zhang, Shize Guo, Tao Wang, Zhijie Shi, Huiying Liu and Keke Ji, "MDASCA : An Enhanced Algebraic Side Channel Attack for Error Tolerance and New Leakage model Exploitation", *Proceedings of 3 rd International Workshop Constructive Side Channel Analysis and Secure Design*, Vol. 7275, pp. 231–248, 2012.
7. Asif Shahab; Faisal Shafait; Andreas Dengel; "ICDAR 2011 Robust Reading Competition Challenge2: Reading Text in Scene Images", *Proceedings of International Conference on Document Analysis and Recognition*, pp. 1491–1496, 2011.
8. Tsung-Fu Lin; Chih-Pin Su; Chih-Tsun Huang; Cheng-Wen Wu; "A High-throughput low-cost AES cipher chip" *Proceedings. IEEE AsiaPacific Conference on ASIC.*
9. C. Sivakumar; A. Velmurugan; "High-Speed VLSI Design CCMP AES Cipher for WLAN (IEEE 802.11i)" 2007 *International Conference on Signal Processing, Communications and Networking.*
10. Vatchara Saicheur; Krerk Piromsopa; "An implementation of AES128 and AES-512 on Apple mobile processor" 2017 *14th International Conference on Electrical Engineering/Electronics, Computer, Telecommunications and Information Technology (ECTI-CON).*

11. S. P. Guruprasad; B. S. Chandrasekar; "An evaluation framework for security algorithms performance realization on FPGA" 2018 *IEEE International Conference on Current Trends in Advanced Computing (ICCTAC)*.
12. N. S. Sai Srinivas; M. D. Akramuddin; "FPGA based hardware implementation of AES Rijndael algorithm for Encryption and Decryption" 2016 *International Conference on Electrical, Electronics, and Optimization Techniques (ICEEOT)*.
13. P. S. Abhijith; Mallika Srivastava; Aparna Mishra; Manish Goswami; B. R. Singh; "High-performance hardware implementation of AES using minimal resources" 2013 *International Conference on Intelligent Systems and Signal Processing (ISSP)*.
14. Wei Wang; Jie Chen; Fei Xu; "An implementation of AES algorithm Based on FPGA" 2012 *9th International Conference on Fuzzy Systems and Knowledge Discovery*.
15. Ashwini M. Deshpande; Mangesh S. Deshpande; Devendra N. Kayatanavar; "FPGA implementation of AES encryption and decryption" 2009 *International Conference on Control, Automation, Communication and Energy Conservation*.

Chapter 10

Design and implementation of LPG gas cylinder management and alerting system using IoT

Sreedhar and G. N. Kodandaramaiah

10.1 INTRODUCTION

Because of a lack of available LPG, pipeline deliveries of LPG aren't possible in India. In view that technology is advancing so quickly, many gasoline companies and vendors have followed interactive voice response system (IVRS). But, because of customers' busy schedules, it could be difficult to keep track of gas usage and to schedule a brand-new cylinder, and it could be extraordinarily dangerous for an LPG gas leak to arise in a home, inside the chemical industry, or in every other utility. This chapter proposes an approach that solves the issue of LPG leakage and offers computerized cylinder ordering. Moreover, it's going to rent global system for mobile communications (GSM) generation to record your reservation by means of sending an SMS to the distributor and simultaneously alerting the user [1–3]. The system is bound to help the elderly who are reliant on others and live by themselves by empowering them and shielding them from any dangerous conditions inside the kitchen. Our idea is to fully automate the LPG ordering process without requiring human participation, to protect clients from dishonest actors. Our system aims to help clients in elevating their safety standards, adhering to environmental regulations, and preventing live- and property-endangering accidents. We use ubiquitous sensors to measure the gasoline in the cylinder when its weight falls below a specified load. The user is notified when the order for a new cylinder is to be placed, as well as the specifics of the ordering procedure. The secondary goal of the system is to report malfunctions in a gasoline system to prevent explosions and fires. The capability to display and manage across sectors has been transformed with the aid of the of Internet of Things (IoT) technologies into several systems. Right here, the creation of a cutting-edge fuel cylinder control and alerting system demonstrates how the IoT can also improve performance and protection in fuel-associated packages.

This device combines a selection of hardware factors, including an electricity supply unit, wirelessly interfaced with an Arduino microcontroller-managed HX711 module, gas sensor, 16 x 2 liquid crystal display, buzzer, Node MCU, and IoT connection via the UBI DOTS platform. The principal intention of this task is to extend a comprehensive solution that tackles the vital elements of gasoline cylinder management by ensuring correct monitoring of fuel use and identification of, and alerting the users to, any leaks or abnormalities. The mixture of the weight cell and HX711 Module permits accurate measurement of the cylinder's weight in real time, which in turn presents a specific estimate of the amount of fuel fed on. Simultaneously, the fuel sensor continuously monitors the environment for any deviations in fuel ranges, directly alerting the machine to capacity leaks or uncommon gas concentrations.

The Arduino-powered vital processing unit manages the gathering of data from several sensors, performs vital calculations, and controls nearby output through the 16 x 2 liquid crystal display and the buzzer for auditory notifications. To facilitate easy communication

 DOI: 10.1201/9781003591788-10

to the UBI DOTS IoT platform and allow remote monitoring, records evaluation, and alarm messages, the Node MCU acts as a bridge to the internet. This project provides a multifaceted method to improve protection, optimize resource utilization, and offer remote accessibility for tracking and timely interventions. It explores the synergistic integration of IoT era and sensor-based complete systems for effective gas cylinder control.

The chapter is organized as follows. Literature overview is provided in Section 10.2. Section 10.3 shows the concept of existing method. Section 10.4 demonstrates the concept of the proposed approach. Section 10.4 presents the simulation effects of present and proposed strategies. Section 10.6 concludes with a summary and future use potential.

10.2 LITERATURE REVIEW

Gas leakage supply detection and level tracking of continuous usage have gained significant research attention both in the academia and the industry because of the loss and harm caused by gasoline leakage at large-scale petrochemical plants. With the advance and rapid adoption of Wi-Fi sensor networks (WSNs), supply localization and boundary estimation have emerged as the focus of research work [1].

With the increase in large outdoor marketing forums, public safety issues arising due to disintegration of outdoor advertising and marketing boards have attracted significant public concern. In this paper, a WSN monitoring system is designed for the structural health monitoring of large outdoor advertising boards [2].

Poisonous and flammable gases are among the most notorious killers of the oil and gas industry workers. Consequently, local governments mandate the usage of gas sensors in all works associated with those gases. Currently, stressed-out gas sensing structures are used [3].

This paper focuses on a leak prognosis and localization method primarily based on infrared photo sequences. Issues associated with false warnings and their poor effect on operations are solved by means of leak detection. An experimental version is mounted for leak prognosis and localization based on infrared picture sequences. Differential background prediction is provided to remove the poor effects of marginal statistics on check vessels primarily based on a kernel regression technique [4].

Detection of gases in industrial contexts is essential for ensuring safety in storage and delivery if you want to restrict atmospheric pollution and precisely control commercial and agricultural techniques. Even though chemical sensors are in wide use, stable-count infrared detectors for gasoline sensing promise numerous advantages over traditional catalytic detectors in terms of sensitivity, calibration requirements, and longevity [5].

Methane is the number-one constituent of naturally produced gasoline and is used in many business methods. Detection of the presence of methane is vital, particularly before it reaches explosive concentrations. Advance sensors are primarily based on catalytic adsorption (which may additionally limit the sensor lifetime) at increased temperatures (requiring extra electricity and probably compromising protection). Lately, optical sensors primarily based on infrared absorption with the aid of hydrocarbon molecules have emerged as an essential research focus [6].

Leak detection is critical for the integrity management of oil and gas pipelines. A pipe leak can prove to be a fatal event, especially when transporting dangerous substances. The effects on the environment and human lifestyles can be devastating, thus a timely detection of pipe leaks is crucial [7].

This paper proposes a small leak detection method based on variational mode decomposition (VMD) and ambiguity correlation classification. The indicators obtained from sensors were broken down using the VMD, and several advantages were achieved. In line with the probability density characteristic, an adaptive de-noising set of rules based totally on VMD is proposed for noise factor processing and de-noised additives reconstruction [8].

In numerous water distribution systems, significant water loss occurs due to leaks during transport from treatment plants to consumers. Consequently, detecting and pinpointing water leaks have been a continuous area of research. Typically, detection systems based on sensor signals involve substantial computational and time expenses, and their effectiveness relies heavily on the features chosen as inputs for classification. In this paper, the authors propose a novel, efficient, and precise water leakage detection system with an adaptive design that integrates a one-dimensional convolutional neural network and a support vector machine [9].

In the evaluation of pipeline leakage alerts, the effectiveness of alerts for 1-mm and 2-mm leaks has proven that the proposed detection approach can detect a small leak accurately and effectively. Moreover, experimental outcomes have proven that the proposed approach produced better performances than SVM and lower back propagation neural network techniques [10].

10.3 EXISTING METHOD

Running out of cooking fuel is a source of significant inconvenience for many families. It may take days to schedule a cylinder and get confirmation from the gasoline software. Many countries utilize LPG for cooking as the most abundant and reasonably priced fuel source. This increased demand produced the need for the more consistent supply. Currently there are no systems that allow automated level tracking and reordering. Fuel leak detection gadgets are usually set up within the wall of a residence and have limited sensitivity. There is no current functionality for automatic or remote LPG cylinder shutoff. If a leak occurs, a servo motor installed within the LPG cylinder can close it off, but it requires on-site activation. Leak sensors are not able to distinguish between flammable or toxic gases.

10.4 PROPOSED METHOD

10.4.1 Block diagram

Figure 10.1 displays the block diagram of the proposed system. The ATMEGA328 microcontroller interfaces with the fuel sensor, load cell, and fire sensor, as indicated in the diagram. These sensors provide inputs to the system. The Arduino manages the entire system operation, including LPG monitoring. Both the fuel sensor module and load cell module generate outputs. The Node MCU connects to the internet. These sensors are highly sensitive with rapid response times. The fuel sensor detects gas leaks, including other gases like cigarette smoke. When gas is detected, the sensor triggers the buzzer, and data are displayed on the LCD screen. Upon detecting a gas leak, the user receives an IoT notification. The load cell continually monitors the LPG cylinder's weight. If the load detected by the load cell drops significantly, a warning is issued to the homeowner, prompting them to reorder a gas cylinder. IoT is used to send alert notifications. Additionally, the LCD display continuously shows the weight of LPG in the cylinder.

The load cell constantly measures the weight of the fuel cylinder, transmitting records to the Arduino. The gas sensor simultaneously displays the state of the fuel environment, sending real-time data to the Arduino. The Arduino analyzes the received statistics, computes fuel intake, exams for anomalies, and controls the neighborhood 16 x 2 LCD screen. In case

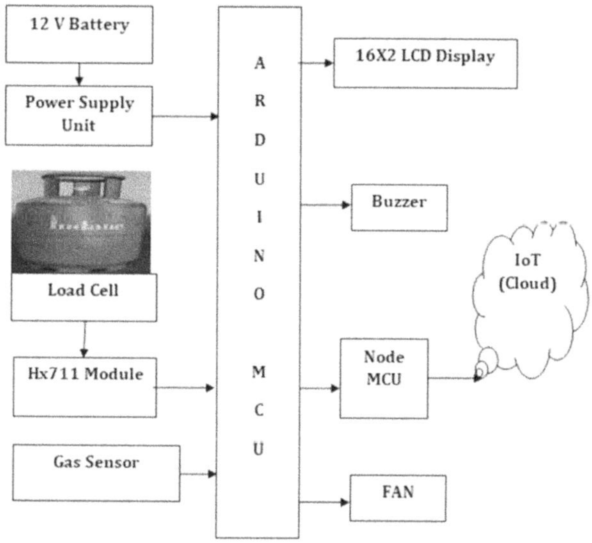

Figure 10.1 Proposed block diagram.

of abnormal fuel ranges or leaks detected via the gasoline sensor, the Arduino triggers the buzzer for fast audible signals. The Node MCU establishes connectivity to the UBI DOTS IoT platform, permitting remote get admission to gasoline cylinder information, real-time notifications, and analytics for comprehensive monitoring and control.

The gasoline cylinder control and alerting gadget offer more desirable protection by means of detecting gasoline leaks or irregularities right away. It allows precise tracking of gas intake, making sure efficient resource control. Additionally, its integration with the IoT platform permits for faraway accessibility, facilitating proactive interventions and statistics-driven selection-making.

This running version creates a comprehensive answer for fuel cylinder control, catering to numerous industrial and domestic applications, prioritizing safety, efficiency, and faraway accessibility.

10.4.2 Working

The operating of the fuel cylinder management and alerting machine entails the seamless integration of various components to display, manipulate, and alert concerning gas cylinder fame and capability hazards. The following is an outline of the system's functioning:

1. Powered delivery unit: the gadget is powered by a 12V battery linked to an energy supply unit, ensuring nonstop operation.
2. Load monitoring and HX711 module: the weight monitor measures the weight of the gas cylinder, and the data are processed by using the HX711 module interfaced with an Arduino microcontroller. The Arduino collects and analyzes the load facts, providing real-time facts on fuel consumption.
3. Gasoline sensor: A gas sensor is hired to detect fuel tiers and deviations inside the surroundings. It continuously monitors for leaks or abnormal gasoline concentrations within the place.

4. 16 × 2 LCD display: This unit works off of the nearby interface, imparting real-time facts on gas tiers, weight measurements, and machine status for real-time tracking and management.
5. Buzzer: The machine consists of a buzzer that generates audible signals in the event of gas leaks or emergency situations, ensuring immediate attention and reaction.
6. Node MCU and IoT (UBI DOTS): The Node MCU helps with IoT connectivity, permitting the device to connect to the UBI DOTS IoT platform. This integration allows for remote monitoring and control of fuel cylinder status. Through the IoT platform, users can get right of entry to real-time records, acquire signals, and track gasoline consumption.

10.4.3 Implementation

Step 1: Hardware assembly and connections

- Load cellular and HX711 module: connect the load mobile to the HX711 module, then interface the HX711 module with the Arduino for weight size.
- Gas sensor: Interface the gasoline sensor with the Arduino for monitoring fuel stages.
- 16x2 LCD display and buzzer: connect the display and buzzer to Arduino for nearby output and indicators.
- Power supply: join the 12V battery or power supply unit to power the system.

Step 2: Firmware development

- Write code for the Arduino to gather facts from the load mobile and fuel sensor.
- Put in force algorithms for gasoline intake calculation, anomaly detection, and triggering signals.
- Integrate the Node MCU for IoT connectivity with UBI DOTS platform.

Step 3: Integration and checking out

- Combine all hardware additives and add firmware to the Arduino and Node MCU.
- Check male and female additives to ensure their correct characteristics.
- Check the setup by trying to validate records accuracy, alert triggering, and IoT connectivity.

Step 4: Deployment and Calibration

- Install the gadget within the desired location, making sure proper calibration of sensors for correct measurements.
- Test-run device parameters to optimize performance.

Step 5: IoT Platform Integration

- Set up an account on the UBI DOTS IoT platform.
- Configure the Node MCU to connect and transmit facts to the UBI DOTS platform.
- Confirm connectivity and facts transmission to the IoT platform.

Step 6: Person interface improvement

- Expand a consumer interface at the UBI DOTS platform to visualize fuel cylinder data, which include fuel tiers, consumption, and alerts.
- Allow remote access for tracking and receiving real-time signals.

10.4.4 Flowchart

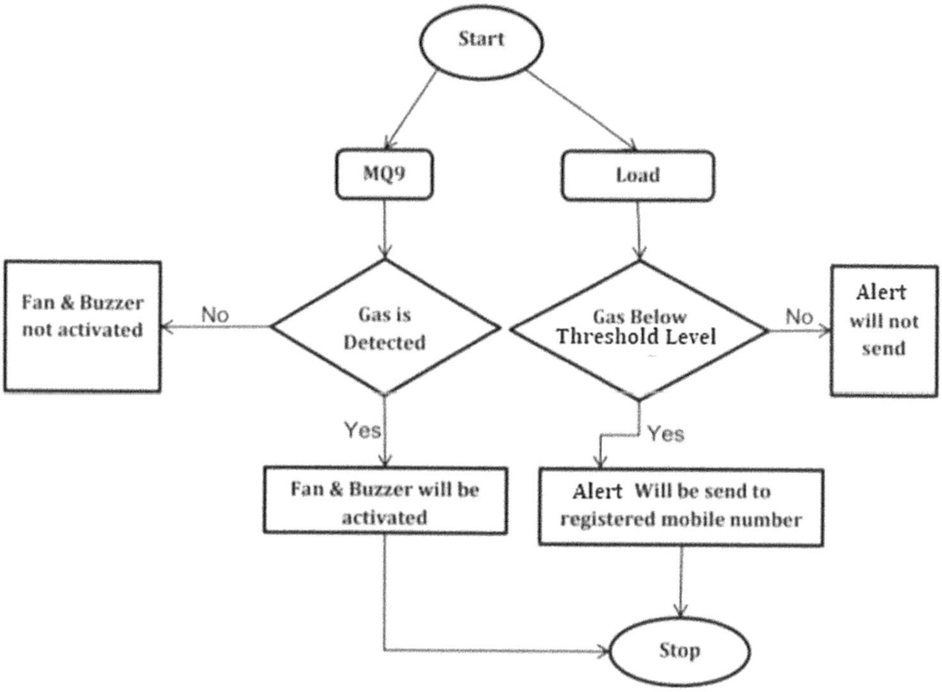

Figure 10.2 Flowchart of LPG gas leakage detection and monitoring system.

The flowchart in Figure 10.2 depicts the workflow of the proposed system. The process steps outlined in the flowchart are as follows:

- Start the process.
- Initialize the load cell and gas sensor.
- Enter the main loop, which may include two sub-loops.
- The load cell monitors the load weight against a fixed threshold value. If the load weight drops below this threshold, it notifies the user automatically.
- Register the user information.
- The gas sensor monitors the gas level against a threshold value. If a gas leak is detected, it activates the exhaust fan and sends an alert message to the user via IoT.
- Stop the process.

Algorithm

1. A load cell, or pressure sensor, is utilized to monitor the weight of the cylinder.
2. When the cylinder weight falls below a predefined threshold value, an SMS is automatically sent to a predefined number, typically the gas agency.

10.4.5 Hardware requirements

10.4.5.1 Arduino UNO

Primarily based on the ATmega328, it is a microcontroller board. Its capabilities include a 16-MHz ceramic resonator, 6 analog inputs, 14 virtual enter/output pins, a USB port, an energy jack, an ICSP header, and a reset button (Figure 10.3).

Figure 10.3 Arduino UNO.

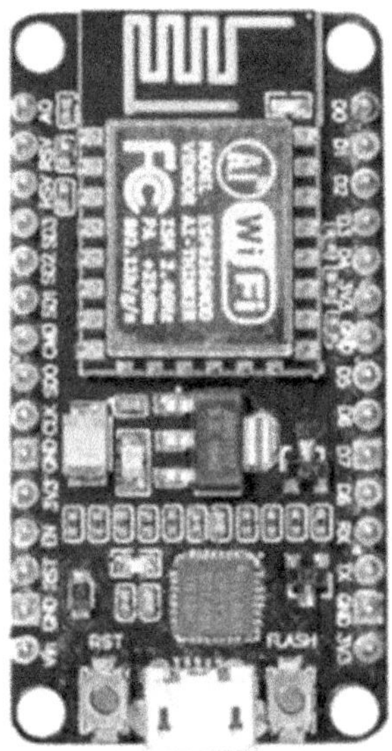

Figure 10.4 Node MCU (ESP8266).

10.4.5.2 Node MCU

The Node MCU (ESP8266) is a microcontroller with an included Wi-Fi module. This tool has 30 total pins, of which 17 are general purpose input/output (GPIO) pins. Those pins are related to a diffusion of sensors that allows you to access data from the sensors and provide output statistics to different devices connected to them. Applications and data may be saved within the 4MB flash reminiscence and 128KB RAM of the Node MCU. Through USB, the code is routed into the Node MCU and stored there (Figure 10.4).

10.4.5.3 Relay

The loadcell seen in parent five has four wires: red, black, green, and white. A load mobile amplifier, such as the HX711 load cell amplifier, is used to extract measurable statistics (Figure 10.5). Due to many elements that include temperature modifications, vibration, flow, and many others, its accuracy is most effective +/–5%.

10.4.5.4 LCD display

Liquid crystals displays are used to reveal application popularity, show values, debug applications, and more. A 16 x 2 LCD display show as many as 16 characters on each of its traces.

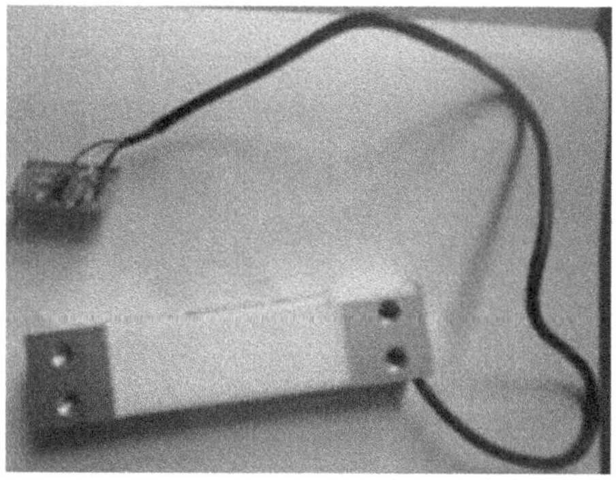

Figure 10.5 Load cell.

Figure 10.6 16 x 2 LCD display.

Each character is shown as a 5 x 7–pixel matrix. There are 224 characters and emblems that may be displayed on the 16 x 2 smart alphanumeric dot matrix display. The display has two characters: command and information (see Figure 10.6).

10.4.5.5 GAS sensor

That is MQ9 LPG, methane, and carbon monoxide. The gas sensor module is able to detect methane and carbon monoxide. The MQ9 gasoline sensor's detection substance, SnO_2, has a reduced conductivity in smooth air, as visible in Figure 10.7. It uses a cycle of high and average temperatures to detect CO while the temperature is low (heated by using 1.5V). As the concentration of fumes rises, so does the conductivity of the sensor. It cleans the alternative gases adsorbed at low temperature and detects flammable gases such as methane and propane while the temperature reaches an excessive factor (heated by 5 V).

10.4.5.6 Buzzer

Figure 10.8 depicts a buzzer, an auditory signaling tool used to deliver alerts. It creates an unmistakable, high-frequency sound by changing the electric current into sound.

10.4.6 Software requirements

10.4.6.1 Arduino IDE

Arduino IDE is an open-source application that simplifies code writing and allows uploading to an Arduino board. The uploaded code includes an application that explains how the system operates. The software's ability to run on any Arduino board is its primary advantage. Several sensors, including the accelerometer, temperature, and heartbeat sensor, can be controlled and communicated with by using the Arduino.

Figure 10.7 Gas sensor.

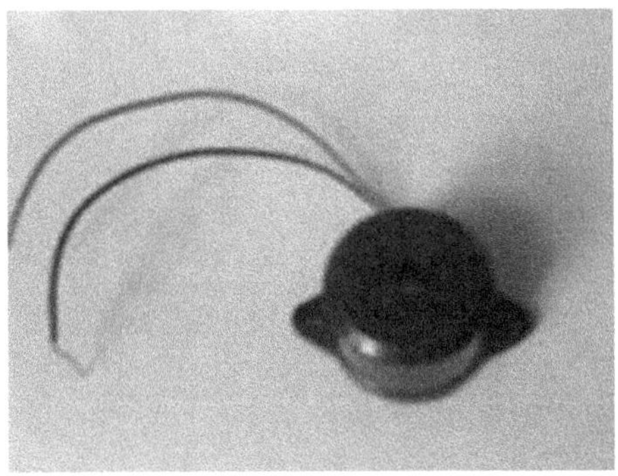

Figure 10.8 Buzzer.

10.4.6.2 UBI DOTS

Any net of factors utility interacting on a UBI DOTS platform must include the following fundamental elements: gadgets, variables, dashboards, activities, and the artificial variables engine. They communicate with each other when it comes to the UBI DOTS IoT development and deployment platform in this text, alongside tips on how to properly set up your UBIDOTS apps to interact customers.

10.5 EXPERIMENTAL RESULTS

The hardware setup of the device during power cycles is illustrated in Figures 10.9 to 10.12.

When the gas sensor detects high levels of LPG in the vicinity, the buzzer sounds to alert neighbors of potential danger, enabling them to take action to mitigate the situation.

Here are the operational scenarios:

- Case 1: In the absence of gas leakage, the alert system remains inactive and no notifications are sent to the user.
- Case 2: If the gas sensor triggers an alert indicating LPG leakage in the vicinity, the alarm is activated, and the user receives a notification stating "LPG DETECTED".

Figure 10.6 depicts the real-time monitoring of liquid fuel level changes online through IoT, indicating either low (0) or high (1) levels. A level of 0 signifies low fuel, whereas a level of 1 indicates high fuel.

Figure 10.9 Hardware kit when power is OFF.

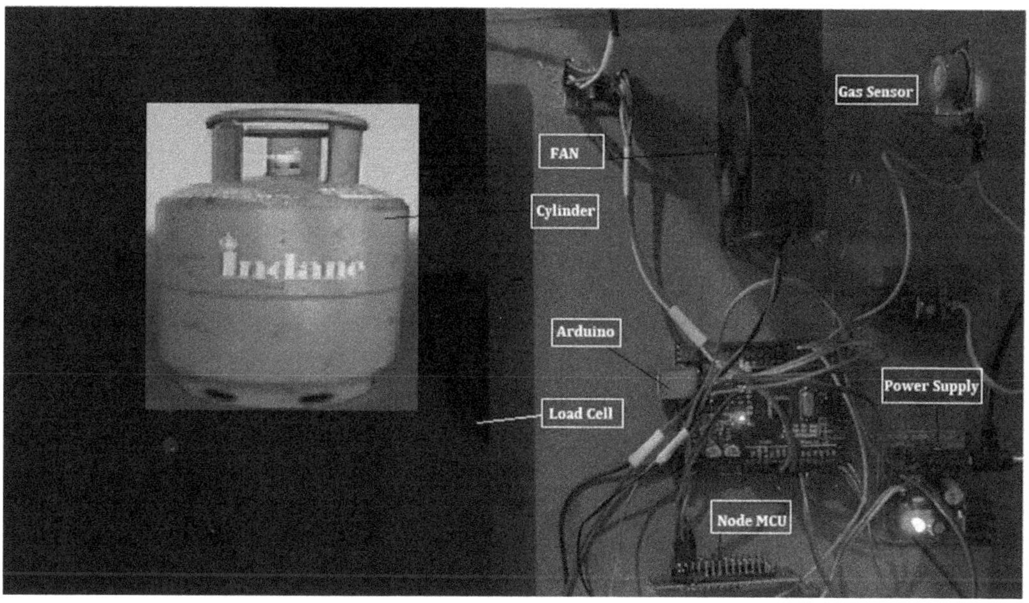

Figure 10.10 Hardware kit when power is ON.

Figure 10.11 When the cylinder is empty, it is displayed on LCD.

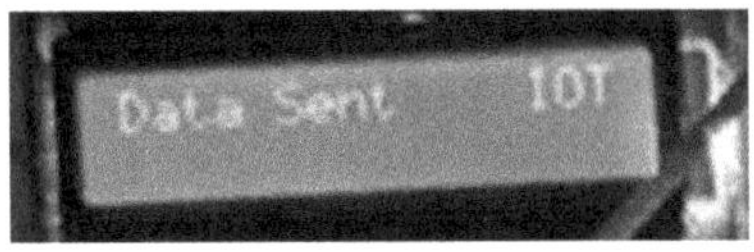

Figure 10.12 LCD showing that data have been sent to IOT.

10.6 CONCLUSION

As the use of LPG continues to increase, so does the risk of leakage and subsequent damage. A smart fuel control system monitors these leaks closely. It alerts users promptly to turn off the gas valve to prevent extensive damage. Additionally, it notifies users when the fuel level in the cylinder drops below a critical threshold. If a leak or gas wastage is detected, a buzzer sounds an alert, and a fan activates to disperse the gas, thereby minimizing potential damages from gas leaks. This IoT-based smart fuel management system aims to reduce the impact of gas leakage incidents significantly.

10.7 FUTURE SCOPE

This project can be expanded into a comprehensive system suitable for industrial applications. It can automate the delivery of refilled cylinders once they are empty and enable automated fire extinguishing in case of gas leaks, operating independently of human intervention.

REFERENCES

[1] Bhatti, D. S., Saleem, S., Imran, A., Iqbal, Z., Alzahrani, A., Kim, H.J., Kim, K.-I. Kingdom Management of Labor Safety, "Data of dangerous chemical accidents", *and Kingdom Administration of Labor Protection*, Retrieved on Dec. 2017.

[2] Wang, W. H., Dong, L., Wei, W., Zhao, W. S., Xu, O., & Wang, G. (Feb.1, 2018), "The WSN monitoring machine for big out of doors advertising forums primarily based on ZigBee and MEMS Sensor," *IEEE Sensors Magazine*, vol. 18, no. 3, pp. 1314–1323.

[3] Brunelli, D., & Rossi, M. (2014), "Improving life of WSN for natural gas leakages detection", *Micro Electron Journal*, vol. 45, no. 12, pp. 1665–1670.

[4] Zhao, L., & Yang, H. (2017). "Small-goal leak detection for a closed vessel through infrared picture sequences," *Infrared Physics & Technology*, vol. 81, pp. 109–116

[5] Made, I., Raj Manes, S., Gavial, A. P., & Nayakwadi, P. V. N. (2018). Gas leakage detection and smart alerting device the usage of IOT. *Worldwide Journal of Innovative Research & Studies*, vol. 2, no. II, pp. 327–333.

[6] Zantalis, F., Koulouras, G., Karabetsos, S., & Kandris, D. (2019). A overview of system learning and IoT in smart transportation. *Future Internet*, vol. 11, no. 4, pp. 94.

[7] Tamizharasan, V., Ravichandran, T., Sowndariya, M., Sandeep, R., & Saravanavel, K. (2019, March). Gas stage Detection and automated booking the use of IoT. In *2019 Fifth Global Conference on Advanced Computing & Verbal Exchange Systems (ICACCS)* (pp. 922–925). IEEE.

[8] Amin, M. M., Nugratama, M. A. A., Maseleno, A., Huda, M., & Jasmi, A. (2018). Layout of cigarette disposal blower and automatic Freshner the use of Mq-five sensor based on atmega 8535 microcontroller. *International Journal of Engineering & Era*, vol. 7, no. three, pp. 1108–1113.

[9] Shrestha, S., Anne, V. Okay., & Chaitanya, R. (2019, April). IoT based totally clever gas management machine. In *2019 third global conference on trends in Electronics and Informatics (ICOEI)* (pp. 550–555). IEEE.

[10] Anandhakrishnan, S., Nair, D., Rakesh, Okay., Sampath, O. K., & Nair, G. S. (2017). IOT based clever fuel monitoring system. *IOSR Journal of Electrical and Electronics Engineering (IOSR-JEEE)*, pp. 82–87.

Chapter 11

A machine learning approach for sentiment analysis of Hindi tweets

Sridhar Reddy Vulapula and Prerana Rangdal

11.1 INTRODUCTION

The use of social media applications such as X (formerly Twitter), Facebook, and others has skyrocketed over the last decade, fundamentally altering how individuals exchange information and remain updated on current events. These platforms have become critical to worldwide communication, with millions of users expressing their thoughts and feelings through postings and comments. Among these sites, X stands out, particularly in India, which ranks third in the world in terms of X usage. Despite broad usage, the analysis of tweets to discern public mood is restricted. Sentiment analysis, which determines whether a piece of text is positive, negative, or neutral, can give useful information regarding public opinion and social trends [1]. Using sentiment analysis on social media data, we may classify remarks and address societal problems and dangers both locally and globally [2].

Sentiment analysis has multiple applications in a variety of fields. In business, it is used to collect feedback on products and services, allowing organizations to better understand client preferences and enhance their offers. This technique, also known as opinion mining or sentiment mining, has been extensively examined, with a variety of methodologies and study disciplines investigated [3]. While several research have focused on Facebook sentiment analysis, this work is primarily concerned with X sentiment analysis [4]. X's unusual structure, with its character restriction and real-time nature, brings new obstacles and opportunities for sentiment research.

The growth of the internet has provided new avenues for individuals to express themselves. Online platforms are increasingly replete with user-generated material, offering a wealth of information and allowing users to examine the viewpoints of others. These views, divided into sentiment classes, are increasingly important in decision-making processes across a wide range of areas [5]. However, analyzing and deriving valuable insights from this unstructured text data is a huge problem. This challenge is being addressed using machine learning approaches, both supervised and unsupervised [6]. Several ways of summarizing text have been developed, including grading the relevance of sentences within a text and producing summaries based on these rankings. Another option is to use end to end generative models, which have showed promise in domains such as image recognition, speech recognition, language translation, and question answering [7].

This study advances the field of sentiment analysis by concentrating on the classification of customer evaluations, especially tweets. Tweets frequently convey extremely unstructured opinions, which might be positive, negative, or somewhere in the between. Our technique starts with preprocessing the dataset to clean and standardize it. We then extract relevant adjectives, also known as feature vectors, from the dataset. The feature vector list is chosen, and machine learning–based classification methods like Naive Bayes, Maximum Entropy,

DOI: 10.1201/9781003591788-11

and content similarity are used to these features. Finally, we evaluate the classifiers' performance in terms of recall, precision, and accuracy.

The relevance of sentiment analysis stems from its capacity to extract actionable insights from enormous amounts of text data. Businesses may make better decisions by monitoring tweets about their goods, policies, and events. Attitude analysis may also assist in uncovering and alleviating societal concerns by evaluating public attitude on a variety of topics. This project's methodology and findings may be extended to different social media platforms and situations, helping advance the science of natural language processing and machine learning.

To summarize, the increasing usage of social media platforms such as X creates both possibilities and obstacles for sentiment research. By inventing and improving algorithms for classifying and understanding attitudes conveyed in tweets, we may use social media data to solve real-world issues and enhance decision-making processes across several domains. This project intends to develop sentiment analysis by offering a strong framework for assessing consumer feedback on X, resulting in a more educated and connected society.

11.2 LITERATURE SURVEY

Social media platforms such as X have transformed the way people interact and exchange information throughout the globe. With the fast proliferation of user-generated material, sentiment analysis has emerged as an essential technique for understanding public opinion and sentiment conveyed on these platforms. Singh, Sawhney, and Kahlon [5] used sentiment analysis to study reactions to big events such as the Indian government's demonetization of 500- and 1,000-rupee banknotes. Their research demonstrated the effectiveness of sentiment analysis in collecting varied public opinions and reactions to government initiatives.

Bagheri and Islam [6] added to the field by focusing on sentiment analysis, especially on X data, and investigating various methodologies and strategies for categorizing sentiments conveyed in tweets. Their research addressed the problems and potential associated with interpreting the massive volume of real-time data created on X. Similarly, Madan and Ghose [7] expanded on this work by concentrating on sentiment analysis in Hindi on X, emphasizing the relevance of linguistic variety in evaluating attitudes across populations.

Laksito et al. [8] investigated several search techniques for gathering X data on pharmacological adverse responses, illustrating the use of sentiment analysis in the context of healthcare and public health. Their findings demonstrated the need for using appropriate data-gathering methods to produce consistent sentiment analysis results.

Alsaeedi and Khan [9] did a thorough study comparing multiple sentiment analysis algorithms applied to X data, demonstrating the usefulness of different approaches in properly categorizing attitudes. Their study helped better grasp the benefits and limits of various machine learning and natural language processing algorithms for sentiment analysis.

Go, Bhayani, and Huang [10] proposed the notion of remote management for X sentiment classification, offering a technique to train sentiment classifiers using hashtags and emoticons. This strategy attempted to harness X's huge volume of user-generated metadata to automatically annotate sentiment data for training purposes.

Tumasjan et al. [11] investigated the use of X data for election forecasting, showing that sentiment analysis of tweets may reflect and predict political views and results. Their research demonstrated the potential of social media data, particularly X, to provide real-time insights into public opinion and political trends.

Sharma and Moh [12] used sentiment analysis to forecast Indian elections using Hindi X data, demonstrating the versatility of sentiment analysis across languages and cultures. Their findings highlighted the relevance of language-specific sentiment analysis methods in collecting subtle feelings expressed in regional languages.

Pandey and Govilkar [13] created a framework for sentiment analysis in Hindi using Hindi SentiWordNet (HSWN), recognizing the necessity for language-specific resources and methods to successfully assess feelings expressed in non-English languages. Their work helped advance sentiment analysis techniques beyond English-centric methodologies, allowing for greater use in different language situations.

Zhou and Fan [14] conducted a sociolinguistic study on American slang on X, investigating how linguistic differences and expressions affect sentiment analysis results. Their findings underlined the complexities of assessing sentiments expressed on social media platforms using informal and colloquial language.

Nakov et al. [15] contributed to sentiment analysis research by taking part in SemEval-2013 Task 2, which focused on sentiment analysis utilizing X data. Their work established benchmark datasets and assessment measures for analyzing sentiment analysis systems, promoting progress in the area through consistent evaluation processes.

Overall, the literature on sentiment analysis of X data indicates a wide range of applications and approaches across several disciplines. Researchers have investigated different areas of sentiment analysis to extract relevant insights from social media data, including evaluating public reactions to governmental policies and elections, as well as linguistic subtleties and language-specific sentiment analysis. These findings highlight the expanding relevance of sentiment analysis in understanding public opinion, improving decision-making processes, and furthering research in natural language processing and machine learning.

11.3 METHODOLOGY

11.3.1 Proposed work

The proposed approach uses dependency parsing to extract sentiment structure, with an emphasis on relationship migration and modified distance measures. This method improves understanding of sentiment in brief texts by examining the various effects of links between modifiers and emotion terms. Each sentence's input to sentiment computation is thoroughly considered, resulting in a thorough sentiment analysis of brief texts. Experimental results validate the methodology's capacity to overcome problems inherent in sentiment analysis of brief textual input, providing a strong framework for reliable sentiment evaluation in real-world applications.

11.3.2 System architecture

The system design begins with data collecting, which involves gathering raw data from social media networks like X. These data are preprocessed, which includes text normalization, tokenization, and the removal of noise like special characters and stopwords. After preprocessing, the processed data are put into machine learning algorithms like Naive Bayes, Maximum Entropy, or Support Vector Machines, which are trained on labeled datasets to categorize attitudes as positive, negative, or neutral as mentioned in Figure 11.1.

Following sentiment categorization, the system presents the results in an understandable fashion, usually through visualizations or structured reports. This final stage guarantees that sentiment analysis results are understandable and actionable. Each component of the architecture contributes significantly to efficient sentiment analysis, from data collection to the display of sentiment-based insights, allowing for informed decision-making across several domains and applications (Figure 11.1).

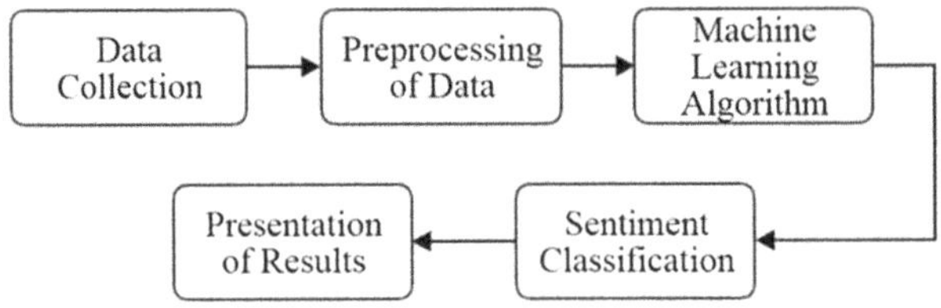

Figure 11.1 Proposed architecture.

11.3.3 Dataset collection

For the sentiment analysis on X data gathering for the Hindi dataset, which contains 25,000 positive and 25,000 negative movie reviews, entails importing the dataset from a reputable source or repository. The dataset should be carefully chosen to cover a wide range of moods and is appropriately classified. Once imported, the data will be analyzed to determine its structure and format. This stage entails confirming data integrity, dealing with any missing numbers, and ensuring a balanced number of positive and negative ratings. The dataset will next be divided into training and testing sets so that the Naive Bayes classifier may be properly trained. The aim is to create a strong classifier that can properly categorize unseen movie reviews as positive or negative feelings based on training data.

11.3.4 Data processing

Data processing for the sentiment analysis project entails converting raw X data into a structured format suitable for categorization. Initially, raw text data collected via X API is unorganized and frequently contains irrelevant letters and phrases. To clean this data, multiple preprocessing procedures are used with Python's Regular Expressions module. This includes deleting typical noise components like hashtags (e.g., #subject), usernames (e.g., @user), retweets, and emoticons, which indicate face expressions or emotions using punctuation.

Stopwords, which are common terms that contribute little to sentiment analysis, are also removed to improve the classification model's accuracy. Once cleaned, the data are tokenized, which divides text into meaningful units such as words and phrases. Stemming is used to reduce words to their basic forms, which simplifies the text for analysis. These preparation processes are critical for refining the data and improving the performance of the Naive Bayes classifier, the method used for this project.

After preprocessing, the structured data is ready to be input into the classification model, which goes through training and testing phases. The Naive Bayes classifier uses the labeled dataset of positive and negative movie reviews to properly categorize unseen reviews based on sentiment. This methodical approach guarantees that the sentiment analysis model is strong and capable of properly classifying tweets into preset sentiment categories, allowing for better-informed decision-making and comprehension of public opinion.

11.3.5 Training and testing

During the Naive Bayes training phase, we import and instantiate the appropriate class/module to fit the model to the training data. The dataset, which contains 2,928 tweets, is divided into training (2,343 tweets) and testing (585) groups. To guarantee model compatibility, these sets are encoded in binary using the 'sklearn' package. Following training, the model's accuracy is evaluated against the testing set. Iterative fine-tuning of parameters is used to attain satisfactory outcomes. During testing, the model predicts sentiment labels for fresh data inputs, modifying algorithmic parameters as necessary to enhance prediction accuracy.

11.3.6 Algorithms

The Naive Bayes method is used to analyze sentiment in the X Hindi dataset, which contains 25,000 movie reviews. Naive Bayes is chosen for its performance in text classification problems, particularly when dealing with very large datasets and high-dimensional feature spaces, which are common in natural language processing. The algorithm determines whether a tweet belongs to a positive or negative sentiment category based on the occurrence of words/features in the training data. Its simplicity and efficacy make it excellent for categorizing unseen tweets as positive or negative, resulting in reliable sentiment analysis conclusions in real-time social media data processing.

11.4 EXPERIMENTAL RESULTS

Recall: ML recall measures a model's ability to catch all class occurrences. The model's ability to recognize a certain type of event is measured by the percentage of precisely anticipated positive prospects that turn into real earnings.

Precision: Precision quantifies the percentage of certain events or tests that are well characterized.

Accuracy: The accuracy of a test is determined by its ability to properly distinguish between diseased and healthy cases. To measure the accuracy of a test, we calculate the proportion of true positives and true negatives among all analyzed cases. Mathematically, this can be expressed as shown in Figures 11.2–11.8.

11.5 CONCLUSION

In this research, machine learning methods and NLTK modules were used to improve sentiment analysis accuracy, revealing whether individual tweets within a loaded dataset are positive or negative. The use of these methodologies is critical for comprehending varied viewpoints throughout India's multilingual terrain, and it ensures that language barriers do not impede public service assessment. However, a major issue remains unresolved: the degree of division in viewpoints expressed on social media sites. This polarization might result in neutralized sentiment scores, which hide the intensity of public feeling on certain themes. Furthermore, the research discovered tweets that were multilingual, containing Devanagari, English, and Romanized Hindi, with only the Devanagari text analyzed, resulting in information loss.

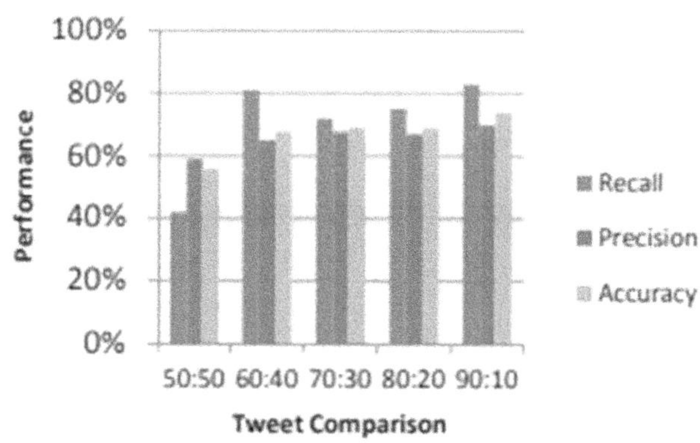

Figure 11.2 Comparison graphs.

```
#loading modules
import numpy as np, pandas as pd, matplotlib.pyplot as plt, random

import string,re

pip install googletrans==3.1.0a0

import nltk
nltk.download('omw-1.4')

foo_nltk=__import__('nltk')
foo_nltk.download('stopwords')
foo_nltk.download('punkt')
foo_nltk.download('averaged_perceptron_tagger')
foo_nltk.download('tagsets')
foo_nltk.download('treebank')
foo_nltk.download('wordnet')
foo_nltk.download('twitter_samples')

del foo_nltk
```

Figure 11.3 Imported required libraries.

```
# load data loader
from nltk.corpus import twitter_samples

# get some random index list
random_indexs=np.random.randint(0,high=5000,size=5)

tweets_data=twitter_samples.strings(fileids='tweets.20150430-223406.json')
# total number of tweets
print('Total number of smaples:',len(tweets_data))
# see random tweets (any five)
for index in np.random.randint(0,high=len(tweets_data),size=5):
    # print random tweet
    print('Tweet number:',index,':',tweets_data[index])
```

Figure 11.4 Import dataset.

Addressing this involves progressing to multilingual emotion analysis and establishing methods for reliably converting Romanized text into Devanagari, which is a difficult process due to the multiple transliteration standards. These issues are critical for developing sentiment analysis technologies that can collect and analyze complex public attitudes across linguistic and cultural boundaries.

11.6 FUTURE SCOPE

Future improvements to this project might include increasing multilingual sentiment analysis skills to better manage the range of languages used on social media sites such as X. This entails creating strong methods for correctly processing and analyzing bilingual and multilingual

```
# make remove - "# tag" and "@ tag" strings
def tagRemover(data:list,to_remove:list=['#[\S]*','@[\S]*','http[\S]*'],
               filler=''):
  for pattern in to_remove:
    data=[re.sub(pattern,filler,tweet) for tweet in data]
  return data

# function to get set of similes in data
def getSimiles(data:list,pattern:str='[a-zA-Z0-9]*',filler=''):
  # make set of all similes used in twitter data
  similes=set()
  for tweet in data:
    for simile in re.sub(pattern,filler,tweet).split():
      similes.add(simile)
  return similes

# function to remove special characters
def specialCharaterRemover(data:list,specialInData:set,to_leave:dict,
                           decodeLeaves:dict,filler=' '):
  #revmove all characters except alphabets
  to_remove=string.printable.replace(string.ascii_letters,'')
  to_remove_trans=str.maketrans(to_remove,filler*len(to_remove))
  # join all special characters in data - get all special characters in twitter data
  special_charters=''.join(specialInData)
  # leave all special in special characters
  for key,value in to_leave.items():
    special_charters=special_charters.replace(key,value)
  special_charters_trans=str.maketrans(special_charters,filler*len(special_charters))
  data=[tweet.translate(special_charters_trans) for tweet in data]
  # convert ':(' or ':)' to word "negative" or "postive"
  for key,value in decodeLeaves.items():
    data=[tweet.replace(key,value) for tweet in data]
  data=[tweet.translate(to_remove_trans) for tweet in data]
  return data
```

Figure 11.5 Data clearing.

```
# load Stemmer and Lemmatizer
from nltk.stem.snowball import SnowballStemmer
from nltk.stem.wordnet import WordNetLemmatizer
from nltk.tag import pos_tag

# function to stem and lemmatize word
def wordCleaner(data:list):
  # make Stemmer
  stemmer_=SnowballStemmer('english')
  # make lemmatizer
  lemmatizer_=WordNetLemmatizer()
  cleanedData=list()

  # make clean - sentence by sentence
  for sentence in data:
    # add pos tags (and clean word by word)
    # make list of cleaned words
    cleanSentences=list()
    for token,tag in pos_tag(sentence):
      # if tag start with NN
      if tag.startswith('NN'):
        tag='n' # make noun
      # if tag start with VB
      elif tag.startswith('VB'):
        tag='v'  # verb

      else:
        tag='a'
      # apply Lemmatization
      token=lemmatizer_.lemmatize(token.lower(),tag)
      # apply stemmer
      token=stemmer_.stem(token)
      # apped words to clean sentences list
      cleanSentences.append(token)
```

Figure 11.6 Data preprocessing.

tweets containing Devanagari, English, and Romanized Hindi. Furthermore, using modern approaches such as deep learning models into sentiment analysis might improve accuracy by capturing subtle linguistic nuances and contextual meanings across several languages and dialects. These developments would allow for more extensive and intelligent research of public opinion, resulting in better decision-making processes in a variety of fields, including governance and public service assessment.

```
# import module
from nltk import classify,NaiveBayesClassifier
# train maodel
classifier_=NaiveBayesClassifier.train(train_set)
# test model
print('Accuracy score:',round(classify.accuracy(classifier_,test_set)*100,3))

# classifier 10 most informative features
classifier_.show_most_informative_features(10)
```

Figure 11.7 Training using Naïve Bayes.

testing on hindi input

```
def conversion(get_inp):
    from googletrans import Translator
    translator = Translator()
    get_inp = translator.translate(text = get_inp,dest = 'en',src = 'hi')
    get_inp = get_inp.text
    return [get_inp]
✓ 0.3s

# sample postive sentence
inp=input("Enter text in hindi")
custom_tweet=conversion(inp)
cleaned_custom_tweet=removeStopWords(specialCharaterRemover(tagRemover(custom_tweet),positive_similes,
                                     to_prevent_positive,positive_similes_code))
# preprocessing
custom_tokens=wordCleaner(cleaned_custom_tweet)

# print results ## Note classifier_ takes only single sample at a time (not like sklearn classifiers)
print(custom_tweet,' <- type:',classifier_.classify([dict([token,True] for token in sample) for sample in custom_tokens][0]))
✓ 5m 25.4s

['What is right will be tweeted, what is wrong will be opposed - Jai Hind | RT follow 100% follow back']  <- type: Positive
```

Figure 11.8 Output screen.

REFERENCES

[1] Jeremy YL Yap, Chiung Ching Ho, and Choo-Yee Ting, "Analytic hierarchy process (AHP) for business site selection," *AIP Conference Proceedings*, vol. 2016, p. 020151, AIP Publishing 2018.

[2] Aurélien Géron, "*Hands-On Machine Learning with Scikit-Learn, Keras, and TensorFlow*," 2nd Edition, 2019, O'Reilly Media, Inc.

[3] Kan Yao and Yuebing Zheng, "Fundamentals of Machine Learning," in *Nanophotonics and Machine Learning: Concepts, Fundamentals, and Applications*. Cham: Springer International, 2023, pp. 77–112.

[4] Amita Jain ,Minni Jain, "Location based twitter opinion mining using common-sense information," *Global Journal of Enterprise Information System*, 9(2), 2017, pp. 28–32.

[5] P. Singh, R. S. Sawhney, and K. S. Kahlon, "Sentiment analysis of demonetization of 500 &1000 rupee banknotes by Indian government," *ICT Express*, vol. 4, no. 3, pp. 124–129, 2018.

[6] Varsha Sahayak, Vijaya Shete, and Apashabi Pathan. "Sentiment analysis of twitter data." *International Journal of Innovative Research in Advanced Engineering*, vol. 2, no. 1 (2015), pp. 178–183.

[7] Anjum Madan and Udayan Ghose, Sentiment analysis for Twitter Data in the Hindi language. In *2021 11th International Conference on Cloud Computing, Data Science & Engineering (Confluence)*, IEEE (2021), pp. 784–789.

[8] A. D. Laksito, Kusrini, H. Sismoro and M. Y. Fita Rahmawati, "A comparison study of search strategy on collecting Twitter data for drug adverse reaction," *International Seminar on Application for Technology of Information and Communication (iSemantic)*, IEEE (2018), pp. 356–360.
[9] A. Alsaeedi and M. Z. Khan, "A study on sentiment analysis techniques of Twitter Data," *International Journal of Advanced Computer Science and Applications*, vol. 10, no. 2, pp. 361–374, 2019.
[10] A. Go, R. Bhayani and L. Huang, "Twitter sentiment classification using distant supervision," CS224N project report, Stanford, vol. 1, no. 12 (2009), p. 2009.
[11] A. Tumasjan, T. O. Sprenger, P. G. S. Sandner and I. M. Welpe, "Election forecasts with Twitter: How 140 characters reflect the political landscape," *Social Science Computer Review*, vol. 29, no. 4 (2011), pp. 402–418.
[12] P. Sharma and T.-S. Moh, "Prediction of Indian election using sentiment analysis on Hindi Twitter," *In 2016 IEEE International Conference on Big Data (Big Data)*, 2016
[13] Pooja Pandey and Sharvari Govilkar. 2015. A framework for sentiment analysis in Hindi using HSWN. *Inter-national Journal of Computer Applications*, vol. 119, no. 19, pp. 23–26, June.
[14] Y. Zhou, and Y. Fan, " A sociolinguistic study of American Slang," *Theory and Practice in Language Studies*, vol. 3, no. 12, pp. 2209–2213, 2013. doi:10.4304/tpls.3.12.2209-2213
[15] P. Nakov, Z. Kozareva, A. Ritter, S. Rosenthal, V. Stoyanov, T. Wilson, Sem Eval- 2013 Task2: Sentiment Analysis in Twitter vol. 2, pp. 312–320, 2013.

Chapter 12

Detection of Alzheimer's disease using deep learning MobileNet model

Thatikonda Radhika and Sridhar Chintala

12.1 INTRODUCTION

The identification process involved the utilization of a deep learning (DL) tool for Alzheimer's patients, which addressed features, preprocessing techniques, biomarkers, and sparse datasets. Enhancing diagnostic accuracy and benchmarking systems is among the obstacles. One such obstacle is the implementation of a DL algorithm-based AI system prototype that assists Alzheimer's patients by triggering reminders for hydration and feeding, thereby enabling remote care from a career perspective [1]. The IoT stabilizes health care, transportation, and smart homes by measuring patient's health and need medical attention, providing customized care and enhancing remote monitoring during the COVID-19 pandemic. They increase the efficiency of health care and protect the patient's data [2]. This chapter shows how machine learning (ML) and DL can be used in medicine to diagnose Alzheimer disease (AD) using magnetic resonance imaging (MRI) sets in the early stages of disease. When the described approach is implemented in Python, an overall accuracy of 95% is obtained through fully automated DL. Using IoT data for accurate categorization of patients affected by AD produces 68% accuracy [3]. When it comes to acute problems, the prototype is designed to diagnose and aid patient suffering from AD. The realization of the wearable prototype involves the use of steganography in decoding image, for the purpose of tracking AD's location; the detected images are categorized as either family or non-family members. As for the assistance feature, it incorporates Google Assistant to help and communicate, resulting in a reduction of social exclusion [4].

AD is a type of dementia that disproportionately affects the elderly, with a diagnosis accuracy of only 85%. Medical reality modeling language (MRML) techniques can employ MRI techniques to enhance diagnosis and prediction throughout the process. Using the DBN-MOA algorithm with multimodal time-series data has demonstrated its efficacy in distinguishing between healthy and diseased patients [5]. AD remains a silent pandemic, but noninvasive techniques like imaging, blood component monitoring, and biosensors can develop precise biomarkers for early detection [6]. AD leads to abnormalities in daily activities for a significant number of elderly individuals worldwide. A proposed approach uses wearable data to identify behavioral abnormalities in Alzheimer's patients. This method enhances performance and prevents the progression of disease by employing conventional methods and multiheaded architectures [7]. We've developed a more refined and compact deep learning model for accurate MRI diagnosis in dementia scans. By combining multiple traditional approaches into one, the model can achieve outstanding detection performance. The model proved its efficacy in detecting AD by outperforming previous models on the Kaggle dataset [8].

The chapter is organized as follows: Section 12.2 presents the relevant literature, Section 12.3 discusses the AD detection system, Section 12.4 introduces methods and approaches, Section 12.5 discusses the results, and Section 12.6 concludes and talks about the future scope.

 DOI: 10.1201/9781003591788-12

12.2 RELATED WORK

To combat the development of dementia resulting in modest mental impairment, Simeon Spasov et al. [9] employed a DL method that was efficient with parameters. The model, which used the pMCI vs. sMCI (comparing mild cognitive impairments) multimodal feature extractor and the AD vs. healthy task, got an area under the curve (AUC) of 0.925, proved to be 86% 10 times more effective, and showed an 87.5% sensitivity. With 85% specificity, it was quite effective. Contrary to expectations, the identical network outperformed all other networks in accurately differentiating between AD patients and healthy controls, achieving an AUC of 1 and a perfect score in all three categories. Data overfitting is still an issue, though. Using neuroimaging data, Jo et al. [10] used DL methods to diagnose AD and predict its prognosis. They used ADNI-1 for model training, ADNI-2 and MIRIAD for testing, and their models achieved 84.2% MCI conversion prediction accuracy and 96% AD classification accuracy. However, this is a huge obstacle for mechanical studies that try to figure out which features are important for model building. Using AD datasets from OASIS and Kaggle, Kavitha et al. [11] trained ML models to forecast the onset of early-stage AD. Application of these classifiers to the AD test data yielded an average validation accuracy of 83%: DT, RF, SVM, GB, and Voting. The data, sourced from multiple sources, may pose a potential issue with this approach due to its increased susceptibility to outliers.

A collection of audio recordings showcases the voices of individuals with and without AD. To identify Alzheimer's dementia, Rohanian et al. [12] used acoustic, lexical, dysfluency, and speech pause features. When tested on the AD ReSSo challenge dataset in 2021, the BiLSTM model achieved an accuracy rate of 84%. To classify AD using MRI scans from the ADNI dataset, Yousry AbdulAzeem et al. [13] created a convolutional neural network (CNN)-based framework. With a classification accuracy of 97.5%, the suggested framework achieved remarkable results. A gradient vanishing problem occurs because classification tasks often have a wide decision boundary. When it comes to AD classification, Sethi et al. [14] came up with a CAD system that makes use of neuroimaging MRI two-dimensional slices. The datasets used for training and testing were OASIS, ADNI, and MRI. On the OASIS dataset, they achieved an outstanding 86.2% accuracy using CNN and hybrid CNN-SVM models. However, compared to the accuracy achieved when AD was differentiated from CN, it dropped to 84.23% and 84.9% when MCI was considered separately. This disparity is likely due to the growing difficulty in differentiating the early stages of the disease.

The purpose of AD classification from MRI brain images using the VGG-16 CNN architecture, Jain et al. [15] have created a mathematical model known as PFSECTL mathematical model, which is based on transfer learning. This approach achieves a three-way classification accuracy of 95.73%. A longer convergence time is one of the downsides of using artificial neural networks (ANNs). Odusami et al. [16] initiated an intelligent system for early recognition of AD. Using the MRI biomarkers Ansys and ResNet18 to look for signs of mild cognitive impairment (MCI), late mild cognitive impairment (LMCI), and non-concussion dementia (NCD). In the context of multiclass classification, the proposed method achieved 98.86% accuracy, 98.94% precision, and 98.89% recall. Their inability to identify changes in the functional connectivity within the functional brain networks of MCI patients is a problem with these algorithms. Using neuroimaging biomarkers, Agarwal et al. [17] performed a comprehensive examination of dementia transfer learning. The study used images from the healthy, AD, and PET datasets. The AD classification using three-dimensional CN and local transfer learning achieved an accuracy of 98.2%. The accuracy of the AD prognostic prediction was 87.78%. This study's complexity of training is a limitation.

Murugan et al. [18] presented a DL model DEMNET for early MR-based diagnosis of Alzheimer's disease and dementia. With a 97% AUC, 0.93 Cohen's Kappa, and an accuracy of 95.23%, the DEMNET model was incredibly successful. The dataset does have some notable limitations, however, one of which is the presence of class imbalance. Borji et al. [19] established a new ensemble method for early AD detection using PET scan images. Two groups participated in the research: one comprised of people with normal cognition and AD, and the other of patients with stable progressive MCI. When tested on patients with MCI, the model produced impressive results with an AUC of 94.4% and an average accuracy of 93.13% thanks to Alex Net, VGG16, and a custom CNN. Using the majority voting technique was essential in overcoming the limitations of single-model predictions. To improve the accuracy of AD diagnosis using MRI scans, Khatun et al. [20] linked CNN with long-term and short-term memory. With Inception V3, Resnet50, Vgg16, and LSTM as their building blocks, the CNN model produced a 98.8% success rate, a 100% sensitivity rate, and a 76% specificity rate. The study used a variety of data sources, including MRI scans, to sharpen its diagnostic precision.

Sriram et al. [21] used DL to classify AD using eye-tracking data. Specifically, VTNet_1000_att, the VT Net with ET model, outperformed the baseline in sensitivity and area under the curve (AUC). Notably, sensitivity improved by 7.7 percentage points from the beginning, reaching 0.7. Because of its balanced but limited accuracy for both metrics, VTNet_1000 presented results either inferior or equivalent, making result analysis difficult.

Oktavian et al. [22] used MRI scans and the CNN architecture, especially ResNet-18, in their research aimed at AD classification with transfer learning. The outcomes demonstrated that their model achieved an accuracy level of 88.3%. When contrasted with the baseline model's accuracy of 69.1%, this represents a considerable improvement. However, a degradation problem arose due to the convergence of the network's deeper layers. Mittal et al. [23] explored how to detect AD from transcripts of both spoken and written language. They created the transcripts from audio clips using an ASR system. The research uses BERT Embeddings, Sentence BERT Embeddings, and Fast Text-CNN. Even after 10 rounds of cross-validation, the suggested method managed an astounding 85.3% accuracy. However, handling datasets to detect AD based on language impairments can present significant challenges.

12.3 ALZHEIMER'S DISEASE DETECTION SYSTEM

Figure 12.1 depicts the overall program for detecting Alzheimer's disease. The difficulty of processing visual data, for example the scans that depict the state of the brain unlike in other methodologies in detecting AD, makes computer vision unique. This could be a direct approach of looking for abnormalities or patterns linked to AD; however, given the complexity of the brain as well as changes in the structure that are hard to decipher, this becomes a real challenge. This is the first problem that computer vision techniques have to solve to

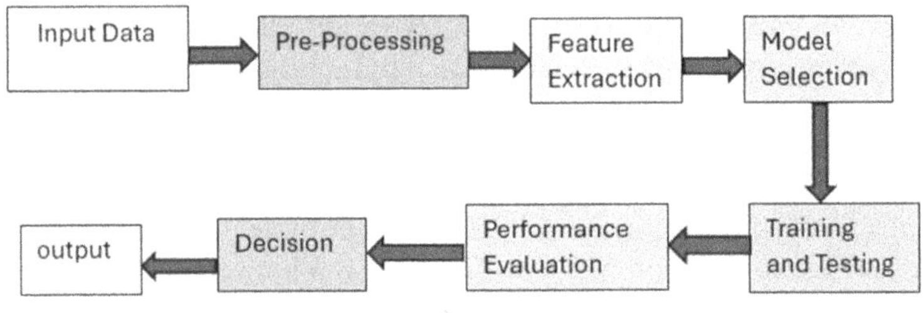

Figure 12.1 A general flow chart for Alzheimer's disease detection.

tackle the learning metric of morphological changes in the brain that may be very subtle and with time are bound to be a bit distorted due to image quality, resolution, and noise. Speaking of analyzing the overall study, it becomes already quite challenging to examine a solitary modality, let alone MRI, PET, and CT scans only. There are some disadvantages in using this kind of technology, but current advancements in DL architectures as well as ML algorithms indicate a brighter future and can increase the ability of computer vision–based AD detection. Concerning the detection of AD, various data sources are preprocessed, including the medical history, cognitive assessment data, genetic information, and neuroimaging data. Then, in the next step, a feature extraction will have to be performed to obtain biomarkers and patterns that may be useful in predicting the evolution of AD among patients. ML algorithms such as support vector machines, random forests, or DL models train on labeled datasets to identify patterns associated with AD. We then test the trained model on unseen data to assess its accuracy in identifying people with AD. Performance indicators such as specificity, sensitivity, and accuracy evaluate the efficiency of the detection system. To help health care providers detect and intervene early during AD, the system generates a diagnostic decision. Incorporating ongoing system refinement and updates is key to ensuring the system's growing accuracy and reliability.

12.4 METHODOLOGIES AND APPROACHES

AD detection using DL is a methodical and rigorous approach to collecting data and analyzing it. To find information about AD detection, DL, neuroimaging, and other related topics, many of them used academic databases such as PubMed, IEEE Xplore, and Google Scholar. We also searched relevant journals and conference proceedings by hand shown in Figure 12.2. The review's inclusion and exclusion criteria consider elements like study design (e.g., original research articles, reviews), publication date (e.g., studies published from 2018 onward), and emphasis on DL methodologies for AD detection using neuroimaging data. I extracted important information from the selected studies, including the study's aims, DL architectures used, neuroimaging modalities (such as MRI and PET), sample size, performance metrics, and important findings shown in Figure 12.4. The literature review for the comprehensive study on DL for AD detection follows a methodical and thorough approach to data collection and analysis.

12.4.1 Data analysis

To evaluate the current status of DL-based AD detection, we evaluated existing data from specific studies. We aggregated the primary research methodologies and approaches that cover DL architectures, preprocessing techniques, feature extraction methods, and performance

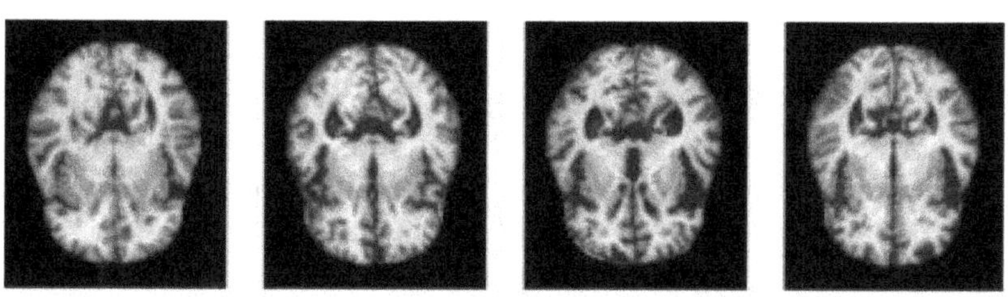

Figure 12.2 MRI samples representing four different stages of dementia: not demented (ND), moderately demented (MoD), mildly demented (MD), and very mildly demented (VmD).

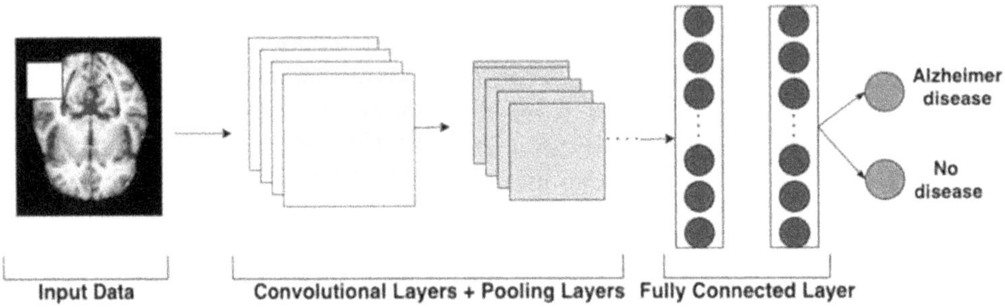

Figure 12.3 CNN-based AD detection system architecture.

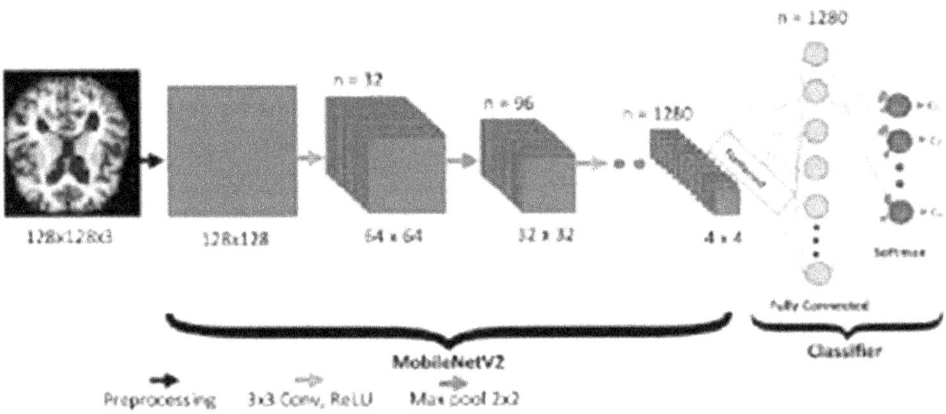

Figure 12.4 AD detection via MobileNet architecture.

assessment techniques. In the process, we focused on observing the general methodologies and approaches incorporated in the selected studies with the intention of identifying the similarities and differences between them. This made it possible to establish the existing patterns, strengths, and weaknesses in the current studies on detection of AD via DL. Therefore, the interpretation of the findings followed the review's main goal, which aims to shed light on the possibilities of DL in detecting AD. Toward the end of the discussion, we asked questions on how the results could impact the clinical practice, where the research can be taken, and the future of innovations. To provide an accurate and comprehensive account of the situation in the field presently, it was quite evident that the methodologies and approaches which were involved in the detection of AD using DL had a system and scientific method to collecting and analyzing the data. The investigations exploring the use of DL for the detection of AD have presented some interesting patterns and outcomes, which reflect the current state of study of this rapidly evolving field. Some of the DL architectures that the review specified for AD detection include generative models, RNNs, and CNNs. CNNs seem to hold potential for extracting features from neuroimaging data, and it becomes feasible to diagnose AD patients from healthy individuals based on the MRI and PET scans. To make the neuroimaging data and the DL model work better, we employed some preprocessing techniques. These include, among others, feature scaling, data augmentation, and picture normalization. In addition, the DL models were comparatively more accurate for the detection of AD because these incorporated better preprocessing techniques such as data smoothening and data balancing, among others. When it comes to AD stratification, feature extraction was needed to obtain relevant data from neuroimaging. Two DNN feature extraction approaches, namely autoencoders and transfer learning, have been observed to learn differentiable features on very large datasets. This should increase the generality of DL models and, therefore, enhance their precision. More often, authors quantified the ability of different DL models for AD detection based on statistical indicators such as F1 score, AUC, sensitivity and specificity, and accuracy. Consequently, different studies' findings indicated that net DL models could be helpful in diagnosing AD using neuroimaging data, with the classification accuracies varying from 85% to more than 95%. For higher accuracy in DL-based AD detection models, there is a growing trend to use multimodal neuroimaging data, MRI, PET, etc., as identified from the literature survey conducted. Currently, the performance of DL models in the diagnosis of early AD is considered insufficient, and one of the potential ways of its enhancement is the utilization of clinical information, including genetic and neuropsychological tests. Therefore, given the analysis of highly complex neuroimaging data through DL, it has the potential to revolutionize AD detection based on the trends and studies highlighted in the literature review. One possible avenue of future research could involve the combination of multiple inputs and DL architectures; a second possibility might be the enhancement of the architecture of the current DL; and the third one might be associated with the utilization of new preprocessing methods to identify a more accurate diagnosis of AD. Several challenges and gaps in knowledge were identified in AD detection by DL. The major challenge that training of DL models poses is the low availability of large and diverse dataset. The shortcomings of DL algorithms to generalize and the bearing of this constraint has seen most models suffer from overfitting. While DL models present relatively good accuracy, the attributes and decisions made by such models are often very hard to explain because the models are not very interpretable. Due to this, it is hard to attain the degree of openness required for attaining high levels of interpretability and explainability, a factor likely to win the hearts of health care providers managing clinical settings. The current number of healthy controls is larger than the number of AD patients; hence, a bias of the models' predictions and low accuracy is expected.

12.4.2 A CNN-based MobileNet alzheimer disease detection system

A CNN-based AD diagnosing system utilizes DL to identify primary MCI signs from neuroimaging information. To eliminate discrepancies and deal with fluctuations, common sources indicate that the initial step in the process often involves scanning and normalization of the input images that can originate from MRI, PET, or CT scans. Subsequently, the system uses a CNN architecture that comprises several layers of convolutional, pooling, and fully connected layers. It can be noted that these layers learn hierarchical representations of features in the input images to identify patterns related to increases in AD. CNN is trained on a set of brain images that are labeled with respect to the existence of AD in the patients. In training, the network will change the parameter of the model to increase the probability of correct classification of the brain scan as healthy or diseased. Once trained, CNN can distinguish AD from new brain images. Performance evaluation metrics such as accuracy, sensitivity, and specificity assess the system's effectiveness. Continuous refinement and optimization of the CNN architecture and training process are required to improve the system's accuracy and extrapolation of unknown data. Furthermore, combining clinical data and biomarkers with imaging data can improve the system's predictive abilities and clinical utility (Figure 12.3).

12.4.3 MobileNet

A CNN architecture model known as MobileNet has been trained specifically for mobile vision and image classification. We construct lightweight deep neural networks using depth-wise separable convolutions, which significantly reduces the parameter count compared to networks using regular convolutions at the same net depth. The classifier's advantages include reduced parameters, smaller networks, and quicker performance. We can size and configure mobile networks to meet the resource requirements of different use cases. They have low power and low latency (Figure 12.4).

12.4.4 Implementation steps for MobileNet

Step 1 Import the necessary libraries, including the device libraries and TensorFlow version 2.8.2. Print out all local devices. After that, use your Gmail login to access Collab Pro Google Drive. Link up with Google Drive.

Step 2 Bring in all classifier-related files: Windows 10, NumPy, openCV2, matplotlib, a few Sk_learn metrics, a single Hot Encoding, Sequential, Dense, Activation, Dropout, Flatten, MobileNet, Model Checkpoint, Early Stopping, Reduce LR On Plateau, Adam, Random Seed = 123, and Classification Report.

Step 3 Add the three classes' image folders to the upload. Make sure to include the test and training folder paths.

Step 4 Sort the training and test images into four folders: mild, very mild, moderate, and non-moderate.

Step 5 Preprocess the input data and photos using 224 x 224–pixel device.

Step 6 Expand the data: rotate it through 20 degrees and the flips in both the vertical and horizontal directions are accurate. The brightness range is from 0.5 to 1.5, the batch size is 16, the shift range is 0.2, and the shear range is 0.2.

Step 7 Use the improved class-labeled images to analyze the sample data.

Step 8 Create MobileNet strategies using precalculated picture weights. The Boolean value "false" is entered above the fully connected layer at the top of the network. Load the MobileNet weight. Layer the result file. It is recommended that the call input() be used as the model's picture input, and make sure to enter (224, 224, 3) for the optional form line and make sure the MobileNet format is correct. After that, see a rundown of the MobileNet method, which includes all 15 Conv blocks and their inverse modules. These blocks consist of seven global average queries: zero padding, rescaling, TFOP lambda, conv, depth-wise conv, batch normalizations, and addition.

Step 9 Depending on the number of classes, construct fully linked layers. To achieve this, use the following steps: flattening (940840), including sequential [20], activation (relu), density (512, 256, 3), dropout (0.6), and MobileNet. As far as the three groups are concerned, SoftMax serves as the final layer's activation function. We can conclude that the MobileNet functionality (7, 7, 1920) in the trainable layers does not accurately represent the model summary. Use the sequential method to build fully connected layers, depending on the number of classes. However, the model summarizes the trainable layers that are prone to errors.

Step 10 Assemble the model with Adam as the optimizer; 0.001 acts as the learning rate, a loss of categorical transverse entropy, and a precision metric of 1. After that, pass the following parameters into the callbacks: To save the best model weights, create a file path, h5. For an early shutdown, you need to run a monitor calculation with the following parameters: mode = max, patience = 25, and verbose = 1. Here are some of the criteria for Plateau: for the monitor calculation, set val_loss = 10, patience = 10, minimum LR = 0.001, and mode = min. You can adjust the model checkpoint's performance in the file directory. Set verbose to 1, mode to max, save best only if true, and use Val accuracy for monitoring. The following three make use of the callbacks list.

Step 11 Plot and show the model's performance using the following parameters: the figure measures 10 by 5. Figure 12.5 shows the subplot labeled (1, 2, 1), which represents accuracy on the y-axis and epochs on the x-axis. Figure 12.6 displays the 4 x 4 confusion matrix readings for the training and testing predictions.

Step 12 Display these.

Step 13 For reference, display the correct and intended class labels next to the correctly classified photos.

Step 14 , use the correctly labeled photographs as a guide, taking into account both the actual and anticipated category labels.

Step 15 Using Table 12.1, the classification report shows the accuracy, recognition, f1 score, and AUC for each class.

12.5 RESULT ANALYSIS

Figure 12.5 illustrates how the training and validation loss distributions of the proposed network converge smoothly over the entire time period, as indicated by the curve.

A confusion matrix is used to evaluate the effectiveness of a detection model using numerical values from the test data. Figure 12.6 shows the detection dataset's confusion matrix. You can see both the right and wrong pictures in the matrix. The matrix's y-axis shows genuine labels, whereas the x-axis shows detected labels that can answer the class's predictions with a yes or no. A positive result here would mean the illness is present, while a negative one would mean it isn't. In addition, we used the F1 score, recall, accuracy, and precision metrics to assess our classifiers.

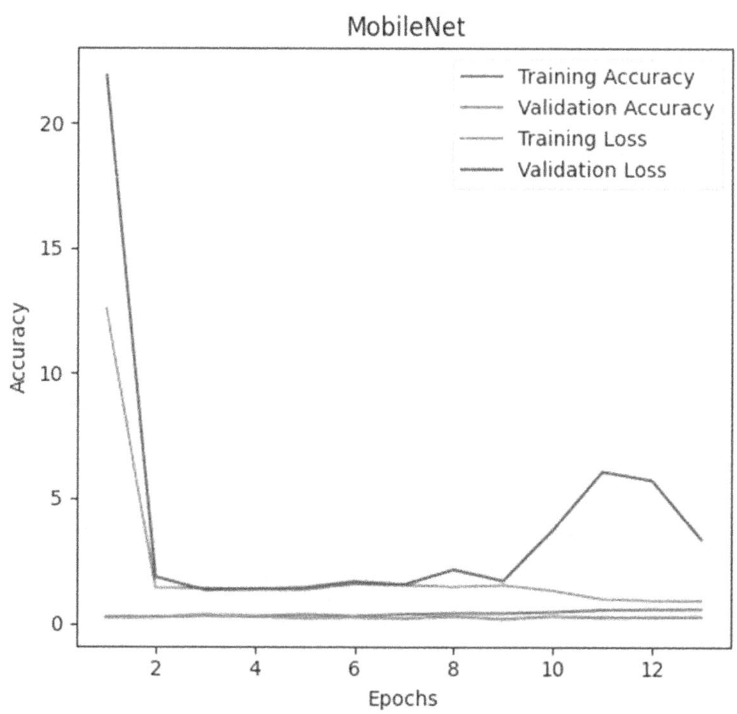

Figure 12.5 Comparing loss and accuracy curves.

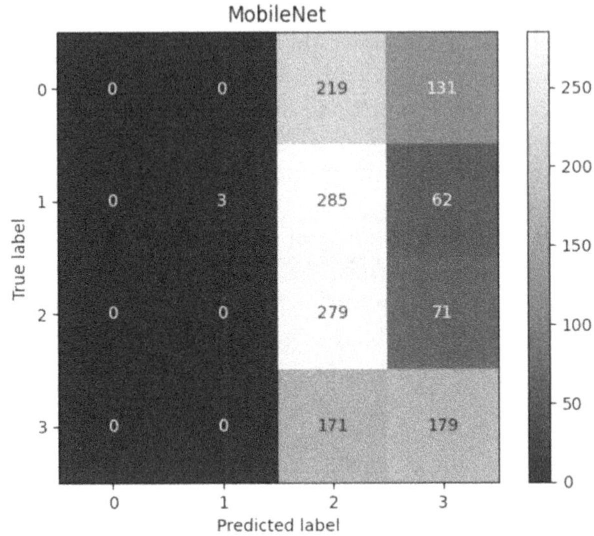

Figure 12.6 Outcomes of the confusion matrix.

Table 12.1 F1 Score, AUC, accuracy, precision, and recall

Classes	*Accuracy*	*Precision*	*Recall*	*F1-Score*	*AUC*
Mild	62.57	0.0	0.0	0.0	59
Very mild	**81.42**	**100**	0.0	0.0	**76**
Moderate	79.71	29.25	**79.71**	42.79	67
Non-moderated	51.14	40.41	51.14	**45.15**	74

Table 12.1 displays the results of the MobileNet model's performance in terms of accuracy, precision, recall, F1 score, and AUC. In the very mild class, MobileNet achieved 81.42% accuracy, 100% precision, 45.51% F1 score in the non-moderate class, and 79.71% recall in the moderate class. When it comes to classification, the very mild class boasts the best AUC at 76%.

12.6 SUMMARY AND PROSPECTS FOR THE FUTURE

This study outlines the major advances in detecting AD using DL methods. This review shows how DL could improve early AD detection and management by analyzing various DP architectures. Despite the current challenges in implementing DL approaches, such as the lack of sufficiently large dataset and the difficulty in interpreting the obtained results, the use of DL can enhance diagnostic precision and promote individualized approaches in AD cases. To facilitate the evolution of this innovative DL-based AD detection and improve patient outcomes in this crucial branch of health care, more studies should be conducted regarding the integration of multiple mitochondrial dysfunction syndrome and the development of benchmarking methodologies.

Future studies that investigate the accuracy of DL models for detecting AD should consider addressing the following factors to help advance the field. First, the enhanced investigation of issues like the combination of MRI, PET, genotypes, phenotypes, and clinical data could help enhance the model's stability. In addition, employing transfer learning and domain adaptation methods could allow the models to be applied to new datasets and hospital environments. Additionally, the work in the area of model interpretability and explainability, especially through attention mechanisms and model-agnostic interpretability techniques, facilitates clinician trust. Thus, the final steps that require expansion are scientific confirmation of the clinical applicability and real-life tests of the proposed DL models. Last, the DL-based model that can be created for long-term analysis of AD progression and early diagnostic characteristics are useful for preventive actions.

REFERENCES

1. Munteanu, D., Bejan, C., Munteanu, N., Zamfir, C., Vasić, M., Petrea, S., & Cristea, D. (2022). Deep-learning-based system for assisting people with Alzheimer's disease. *Electronics*, 11(19), 3229. https://doi.org/10.3390/electronics11193229
2. Oskouei, R. J., MousaviLou, Z., Bakhtiari, Z., & Jalbani, K. B. (2020). IoT-based healthcare support system for Alzheimer's patients. *Wireless Communications and Mobile Computing*, 20(12), 1–15. https://doi.org/10.1155/2020/8822598
3. Yalamanchili, A.D.V.G.V.K., (2023). Attn_CNN_LSTM: IoT-based automated Alzheimer's disease classification using deep learning approach. *International Journal of Engineering Trends and Technology*, 71(7), 132–146 https://doi.org/10.14445/22315381/ijettv71i7p214
4. Chokri, R., Hanini, W., Daoud, W. B., Chelloug, S. A., & Makhlouf, A. M. (2022). Secure IoT assistant-based system for Alzheimer's disease. *IEEE Access*, 10(11), 44305–44314. https://doi.org/10.1109/access.2022.3168311
5. Alqahtani, N., Alam, S., Aqeel, I., Shuaib, M., Mohsen Khormi, I., Khan, S. B., & Malibari, A. A. (2023). Deep belief networks (DBN) with IoT-based Alzheimer's disease detection and classification. *Applied Sciences*, 13(13), 7833. https://doi.org/10.3390/app13137833
6. Vrahatis, A. G., Skolariki, K., Krokidis, M. G., Lazaros, K., Exarchos, T. P., & Vlamos, P. (2023). Revolutionizing the early detection of Alzheimer's disease through non-invasive biomarkers: The role of artificial intelligence and deep learning. *Sensors*, 23(9), 4184. https://doi.org/10.3390/s23094184
7. Meenakshi Ammal, S., & Manoharan, P. (2023). Multi-headed deep learning models to detect abnormality of Alzheimer's patients. *Computer Systems Science and Engineering*, 44(1), 367390. https://doi.org/10.32604/csse.2023.025230
8. El-Latif, A. A., Chelloug, S. A., Alabdulhafith, M., & Hammad, M. (2023). Accurate detection of Alzheimer's disease using lightweight deep learning model on MRI data. *Diagnostics*, 13(7), 1216. https://doi.org/10.3390/diagnostics13071216
9. Spasov, S., Passamonti, L., Duggento, A., Liò, P., & Toschi, N. (2019). A parameter-efficient deep learning approach to predict conversion from mild cognitive impairment to Alzheimer's disease. *NeuroImage*, 189(18), 276–287. https://doi.org/10.1016/j.neuroimage.2019.01.031
10. Jo, T., Nho, K., Risacher, S. L., & Saykin, A. J. (2020). Deep learning detection of informative features in tau PET for Alzheimer's disease classification. https://doi.org/10.1101/2020.07.20.212852
11. Kavitha, C., Mani, V., Srividhya, S. R., Khalaf, O. I., & Tavera Romero, C. A. (2022). Earlystage Alzheimer's disease prediction using machine learning models. *Frontiers in Public Health*, 10(8), 1–13. https://doi.org/10.3389/fpubh.2022.853294
12. Rohanian, M., Hough, J., & Purver, M. (2021). Alzheimer’s dementia recognition using acoustic, lexical, Disfluency and speech pause features robust to noisy inputs. *Inter Speech 2021*, 11(4), 1–12. https://doi.org/10.21437/interspeech.2021-1633
13. AbdulAzeem, Y., Bahgat, W. M., & Badawy, M. (2021). A CNN based framework for classification of Alzheimer's disease. *Neural Computing and Applications*, 33(16), 10415–10428. https://doi.org/10.1007/s00521-021-05799-w
14. Sethi, M., Rani, S., Singh, A., & Mazón, J. L. (2022). A CAD system for Alzheimer's disease classification using neuroimaging MRI 2D slices. *Computational and Mathematical Methods in Medicine*, 22(16), 1–11. https://doi.org/10.1155/2022/8680737

15. Jain, R., Jain, N., Aggarwal, A., & Hemanth, D. J. (2019). Convolutional neural network-based Alzheimer's disease classification from magnetic resonance brain images. *Cognitive Systems Research*, 57(7), 147–159. https://doi.org/10.1016/j.cogsys.2018.12.015
16. Odusami, M., Maskeliūnas, R., & Damaševičius, R. (2022). An intelligent system for early recognition of Alzheimer's disease using neuroimaging. *Sensors*, 22(3), 740. https://doi.org/10.3390/s22030740
17. Agarwal, D., Marques, G., De la Torre-Díez, I., Franco Martin, M. A., García Zapiraín, B., & Martín Rodríguez, F. (2021). Transfer learning for Alzheimer's disease through neuroimaging biomarkers: A systematic review. *Sensors*, 21(21), 7259. https://doi.org/10.3390/s21217259
18. Murugan, S., Venkatesan, C., Sumithra, M. G., Gao, X., Elakkiya, B., Akila, M., & Manoharan, S. (2021). DEMNET: A deep learning model for early diagnosis of Alzheimer diseases and dementia from MR images. *IEEE Access*, 9(4), 90319–90329. https://doi.org/10.1109/access.2021.3090474
19. Arezoo, B., Taha, H & Abbas, S (2024). Introducing an ensemble method for the early detection of Alzheimer's disease through the analysis of PET scan images. arXiv, 13(8), 1–https://doi.org/10.1016/j.cogsys.2018.12.015
20. Khatun, M., Islam, M. M., Rahman Rifat, H., Bin Shahid, M. S., Talukder, M. A., & Uddin, M. A. (2023). Hybridized Convolutional neural networks and long short-term memory for improved Alzheimer's disease diagnosis from MRI scans. *2023 26th International Conference on Computer and Information Technology (ICCIT)*, 13(8), 10415–10428. https://doi.org/10.1109/iccit60459.2023.10441274
21. Sriram, H., Conati, C., & Field, T. (2023). Classification of Alzheimer's disease with deep learning on eye-tracking data. *International Conference on Multimodal Interaction*, 24(12), 147–159. https://doi.org/10.1145/3577190.3614149
22. Oktavian, M. W., Novanto, Y. & Achmad, R. Classification of Alzheimer's Disease Using the Convolutional Neural Network (CNN) with Transfer Learning and Weighted Loss (2022). *arXiv*, 13(3), 1–12. https://doi.org/10.1101/2020.06.24.20139592
23. Amish, M., Sourav, S., Arnhav, D. Multi-Modal Detection of Alzheimer's Disease from Speech and Text (2021). arXiv 22(16), 1–11. https://doi.org/10.1155/2022/8680737

Chapter 13

Leveraging machine learning and web applications for heart disease prediction

Ravi Boda, B. Mohan Rao, Gudi Srikanth, Bommidi Sathvik, Kotha Ajay Kumar, and Kurma Srujan

13.1 INTRODUCTION

Cardiovascular diseases represent a major global health challenge, straining health care systems and significantly affecting people's lives. Accurate and timely prediction of heart disease is crucial for enabling proactive interventions and ensuring optimal patient care. The integration of machine learning techniques in health care has become a promising approach, enhancing diagnostic capabilities and revolutionizing traditional disease prediction methods [1, 2].

This chapter contributes to the expanding field of heart disease prediction using machine learning methodologies. It seeks to advance existing research by investigating and assessing a range of algorithms aimed at enhancing accuracy while mitigating computational costs in prediction tasks. Given the paramount importance of early detection and intervention in mitigating the health risks associated with cardiovascular diseases, our study is dedicated to exploring innovative approaches that can facilitate timely and precise identification of potential risks [3–5].

Recognizing the intricate nature of heart disease prediction, this study delves into the complexities within the medical domain, addressing the multifaceted challenges involved. To explore the best approach for predicting heart disease, we're investigating a variety of machine learning algorithms. These include Logistic Regression, Naive Bayes, Random Forests, XGBoost, K-Nearest Neighbors, Decision Trees, and Support Vector Machines [6, 7]. Each algorithm has its own strengths, and by evaluating them all we hope to identify the most effective technique for accurately predicting the presence or absence of heart disease based on patient data [7, 8].

The machine learning algorithms we've selected each offer unique advantages and have been widely applied across various domains. Logistic Regression, a fundamental yet powerful linear model, is well suited for binary classification tasks, making it an excellent starting point for our analysis. Naive Bayes, grounded in the probabilistic principles of Bayes' theorem, is known for its simplicity and efficiency, particularly when dealing with datasets featuring categorical variables. Moving beyond linear models, algorithms like Random Forest and Decision Tree offer robust capabilities by integrating information from multiple sources to detect complex patterns within the data [9–11]. This makes them particularly effective in situations where the factors influencing heart disease exhibit intricate, nonlinear relationships. Extreme Gradient Boosting, a gradient-boosting algorithm known for its speed and high performance, serves as a powerful tool for enhancing predictive accuracy. K-Nearest Neighbors, an instance-based learning algorithm, provides an intuitive approach to classification by identifying similar instances in the feature space. Lastly, Support Vector Machines, which excel at finding optimal hyperplanes for classification, are especially effective in handling high-dimensional data and complex decision boundaries [12–15].

DOI: 10.1201/9781003591788-13

Furthermore, in line with our research objectives, we have developed a user-friendly website that integrates the predictive models generated, offering individuals an accessible platform to assess their cardiovascular health status with ease and accuracy.

13.2 MOTIVATION

Cardiovascular diseases (CVDs) remain a significant global health threat, driving the need for innovative strategies to improve early detection and intervention.

This research is motivated by the pressing need to transform health care practices, particularly in predicting heart disease and ensuring proactive patient care. The rising prevalence of CVDs highlights the urgent necessity to develop advanced decision support systems for accurate risk assessment.

13.3 LITERATURE REVIEW

This research is based on a comprehensive review of existing literature. By analyzing scholarly articles and established methodologies, we aim to expand upon the current knowledge in the field. This involves a critical evaluation of machine learning algorithms, including Random Forest, Decision Tree, Logistic Regression, Naive Bayes, and various ensemble methods. Through synthesizing insights from related studies, our goal is to identify gaps and opportunities for creating more effective tools for the early detection of cardiovascular disease.

Golande and Pavan Kumar [16] conducted a study examining machine learning algorithms suitable for heart disease classification, focusing on Decision Tree, K-Nearest Neighbors (KNN), and K-Means. They found Decision Tree to perform best, suggesting potential improvements through technique combinations and parameter tuning. The methodology involved preprocessing data to handle NaN values, splitting it into training and testing sets, and training with four algorithms. Decision Tree utilized gain ratio for feature selection. KNN relied on proximity for classification. K-Means clustered data based on similarity. Adaboost enhanced Decision Tree's performance. The study concluded by emphasizing the importance of exploring various techniques and tuning parameters for accuracy enhancement.

The study conducted by Nagamani et al. [17] implemented a comparative analysis, employing the MapReduce algorithm alongside a new approach that combines advanced optimization techniques with a powerful learning model to analyze data from a well-established heart disease dataset. This approach aims to improve the accuracy of predicting the presence or absence of heart disease. Remarkably, the analysis demonstrated a significant improvement in accuracy, achieving 98.12% for the testing set instances compared to conventional methods. This enhancement was attributed to the dynamic schema and linear scaling utilized within the proposed MapReduce algorithm.

In a recent study conducted by Alotaibi [18], five machine learning models were employed to predict heart disease using collected data. The research meticulously assessed the performance of each classifier, comparing it with previous studies. After successful data preprocessing, Alotaibi discussed the selection of machine learning algorithms and the research methods employed. The study aimed to improve accuracy by incorporating techniques such as data expansion and cross-validation. The selected models included Decision Tree, Naive Bayes, Random Forest, Logistic Regression, and Support Vector Machine, all chosen for their classification capabilities and suitability for the dataset.

A study by Repaka et al. [19] analyzed heart disease risk using four classification algorithms. Leveraging the UCI Cleveland dataset's 14 features, the research investigated the effectiveness of Random Forest, Decision Tree, Logistic Regression, and Naive Bayes algorithms. The Random Forest algorithm stood out with an impressive 90.16% accuracy score. This research underscores the critical role of predictive modeling in health care and suggests potential enhancements.

13.4 METHODOLOGY

1. Dataset Description: The dataset utilized in this study is publicly accessible via the Kaggle platform and originates from an ongoing cardiovascular investigation conducted among residents of Framingham, Massachusetts. The primary objective of classification is to forecast whether patients face a 10-year risk of developing coronary heart disease (CHD). Comprising more than 4,000 entries, the dataset encompasses 15 attributes, offering a comprehensive array of patient information for analysis.
2. Data Preprocessing: The dataset undergoes meticulous preprocessing to ensure data quality and consistency, beginning with the handling of missing values (if any). Any missing data points are systematically addressed through appropriate imputation techniques to maintain the integrity of the dataset [20]. Furthermore, numerical attributes undergo standardization or normalization procedures to mitigate potential variations in scale among different features. Specifically, the data is standardized to achieve a mean of 0 and a standard deviation of 1, facilitating comparability and enhancing the effectiveness of subsequent modeling techniques. Additionally, irrelevant columns, such as the 'education' attribute, are excluded from the analysis to streamline the dataset and focus on pertinent features for heart disease prediction (see Figure 13.1).
3. Training–Testing Split: For model training and evaluation, data are divided into an 80–20 ratio, where 80% of the data is used for model training and 20% for evaluation.
4. Model Selection: A variety of machine learning models are utilized for heart disease prediction, including Logistic Regression, Naive Bayes, Random Forest Classifier, Extreme Gradient Boosting, K-Nearest Neighbors, Decision Tree, and Support Vector Machine. Each model is trained on the training dataset and evaluated on the testing dataset, with accuracy serving as the primary performance metric (Figure 13.2).
5. Evaluation Metrics: Model performance is evaluated using accuracy, which quantifies how well the model performed on the testing set by measuring the proportion of correct classifications. Performance scores are documented for each model to enable comparison and identify the top-performing model(s).
6. Result Analysis: The accuracies of various models are compiled into a table for comparison, with the model achieving the highest accuracy identified as the leading candidate

	male	age	education	currentSmoker	cigsPerDay	BPMeds
0	1	39	4.0	0	0.0	0.0
1	0	46	2.0	0	0.0	0.0
2	1	48	1.0	1	20.0	0.0
3	0	61	3.0	1	30.0	0.0
4	0	46	3.0	1	23.0	0.0

Figure 13.1 Dataset overview.

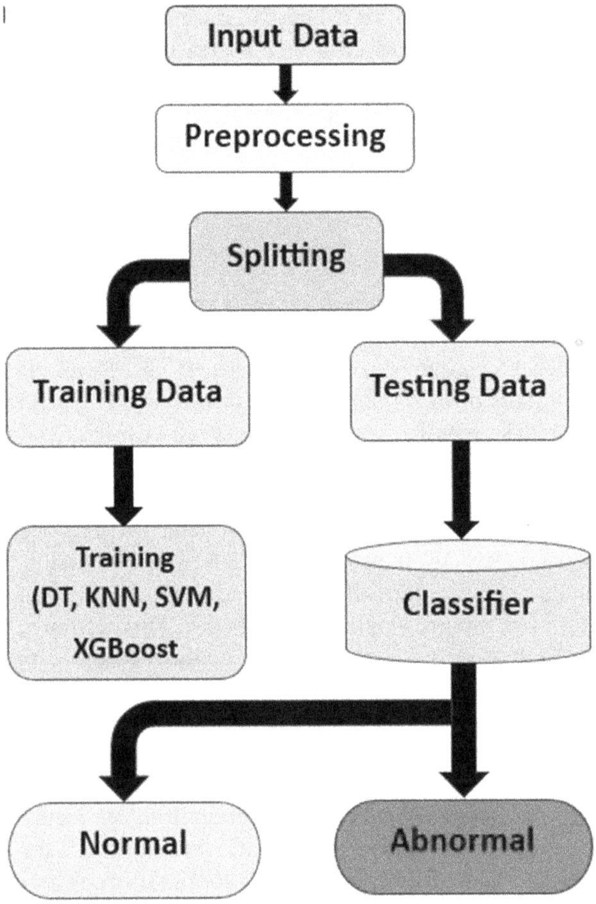

Figure 13.2 Machine learning framework for data analysis.

Table 13.1 Model accuracies

Model	*Accuracy (%)*
L R	85.25
N B	85.25
R F	86.89
XG Boost 90.16	
KNN	88.52
DT	81.97
SVM	88.52

for heart disease prediction. Further analysis may involve examining confusion matrices, precision-recall curves, and ROC curves to gain a deeper understanding of model performance across different evaluation metrics.

To improve predictive accuracy, we applied an ensemble learning technique called stacking. Stacking involves combining the predictions of multiple base models through the use of a meta-classifier (Table 13.1).

13.4.1 Stacking technique

We utilized the StackingCVClassifier implementation from the mlxtend library in Python to implement the stacking ensemble method. This classifier allows us to stack multiple base classifiers and use a meta-classifier to combine their predictions.

$$\text{scv} = \text{StackingCVClassifier}(\text{classifiers} = [\text{xgb}, \text{knn}, \text{svc}],$$

$$\text{meta classifier} = \text{svc}, \text{random state} = 42)$$

$$\text{scv.fit}(X_{\text{train}}, y_{\text{train}})$$

$$\text{scv predicted} = \text{scv.predict}(X_{\text{test}})$$

The classifiers parameter specifies the base classifiers to be stacked, which in our case include XGBoost, KNN, and Support Vector Classifier (SVC). The meta-classifier parameter specifies the meta-classifier used to combine the predictions, which is another SVC in our implementation.

13.4.2 Results

Upon training and evaluating the stacking classifier, we obtained the following results:

– Accuracy of StackingCVClassifier:	91.8%
– Confusion Matrix:	
	24 3
	2 32

	precision recall support f1-score				
– Classification Report:	0	0.92	0.89	27	0.91
	1	0.91	0.94	34	0.93

Model 1:	**Logistic Regression**
Confusion Matrix:	
`	21 6
	3 31

Accuracy of L R:	85.25%			
Classification Report:				
	precision recall support f1-score			
0	0.88	0.78	27	0.82
1	0.84	0.91	34	0.87

Model 2:	**Naive Bayes**
Confusion Matrix:	
	21 6
	3 31

Accuracy of N B:	85.25%			
Classification Report:				
	precision recall support f1-score			
0	0.88	0.78	27	0.82
1	0.84	0.91	34	0.87

Model 3:	**Random Forest**
Confusion Matrix:	
	22 5
	3 31

Accuracy of R F:	86.89%			
Classification Report:				
	precision recall support f1-score			
0	0.88	0.81	27	0.85
1	0.86	0.91	34	0.89

Model 4:	**Extreme Gradient Boost**
Confusion Matrix:	
	24 3
	3 31

Accuracy of XG Boost:	90.16%			
Classification Report:				
	precision recall support f1-score			
0	0.89	0.89	27	0.89
1	0.91	0.91	34	0.91

Model 5	**K-Nearest Neighbour**
Confusion Matrix:	
	24 3
	4 30

Accuracy of KNN:	**88.52%**			
Classification Report:				
	precision recall support f1-score			
0	0.86	0.89	27	0.87
1	0.91	0.88	34	0.90

Model 6:	**Decision Tree**
Confusion Matrix:	
	23 4
	7 27

Accuracy of D T:	**81.97%**			
Classification Report:				
	precision recall support f1-score			
0	0.77	0.85	27	0.81
1	0.87	0.79	34	0.83

Model 7:	**Support Vector Classifier**
Confusion Matrix:	
	23 4
	3 31

Accuracy of SVC:	**88.52%**			
Classification Report:				
	precision recall support f1-score			
0	0.88	0.85	27	0.87
1	0.89	0.91	34	0.90

The stacking technique yielded an accuracy of 91.8%, demonstrating its effectiveness in improving the predictive performance of our model. Additionally, a comprehensive comparison of the models will include metrics like precision, recall, and F1 score, indicating a balanced performance across the positive and negative instances.

13.4.3 Web application

Developed the front end of the web application using Hypertext Markup Language (HTML) and Cascading Style Sheets (CSS), the foundational technologies for building web pages. HTML provided the structure and content of the web interface, while CSS was used for styling and layout, ensuring a visually appealing and user-friendly design (Figure 13.3).

- Implemented a responsive and interactive user interface through HTML forms, allowing users to input their demographic and clinical data necessary for heart disease prediction. The form fields were carefully designed to collect a comprehensive range of information, including age, gender, blood pressure readings, cholesterol levels, body mass index, and smoking status, ensuring the model receives pertinent data for accurate predictions.
- Employed Python, a versatile and powerful programming language, for the back-end development of the web application. Python's extensive ecosystem of libraries and

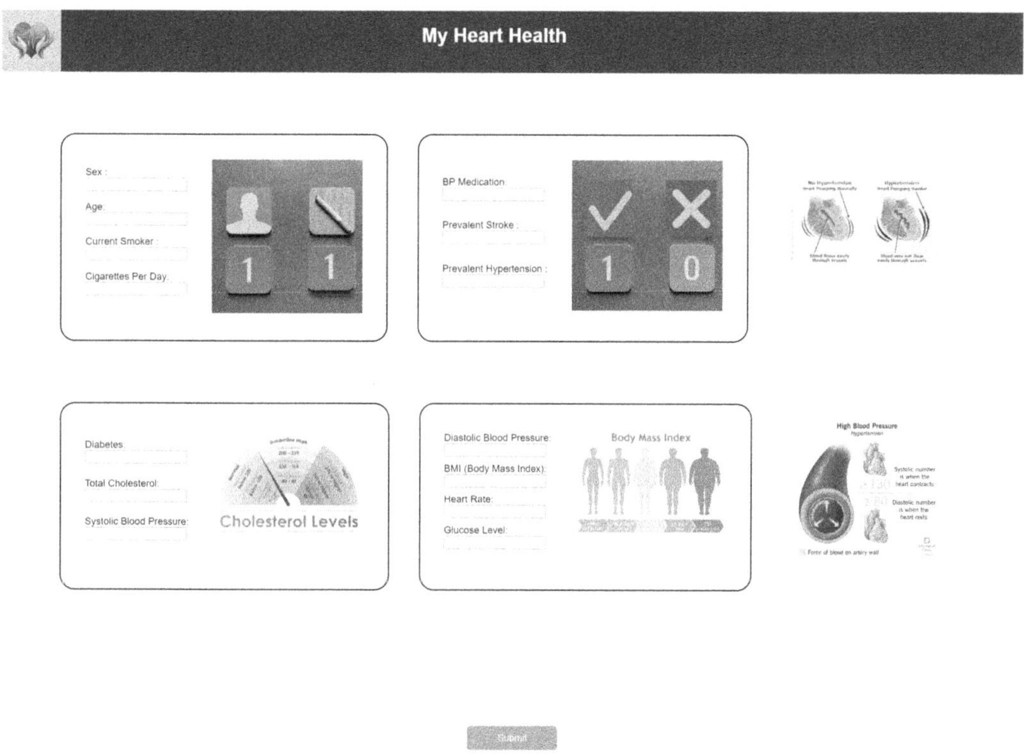

Figure 13.3 Front end of the web application.

frameworks made it an ideal choice for handling data processing tasks and implementing the server-side logic.

- Leveraged Flask, a lightweight and extensible web framework for Python, to build the back-end infrastructure of the web application. Flask's simplicity and flexibility allowed for rapid development of RESTful APIs (Application Programming Interfaces) and URL routing, enabling seamless communication between the front-end and back-end components.
- Integrated a pretrained Stacking Classifier model into the Flask application to facilitate real-time prediction of heart disease risk. The Stacking Classifier model, trained using machine learning algorithms such as Random Forest, Decision Tree, and Logistic Regression, was serialized as a .pkl file and loaded into the Flask application. This enabled the web application to utilize the predictive power of machine learning for assessing cardiovascular health risks.
- Upon submission of the user input form, the data was transmitted via HTTP POST request to the back-end server implemented with Flask. The Flask application processed the incoming data, performing any necessary data transformations and invoking the Stacking Classifier model to generate predictions.
- The prediction outcome, indicating the likelihood of the user having a risk of obtaining a heart disease, was then communicated back to the user through the web interface. The user-friendly output interface provided clear and actionable insights into the individual's cardiovascular health status, aiding in informed decision-making and risk management.
- Implemented robust error handling mechanisms and informative feedback features to enhance the reliability and usability of the web application. Error messages and prompts were strategically designed to guide users in case of invalid inputs or technical issues, ensuring a seamless and intuitive user experience.

Interpretation and Conclusion: The results from comparing the models and applying ensemble techniques were analyzed to assess the effectiveness of machine learning approaches for predicting heart disease. Notably, the ensemble technique, especially stacking, has shown significant improvements in predictive accuracy over individual models.

Ensemble methods, such as stacking, highlight the potential for synergistic effects among various machine learning algorithms. By combining multiple models, akin to assembling a high-performing team, these methods mitigate the weaknesses of any single model and enhance the accuracy of heart disease predictions, leading to improved overall performance.

In parallel with model development, a web application was constructed to facilitate user-friendly access to the predictive model. This application allows individuals to input their demographic and clinical data through a simple form accessible via a web browser. The data is then transmitted to a back-end server implemented using the Flask web framework in Python.

Upon submission of the form, the bacend server processes the user input and invokes the pretrained ensemble model, stored as a serialized file. The model predicts the likelihood of the user having a risk of obtaining a heart disease based on the input data. The prediction outcome is then communicated back to the user through the web interface, providing clear and actionable insights into their cardiovascular health status (Figures 13.4 and 13.5).

Recommendations are given based on the dataset characteristics and application needs to identify the most suitable machine learning approach for predicting heart disease risk.

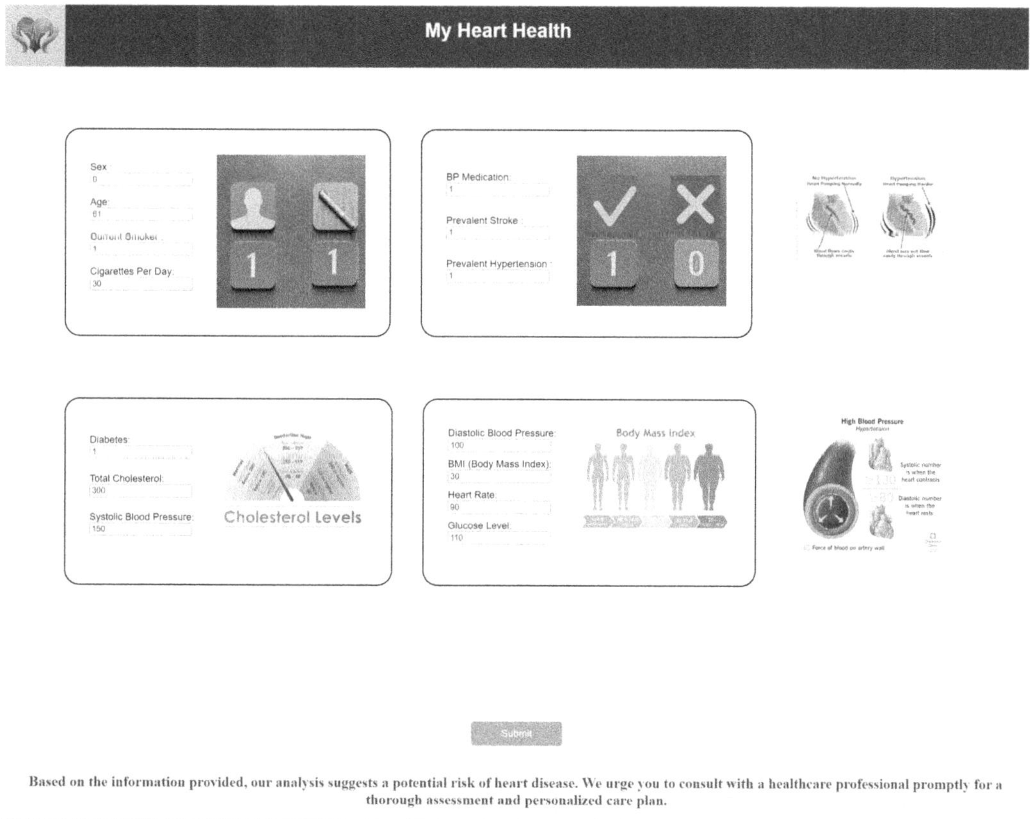

Figure 13.4 When the user has heart disease.

Although individual classifiers demonstrate strong performance, ensembling techniques are highlighted as the optimal choice for achieving the highest predictive accuracy and robustness.

Future research could explore new ensemble strategies, integrate additional base classifiers, or include domain-specific features to further enhance heart disease prediction accuracy. Additionally, advancements in computational methods and data availability present opportunities for refining predictive models and supporting personalized health care interventions.

13.5 CONCLUSION

This study underscores the transformative potential of ensemble learning in predicting heart disease. By combining diverse machine learning algorithms through the StackingCVClassifier, we achieved an impressive accuracy of 91.8%, significantly enhancing health care analytics and paving the way for personalized medicine. The development of a user-friendly website further amplifies the impact of our research, providing accessible tools for individuals to assess their cardiovascular health with ease and accuracy. Future research should continue to explore and refine ensembling techniques to further improve predictive models and patient outcomes.

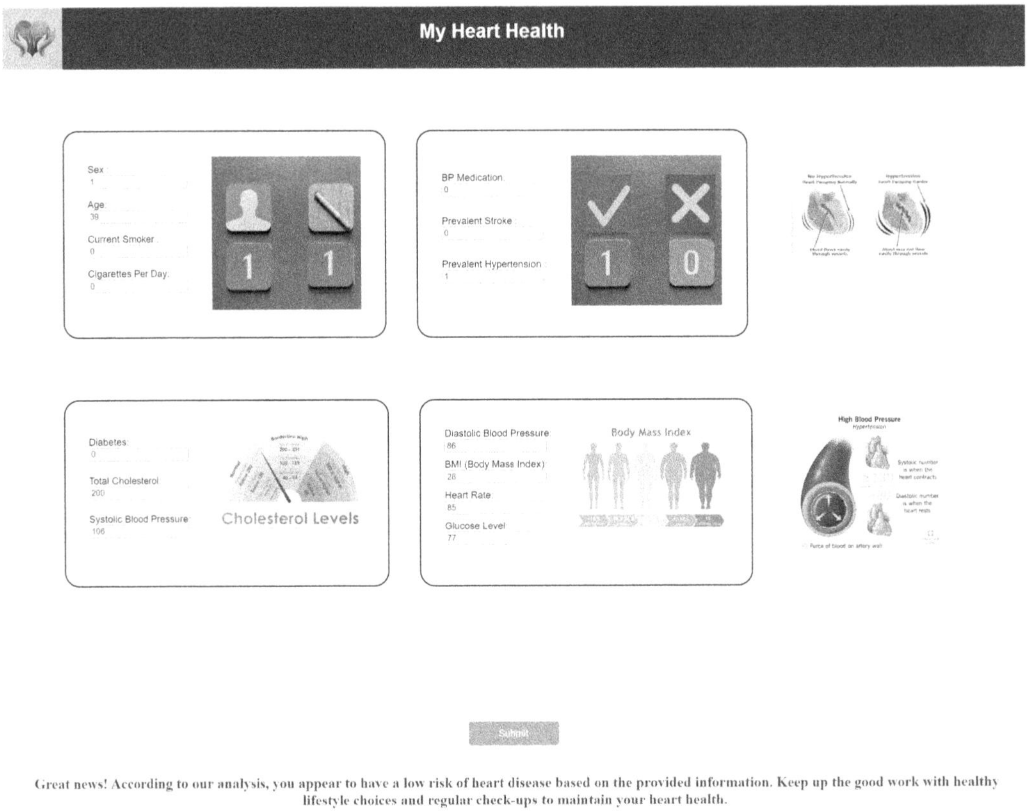

Figure 13.5 When the user doesn't have heart disease.

REFERENCES

1. Avinash Golande, Pavan Kumar T, "Heart Disease Prediction Using Effective Machine Learning Techniques", *International Journal of Recent Technology and Engineering*, Vol 8, pp.944–950,2019.
2. T. Nagamani, S. Logeswari, B. Gomathy," Heart Disease Prediction using Data Mining with Mapreduce Algorithm", *International Journal of Innovative Technology and Exploring Engineering (IJITEE)* ISSN: 2278-3075, Vol. 8, No. 3, January 2019.
3. Fahd Saleh Alotaibi," Implementation of Machine Learning Model to Predict Heart Failure Disease", *(IJACSA) International Journal of Advanced Computer Science and Applications*, Vol. 10, No. 6, 2019.
4. Anjan Nikhil Repaka, Sai Deepak Ravikanti, Ramya G Franklin, "Design And Implementation Heart Disease Prediction Using Naives Bayesian", *International Conference on Trends in Electronics and Information(ICOEI 2019).*
5. V. Krishnaiah,G. Narasimha, N. Subhash Chandra," Heart Disease Prediction System using Data Mining Techniques and Intelligent Fuzzy Approach: A Review" *IJCA* 2016.
6. Niti Guru, Anil Dahiya, Navin Rajpal, "Decision Support System for Heart Disease Diagnosis Using Neural Network", *Delhi Business Review*, Vol. 8, No. 1, January - June 2007.
7. C. S. Dangare and S. S. Apte (2012). "Improved study of heart disease prediction system using data mining classification techniques," *International Journal of Computer Applications*,47(10), 44–48.

8. A. Gavhane, G. Kokkula, I. Pandya, and P. K. Devadkar, "Prediction of Heart Disease Using Machine Learning," In *Proceedings of the 2nd International Conference on Electronics, Communication and Aerospace Technology, ICECA 2018*, 2018, pp. 1275–1278.
9. S. Kodati, R. Vivekanandam, and G. Ravi, "*Comparative Analysis of Clustering Algorithms with Heart Disease Datasets Using Data Mining Weka Tool, in Soft Computing and Signal Processing*, Singapore: Springer, 2019, pp. 111–117.
10. Theresa Princy R,J. Thomas, "Human heart Disease Prediction System using Data Mining Techniques", In *International Conference on Circuit Power and Computing Technologies*,Bangal ore,2016.
11. V. Krishnaiah, G. Narasimha, N. Subhash Chandra, "Heart Disease Prediction System using Data Mining Techniques and Intelligent Fuzzy Approach: A Review" *IJCA* 2016.
12. Ankita Dewan, Meghna Sharma, "Prediction of Heart Diseases using a hybrid technique in Data Mining Classifiscation", *2nd International Conference on Computing for Sustainable Global Development (INDIACom)*, 2015
13. Syed Umar Amin, Agarwal, K., and Beg, R., "Genetic neural network based data mining in prediction of heart disease using risk factors", *IEEE Conference in Information and Communication Technologies (ICT)*, 1227–1231, 2013
14. S. Shilaskar and A. Ghatol, "Feature selection for medical diagnosis: Evaluation for cardiovascular diseases," *Expert Syst. Appl.*, vol. 40, no. 10, pp. 4146–4153, Aug. 2013
15. A. Gavhane, G. Kokkula, I. Pandya, and P. K. Devadkar, "Prediction of Heart Disease Using Machine Learning," In *Proceedings of the 2nd International Conference on Electronics, Communication and Aerospace Technology, ICECA 2018*, 2018, pp. 1275–1278.
16. H. Murthy and M. Meenakshi, "Dimensionality reduction using neurogenetic approach for early prediction of coronary heart disease," In *International Conference on Circuits, Communication, Control and Computing (I4C)*, 2014, pp. 329–332.
17. M. Gjoreski, A. Gradiˇsek, M. Gams, M. Simjanoska, A. Peterlin, and G. Poglajen, "Chronic heart failure detection from heart sounds using a stack of machine-learning classifiers," in *Proceedings - 2017 13th International Conference on Intelligent Environments*, IE 2017, 2017, pp. 14–19.
18. V. V. Ramalingam, A. Dandapath, and M. Karthik Raja, "Heart disease prediction using machine learning techniques: A survey," *Int. J. Eng. Technol.*, vol. 7, no. 2.8, pp. 684–687, 2018.
19. Hongyu Lee, Ki Yong Noh, Keun Ho Ryu, "MiningBiosignal Data: Coronary Artery Disease Diagnosis using Linear and Nonlinear Features of HRV," *LNAI 4819: Emerging Technologies in Knowledge Discovery and Data Mining*, May 2007, pp. 56–66
20. Sellappan Palaniappan, Rafiah Awang, "Intelligent Heart Disease Prediction System Using Data Mining Techniques", *(IJCSNS)*, Vol.8 No.8, August 2008.

Chapter 14

Smart food donation

An Android app for efficient waste management

C. Kavitha, Shanthi Makka, S. Bharath Reddy, A. Sowmya, S. B. Goyal, and Budati Anil Kumar

14.1 INTRODUCTION

We face a daunting challenge in today's world whose systems are intertwined and intricate: food shortages combined with uncontrolled food dumping on a worldwide scale. The harsh realities of hunger and inadequate access to essential sustenance contrasts with the loss or disposal of about 33% of all the food produced in the world today. Current research has begun investigating innovative and transformative use of targeted smartphone apps to face this global crisis. This app introduced in this chapter is a dynamic platform that connects food donors, which could be hostels, hotels, and restaurants, among others, with those who need it through active nongovernmental organizations (NGOs) and dedicated volunteers. Moreover, this pioneering system also includes mechanisms for safe money transactions accompanying every donated foodstuff. This therefore represents an outstanding example where technology is used to solve real-life challenges, making our food distribution system more fair and sustainable.

At its core, this project intends to redefine how people donate and distribute their foods. It is not just about treating symptoms of scarcity of these products, but rather using advanced mapping technologies to maximize inputs into their collection as well as dissemination processes. This means that there will be both timely delivery of emergency aid supplies alongside increased transparency during distribution processes resulting in efficient allocation mechanisms of these inputs into useable forms. It also shows how innovative solutions can span the gap between surplus and scarcity, increasing both the efficiency and efficacy of donations. This groundbreaking app embodies a shift toward technology-driven food donation in its marriage of volunteerism and technological platforms. It is a hopeful indicator for change, as it demonstrates that through innovation one can balance the excesses of abundance with extreme want to produce effective solutions.

The landscape of waste food management applications and food donation solutions is explored in the literature review (Section 14.2), stressing the importance of incorporating technology, payment gateways, and mapping features into their operational framework to enhance efficiency and impact.

14.2 LITERATURE REVIEW

An Android app created by Sudheepa et al. [1] takes on food wastage management by connecting donors such as hostels, hotels, and restaurants with those who need it via NGOs and volunteers. Nukala et al. [2] aimed their efforts at designing a system for managing leftover food using effective hunger search techniques. This study stresses the significance of efficient

 DOI: 10.1201/9781003591788-14

food distribution and introduces new approaches to aid the process; it doesn't, however, involve an exploration of payment gateways.

A comprehensive review on food waste–reducing platforms was performed by de Almeida Oroski and da Silva [3]. Without examining any particular application (and also without discussing payment gateways), Prova et al. [4] offer great insights into what constitutes garbage management frameworks by just introducing a web and mobile-based approach of redistributing consumable food waste. "Helping Hands" is an approach for food wastage reduction through donation discussed by Anusha and Bhargavi [5]. Although specific details concerning strategy are not provided, it emphasizes the reduction of wastage as a result of donation. Hajjdiab et al.'s [6] analysis focused on reducing food wastes. The study brings out how important it is to reduce food waste, and that it can be best achieved with the use of waste food management applications—the point emphasized by Hossain et al. as well [7].

"SeVa," a smart living–oriented Feeding India app, was put forward by Varghese et al. [8]. The app underscores the ease in giving away or sharing surplus foods using smartphone applications. "Foodernity" [9] details a mobile and web-based application for food sharing. It matches well with the fundamental principles of waste food management applications that target connecting donors with those in need. "FoodX," a system for reducing food wastage, is discussed by Shinta Oktaviana et al. [10]. This system aims are ensuring simplicity in the distribution of food, thus leading to reduction of waste. Bhardwaj et al. [11] discussed a food waste management Android app. Alblihed et al. [12] introduced a food charity operations management system. The system is designed to improve efficiency in the operations relating to charity when it comes to food, which highlights how important it is to have efficient modes of food distribution and donation. Collectively, the reviewed literature underscores the multifaceted nature of waste food management applications and food donation solutions. Some applications [13] stress sharing and distribution of foods while others focus on decreasing their wastages. It further argues that current roadblocks in lowering food wastage can and should be overcome.

14.3 PROPOSED METHODOLOGY

Our methodology revolves around a systematic approach to investigating and analyzing the innovative Android app designed to enhance waste food management. Using this app allows overseeing both donors and NGOs distributing the donations. Donors, including hostels, restaurants, hotels, function halls, or individuals, must initially register on the application, providing details such as name, email, address, and other contact information. The registration data is securely stored in an SQLite database. To enhance security, password-hashing techniques are implemented alongside SQLite databases. Hashing algorithms like SHA-256 transform passwords into irreversible hash values, significantly reducing the risk of plaintext exposure in case of a data breach. Figure 14.1 represents the architecture of the proposed system.

The cryptographic approach ensures that even if the database is compromised, sensitive passwords remain protected and unreadable to unauthorized parties [14–16]. During login, the input password undergoes the same hashing process, and the resulting hash is compared to the stored hash in the database for the corresponding username. If the hashes match, the login credentials are deemed valid, affirming the user's authenticity without storing or transmitting plaintext passwords, thereby maintaining robust security standards. Donors can use their valid credentials to log in and click on the "Donate Food" button [17] if they have excess food items. They can then specify the food items, quantity, location, and contact details before submitting. Donors have the flexibility to edit donated details and view past donation history by clicking the "History" button. See Figure 14.2 for the architectural diagram.

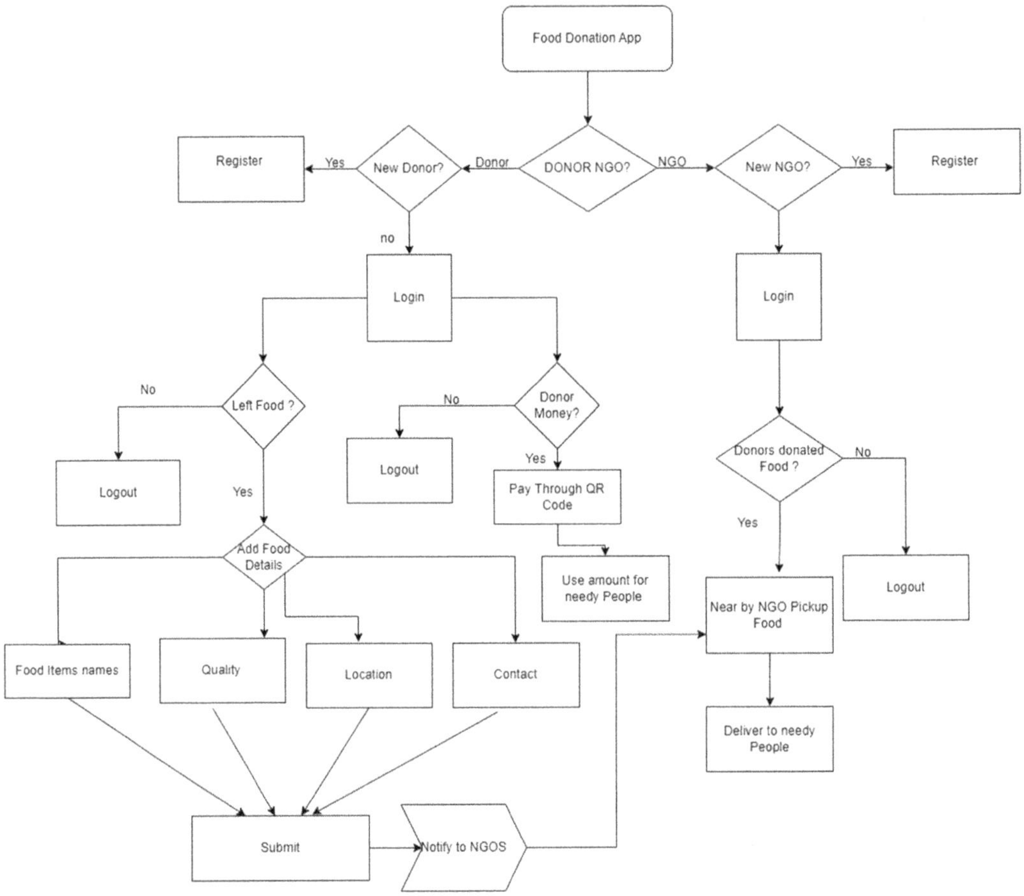

Figure 14.1 Architecture representing the proposed approach.

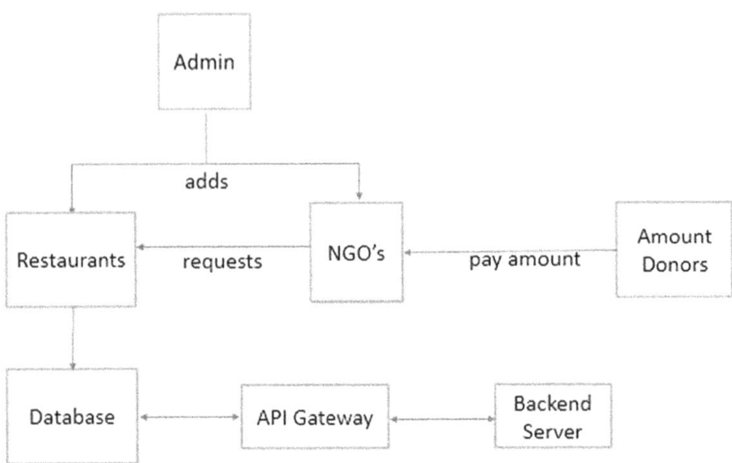

Figure 14.2 Architectural diagram.

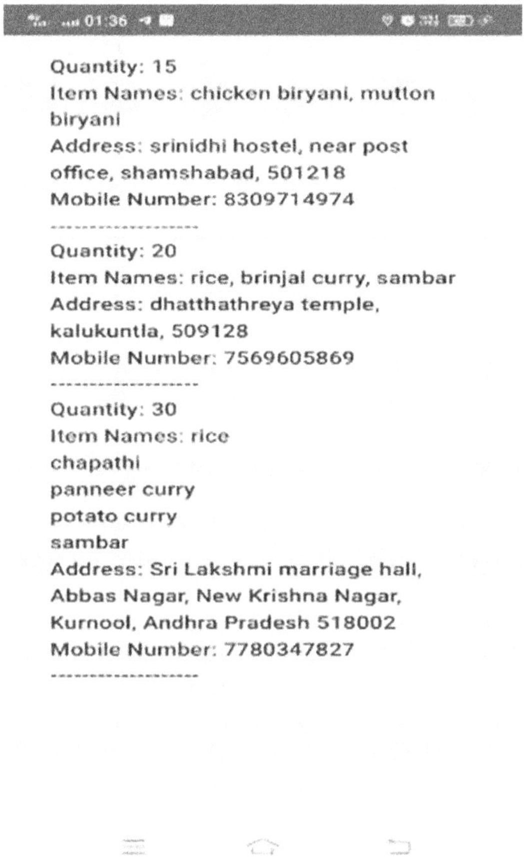

Figure 14.3 Donors donate their leftover food items.

The integration of Google Maps Android API [18–20] facilitates location selection, providing interactive maps, markers for specific locations, and user interaction capabilities. The application utilizes Firebase Cloud Messaging (FCM) to send notifications to NGOs when donations are made, even if the app is not actively in use. NGOs can then collect donations from the specified locations and distribute them to those in need, including roadside dwellers, elderly individuals, and orphanages (Figure 14.3).

Donors also have the option to contribute monetary donations directly through the application, facilitated by integrating payment gateway SDKs such as PayPal, ensuring secure handling of transactions. The user interface is developed using extensible markup language (XML), with all activity code written in Java. Explicit intents are employed for navigating within the application, while implicit intents are utilized to request functionality from other applications on the device.

14.4 RESULTS AND DISCUSSION

A great challenge to the world, according to the literature review carried out in this study, is that food scarcity and substantial waste of food currently coexist. This emphasizes how urgent this problem is, given that almost one-third of the global food supply is wasted. A range of crucial research findings have been brought to the fore through a survey on existing waste food management applications and related studies. First, it is evident from reviewed sources that many waste food management apps are focusing on streamlining processes for donating foods without having secure payment gateways. Nevertheless, an emerging trend in the literature recommends utilization of payment gateways for making huge differences in terms of donation system's efficiency. The above-named gateways enable donors not only to donate food but also to offer financial resources, thus providing a flexible approach to addressing hunger issues.

Meanwhile, variations in sample sizes, research methods, and data sources are apparent despite a wide range of studies and sources found in literature. In some instances variations may impact credibility and reliability of such findings. Literature-based insights also have practical implications for Android app development being proposed here. By integrating payment gateways with mapping technology, there are possibilities for significantly enhanced performance of the app by allowing online ordering even from local restaurants via mobile phone with instant delivery services.

This review of literature has brought to light significant global issues surrounding food waste and food scarcity, offering valuable insights into the current landscape of waste food management and the potential for innovative solutions. The coexistence of a substantial amount of wasted food alongside food scarcity highlights the urgency of addressing this paradox. Through our analysis, we have identified key findings that emphasize the transformative impact of integrating payment gateways and mapping technology into waste food management systems.

The literature consistently emphasizes the importance of payment gateways in enhancing the efficiency of food donations by enabling donors to contribute both food and financial resources. This flexible approach shows promise in addressing food scarcity more effectively. Furthermore, the literature reveals the untapped potential of mapping technology in optimizing food distribution, presenting a significant opportunity for innovation. Given the proven effectiveness of mapping technology in various sectors, its application in food collection and distribution could further aid in reducing waste and alleviating food scarcity (Figure 14.4).

The research gap identified in the literature, particularly the lack of payment gateways and mapping features in current waste food management applications, underscores the necessity for innovation in this field. Closing this gap is crucial in establishing a more efficient and equitable food distribution system that promotes sustainability and waste reduction. While the literature review demonstrated diversity in strengths, it also highlighted variations in sample sizes, research methods, and data sources, indicating the importance of rigorous research and standardization in this area (Figures 14.5–14.7).

14.5 FUTURE SCOPE

The insights gained from this literature review present several promising avenues for future research and development. These areas of future exploration hold great potential for further advancements in addressing food waste and scarcity. The future scope of the presented project is vast and promising. Expanding the app's functionalities to include advanced analytics and machine learning can optimize donation matching and predict surplus food availability. Integrating with local government and nonprofit databases can enhance the app's reach and impact, fostering a community-driven approach to food waste reduction. Additionally, incorporating real-time tracking and feedback mechanisms will improve transparency and trust among users. Exploring partnerships with more businesses and enhancing user engagement through gamification and incentives can further increase participation, ultimately leading to a more sustainable and efficient food donation ecosystem.

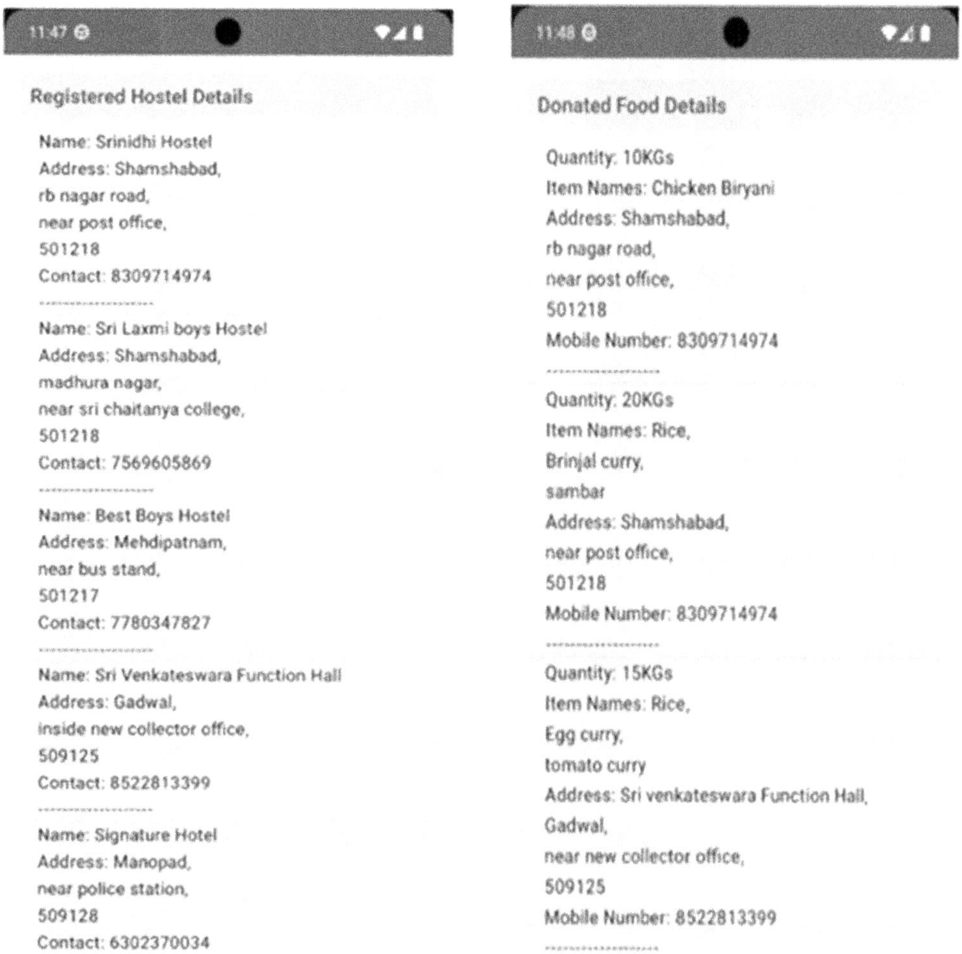

Figure 14.4 Outcomes of proposed approach.

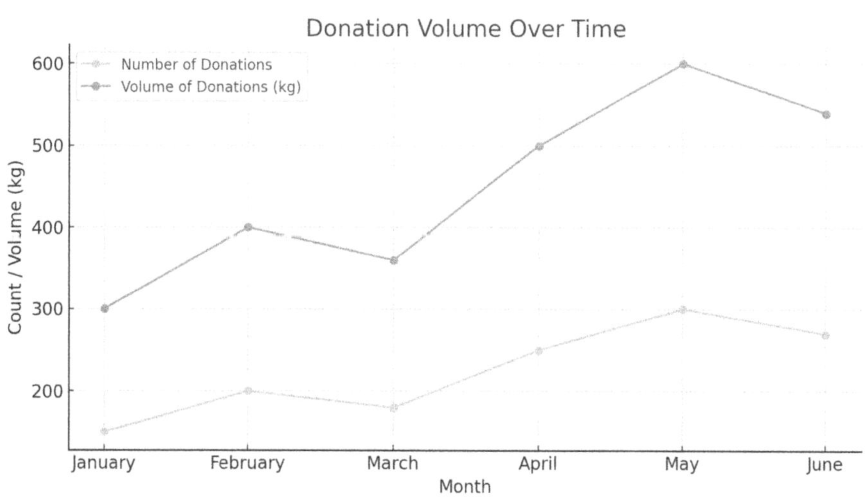

Figure 14.5 Donation volume over time.

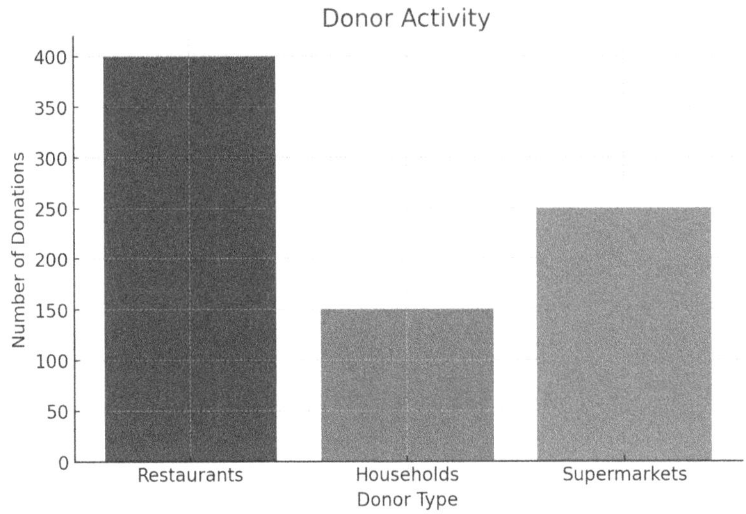

Figure 14.6 Donor activity.

Figure 14.7 Food waste reduction over time.

REFERENCES

[1] K. Sudheepa, P. Rashmitha and P. S. Maran, "Food Wastage Management Application using Android Studio," *2023 2nd International Conference on Applied Artificial Intelligence and Computing (ICAAIC)*, Salem, India, 2023, pp.1059–1064,doi: 10.1109/ICAAIC56838.2023.10140489

[2] Naveen Kumar G. N., Jeevith R., Nukala S. S., Manoj Kumar V., Shankar Sahana P., and Kandarp S., "Development of Leftover Food Management System Using Efficient Hunger Search Techniques," *2021 IEEE Mysore Sub Section International Conference (MysuruCon)*, Hassan, India, 2021, pp. 312–321, doi: 10.1109/MysuruCon52639.2021.9641624

[3] De Almeida Oroski F., da Silva J. M. Understanding Food Waste-Reducing Platforms: A Mini-review. Waste Management Research.2023;41(4):816827.doi:10.1177/0734242X221135248

[4] R. R. Prova, A. Rayhan, R. S. Shilon and M. M. Khan, "A Web and Mobile Based Approach to Redistribute Consumable Food Waste," *2021 12th International Conference on Computing*

Communication and Networking Technologies (ICCCNT), Kharagpur, India, 2021, pp. 1–6, doi: 10.1109/ICCCNT51525.2021.9579645

[5] Anusha K., Bhargavi R. Food Wastage Reduction through Donation using New Approach: Helping Hands. *Volume VIII, Issue III. 2019 MarSV, Narayanan, and Maheshwaran KS. "Food Waste Reduction and Analysis."* (2021).

[6] H. Hajjdiab, A. Anzer, H. A. Tabaza and W. Ahmed, "A Food Wastage Reduction Mobile Application," *2018 6th International Conference on Future Internet of Things and Cloud Workshops (FiCloudW)*, Barcelona, Spain, 2018, pp. 152–157, doi: 10.1109/W-FiCloud.2018.00030

[7] Hossain, I., Haque, A. M., & Ullah, S. A. (2024). Assessing Sustainable Waste Management Practices in Rajshahi City Corporation: An Analysis for Local Government Enhancement Using IoT, AI, and Android Technology. *Environmental Science and Pollution Research*, 1–19.

[8] C. Varghese, D. Pathak and A. S. Varde, "SeVa: A Food Donation App for Smart Living," 2021 *IEEE 11th Annual Computing and Communication Workshop and Conference (CCWC)*, NV, USA, 2021, pp. 0408–0413, doi: 10.1109/CCWC51732.2021.9375945

[9] J. A. R. Morilla, F. C. Bagsic, M. K. Dela Cruz, C. D. A. Patio and E. R. Yabut, "Foodernity: A Mobile and Web Application for Food Sharing," *2021 1st International Conference in Information and Computing Research (iCORE)*, Manila, Philippines, 2021,pp: 90–95,doi: 10.1109/iCORE54267.2021.00035

[10] R. Shinta Oktaviana, D. A. Febriani, I. Yoshana and L. R. Payanta, "FoodX, a System to Reduce Food Waste," *2020 3rd International Conference on Computer and Informatics Engineering (IC2IE)*, Yogyakarta, Indonesia, 2020, pp.361–365,doi: 10.1109/IC2IE50715.2020.9274576

[11] Bhardwaj, Sonali and Kumar, Utkarsh and Kumar Dr, Yogesh, Food Waste Management Android App (July 14, 2022). *Proceedings of the Advancement in Electronics & Communication Engineering* 2022.

[12] N. Alblihed, M. Almutairi, R. Almahmoud, S. Aladhadh and A. Alabdulatif, "Developing Food Charity Operations Management System," *2022 2nd International Conference on Computing and Information Technology (ICCIT)*, Tabuk, Saudi Arabia, 2022, pp. 93–96, doi: 10.1109/ICCIT52419.2022.9711609

[13] Yogananth, V. S., & Balasubramani, M. (2024, February). IoT-Aided Charity-Redistribution of Excess Food. In *2024 Second International Conference on Emerging Trends in Information Technology and Engineering (ICETITE)* (pp. 1–6). IEEE.

[14] D Dilkhush Mihirsen, Josephine Taniha Joseph, B Renisha, "Time Series Analysis for Supply Chain Planning in Restaurants", *2020 5th International Conference on Computing, Communication and Security (ICCCS)*, pp.1–5, 2020.

[15] Bharani, S., Mohanraj, E., Sujith, M., & Vinothkumar, P. (2024, February). Optimizing Surplus Food Management: A User-Centric Application Approach. In *2024 Second International Conference on Emerging Trends in Information Technology and Engineering (ICETITE)* (pp. 1–6). IEEE.

[16] Varghese, C., Pathak, D., & Varde, A. S. (2021, January). SeVa: a food donation app for smart living. In *2021 IEEE 11th Annual Computing and Communication Workshop and Conference (CCWC)* (pp. 0408–0413). IEEE.

[17] Usharani, S., Puneeth, T., Sugavanan, K., & Depuru, S. (2023, August). Food Waste Management using IoT & Android Interface. In *2023 Second International Conference on Augmented Intelligence and Sustainable Systems (ICAISS)* (pp. 1504–1513). IEEE.

[18] Elavarasan, M. S., & Nesakumar, C. D. (2019). Food Wastage Reduction Mobile Application. *International Journal of Computer Science and Mobile Computing*, 8(10).

[19] Pardini, K., Rodrigues, J. J., Diallo, O., Das, A. K., de Albuquerque, V. H. C., & Kozlov, S. A. (2020). A Smart Waste Management Solution Geared Towards Citizens. *Sensors*, 20(8), 2380.

[20] Kavitha, R., Prasad, V. N., Gowda, D., Umayal, M., Subhiksha, K., & Anitha, K. (2023, August). A Novel Approach for Identification and Donation of Surplus Food using Machine Learning-based Replate App. In *2023 Second International Conference on Augmented Intelligence and Sustainable Systems (ICAISS)* (pp. 552–558). IEEE.

Chapter 15

Counterfeit products detection using blockchain technology

A. Sowmya, Shanthi Makka, Keerthi Pendam, C. Kavitha, Gagandeep Arora, S. B. Goyal, and Budati Anil Kumar

15.1 INTRODUCTION

Retail systems across the globe are faced with a great problem of counterfeit products. It has been pointed out in a recent study that 3.3% of the entire merchandise sold worldwide is fake [1]. The availability of such items results in huge financial losses: in 2022, for example, an estimated 2.3 trillion USD in revenue has been lost globally [2]. In addition to a significant negative effect on an organization's revenue, it influences its reputation and customer safety because counterfeit products fail to meet quality standards and safety regulations. Electronics, beauty products, and medicines are examples of industries seriously affected by counterfeiting. These fake goods contain wrong ingredients, doses, or harmful substances that can cause harm to those who are using them. Counterfeit drugs may result in ineffective treatment for illness, while bogus cosmetics may contain dangerous substances such as mercury and lead that can irritate skin, cause allergic reactions, and leave users with long-term health issues [3].

Blockchain technology comes into play as a solution. Blockchain is a decentralized digital ledger technology that monitors transactions across the network of computers. It provides a transparent, immutable, secure, and efficient way to record and verify transactions. This means as soon as data is recorded by this arrangement, it cannot be changed, thus protecting its integrity from any form of forgery or changing in future. A network of computers operates to keep transaction records on a distributed ledge system. All such transfers remain as blocks in a chain connected with each other by linking one block after another onto it, together forming the chain of interconnected blocks. Altering one block would necessitate changing all subsequent ones—something that is impractical in terms of computation complexity. The blockchain achieves transparency while resisting tampering through a distributed node network. While offering a viable solution to the problem of counterfeit products, this technology introduces a safe and dependable method for recording transactions that cannot be compromised because they are hack-proof.

Consensus is the process whereby a network of computers verifies any new transaction. It is this process that assures integrity and security of a system by making sure that all nodes in the network agree on the state of blockchain [4]. Once verification has been done, transactions are combined into blocks, which are then chained together to form an unchangeable ledger. When this ends, the transaction is over. Blockchain acts as a decentralized database that does not depend on any central authority for adding data records. Instead, it operates by its own consensus algorithms to authenticate algorithms. It also improves transparency and eliminates the need for intermediaries. Besides cryptocurrencies, blockchain has many other applications such as in supply chain management, fraud and counterfeiting prevention, smart contracts, identity management, and many others [5]. Given its potential, we have decided to integrate our project with blockchain technology.

 DOI: 10.1201/9781003591788-15

The use of blockchain technology ensures product tracking and monitoring, making sure that customers get the right products. The goal of this project is to bring consumer transparency during their entire purchasing process and allow them to verify the products they want purchase. This system adopts quick response (QR) codes as a promising measure against fake items. In recent times, advancements in wireless and mobile technologies have made QR codes an efficient tool in combatting product counterfeiting. The encrypted information stored within QR codes proves that the product is genuine and helps stop counterfeiting. Also, this QR code contains a copy-sensitive digital image for added security. This process enables capturing product information with unique identifiers for each one in a central database. The authenticity of the item can be established by querying blockchain database using the user's unique code. If this code matches an entry, then it is true; otherwise it is false. Application of blockchain technologies allows following and watching of products, ensuring that customers receive correct items. The primary aim behind this project is to give clarity to consumers during their whole buying journey, thus enabling them to authenticate what they want to buy themselves. QR codes are utilized in this system as an encouraging method that fights against counterfeit goods. The recent innovations represented by wireless and mobile technologies have made QR codes effective instruments in controlling piracy of goods on worldwide markets. By containing coded contents about items' legitimacy within them, such QR codes prevent illegal trade as well as guarantee legitimation. Moreover, this specificity improves its sophistication through embedding copy-sensitive digital image inside it. This enables record keeping for specific product features assigning each single entity in the database a unique identifier only known by creator The product's authenticity can be confirmed by querying the blockchain database with your individual code, if such exists. If it checks in with one of the entries, then it is original; otherwise, it is an imitation.

An Ethereum blockchain-based decentralized application (DApp) has been developed to identify counterfeit products within the supply chain system. This DApp utilizes Ethereum blockchain technology to establish a secure and transparent method for documenting and transferring product ownership. Every transaction is recorded on the blockchain, ensuring a transparent and unchangeable history of product ownership, similar to an immutable digital ledger. The use of smart contracts enables the system to automatically execute agreements, eliminating the need for intermediaries and improving system efficiency. In addition to supply chain management, this technology can also be utilized to provide consumers with transparent information about the origins and ownership of products on retail and e-commerce platforms, fostering trust and increasing customer satisfaction.

Blockchain technology facilitates a transparent and interconnected network among distributors, suppliers, and manufacturers. All relevant parties have access to transaction, MetaMask, and smart contracts forms a robust records and other essential information, with reduced risk of tampering. Our goal is to address supply chain gaps, minimize costs, and provide a secure, decentralized, and verifiable solution. Leveraging these technologies, we have developed a system to identify and prevent the spread of fake products, ultimately enabling manufacturers to produce genuine goods without reliance on retailers, leading to a significant reduction in quality maintenance costs.

15.2 RELATED WORK

An Android application was proposed to detect counterfeit products using the SHA-256 algorithm, an improvement over SHA-1 developed by the National Security Agency in 2001. This app aimed to create a system for identifying fake products through the use of QR codes. It consists of two main components: the customer/user end and the manufacturer end.

Manufacturers utilize the SHA-256 algorithm to generate a QR code, which customers can scan to verify the authenticity of the product. A recently introduced blockchain-based management system utilizes blockchain technology for data storage and management. The objective is to combat counterfeit products by associating their information with the blockchain, assigning each product a unique code for secure storage. The authenticity of the product is confirmed, and the user is notified accordingly.

The integration of the Elliptic Curve digital signature algorithm into the blockchain framework aimed to enhance traceability and transparency in order to protect against counterfeit drugs in the pharmaceutical industry. This initiative sought to establish a reliable and transparent drug supply chain while addressing the challenges encountered in the current system. The rise in counterfeit medicines has posed significant problems in recent years, making this research particularly relevant for the pharmaceutical sector. Tsang et al. [6] proposed a method to tackle counterfeit products, involving two key actions: verifying the authenticity of the product and updating the database accordingly. To address the limitations of UHF Gen-2 tags in handling complex algorithms, simpler solutions like a pseudo-random number generator (PRNG) and cyclic redundancy check (CRC) were utilized, along with near field communication (NFC). NFC, a widely used feature in smartphones, enables mobile payments and product information retrieval. NFC employs lightweight protocols, including unique serial numbers for each item. As a result, both NFC and electric product code (EPC) tags work together to combat counterfeiting.

Blockchain technology enables food traceability and verification of the food source to ensure its safety and quality. It offers a solution by revolutionizing the way food is tracked in supply chains. Mean arterial pressure (MAP), introduced by Anandhi et al. [7], enhances security with EPC tags, which are similar to barcodes but include an extra blockchain-IoT-based food traceability system (BIFTS). BIFTS combines blockchain, IoT technology, and fuzzy logic to manage perishable food items. It utilizes a lightweight blockchain and a unique consensus-building mechanism. IoT is integrated and coordinated with data flow to track food at various stages. In addition, Toyoda et al. [8] have proposed a new method for transferring product ownership using radiofrequency identification (RFID) tags through blockchain technology. This process involves two steps: the customer initially purchases the product, and then ownership is transferred from the seller to the buyer. Unlike most existing RFID-based ownership transfer protocols, which rely on trusted third parties or centralized reader-to-reader communication, this method mitigates the associated security risks. Therefore, the protocol offers improved security and a transparent method for tracking product ownership.

The profile of mood states (POMS) protocol, as introduced by Nakasumi [9], was created to detect counterfeit products and prevent retailers from replicating genuine tags. Bitcoin's concept of "proof of possession of balance" was implemented to establish a means of proving product ownership. POMS was specifically designed to oversee the process of halting counterfeits once they have left the factory. By ensuring that legitimate manufacturers have initial ownership, the authenticity of products can be effectively monitored. Through RFID tags, all parties in the supply chain can transfer and confirm ownership of products. Customers are empowered to reject products if the seller fails to provide proof of ownership. Supply chain management systems allow companies to exchange and analyze information, aiding in their planning processes. However, these systems often face challenges due to incomplete data caused by information imbalances between companies, which can disrupt planning algorithms. Effective data sharing among manufacturers, suppliers, and customers is essential for adapting to market fluctuations. Double marginalization poses a significant obstacle in supply chain management. Research on decentralized systems utilizing wholesale price contracts has shown how double marginalization can lead to supply shortages, regardless of whether demands are predictable or stochastic. Rahmadika et al. [10] proposed leveraging blockchain technology as a potential solution to address supply chain issues such as double marginalization and information imbalances.

The integration of IoT and blockchain technology has bolstered the reliability of supply chain systems. Blockchain's inherent characteristics make it well suited for elevating service standards and ensuring the integrity and security of data within supply chains. Mohanta et al. [11] integrated blockchain into the supply chain using Ethereum smart contracts to oversee product ownership and tracking. The proposed model aims to reduce fraudulent online trading activities and shield users from purchasing counterfeit products. The products documented in the blockchain are guaranteed to be tamper-proof and permanent, providing enhanced security and safety. Future research also suggests that leveraging IoT devices and blockchain networks enhances the operational effectiveness and efficiency of decentralized supply chain systems.

15.3 PROPOSED WORK

15.3.1 Architecture

We present a blockchain network that establishes a peer-to-peer system utilizing the proof-of-stake consensus mechanism. Ethereum offers a versatile platform for creating applications using its native Solidity scripting language. Introduced in 2015, Ethereum rapidly emerged as the second most prominent blockchain network with an extensive and effective system for identifying counterfeit products based on blockchain technology.

This system is a DApp constructed on the Ethereum network, intended to store all records and oversee transactions (Figure 15.1). The system under consideration utilizes Ethereum as its underlying blockchain platform and utilizes Solidity, Ethereum's specialized programming language [12], for developing smart contracts. Solidity is specifically designed for the Ethereum virtual machine and incorporates functionalities like inheritance and libraries [14]. These smart contracts operate publicly on Ethereum's blockchain. For development purposes, we use Ganache to create a private Ethereum blockchain where smart contracts can be deployed. Ganache enables the setup of a local private blockchain network on a development machine. The user interface, presented as a web page, is developed using React.js. Interaction with the Ethereum blockchain is facilitated by Web3.js [13], which handles transactions, ether transfers, and data management within the smart contracts.

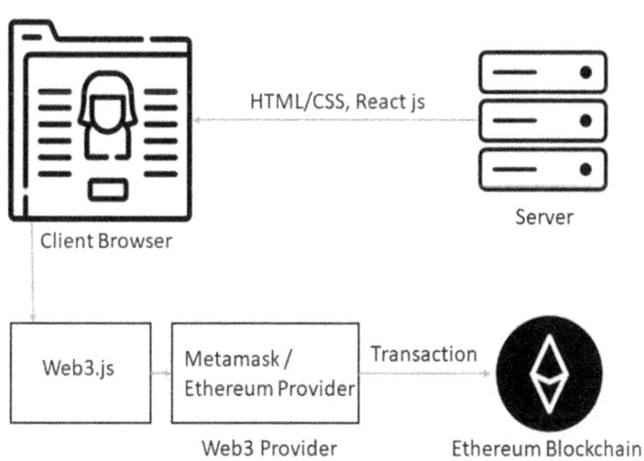

Figure 15.1 System architecture.

The manufacturer and supplier smart contracts are written in Solidity and tested on a local network using the Ganache platform. The host configuration is managed through the truffle-config.js file. Truffle, an Ethereum development framework, provides MetaMask, a well-known cryptocurrency wallet and browser extension, which allows direct interaction with Ethereum-based DApps from users' web browsers. It serves as a tool for building, testing, and deploying smart contracts on the Ethereum blockchain, as well as a digital wallet for securely storing, sending, and receiving Ethereum (ETH). Users can access this wallet directly through their browser. Ganache accounts are imported into MetaMask using the "add network" feature, establishing a new connection between MetaMask and the application. To integrate the supplier and manufacturer blocks, users must confirm transactions through their MetaMask wallet, which is linked to the application using Web3.js.

Web3.js is a JavaScript library designed for developers to interact with the Ethereum blockchain and Ethereum-based DApps. It provides APIs that enable connections to Ethereum nodes using different protocols, allowing direct interaction with the blockchain from web applications. In the server-side setup, the web page is constructed using the http-server suite from Node.js, with Web3.js acting as the intermediary linking the smart contract to the user interface.

This entire architecture provides a fully flexible and efficient fake product detection system that can be used to detect any counterfeited products and avoid them from being sold to consumers. The use of above technology has made it transparent and secure to use. Integration of the mentioned technologies leads to secure and immutable execution of actions.

Our blockchain-based counterfeit product detection system is structured around three main components: the manufacturer end, the seller end, and the consumer end. Here's a breakdown of each component:

- **Manufacturer End:** The manufacturer starts by logging into their account and inputting product details. This process generates a unique QR code for the product. It undergoes authentication when the manufacturer employs the MetaMask wallet to record a block on the Ethereum blockchain. Product information is stored in a database, and the QR code is protected with secure graphic techniques to prevent tampering and copying. Serialized QR codes are also recommended for added security and tracking.
- **Seller End:** The supplier logs into their account and scans the product's QR code to access the information entered by the manufacturer. The seller can then add their own details and update the consumer code. These updates are visible to the buyer.
- **Customer End:** Customers play a vital role in the system as they verify the authenticity of the product by scanning its QR code. The scan results provide comprehensive details, confirming the product's genuineness. Moreover, customers are alerted if the QR code is counterfeit, aiding in the detection of fraudulent copies. They can also verify the legitimacy of the seller's relationship with the manufacturer, check product availability, and access their purchase history and product details.

The proposed study attempts to harness blockchain technology, primarily Ethereum, for the construction of a robust and transparent system for detecting counterfeit products. By utilizing Ethereum's smart contract capabilities and Solidity programming language, the system enables the creation of immutable records of product authenticity and traceability on the blockchain. Throughout the development and testing phases, the system demonstrated its effectiveness in providing a tamper-proof solution for verifying the authenticity of products and tracking their journey from production to consumption (Figure 15.2).

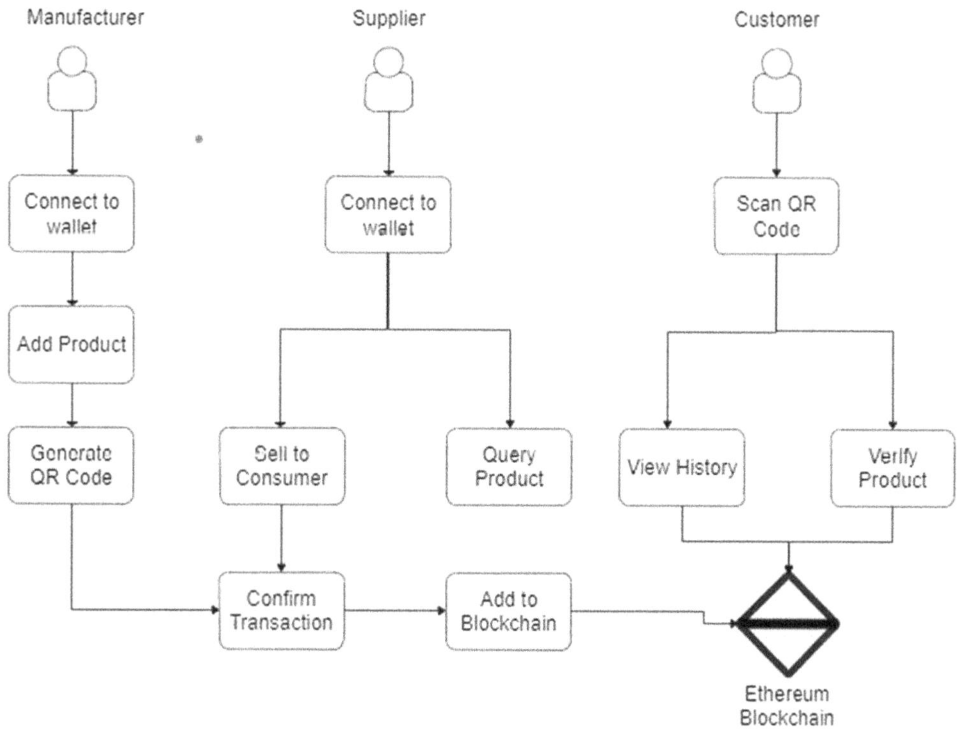

Figure 15.2 Proposed approach.

15.4 RESULTS AND DISCUSSION

The counterfeit product detection system utilizing blockchain technology ensures transparency and integrity throughout the supply chain, enabling stakeholders to trace and track the movement of products and verify their authenticity. The proposed system enables both manufacturers and suppliers to engage with the platform and insert their own blocks with transaction details into the blockchain, while preserving the integrity of existing blocks. Utilizing Ganache for local testing and Truffle for compiling and deploying contracts streamlines the process and allows the developers to quickly complete the process and check for integrity and security. The interface created using ReactJS provides a rich an intuitive interface for engaging with the system. By leveraging blockchain technology with MetaMask and Web3.js this project enhances transparency and trust in purchasing of products online by detecting and verifying if they are fake or genuine.

Here, SHA-256 emerges as the preferred choice among all the other listed algorithms due to its higher security level compared to SHA. With a larger hash size of 256 bits, SHA-256 offers enhanced security against cryptographic attacks, making it more suitable for applications that involve data integrity and security. It is also essential to understand that SHA-256 may incur slightly higher computational overhead when compared to SHA because of its larger output size. After SHA-256, we have analyzed that SHA is the second-best option in situations where speed is considered and given more importance. This makes it applicable for systems that involve quicker and faster data processing with reduced security requirements. Hence, we can conclude that SHA-256 is a better and more viable choice for the fake product detection system when compared to SHA. In addition to cryptographic hashing algorithms, proof of stake (PoS) and proof of work (PoW) offer distinct consensus mechanisms

Table 15.1 Survey on algorithms in blockchain

S. No.	*Algorithm used*	*Time complexity*	*Space complexity*	*Advantages*	*Disadvantages*
1.	Secure hash algorithm (SHA-256)	O(n)	O(1)	More secure due to 256-bit output	Slower than SHA
2.	Secure hash algorithm (SHA)	O(n)	O(1)	Fast hashing speed	Limited to 160-bit output
3.	Proof of stake	Faster than proof of work	Depends on network size and traffic	Energy-efficient consensus mechanism	Security risk

for blockchain networks. PoS presents a better alternative to PoW by offering energy efficiency and scalability. It also eliminates the need for higher computational activities. But it brings along a potential challenge such as the "nothing-at-stake" problem, where validators in the blockchain network might have nothing to lose if they behave dishonestly or try to manipulate the consensus mechanism. PoW is said to be effective in providing security to the blockchain network like Bitcoin but is criticized for its high energy consumption. Hence, the choice of algorithm to be used depending on the specific requirements is SHA-256, which offers higher security and faster processing speed (Table 15.1).

Transmitting data to the blockchain incurs a fee known as a transaction cost. The miners or validators who manage and verify network transactions receive this charge. Gas fees have many uses, including paying miners for their processing power and protecting against any misuse. A user specifies a price and a limit for gas when they start a transaction. The gas price indicates how much a user is prepared to pay for each unit of gas, while the gas limit specifies the maximum amount of computational resources (gas) that a transaction is allowed to consume. The total transaction cost is calculated by multiplying the gas price by the gas limit. Higher gas charge transactions are given priority by miners, since incorporating them in the blocks they mine will increase their earnings. Transactions with higher fees are processed quickly and have higher chances of being included in the next block that is being added to the blockchain.

Figure 15.3 indicates the gas fees for the proposed system amount to 0.00203827 ETH, which equals approximately 6.05 USD, demonstrating the cost efficiency of the proposed model. The values mentioned reflect the amount of ETH needed to carry out each operation, which must be controlled to demonstrate the system's efficiency. This ensures that the gas fees remain optimized and maintain scalability of the system. With these promising results, the counterfeit product identification system proves to be very useful not only for the business organizations but also for consumer safety.

15.5 CONCLUSION

The fully functional counterfeit product detection system represents a significant advancement in ensuring product authenticity and consumer safety. Due to rapid growth in online shopping and e-commerce, it is essential to safeguard the users from purchasing counterfeit products, which is offered by the proposed system. The implemented DApp guarantees immutability and transparency, allowing for the verification of product information and ensuring that consumers receive accurate details. This system helps consumers easily confirm the authenticity of products, significantly reducing the risk of purchasing counterfeit or

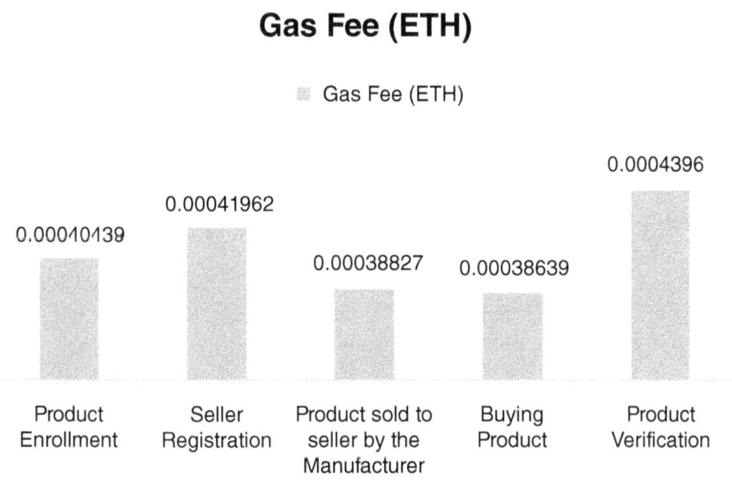

Figure 15.3 Proposed model-gas fee values.

Table 15.2 Gas values of various actions in blockchain

S. No.	*Action description*	*Gas fee (ETH)*
1.	Product Enrollment	0.00040439
2.	Seller Registration	0.00041962
3.	Product sold to seller by the Manufacturer	0.00038827
4.	Buying Product	0.00038639
5.	Product Verification	0.0004396
	Total Gas Fee = 0.00203827 ETH	
	Total in USD = 6.05	

fake items. According to Table 15.2, the operational cost amounts to just 6.05 USD, which is notably low. The model enables end-user verification using a QR code, with transactions validated through ScanApp. This method helps lower counterfeiting rates and bolsters financial resources and the economy.

The system could be expanded to address fraud in areas such as health care, voting, online shopping, and banking. The simplicity of the distributed application's code significantly impacts its operational cost on the Ethereum public chain. The straightforward and non-redundant code of the application fosters confidence in its efficiency and minimal resource requirements. Furthermore, real-time systems like this one can support the creation of decentralized marketplaces that prioritize authenticity and transparency, thereby mitigating fraud and counterfeiting risks in online transactions.

REFERENCES

[1] G. Shobana, R. Shaarmitha, and R. Akhash, "Fake Product Detection using Anonymity and Supply Chain in Blockchain," *2023 2nd International Conference on Advancements in Electrical, Electronics, Communication, Computing and Automation (ICAECA)*, Coimbatore, India, 2023, pp. 1–6,

[2] Y. X. Lo and C. C. Tan, "Blockchain-Based Anti-Counterfeit Product Identification System," *2023 IEEE International Conference on Artificial Intelligence in Engineering and Technology (IICAIET)*, Kota Kinabalu, Malaysia, 2023, pp. 200–205.

[3] K. G. N. Rohith, H. Bg, A. D. Nayak and D. B. Srinivas, "Enhancing Product Authentication and Counterfeit Detection Using QR Codes and Blockchain Technology," *2023 2nd International Conference on Edge Computing and Applications (ICECAA)*, Namakkal, India, 2023, pp. 262–267

[4] K. Vyas and A. De The values mentioned reflect the amount of ETH needed to carry out each operation, which must be controlled to demonstrate the system's efficiency.hmukh, "A Survey Paper on Blockchain Technology and Consensus Algorithms," *2023 11th International Conference on Emerging Trends in Engineering & Technology - Signal and Information Processing (ICETET - SIP)*, Nagpur, India, 2023, pp. 1–6

[5] M. Mallegowda, A. Kanavalli, M. N. Thippeswamy, *et al.*, "Fake Product Identification System Using Blockchain," *2022 4th International Conference on Circuits, Control, Communication and Computing (I4C)*, Bangalore, India, 2022, pp. 163–167

[6] Y. P. Tsang, K. L. Choy, C. H. Wu, G. T. S. Ho and H. Y. Lam, "Blockchain-Driven IoT for Food Traceability with an Integrated Consensus Mechanism", *IEEE Access*, vol. 7, pp. 129000–129017, 2019.

[7] S. Anandhi, R. Anitha and S. Venkatasamy, "RFID Based Verifiable Ownership Transfer Protocol Using Blockchain Technology," *2018 IEEE International Conference on Internet of Things (iThings) and IEEE Green Computing and Communications (GreenCom) and IEEE Cyber, Physical and Social Computing (CPSCom) and IEEE Smart Data (SmartData)*, Halifax, NS, Canada, 2018, pp. 1616–1621.

[8] K. Toyoda, P. T. Mathiopoulos, I. Sasase and T. Ohtsuki, "A Novel Blockchain-Based Product Ownership Management System (POMS) for Anti-Counterfeits in the Post Supply Chain," in *IEEE Access*, vol. 5, pp. 17465–17477, 2017.

[9] M. Nakasumi, "Information Sharing for Supply Chain Management Based on Block Chain Technology," *2017 IEEE 19th Conference on Business Informatics (CBI)*, Thessaloniki, Greece, 2017, pp. 140–149.

[10] S. Rahmadika, B. J. Kweka, C. N. Z. Latt and K.-H. Rhee, "A Preliminary Approach of Blockchain Technology in Supply Chain System," *2018 IEEE International Conference on Data Mining Workshops (ICDMW)*, Singapore, 2018, pp. 156–160.

[11] B. K. Mohanta, S. S. Panda and D. Jena, "An Overview of Smart Contract and Use Cases in Blockchain Technology," *2018 9th International Conference on Computing, Communication and Networking Technologies (ICCCNT)*, Bengaluru, India, 2018, pp. 1–4.

[12] *Web3.js*, 2018, [online] Available: https://github.com/ethereum/web3.js/

[13] *HTTP-Server*, 2018, [*online*] Available: https://www.npmjs.com/package/http-server

[14] *Node.js*, 2018, [*online*] Available: https://www.myetherwallet.com/

Chapter 16

Advanced deep learning framework for accurate analysis of benign and malignant skin cancer

Prasanna Lakshmi Akella, R. Kumar, and Ramakrishna Akella

16.1 INTRODUCTION

Skin disease is one of the most well-known types of cancer. It is the most common type of cancer in the United States and affects a significant proportion of the population [1]. Every year, many people lose their lives due to the skin cancer known as lymphoma. However, if identified early enough, it can be successfully treated using simple extraction techniques. Late-stage diagnosis, on the other hand, is linked to a higher risk of death, with a survival rate of less than 20% following luminary stage identification. Dermatologists can diagnose patients with a variety of noninvasive methods, such as visible photos taken with cameras or smartphones [2, 3]. Unfortunately, there is often a lack of quality in these images. In order to overcome this limitation, dermatoscopic instruments offer the best visual depiction and are useful noninvasive instruments for identifying dangerous skin lesions. Dermoscopy enables the more accurate distinction of different types of sores based on their appearance and morphological characteristics.

The diagnosis of melanoma, a highly malignant illness, is quite difficult when using traditional techniques like ordinary cameras [4]. This condition impacts the DNA, causing an overexposure of skin cells to harmful ultraviolet radiation and subsequent skin pigmentation [5]. If melanoma is not detected early, it can spread deeper into the body, causing damage to blood vessels and lymph nodes. Convolutional neural networks (CNNs) and Inception Net, two prominent deep learning methodologies, play a crucial role in these scenarios by offering accurate diagnosis and treatment.

In the last few years, skin cancer identification and classification have seen a tremendous revolution because of deep learning (DL) and machine learning (ML) [6–8]. Deep learning is a great method for analyzing large amounts of medical data and extracting useful information. This sophisticated artificial intelligence has the capacity to produce initial radiological reports, make predictions for various diagnoses, and automatically detect abnormalities. For example, the well-known multinational corporation IBM is already using its Dr. Watson technology to develop radiological applications. This system includes all of the capabilities mentioned earlier, especially automatic identification and quantitative analysis of medical images for identifying abnormalities. The rapid growth of AI technology requires that radiologists become acquainted with it in order to comprehend its capabilities and the potential impact on radiological practice [9]. We are inclined to believe that the integration of ML-based analytical tools into radiology practice is bound to grow. We do not believe that this equates to completely replacing radiologists, but certain specific duties may be automated. These methods will not be a complete alternative, but rather a valuable addition to the field of radiology, complementing the indispensable and unique skills of human radiologists.

DOI: 10.1201/9781003591788-16

16.2 LITERATURE SURVEY

According to the World Health Organization, it is estimated that by 2030, skin cancer would be responsible for 13.1 million annual deaths globally, making it the primary cause of cancer-related death [10]. Due to the worldwide scope of this issue, research on skin cancer categorization has increased on an international level, with significant contributions originating from many locations. These findings, which encompass classification across a diverse variety of skin types and ethnic groups, emphasize the significance of comprehensive and adaptable diagnostic solutions. Skin cancer is a prevalent condition primarily caused by abnormal cell growth that can rapidly infiltrate and metastasize throughout the body [11].

A system for classifying skin lesions into benign and malignant groups was developed by Xie et al. [12]. There are three separate phases to the mechanism. Initially, a self-generating neural network is used to extract lesions from images. Other attributes observed include tumor borders, texture, and minor color changes; there are a total of 57 features, 7 of which are unique to lesion boundaries. The dimensionality of these features is subsequently reduced using principal component analysis, and the best set is chosen. Consequently, to increase classification accuracy, lesions are identified using a combination of fuzzy and backpropagation neural networks. Various classifiers, including random forest, Adaboost, k-nearest neighbors, and support vector machines, were employed to evaluate the system's performance. With a precision of 91.11%, the suggested approach performed at least 7.5% better in terms of sensitivity than the other classifiers.

An artificial neural network (ANN)-based skin cancer screening approach was proposed by Masood et al. [13]. The study emphasized three ANN learning algorithms: Levenberg-Marquardt (LM) [14], robust backpropagation (RP) [15], and scaled conjugate gradient (SCG) [16]. The LM algorithm had a high specificity score of 95.1% for correctly identifying benign lesions. However, the SCG method performed better with more epochs, obtaining a sensitivity rate of 92.6%. Furthermore, a mole classification system was established to aid in the early diagnosis of melanoma [17]. This method extracted features using the asymmetry, border, color, and diameter rule. Asymmetry was calculated using the Mumford-Shah technique, and borders were defined using the Harris-Stephen method. Additional testing was required for moles with colors other than black, cinnamon, or brown, as well as dimensions greater than 6 mm. The system, which used a backpropagation feed-forward ANN, had an accuracy of 97.51%.

The use of CNNs was investigated in the field of image classification for object identification by gender [18]. Three pretrained models—VGG-16, Inception-V3, and MobileNet-V2—were tested using transfer learning to determine the most successful architecture. In the trials, RMSProp and Adam's optimization techniques were used. The Inception-V3 model performed the best, with a validation loss of 0.1550 and an accuracy of 0.9350. In contrast, the VGG-16 and MobileNet-V2 models performed poorly, with accuracy scores of 0.9320 and 0.1660 and 0.8760 and 0.3000, respectively. Furthermore, the Nas Net model was utilized to categorize benign and malignant skin images using the same dataset [19] as in this experiment.

16.3 METHODOLOGIES

16.3.1 Dataset description

The efficacy of DL techniques relies on the presence of an appropriate and reliable dataset. This research utilizes the dataset provided below.

The dataset [20] comprises 2,637 dermoscopic images, consisting of 1,197 images depicting malignant skin lesions and 1,440 images depicting benign skin lesions. Each image is

Table 16.1 Summary of images distribution of training and testing

Class levels	Training set	Testing set
Malignant	949	248
Benign	1,160	280
Total	2,109	528

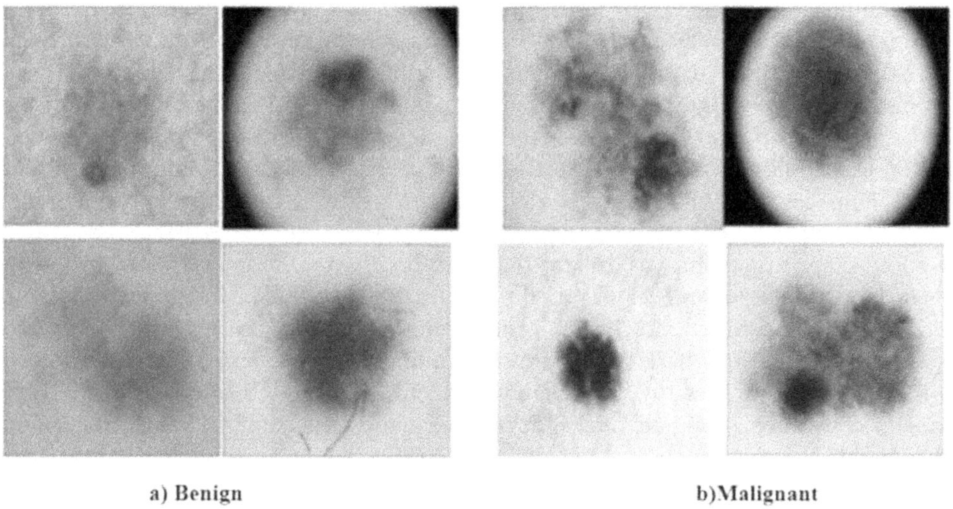

Figure 16.1 (a) Benign and (b) Malignant lesions sample images.

linked to one of these patients using a distinct patient identification. The distribution of the data is shown in Table 16.1. Additionally, a range of data augmentation techniques were implemented, such as rescaling, width shifting, rotation, shear range, horizontal flipping, and channel shifting. Figure 16.1 shows a sample images representation of the benign and malignant skin cancer.

16.3.1.1 Preprocessing of images

Preprocessing is used on each of the dataset's input photos in order to produce enhanced features and a higher degree of consistency in the classification results. Massive amounts of recurrent training are necessary for the DL technique, and in order to avoid the risk of overfitting, a large-scale image dataset was needed.

16.3.1.2 Resizing images

Every photograph in the collection has been scaled to 224 × 224. It will expedite the processing procedure and significantly decrease the model's performance.

16.3.1.3 Data augmentation

Annotating skin images in medical image data is a challenge because skilled specialists are scarce. The ultimate success of skin image categorization depends critically on the caliber of the data augmentation procedure. Because they are classified as medical images, skin photos are subject to the same restrictions. Medical photo labeling cannot be contracted out to a third party, unlike speech or text data. The only people qualified to label these data are experienced radiologists, and it takes them at least 30 minutes to meticulously go over each image several times and manually label each one with the position of each nodule. The annotation of skin images in medical image data will remain challenging because of this specialist scarcity. Data augmentation is important because it makes it possible to expand the training dataset in a reasonable and sufficient way, which enhances the model's capacity for generalization. The model's stability is improved when adequate and acceptable noise data are included.

Using the image data generator function of the Python Keras library, different data augmentation techniques have been applied to the training set in order to reduce overfitting and improve the variety of the dataset. To reduce computing costs, scale transformation was used, utilizing smaller pixel values within the same range. Each pixel's value ranged from 0 to 1 when the parameter value was set to 1. To rotate the images by 15 degrees, a rotation transformation was applied. With a width shift value of 0.1, the width shift range transformation enabled the images to be shifted horizontally in any direction. To move the training images vertically, the height shift range parameter value of 0.1 was used. The photos were magnified if the zoom range argument was greater than 1.0; otherwise, the images were zoomed out. In this instance, a 0.2-zoom level was used to enlarge the image. The image was horizontally flipped using the flip function. The brightness transformation was applied, and the zoom range was set to 0.5–1.0, where 1.0 denotes maximum brightness and 0.0 denotes no brightness. Table 16.1 shows that the 0.05 channel shift range was used to obtain the closest fill mode. This is because during channel shift transformation, the channel values are randomly changed within the given range.

16.3.2 Inception V3 model

A CNN is used to classify data in images, specifically designed for image recognition tasks [21]. The CNN model's primary advantage is its hierarchical learning layer, which can be extensively trained if the model topology aligns with the input characteristics. By utilizing the spatial correlation of visual patterns, the model effectively reduces the number of parameters, thereby improving performance accuracy. Inception V3, created by Google, is a CNN structure specifically tailored for the purpose of picture classification. The Inception architecture's third iteration was launched in 2015. Inception V3 builds on the principles of its previous versions and strives to improve both the effectiveness and efficiency of picture classification tasks. The structure of Inception V3 is complex and detailed, comprising a series of interrelated inception modules. Each module utilizes a combination of convolutional and pooling layers to extract diverse information from the input image. Inception V3 is distinguished by its use of factorized convolutions, which reduce the number of parameters in the network without compromising its accuracy. By utilizing factorized convolution, the network is able to acquire knowledge about both the local and global characteristics of a picture, resulting in an enhancement of the model's accuracy. Inception V3 utilizes a blend of 1×1, 3×3, and 5×5 convolutional filters to extract characteristics from the input image. The 1×1 filters are employed to decrease the dimensionality of the input, while the 3×3 and 5×5 filters capture more complex information from the image [22].

Inception V3 also stands out for its implementation of batch normalization, a method used to normalize the inputs to the network. Batch normalization helps stabilize the training process and reduce the internal covariate shift, which is the change in the distribution of the network's inputs during training. Inception V3 undergoes its initial training on a comprehensive dataset called ImageNet, which consists of more than 14 million images and encompasses 1,000 different categories. This allows the model to be used for transfer learning in other image classification tasks that have a smaller dataset. In such cases, the model can be adjusted and optimized for a particular task. Transfer learning is a method that allows a pretrained model to be adapted for a different task by modifying the model using a new dataset. This can greatly decrease the quantity of data and processing resources needed to train a new model from the beginning. The utilization of Inception V3 for image classification tasks has been extensive, and it has demonstrated outstanding performance on a range of benchmarks. It has been utilized in several applications, including object identification, picture segmentation, and video classification. The model's utilization of factorized convolutions and Inception modules results in a highly efficient and precise approach for picture classification problems. Furthermore, the model's prior training on the ImageNet dataset makes it very adaptable and capable of achieving a remarkable level of accuracy across many applications. Inception V3 is a powerful CNN design that has been widely used for tasks involving image categorization. It has consistently performed exceptionally well in numerous benchmark tests. The model's utilization of factorized convolutions and Inception modules renders it a remarkably efficient and accurate tool for picture classification tasks. The pretraining on the ImageNet dataset facilitates transfer learning for other image classification tasks using a smaller dataset. This allows the model to be fine-tuned for a given job, reducing the need for extensive data and processing resources to train a new model from the beginning. The Inception-V3 architectural model has an advantage over other models due to its complex and efficient architecture. It contains approximately 4 million parameters, which is significantly smaller than VGG. Unlike other models, Inception-V3 does not use a fully connected layer but instead replaces it with a pooling layer. The reduced number of parameters results in a smaller model size, which allows for faster model calculations [21]. Figure 16.2 illustrates the structural schematic diagram of the Inception-v3 model. InceptionV3 architectures aim to address the issue of excessive variability in the position of salient elements in images under analysis by enabling the network to combine many kernel types at the same level, thereby expanding the network.

The process for optimizing the Inception V3 model is shown in Figure 16.3, which illustrates the process of optimizing the Inception V3 model through the use of a 2D GAP layer. The two-dimensional global average pooling layer's output is then used as the input for a compact layer. On the activation layer, Sigmoid, Relu, and Tanh are among the activation function alternatives. Its nonlinear character is required, since its aim is to add nonlinear components to increase the expressiveness of the models. As a result, the first stage's activation function is the Relu function, which is well known for its exceptional performance in nonlinear systems, while the second dense layer makes use of the Sigmoid activation. After that, a dropout layer with a 0.5 dropout rate is implemented. After that, a further series of dropout layers and compact layers are used. Finally, SoftMax is used for categorization purposes.

16.4 RESULTS AND DISCUSSION

The Inception model's performance was assessed using two distinct optimizers, Adam and Nadam, on a dataset of skin cancer images. The purpose was to divide the images into two categories: malignant and benign. The evaluation metrics are accuracy, precision, sensitivity (recall), specificity, and the F1 score. Furthermore, the model's learning process was examined throughout 50 epochs, identifying changes in loss and accuracy.

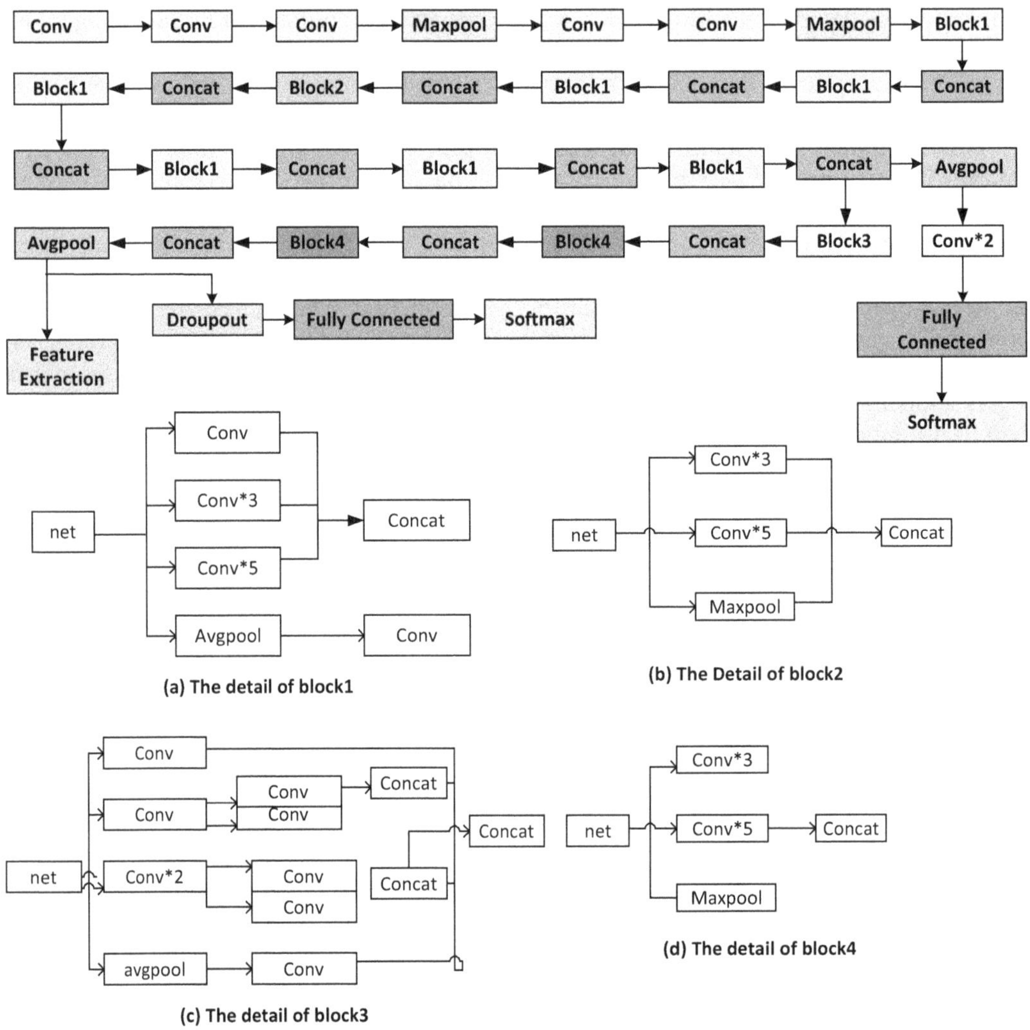

Figure 16.2 The Inception V3 model's structural schematic diagram. (a–d) depict the details of block 1–4.

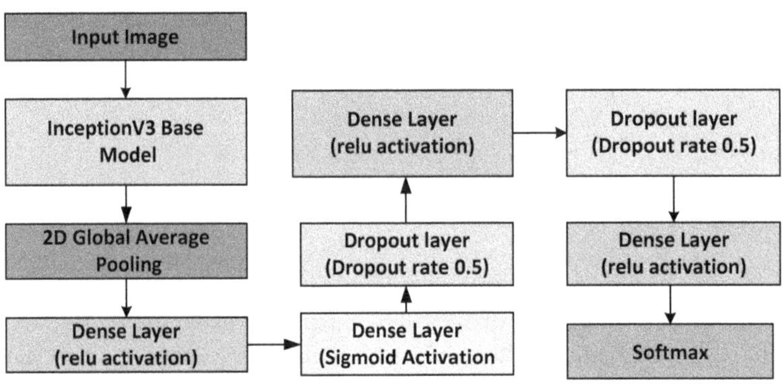

Figure 16.3 Optimization of inception V3 model.

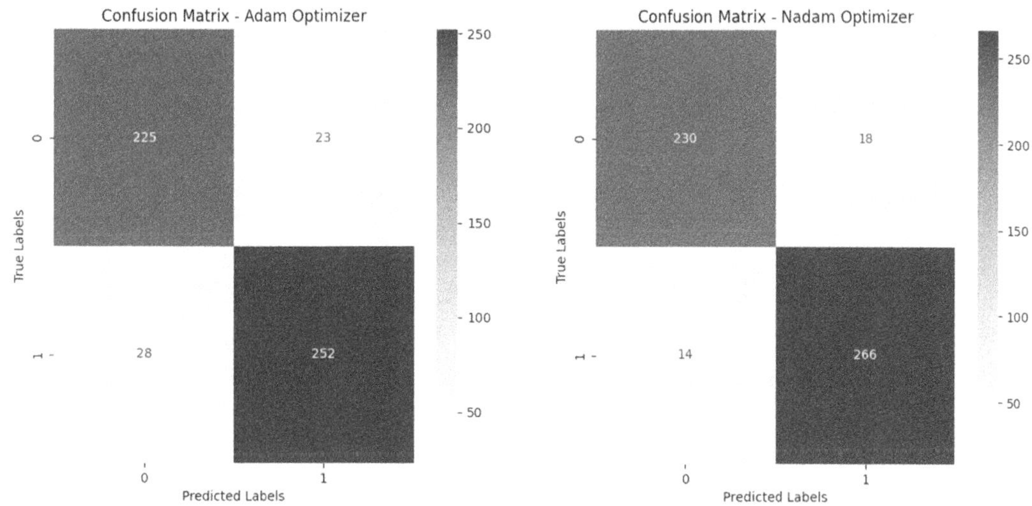

Figure 16.4 Confusion matrix for Adam and Nadam optimizers.

16.4.1 Confusion matrix analysis

Figure 16.4 displays the confusion matrices for the Adam and Nadam optimizers, which offer a comprehensive summary of the model's classification performance. With 225 out of 248 malignant cases accurately identified, the Adam optimizers yielded a 91% true-positive rate. The model correctly detected 252 out of 280 instances on the benign side for a 90% true-positive rate.By contrast, the Nadam optimizers performed better, accurately identifying 230 instances as cancer (93% true-positive rate) ane 266 out of 280 benign cases (95% true-positive rate). These findings suggest that the Nadam optimizer is a more dependable choice for skin cancer classification jobs because it not only increases the detection of malignant cases but also dramatically lowers the number of false positives.

16.4.2 Comparison of accuracy, sensitivity, and specificity

A comparative analysis of the performance metrics further underscores the effectiveness of the Nadam optimizer over the Adam optimizer. As shown in Figure 16.5, the accuracy achieved with the Nadam optimizer was 93%, compared to 90% with the Adam optimizer. This 3% improvement is significant in the context of medical diagnostics, where every percentage point can contribute to better patient outcomes. The precision of the Nadam optimizer was also higher at 94%, compared to 89% for Adam, indicating that Nadam is more effective in reducing false positives, which is critical when the goal is to minimize unnecessary alarms in clinical practice.

Sensitivity (recall) is particularly important in medical diagnosis, as it measures the model's ability to correctly identify all malignant cases. The Nadam optimizer achieved a sensitivity of 93%, slightly higher than the 91% achieved by Adam. This improvement, though modest, could have significant implications in real-life situations.

16.4.3 Epochs vs. loss and accuracy

The Inception model's training progress, as measured over 50 epochs, sheds light on the learning dynamics of the Adam and Nadam optimizers. The loss curves, shown in Figure 16.6,

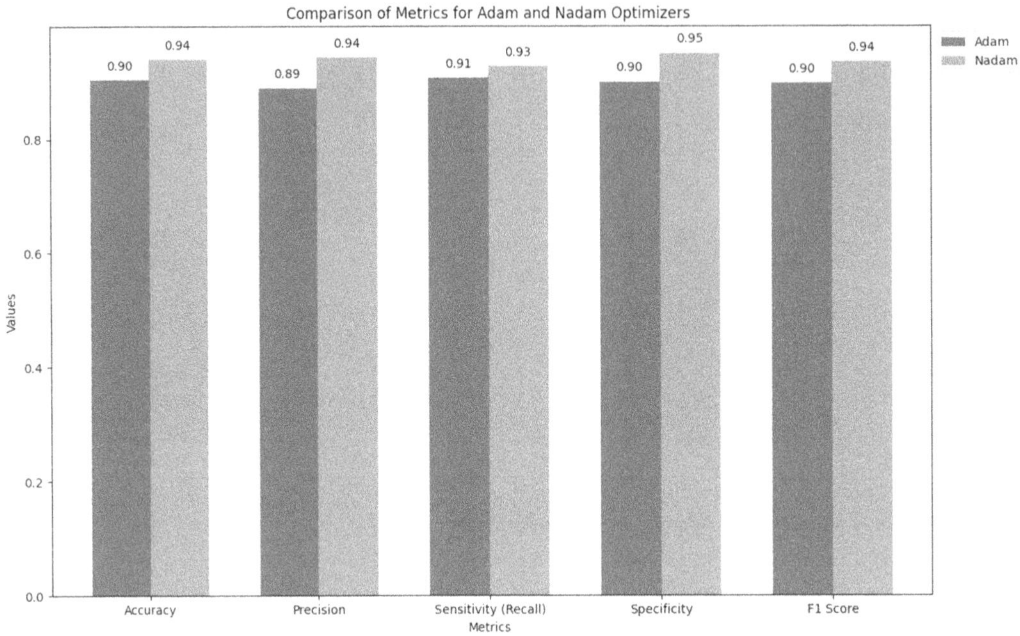

Figure 16.5 Comparison of accuracy, sensitivity, specificity, precision for Adam and Nadam.

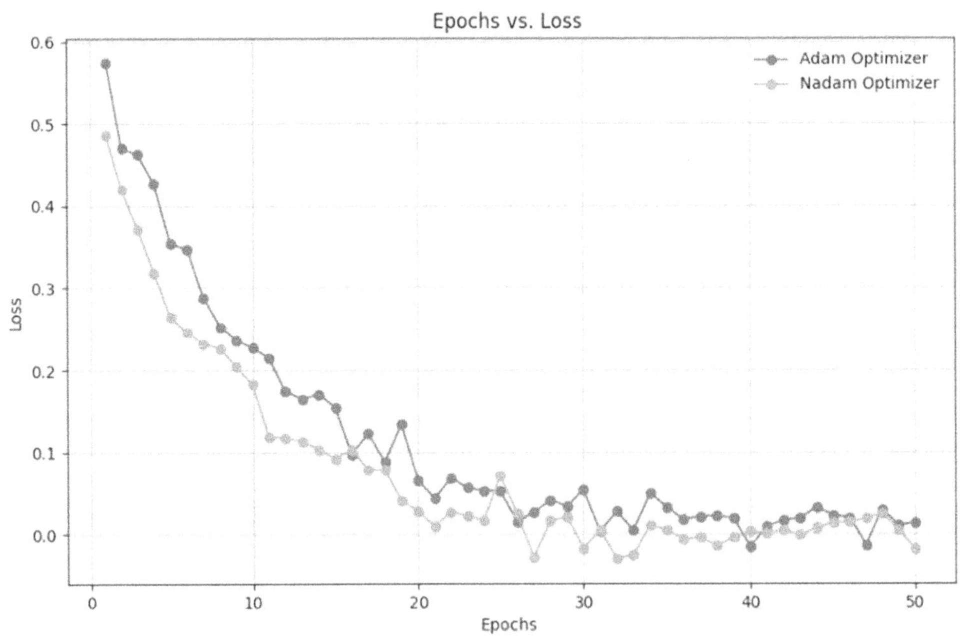

Figure 16.6 Epochs vs. loss.

demonstrate a consistent decrease in loss for both optimizers. This is a natural outcome as the model becomes more proficient in accurately classifying the images. On the other hand, the Nadam optimizer consistently achieved lower loss values throughout the epochs, suggesting a more efficient optimization process. It is suggested that Nadam could potentially result

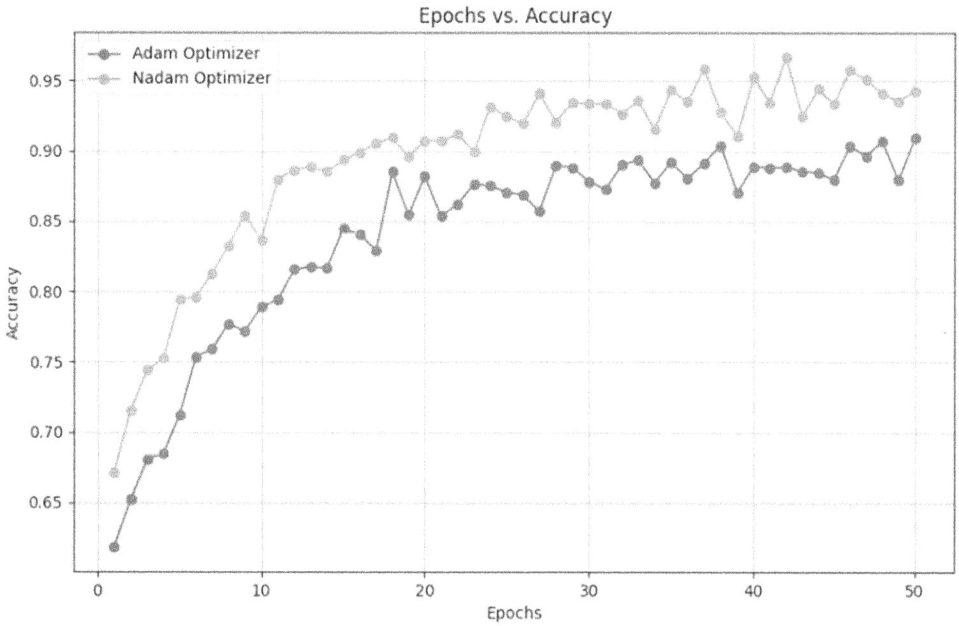

Figure 16.7 Epochs vs. accuracy.

in more reliable and efficient convergence, reducing the risk of overfitting and improving overall performance on the test set.

The accuracy curves confirm these observations, as the Nadam optimizer achieves higher accuracy faster than the Adam optimizer. In Figure 16.7, it can be observed that Nadam's accuracy reached a plateau of approximately 93% before the 50th epoch. On the other hand, Adam's accuracy displayed fluctuations before eventually stabilizing at around 90%. The faster convergence and higher final accuracy of Nadam demonstrate its efficiency and reliability in training DL models for complex classification tasks, such as skin cancer detection. Based on its exceptional accuracy and ability to reduce loss, it appears that Nadam is the ideal option for optimizing the Inception model in this particular application.

16.4.4 Discussion

The comparison of the Adam and Nadam optimizers for the Inception model demonstrates Nadam's clear benefits in skin cancer classification. In analyzing the confusion matrix, performance metrics, and training curves, it becomes evident that Nadam significantly improves accuracy and precision. Moreover, it enhances the model's capability to accurately identify both malignant and benign cases, resulting in a reduction of false positives and false negatives. Precision and dependability are of utmost importance in the medical domain, where precise and trustworthy diagnostics are absolutely crucial.

The enhanced loss and accuracy trends observed with Nadam indicate a more efficient learning process, enabling the model to converge faster toward an optimal solution. This leads to a model that is not only more precise but also more effective, making it a superior option for practical applications where computational resources and time are frequently restricted.

Ultimately, the Nadam optimizers offers a stronger and more dependable method for training DL models in the realm of medical image classification. The optimizers are highly favored for tasks that demand high accuracy and precision, like skin cancer detection, due to their exceptional performance metrics and faster convergence. Further research could investigate the combination of Nadam with other advanced architectures to improve diagnostic accuracy and efficiency in clinical settings.

16.5 CONCLUSION

This study presents a novel approach for classifying skin cancer by utilizing the Inception V3 architecture on skin images. It also evaluates the performance of this technique in comparison to existing methods. Employing migration-based learning techniques and advanced image categorization methods can greatly enhance the accuracy of skin cancer classification. In classifying skin images within the dataset, the transfer learning approach applied to neural network models has shown remarkable performance compared to traditional deep CNNs. In situations where there is a scarcity of skin image data, the use of transfer learning models can be extremely valuable. These models, especially when applied to datasets like ISIC or other skin image datasets, can greatly assist in accurately diagnosing skin conditions with the help of computer-assisted systems. Applying fine-tuning techniques to improve the accuracy of skin image classification through Inception Net learning can yield significant benefits. It is crucial to understand that choosing the wrong transfer learning network can have adverse effects, such as decreased accuracy and longer training durations. Therefore, there is a great potential for additional research to concentrate on enhancing network selection for skin imaging tasks, guaranteeing the development of more powerful and efficient diagnostic tools.

REFERENCES

1. Oliveira, Roberta B., et al. "Computational methods for pigmented skin lesion classification in images: review and future trends." *Neural Computing and Applications* 29 (2018): 613–636.
2. Rogers, Howard W., et al. "Incidence estimate of nonmelanoma skin cancer (keratinocyte carcinomas) in the US population, 2012." *JAMA dermatology* 151.10 (2015): 1081–1086.
3. Esteva, Andre, et al. "Dermatologist-level classification of skin cancer with deep neural networks." *nature* 542.7639 (2017): 115–118.
4. Gouda, Niharika, and J. Amudha. "Skin cancer classification using ResNet." *2020 IEEE 5th International Conference on Computing Communication and Automation (ICCCA)*. IEEE, 2020.
5. Harrison, Shannon C., and Wilma F. Bergfeld. "Ultraviolet light and skin cancer in athletes." *Sports health* 1.4 (2009): 335–340.
6. Ahmmed, Syed, et al. "Enhancing brain tumor classification with transfer learning across multiple classes: An in-depth analysis." *BioMedInformatics* 3.4 (2023): 1124–1144.
7. Kato, Junji, et al. "Dermoscopy of melanoma and non-melanoma skin cancers." *Frontiers in medicine* 6 (2019): 180.
8. Alam, Fatema Binte, Prajoy Podder, and M. Rubaiyat Hossain Mondal. "RVCNet: A hybrid deep neural network framework for the diagnosis of lung diseases." *PLoS one* 18.12 (2023): e0293125.
9. Bazgir, Ehsan, et al. "Security aspects in IoT based cloud computing." *World Journal of Advanced Research and Reviews* 20.3 (2023): 540–551.
10. Manandhar, M., Hawkes, S., Buse, K., Nosrati, E., & Magar, V. (2018). Gender, health and the 2030 agenda for sustainable development. *Bulletin of the World Health Organization*, 96(9): 644.
11. Erol, R. (2018). *Skin Cancer Malignancy Classification with Transfer Learning*. Conway, AR: University of Central Arkansas.
12. Xie, Fengying, et al. "Melanoma classification on dermoscopy images using a neural network ensemble model." *IEEE Transactions on Medical Imaging* 36.3 (2016): 849–858.

13. Masood, Ammara, Adel Ali Al-Jumaily, and Tariq Adnan. "Development of automated diagnostic system for skin cancer: Performance analysis of neural network learning algorithms for classification." *Artificial Neural Networks and Machine Learning–ICANN 2014: 24th International Conference on Artificial Neural Networks, Hamburg, Germany*, September 15–19, 2014. *Proceedings 24*. Springer International Publishing, 2014.
14. Transtrum, Mark K., and James P. Sethna. "Improvements to the Levenberg-Marquardt algorithm for nonlinear least-squares minimization." *arXiv preprint arXiv:1201.5885* (2012).
15. Al-Naima, Fawzi M., and Ali H. Al-Timemy. "Resilient back propagation algorithm for breast biopsy classification based on artificial neural networks." *Computational Intelligence and Modern Heuristics. IntechOpen*, 2010.
16. Møller, Martin Fodslette. "A scaled conjugate gradient algorithm for fast supervised learning." *Neural Networks* 6.4 (1993): 525–533.
17. Cueva, Wilson F., et al. "Detection of skin cancer" Melanoma" through computer vision." *2017 IEEE XXIV International Conference on Electronics, Electrical Engineering and Computing (INTERCON)*. IEEE, 2017.
18. Wirayasa, I. Ketut Adi, Handri Santoso, and Eko Indrajit. "Comparison of Convolutional Neural Networks Model Using Different Optimizers for Image Classification." *International Journal of Sciences: Basic and Applied Research (IJSBAR)* 60.2 (2021): 116–126.
19. Rahman, Mohammad Atikur, et al. "Skin cancer classification using NASNet." *International Journal of Science and Research Archive* 11.1 (2024): 775–785.
20. https://www.kaggle.com/datasets/fanconic/skin-cancer-malignant-vs-benign (Accessed on 10th April, 2024)
21. Mijwil, Maad M. "Skin cancer disease images classification using deep learning solutions." *Multimedia Tools and Applications* 80.17 (2021): 26255–26271.
22. Szegedy, Christian, et al. "Rethinking the inception architecture for computer vision." *Proceedings of the IEEE conference on computer vision and pattern recognition*. 2016.

Chapter 17

Revolutionizing healthcare with smart syringe pump

Design and implementation

Winnie Ann Thomas, C. Joshitha, Abhishek Kumar Shrivastava, S. Yazhini, V. K. Pooja, C. V. Kavya, T. P. Nimmy, and Irene Lee Joseph

17.1 INTRODUCTION

Syringe pumps have long been used in the medical field to deliver precise and controlled amounts of fluids or medications to patients. These devices typically consist of a syringe with a mechanism that applies pressure to the syringe barrel at a controlled rate, ensuring accurate dosing over a specified period [1]. Initially, syringe pumps were manually operated, requiring the operator to push the syringe plunger to administer fluids. However, these manual pumps lacked accuracy and consistency, as they depended heavily on the skill and attention of the operator to maintain a steady flow rate [2, 3].

Automation of syringe pumps can significantly reduce errors made by doctors, especially in high-stress environments with critically ill patients [4]. This automation frees nurses from time-consuming tasks, allowing them to focus on other essential duties and increasing their overall efficiency [5].

This chapter introduces an integrated system combining a patient monitor with a smart syringe infusion pump, referred to as the smart self-monitored syringe infusion pump. The system uses an Arduino-based microcontroller to control the speed and velocity of the suction pump. It features a drop counter, tube blockage detection, and drip bag monitoring, utilizing low- and high-power laser diodes and optical sensors for these tasks. The flow rate (measured in drops per minute) and any infusion interruptions are remotely observed through wireless data transmission to users' smartphones via the Blynk mobile application and a computer-based application [6–11].

For over a century, drugs have been administered intravenously using various types of needles and syringes. Early intravenous devices were basic and manual, requiring constant monitoring by medical staff. These manual treatments were typically administered only by physicians, requiring extensive medical staff to assist and guide them.

The objective of this research work is to develop an economically viable wireless microcontroller syringe pump that uses Bluetooth to control and monitor the flow of medication through a connected mobile app. This infusion pump includes robust features such as an alert system with visual and sound alarms. These alarms activate when the fluid reservoir is nearly empty or when the administration of the drug is complete. The mobile app enhances hospital operations by providing alert notifications, ensuring timely interventions and improved patient care.

17.2 MATERIALS AND METHODOLOGY

This section discusses the materials and devices used during the design and construction of the syringe pump, as well as the principles and processes involved in the project's development and manufacturing.

 DOI: 10.1201/9781003591788-17

The design of the syringe pump leverages historical developments, aiming to create a fast, efficient, and cost-effective solution. The project begins with brainstorming strategies and hardware selection, using various components as templates for the syringe pump development. The key hardware components include the motor, Bluetooth module, resistors, capacitors, and the PIC 18F2550 microcontroller, which acts as the system's brain.

The process starts with the creation of an algorithm for the microcontroller, which is crucial for controlling the infusion process. This is followed by hardware design and algorithmic development, leading to hardware realization. Once the prototype is developed, it is used to verify the hardware, identify and fix any errors, and improve its performance. It is well known in digital project development that initial versions rarely work perfectly, and iterative testing and refinement are essential to achieve the desired outcome.

Hardware Requirements

Microcontroller PIC 18F2550
DMOS microstepping driver
Bluetooth module HC05
Seven-segment display
LED
Resistor, capacitor
Switch, button
Power source

Software Requirements

Mobile app

17.3 COMPONENTS

17.3.1 Microcontroller PIC18F2550

The PIC18F2550 microcontroller features design enhancements that make it an ideal choice for many high-performance, power-sensitive applications. Its power consumption is reduced by up to 90% during code execution and normal operations. The microcontroller operates at a frequency of 48MHz and includes built-in direct instruction capabilities. The top view of the IC is shown in Figure 17.1.

17.3.2 DMOS microstepping driver (A4988)

The A4988 is a comprehensive microstepping motor driver designed for easy operation. It supports stepper motors with various step modes and has an output driver capacity of 35V

Figure 17.1 PIC 18F2550 microcontroller (Microchip Technology Inc.).

Figure 17.2 DMOS microstepping driver-A4988 (Allegro Microsystems Inc.).

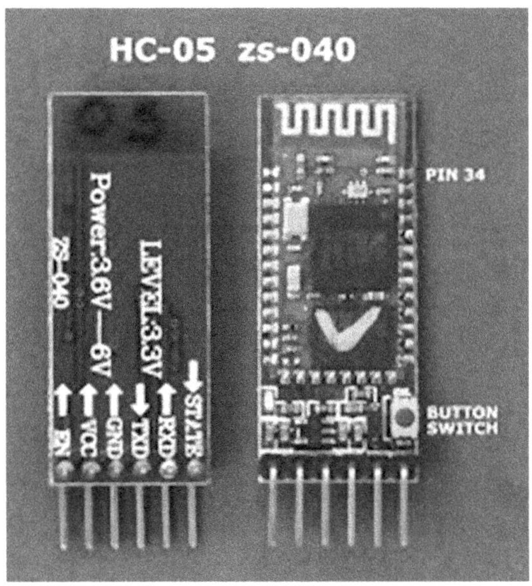

Figure 17.3 HC-05 Bluetooth module.

and ±2A. Additionally, it features a current regulator and overcurrent protection. The photograph of the DMOS microstepping module is shown in Figure 17.2.

17.3.3 Bluetooth module

The HC-05 Bluetooth module provides transparent wireless serial communication. It operates as a slave Bluetooth device, and when connected to smartphones or tablets (masters), its operation becomes seamless and transparent. Figure 17.3 shows the images of Hc-05 Bluetooth module.

17.3.4 Stepper motor

A stepper motor, also called a step or stepping motor, is an electric motor that rotates in precise, incremental steps rather than moving continuously. These motors are a type of digital

Figure 17.4 Stepper motor.

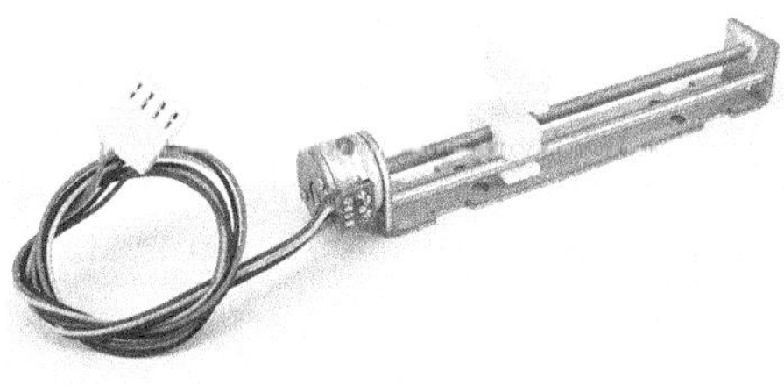

Figure 17.5 Plunger.

actuator, converting electrical energy into mechanical motion. Unlike other electromagnetic actuators, stepper motors can be commanded to move and hold at specific positions without needing a position sensor for feedback, thanks to their open-loop control system—provided that the motor's torque and speed are appropriately matched to the application's requirements. The photograph of a stepper motor is shown in Figure 17.4.

In our system:

- The stepper motor will rotate 1.8 in one step.
- There are 20 pulses (so 20 pulses × 1.8 = 360 [one full rotation]).
- Time for one pulse = 0.02 s.
- Time for one full rotation = 20 × 0.02 = 0.4 s.
- So in one full rotation it will move = 0.5 mm.

17.3.5 Plunger

The plunger, also known as the piston, is the part of the prefilled syringe that, when pressed, expels the vaccine-containing liquid through the needle into the patient. The image of the plunger is shown in Figure 17.5.

17.3.6 Mobile app

A syringe pump controlled by a mobile app allows health care professionals to remotely manage and monitor the administration of medications or fluids. The mobile app provides a user-friendly interface to set infusion rates, monitor progress, and adjust settings as needed. This integration enhances precision and convenience in medical treatments, especially in critical care or home health care environments. In this work, the mobile app named "Smart syringe" is implemented.

17.4 HARDWARE DESIGN

17.4.1 Block diagram

The smart syringe pump is powered by a PIC18F2550 microcontroller, which manages key functions such as pump movement and output indications. The microcontroller receives input from a mobile app via a Bluetooth module, enabling wireless communication between the app and the device. This setup allows for remote control and monitoring, creating a safe separation between the user and the device.

Through the mobile app, users can send commands to the microcontroller to control the stepper motor and the pump. A seven-segment display on the device provides real-time numerical information, such as the status of the infusion, allowing users to monitor the process directly. Additionally, manual inputs can be made using control keys connected to the microcontroller, which also send commands directly to control the stepper motor's rotation. The pump, driven by the stepper motor, is responsible for dispensing fluids accurately.

LED indicators offer visual feedback on system status, including power state, error conditions, and operational modes. The microcontroller controls these LEDs, turning them on or off based on the current state of the system.

17.4.2 Circuit diagram

A circuit diagram provides a detailed electronic setup, showcasing how the microcontroller connects to various components via multiple input/output (I/O) pins to interface with other modules. The microcontroller controls the stepper motor, processes commands, and manages display outputs.

The stepper motor driver circuit translates signals from the microcontroller into appropriate power levels to drive the stepper motor. This circuit typically includes a series of transistors or an integrated driver IC, enabling precise control of the motor's steps. Mechanically connected to the syringe pump, the stepper motor's movement is controlled by signals from the microcontroller via the motor driver.

Wireless communication with the microcontroller is established through a Bluetooth module, connected serially via TX/RX pins. Commands from a mobile app are received by the microcontroller. The amount of fluid dispensed and system status are shown numerically on a seven-segment display. Physical control keys are connected to the microcontroller's input pins for manual operation.

An LED indicator provides visual feedback on the system's status. Resistors are used for current limiting, while diodes offer protection from reverse polarity and aid in rectification. The block diagram of the proposed system is shown Figure 17.6 and the circuit diagram of the same is given in Figure 17.7. The flow chart representation of the prototype is mentioned in Figure 17.8.

17.4.3 Interfacing with microcontroller

The system begins with an initialization phase, which includes setting up pin directions, clearing registers, initializing USART for serial communication, and configuring interrupts to ensure smooth operation. After initialization, the system continuously monitors the status of two buttons. Pressing the reverse button sets the motor direction to reverse, while pressing the forward button sets it to forward.

Once the direction is determined, the system processes data received through USART, moving it to a safe memory location. This data is then used to update the segment display. The

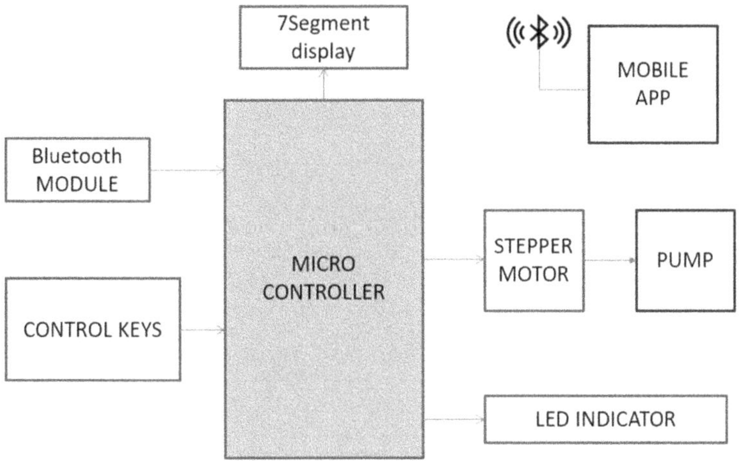

Figure 17.6 Block diagram of proposed system.

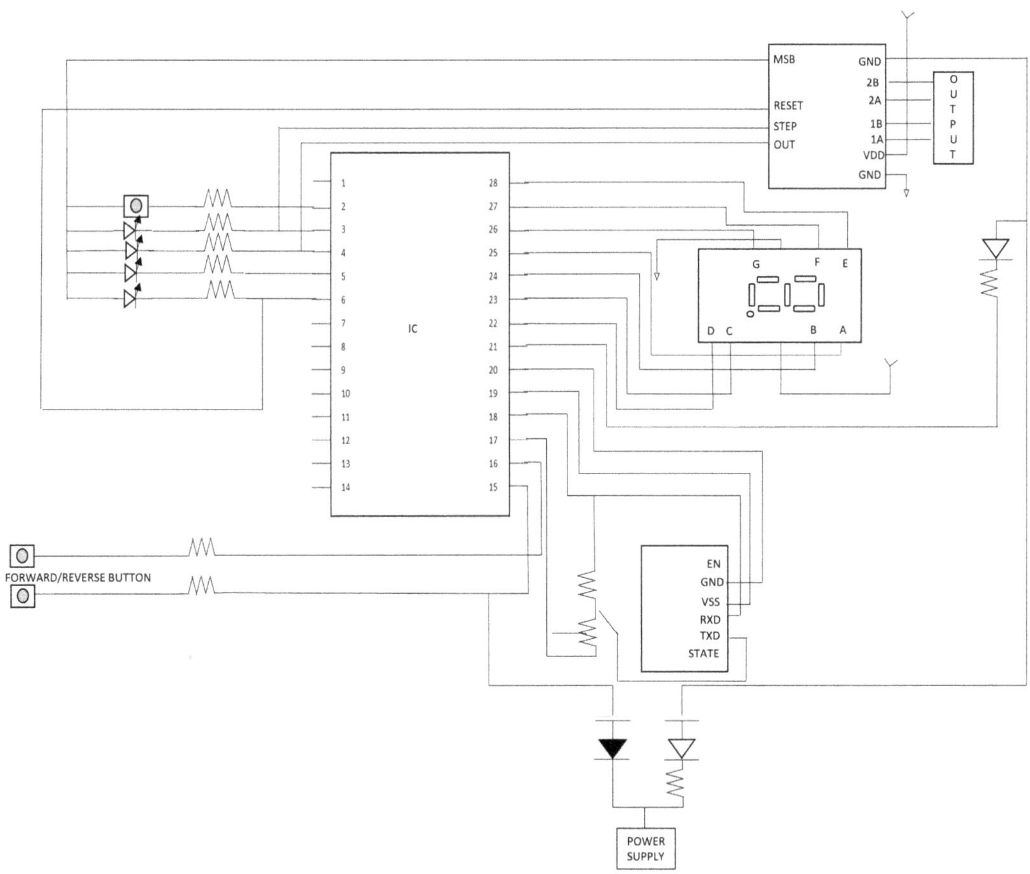

Figure 17.7 Circuit diagram of the proposed system.

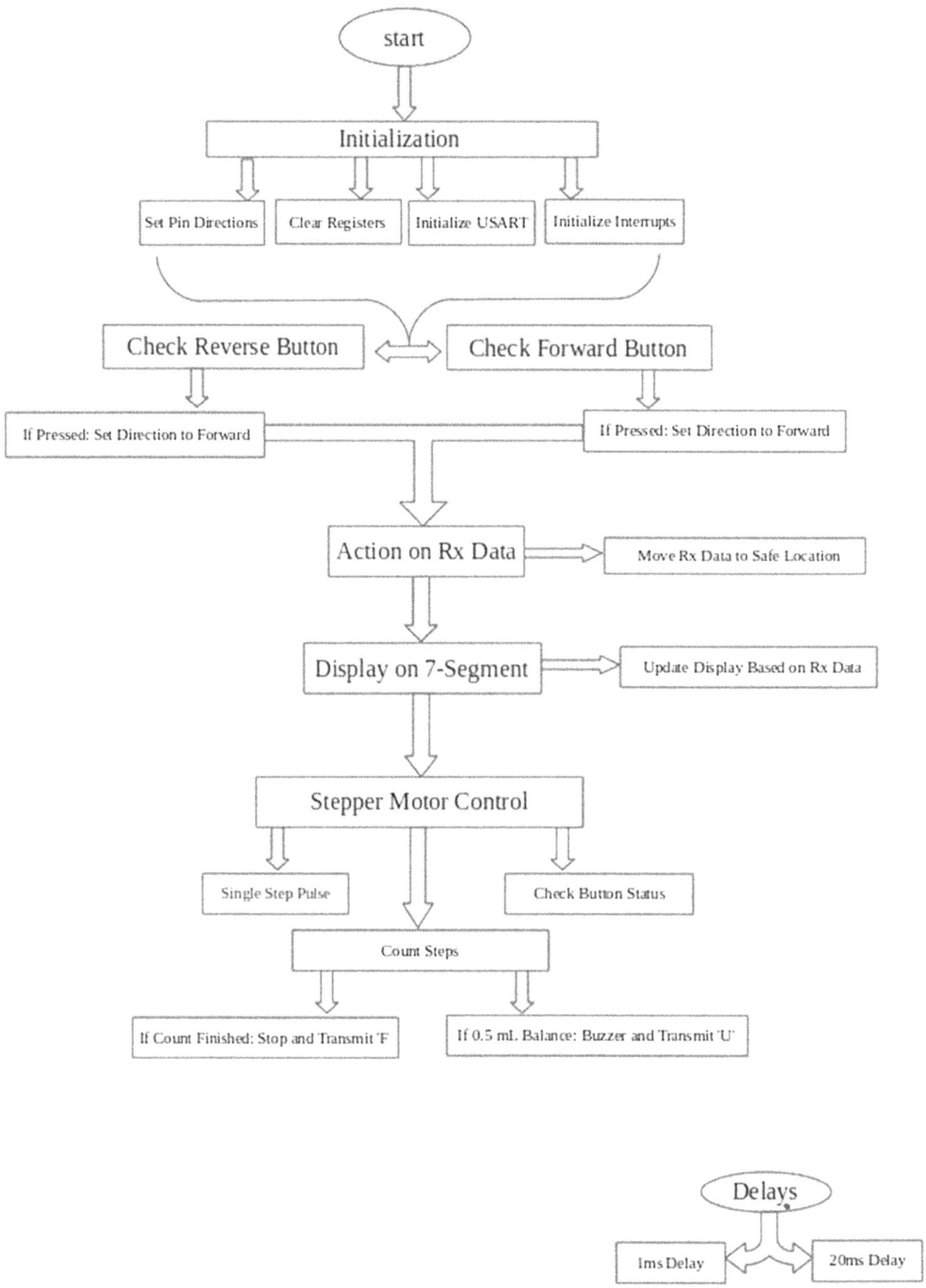

Figure 17.8 Flow chart of proposed device process.

core of the system generates pulses to control the stepper motor. There are two specific conditions during motor control:

1. When the count reaches its endpoint, an 'F' character is displayed, the motor stops, and the buzzer is activated.
2. When a balance of 0.5 ml is detected, a 'U' character is transmitted.

The system uses short (1 ms) and long (20 ms) delays to manage precise timing requirements, ensuring coordinated operation of all components.

17.5 HARDWARE IMPLEMENTATION

17.5.1 Bread board connection

All the components like resistor, capacitor, diode, microcontroller, Bluetooth module, motor driver, seven-segment display, and LED are connected in a bread board using wires. Power for the working of the motor is given via a battery and an AC power supply. The initial testing model is implemented and shown the photograph of the same in Figure 17.9.

17.5.2 Printed circuit board design

A PCB is crucial in a syringe infusion pump, serving as the foundation for the electronic circuits that govern its operation. The PCB plays several key roles in ensuring the pump functions accurately and reliably.

Roles and Components of the PCB in a Syringe Infusion Pump:

1. **Control and Regulation:**
   - **Microcontroller:** The microcontroller manages the pump's software algorithms, controlling the motor that drives the plunger to ensure precise dosage delivery.

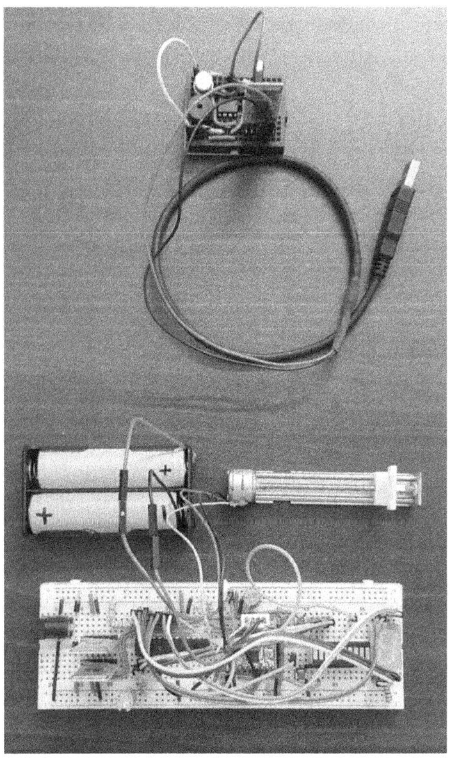

Figure 17.9 Hardware implementation during testing stage.

2. **Sensors and Feedback Mechanisms:**
    - **Integrated Sensors:** Pressure, flow rate, and position sensors are embedded in the PCB, providing essential data to maintain consistent and accurate infusion rates.
3. **Power Management:**
    - **Power Supply Circuits:** These circuits provide stable power to the pump and its peripheral devices, whether from batteries or an external source. Proper power management is crucial for the pump's reliability and longevity.
4. **Connectivity:**
    - **Bluetooth Module Integration:** The PCB includes a Bluetooth module for wireless communication with external devices, enabling remote monitoring and control. This module also manages data transmission securely.
5. **User Interface:**
    - **Display and Buttons:** The PCB supports a touch screen display and buttons, allowing health care providers to set infusion parameters and monitor them on the screen.

Key Components on the PCB:

- **Microcontroller Unit (MCU):** Acts as the central processing unit, running the pump's firmware and controlling overall operation.
- **Motor Driver:** Regulates the electrical power sent to the motor that drives the syringe plunger, ensuring precise control over the motor's speed and movement.
- **Sensors:**
    - **Flow Sensors:** Monitor the flow rate to ensure accurate medication delivery.
    - **Pressure Sensors:** Detect occlusions or blockages in the tubing.
    - **Position Sensors:** Track the position of the syringe plunger to ensure accurate movement.
- **Communication Module:**
    - **Bluetooth Module:** Provides a wireless link for remote supervision and control.
- **Voltage Regulators:** Maintain constant power levels to various components, ensuring stable operation.
- **Battery Management System:** Monitors and manages battery charge and discharge cycles.
- **User Interface Elements:**
    - LED Display: It shows vital details such as infusion rates, volume infused, and warnings. Buttons/Keypad: They let users put in settings and interact with the pump.
- **PCB Design Considerations**
    - Size and Form Factor: The infusion pump housing has limited space that must be filled compactly by the PCB while embracing all essential components.
    - Reliability and Durability: Medical devices need a high level of reliability. The PCB should be able to work continuously under different environmental conditions without breakdowns. **Compliance and Safety:** The design must adhere to medical device rules ensuring patient safety and effectiveness of the device.
    - **Signal Integrity:** Proper routing of signals and minimizing interference are essential for correct sensor readings and reliable Bluetooth communication.

The PCB layout of the proposed device is shown in Figure 17.10. Front view of the working prototype along with mobile app display is shown in Figure 17.11.

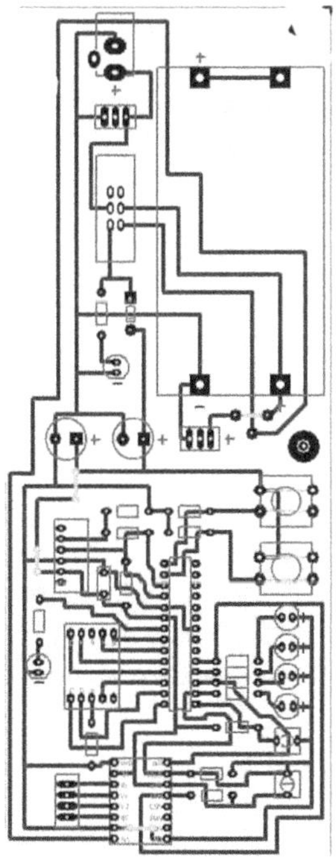

Figure 17.10 PCB layout of the proposed system.

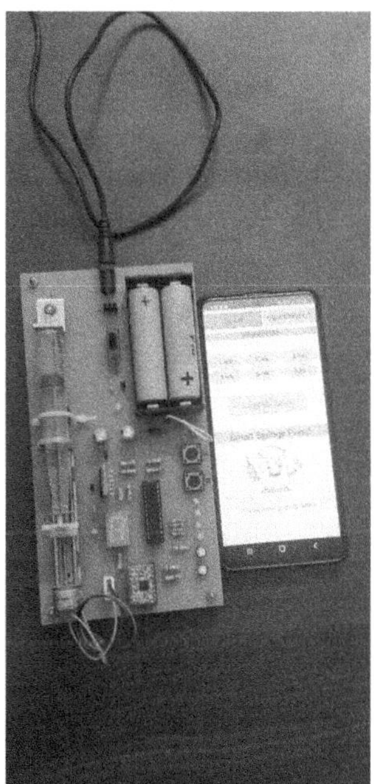

Figure 17.11. Front view of the prototype along with mobile app display.

17.6 CONCLUSION

Connectivity is transforming medication administration with the advent of wirelessly controlled syringe pumps, managed via a mobile app. These pumps deliver medication with remarkable precision, maintaining a consistent flow rate of 1–6 ml per hour. The integrated stepper motor drives the pump head, ensuring accurate medication delivery. This innovative system enhances reliability by providing timely and accurate doses, significantly reducing dosage errors, and boosting productivity.

The introduction of smart syringe pumps marks a significant advancement in convenience, eliminating the time and effort health care professionals previously spent on double-checking volume calculations. This technology streamlines medication delivery, aligning perfectly with the health care industry's increasing adoption of AI and wireless connectivity. It emphasizes patient safety by enforcing stringent safety and quality standards, a responsibility shared by governments, producers, and consumers alike. The syringe pump is compatible with standard reservoirs, offering a flexible solution for various medication needs while ensuring a high standard of care. Its design also prioritizes user comfort, with an adjustable flow rate that adapts to the specific requirements of health care professionals.

REFERENCES

[1] L.J. Murdoch, & V. Cameron (2008). Smart infusion technology: a minimum safety standard for intensive care?, *British Journal of Nursing*, 17(10): 630–636.

[2] B. Jung, K. S. Seo, S. J. Kwon, K. Lee, S. Hong, H. Seo, G. Y. Kim, G. M. Park, J. Jeong, S. Seo (2016). Efficacy evaluation of syringe pump developed for continuous drug infusion. *J Dent Anesth Pain Med*, 16(4): 303–307.

[3] M. M. Struys, T. De Smet, J. I. Glen, H. E. Vereecke, A. R. Absalom, T. W. Schnider. (2016), The history of target-controlled infusion. *Anesth Analg*; 122: 56–69.

[4] K.O. Schnock, P.C. Dykes, J. Albert, D. Ariosto, R. Call, C. Cameron, D.L. Carroll, A.G. Drucker, L. Fang, C.A. Garcia-Palm, et al. (2017), The frequency of intravenous medication administration errors related to smart infusion pumps: A multihospital observational study. *BMJ Qual. Saf.*, 26, 131–140.

[5] Neha Shah & Yogini Jani. (2020). Implementation of Smart Infusion Pumps: A Scoping Review and Case Study Discussion of the Evidence of the Role of the Pharmacist. *Pharmacy*. 8. 239. 10.3390/pharmacy8040239

[6] Karen Kan, Wilton C. Levine, (2021), *16 - Infusion Pumps, Anaesthesia Equipment* (Third Edition), W.B. Saunders, pp. 351–367.

[7] M. U. Sapatnekar and P. M. Mainkar, "Design and Development of IOT Controlled Intravenous Infusion Device," *2022 13th International Conference on Computing Communication and Networking Technologies (ICCCNT)*, Kharagpur, India, pp. 1–7.

[8] M. G. Saqlain, M. R. Uddin, A. Mahmood and M. Hasan, "IoT-Enabled Syringe Pump System: Enhancing Medication Accuracy and Optimizing Drug Delivery with Real-Time Alert System," *2023 26th International Conference on Computer and Information Technology (ICCIT)*, Cox's Bazar, Bangladesh, 2023, pp. 1–5.

[9] R. Rogosic, M. Poloni, R. Marroquin-Garcia, D. Dimech, J. Passariello Jansen, T.J. Cleij, K. Eersels, B. van Grinsven, H. Diliën, (2022) ,Cost-effective, scalable and smartphone-controlled 3D-Printed syringe pump - From lab bench to point of care biosensing applications, *Physics in Medicine*, 14: 100051, ISSN 2352-4510

[10] Komal Ashok Dhone et al (2024) J. Phys.: Conf. Ser. 2763, 012028.

Chapter 18

Advanced lung cancer detection using EfficientDet

A deep learning approach

G. Krishna Subramanyam, Rajib Debnath, and Akella Ramakrishna

18.1 INTRODUCTION

Lung cancer represents the leading cause of cancer-related mortality worldwide. The disease's substantial burden is underscored by the American Cancer Society's 2024 projections, which estimate 234,580 new cases and about 125,070 deaths in the United States, emphasizing the ongoing challenge and the crucial demand for medical breakthroughs [1–4]. Lung cancer affects 1 in 16 men and 1 in 17 women over their lifetime, spotlighting the imperative for advancements in early detection and treatment strategies [5]. The advent of artificial intelligence (AI) and deep learning (DL) marks a significant advance, offering new hope through their ability to intricately analyze imaging data for early cancer detection with remarkable accuracy. This technological evolution is vital, considering lung cancer's propensity to progress silently, making the development of accurate, early detection methods a cornerstone for enhancing patient survival rates [6].

The capabilities of AI and DL are set to revolutionize the field of lung cancer screening and diagnosis. By leveraging automation to enhance the precision of screenings, these technologies promise a reduction in the occurrence of false positives often associated with manual assessments. This improvement is poised to streamline the diagnostic process, facilitating quicker and more accurate care for patients. Additionally, the diverse nature of lung cancer, influenced by a mix of genetic factors, environmental conditions, and lifestyle choices, calls for a move toward more tailored diagnostic and treatment plans. Recent research is increasingly focused on developing advanced, integrated methods that not only elevate detection accuracy but also offer sharper prognostic insights. Such progress seeks to pave the way for a more effective, encompassing strategy in the fight against lung cancer [3].

This study introduces a model that leverages the EfficientDet framework for superior lung cancer detection from CT scans. It begins with a literature review on computational models in lung cancer diagnostics (Section 18.2). The methodology section (Section 18.3) outlines the development and optimization of the model. Experimental procedures and a detailed performance evaluation are presented in Section 18.4, showcasing the model's accuracy in detecting lung nodules. Section 18.5 offers a comparative analysis with existing technologies, highlighting the model's advanced detection capabilities. The study concludes (Section 18.6) by emphasizing the EfficientDet model's contributions to the field and proposing future research directions to further improve diagnostic processes.

18.2 LITERATURE SURVEY

The transformation of lung cancer detection has been significant, propelled by the integration of digital imaging and computational models to surmount the limitations inherent in traditional diagnostic techniques. Traditional methods, reliant on CT scans and expert

DOI: 10.1201/9781003591788-18

interpretation, confront challenges due to a high incidence of false positives. This issue has prompted a transition toward computer-aided detection (CAD) systems and the burgeoning field of DL for enhanced diagnostic accuracy and efficiency [7, 8]. CAD systems have evolved from elementary rule-based algorithms to sophisticated machine learning techniques, ultimately embracing DL models such as convolutional neural networks (CNNs), renowned for their unmatched precision in image analysis [9]. A pivotal development in this field is the incorporation of spatial pyramid pooling and three-dimensional convolution, significantly improving diagnostic accuracy [10].

Simultaneously, digital pathology has greatly benefited from DL, especially in analyzing whole slide images (WSIs) [11], facilitating detailed examination at both the cellular and image levels. Despite these advances, the application of DL in lung cancer histopathology is still nascent, offering a promising direction for future research [12]. Epidemiological modeling has also progressed, integrating a wide array of clinical and lifestyle factors to identify individuals at high risk. Even with enhancements, these models encounter challenges in data collection and accuracy, indicating the potential benefits of merging machine learning and DL to refine lung cancer risk assessments [13, 14, 15].

In the domain of lung cancer detection, DL models have demonstrated remarkable efficacy. Research by Niyaz et al. [16] and others has shown DL's ability, particularly CNN and deep belief networks (DBN), to distinguish between malignant and benign nodules [17]. Subsequent studies have further leveraged CNNs for straightforward lung tumor classification, while additional research found CNN-based models to surpass other DL approaches in tumor detection [18, 19]. Ciompi et al. introduced multiscale CNNs for classifying lung cancer types, employing a multistream neural network to analyze lung nodules from multiple perspectives [20]. Contributions by Yu et al. [22] and Shakeel et al. [21] underscore the importance of preprocessing steps such as bone exclusion, lung segmentation, and image enhancement for effective CNN training and classification.

Ardila et al. developed a comprehensive system that integrates segmentation, detection, and risk estimation models for lung cancer, illustrating the complex approach needed for precise diagnosis [23]. This effort is supported by research from Chen et al. [24] and Hosny et al. [25], focusing on nodule recognition and the use of data augmentation to boost CNN performance. The scope of DL in cancer detection extends beyond CT imaging. Techniques involving temporal attention mechanisms and transfer learning have yielded promising results, with one study achieving an area under the curve (AUC) of 86.4% using visual simple temporal attention (ViSTA) [26]. Transfer learning has further enriched model training, demonstrating high accuracy in nodule detection [27]. DL's applicability has also been explored in histopathology imaging and X-ray imaging, broadening cancer detection's horizons. CNNs integrated with long short-term memory (LSTM) networks have been successful in lesion detection, evidencing DL's capability to accurately predict cancer [28]. Additionally, systems employing EfficientNet and other DL architectures have shown versatility in diagnosing various lung diseases [29].

Advanced computational techniques, such as the guaranteed convergence particle swarm optimization (GCPSO) algorithm and the Bag of Visual Words (BoVW), have pushed the accuracy of lung malignancy detection further, achieving near-perfect accuracy rates [30]. The utilization of data-driven feature selection methods, combined with deep feature extraction from CNNs, has further underscored the effectiveness of DL in leveraging complex patient data for lung cancer detection, achieving significant accuracy [31]. The exploration of advancements in lung cancer detection, particularly through DL and computational models, has illuminated significant progress alongside notable challenges. Traditional diagnostic methods, such as CT scans, are foundational yet troubled by high false-positive rates, leading to unnecessary biopsies and increasing patient anxiety and system inefficiencies. Meanwhile, the promising yet nascent applications of DL in digital pathology, especially in analyzing WSIs, encounter difficulties in providing consistent, nuanced analyses due to the complex and varied nature of lung cancer histopathology. The field of epidemiological modeling, which plays a crucial role in identifying high-risk individuals, faces additional hurdles in data collection and model accuracy, complicating accurate risk assessments. The extensive preprocessing required for DL models, including bone exclusion and lung segmentation, further complicates these challenges by consuming resources and limiting the scalability and practical application of DL in clinical settings.

In response to these multifaceted challenges, we propose a model that integrates the EfficientDet framework, specifically designed to address the limitations identified in current diagnostic approaches. This model harnesses EfficientDet's advanced image recognition capabilities to navigate the complexities of lung tissue images more accurately, without the need for extensive preprocessing.

18.3 METHODOLOGY FOR INTEGRATED DL FRAMEWORK IN LUNG CANCER DETECTION

18.3.1 Data collection and preprocessing

The integrated DL framework for lung cancer detection is outlined beginning with a comprehensive data flow diagram that delineates the proposed study's methodology, from data acquisition through model evaluation. This initial overview, as illustrated in the data flow diagram (Figure 18.1), sets the stage for a deeper understanding of the dataset utilization and preprocessing techniques employed in the research.

This study leverages key datasets for its analysis, particularly emphasizing the Lung Image Database Consortium and Image Database Resource Initiative (LIDC-IDRI). Within the LIDC-IDRI collection, there are diagnostic CT scans from 1,018 individuals, rich with varied instances of lung nodules. Experienced thoracic radiologists have meticulously annotated these scans, categorizing nodules based on size—either greater than or less than 3 mm—and identified others as non-nodules. For those nodules larger than 3 mm, additional details such as malignancy ratings and precise segmentation are provided. These classification efforts are crucial, forming the foundation for the model's training and testing phases, and are detailed within a specific annotations Table 18.1.

Preprocessing of these datasets is crucial for the model's effectiveness and robustness. This involves several key steps, such as cleaning, normalizing, and augmenting the data.

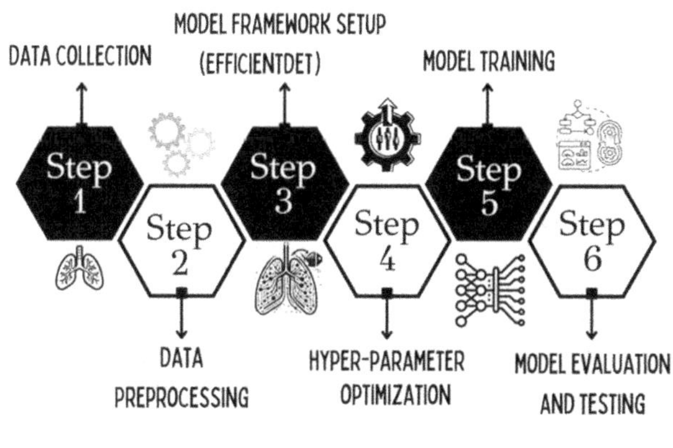

Figure 18.1 Workflow diagram of the hybrid model for lung cancer detection.

Table 18.1 Annotation categories in lung cancer imaging datasets

Annotation category	*Description*	*Details*
Nodules ≥ 3 mm	Lesions identified as nodules with a diameter equal to or greater than 3 mm.	Each nodule is given a malignancy score and detailed segmentation.
Nodules < 3 mm	Lesions identified as nodules with a diameter less than 3 mm.	These nodules are annotated but not given a malignancy score due to their small size.
Non-nodules	Areas identified by radiologists that do not qualify as nodules.	These could include benign masses, scars, or other non-nodule lung abnormalities.

Techniques like noise reduction, resolution standardization, and various data augmentation methods (rotation, flipping, scaling) are meticulously applied. These preprocessing efforts ensure the data is of the highest quality for training the DL model, directly impacting its ability to accurately detect and classify lung nodules.

18.3.2 EfficientDet: deep learning model for lung cancer detection

EfficientDet is a state-of-the-art model optimized for object detection, renowned for its efficiency and accuracy across varying computational constraints. Developed by Tan and Le [32], this model integrates a novel compound scaling method with the EfficientNet backbone to enhance feature extraction and object detection capabilities as illustrated in Figure 18.2.

18.3.2.1 Compound scaling method

The compound scaling method is central to EfficientDet's design, offering a principled approach to scaling the network's depth (d), width (w), and resolution (r). This is mathematically represented by

$$d = \alpha^{\phi} \tag{18.1}$$

$$w = \beta^{\phi} \tag{18.2}$$

$$r = \gamma^{\phi} \tag{18.3}$$

where α, β, and γ are coefficients determined through empirical research, and ϕ is the compound coefficient controlling the scaling.

18.3.2.2 EfficientNet backbone and BiFPN

EfficientNet serves as the backbone for feature extraction in EfficientDet, utilizing a scalable architecture to effectively process input images and extract comprehensive, multiscale features. This scalability enables EfficientNet to adjust its complexity through the compound scaling method, striking an effective balance between computational efficiency and detection performance. EfficientDet further enhances its capability to identify objects of various sizes by incorporating BiFPN for the integration of features across multiple scales. BiFPN

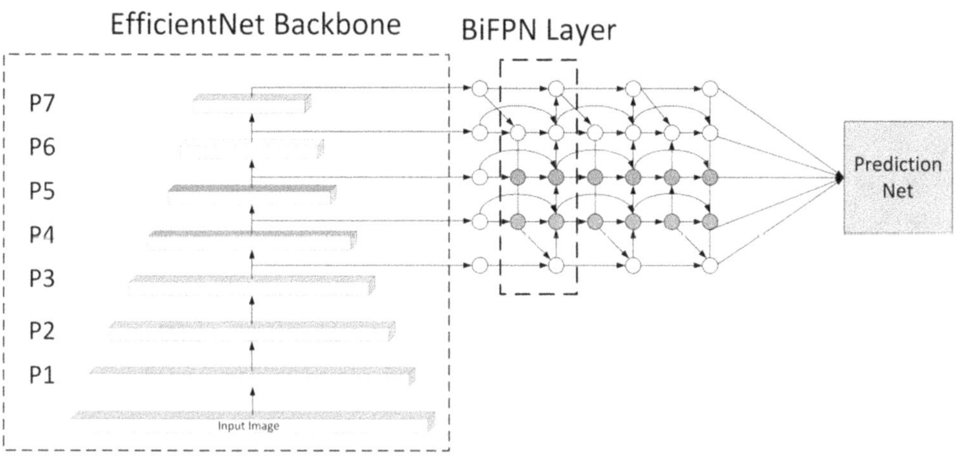

Figure 18.2 EfficientDet architecture.

improves the model's performance by facilitating bidirectional information exchange, which is mathematically optimized through the weighted combination of features.

$$F_i = w_1 \cdot F_{i,high} + w_2 \cdot F_{i,low} \tag{18.4}$$

where F_i denotes the fused feature at level i, and w_1 and w_2 are learnable weights that determine the significance of features from higher ($F_{i,high}$) and lower ($F_{i,low}$) levels, respectively.

18.3.2.3 Anchor optimization and training

EfficientDet optimizes anchor boxes to enhance detection accuracy by utilizing a k-means clustering approach. This method minimizes the average internal optical urethrotomy loss between the anchor boxes and the ground truth, thereby increasing the model's precision in localizing objects. To maintain high efficiency during both training and inference phases, EfficientDet incorporates advanced techniques such as stochastic depth and efficient batch normalization. These methods are instrumental in reducing overfitting and computational overhead, ensuring that EfficientDet remains a highly effective and efficient choice for object detection tasks across a variety of application areas. Structured around a scalable architecture, the EfficientDet model can adapt effectively to varying computational resources and accuracy requirements. This scalability is facilitated through the compound coefficient (ϕ), which determines the model's depth, width, and resolution. Adjustments to the compound coefficient (ϕ) significantly influence the model's complexity and performance, as demonstrated by the parameters, and their optimal values for different configurations of the EfficientDet model presented in Table 18.2.

18.4 EXPERIMENTS AND RESULTS

18.4.1 Model training

The model's training process utilized a dataset split into distinct sets for training, validation, and testing. This dataset was carefully categorized to reflect the critical distinction in lung cancer diagnosis, namely the presence or absence of lung nodules. It includes a total of 40,772

Table 18.2 Optimal parameters for different EfficientDet configurations

Model	*Φ*	*Input size*	*Depth*	*Width*	*BiFPN layers*
EfficientDet-D0	0	512	3	88	3
EfficientDet-D1	1	640	4	112	4
EfficientDet-D2	2	768	5	160	5
EfficientDet-D3	3	896	6	192	6
EfficientDet-D4	4	1024	7	224	7
EfficientDet-D5	5	1280	7	256	7
EfficientDet-D6	6	1280	8	288	8
EfficientDet-D7	7	1536	8	384	8

Table 18.3 Dataset distribution in lung cancer imaging studies

Dataset distribution	*Malignant class*	*Benign class*
Training Images	28,540	15,204
Testing Images	8,154	4,344
Validation	4,078	2,172

Table 18.4 Performance metrics before and after tuning

Metric	*Before tuning*	*After tuning*
Accuracy	97.5%	99.8%
Precision	97.0%	99.4%
Recall	96.8%	99.3%
F1 Score	96.9%	99.5%
AUC	0.961	0.989

images marked as containing nodules (classified as malignant) and 21,720 images identified as lacking nodules (classified as benign), facilitating a comprehensive training regime.

The model underwent training with this data, optimizing its parameters through the application of suitable loss functions and the back-propagation method. Performance monitoring occurred on the validation set to ensure the model's accuracy and efficiency throughout the training phase. The distribution of the dataset into training, testing, and validation sets is detailed in Table 18.3, providing insight into the model's training and evaluation framework.

18.4.2 Impact of model tuning on performance

The integration of EfficientDet into our model tuning process led to remarkable improvements in detection performance. By optimizing the hyperparameters dynamically, EfficientDet ensured the model efficiently learned from the training data, resulting in enhanced diagnostic accuracy. The comparative results, presented in Table 18.4, quantitatively illustrate the impact of tuning on the model's performance. Prior to tuning, the model achieved an accuracy of 97.5%, which, post-tuning, surged to 99.8%. Precision, a measure of the model's exactness, also saw a notable increase from 97.0% to 99.4%, indicating a reduction in false positives. Similarly, recall improved from 96.8% to 99.3%, reflecting the model's enhanced

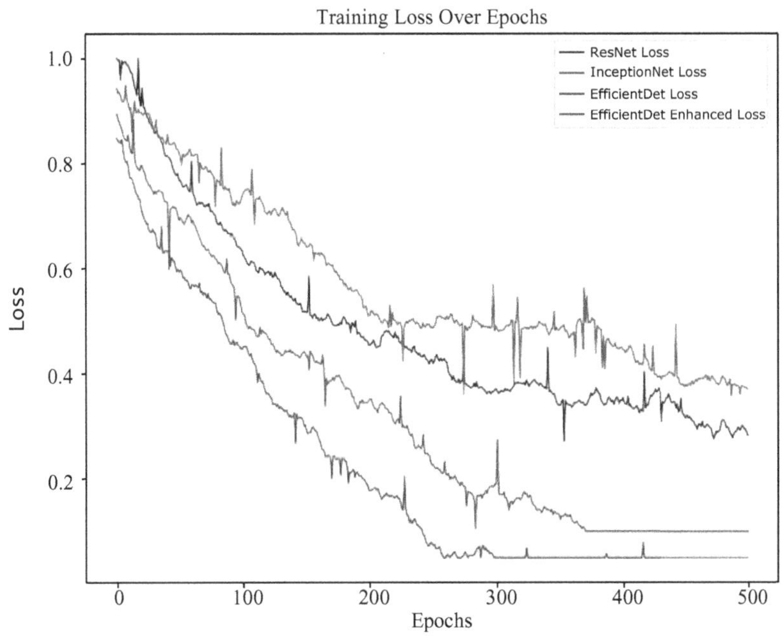

(a) Loss over epochs

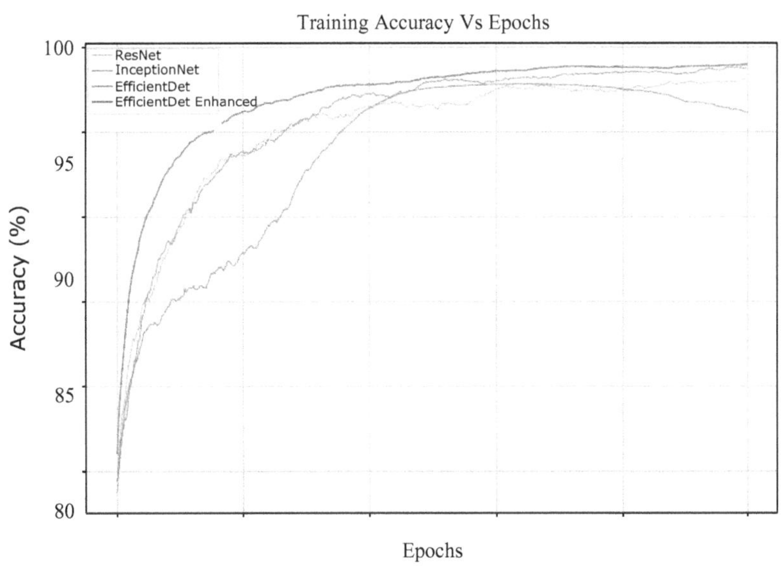

(b) Accuracy over epochs

Figure 18.3 Comparison of loss and accuracy over epochs for various models.

ability to detect all relevant instances of lung nodules. The F1 score, which balances precision and recall, increased to 99.5%, affirming the model's improved reliability. Additionally, the area under the curve (AUC) metric rose from 0.961 to 0.989, showcasing the model's strengthened discriminatory power between the classes of interest post tuning.

The training dynamics of the models under comparison are captured through the loss and accuracy graphs displayed in Figure 18.3. As shown in Figure 18.3a, the EfficientDet model

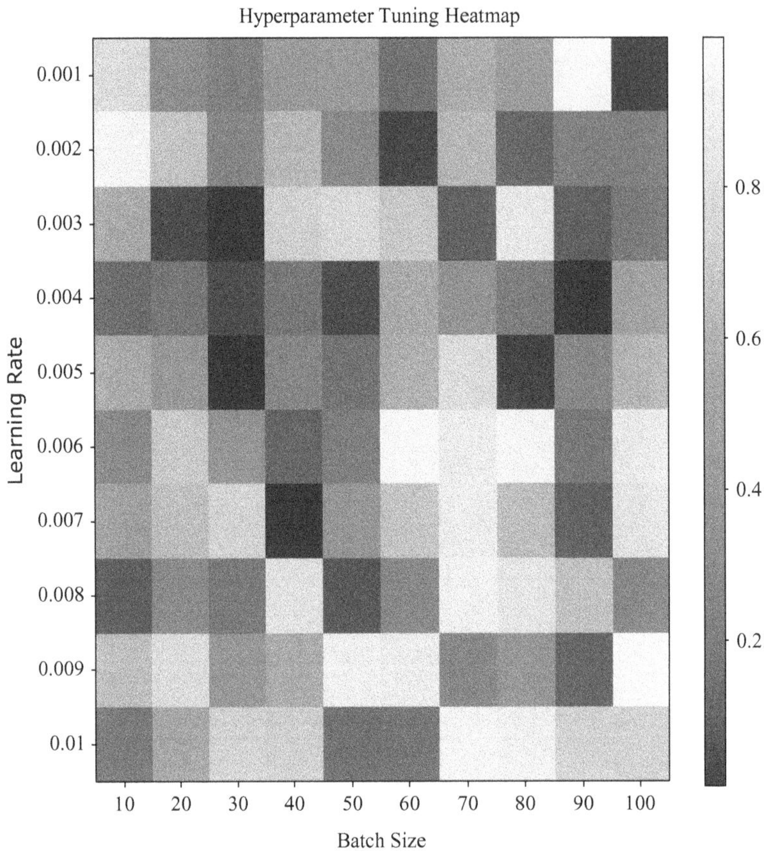

Figure 18.4 Heatmap representation for hyperparameter tuning.

demonstrates a rapid decline in loss, stabilizing at a lower value compared to the other models. This indicates a swift convergence and effective optimization, outperforming the standard EfficientDet, Resnet, and InceptionNet models, particularly after the initial epochs. Conversely, Figure 18.3b illustrates that the EfficientDet model consistently maintains the highest accuracy across epochs, affirming its superior capacity for correct classification as training advances. Following the initial surge in accuracy, the EfficientDet model approaches a plateau, indicating a high level of generalization. This dual depiction in Figure 18.3 accentuates the benefits of incorporating EfficientDet, showcasing marked improvements in convergence rate and accuracy, pivotal for the practical application of lung cancer nodule detection.

18.4.2.1 Hyperparameter optimization visualization

Visualizing the hyperparameter tuning process is critical for understanding the efficiency and effectiveness of EfficientDet optimization. The heatmap (Figure 18.4) illustrates the results of hyperparameter tuning for a deep learning model. Each cell represents a combination of learning rates and batch sizes, with color intensity indicating model accuracy. Brighter colors denote higher accuracy, guiding the identification of optimal configurations. Notably, the best learning rate and batch size are determined to be 0.009 and 60, respectively. This visualization facilitates informed decision-making in hyperparameter optimization, enhancing model performance.

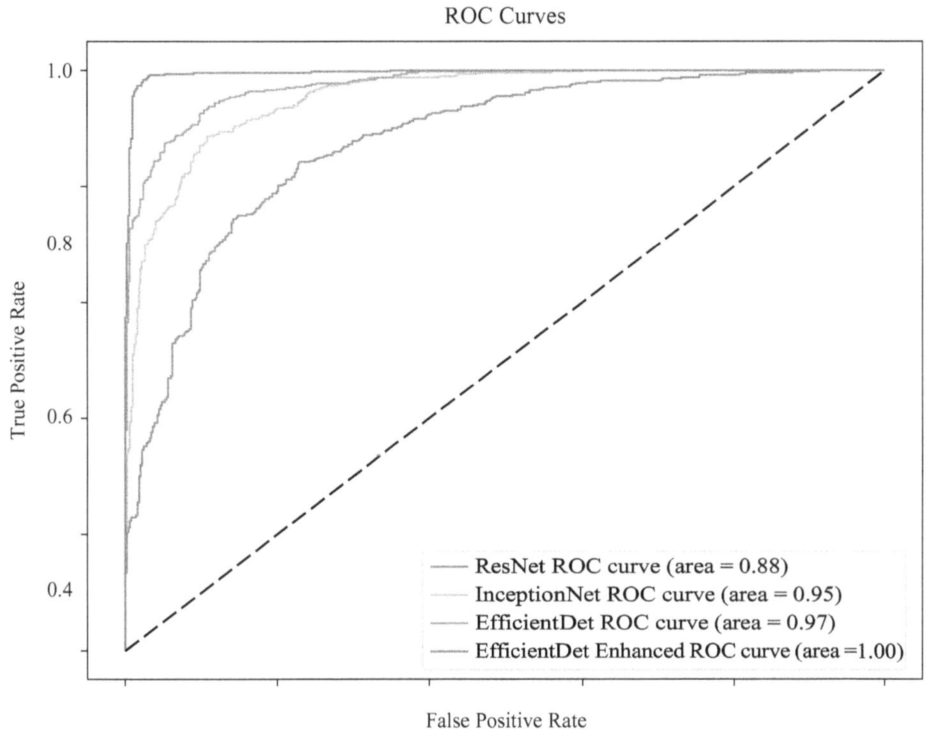

Figure 18.5 ROC curves of state-of-the-art models.

The results underscore the model's ability to discern between malignant and benign nodules with high precision. Figure 18.5 illustrates the Receiver Operating Characteristic (ROC) curve.

Table 18.5 presents a comprehensive analysis of the model's performance in detecting lung cancer nodules of varying sizes. The results underscore the exceptional accuracy, precision, recall, and F1 scores across all categories. Specifically, for small nodules (less than 3 mm), the model achieves an accuracy of 99.6%, with precision, recall, and F1 scores closely aligned, demonstrating its ability to accurately identify even the most challenging, minute nodules. The performance slightly improves for medium-sized nodules (3–10 mm), indicating a 99.8% accuracy and a consistent balance between precision and recall, leading to a 99.5% F1 score. Remarkably, for large nodules (greater than 10 mm), the model reaches a perfect score of 100% across all metrics, reflecting its robustness in identifying more conspicuous nodules. These results affirm the model's comprehensive capabilities in accurately detecting lung cancer nodules across a spectrum of sizes, marking a significant advancement in diagnostic methodologies for lung cancer.

18.5 COMPARATIVE ANALYSIS WITH STATE-OF-THE-ART MODELS

A comparative performance analysis, as outlined in Table 18.6, evaluates the effectiveness of various models, such as EfficientDet, ResNet, and InceptionNet, against the enhanced EfficientDet model. The enhanced model exhibits superior performance across all evaluated metrics achieving an accuracy of 99.8%, precision of 99.4%, recall of 99.3%, and an F1 score of 99.5%, alongside an AUC of 0.989. This contrasts notably with the standard EfficientDet

Table 18.5 Model performance across different nodule sizes

Nodule size	*Accuracy*	*Precision*	*Recall*	*F1 Score*
Small (< 3 mm)	99.6%	99.1%	98.8%	99.0%
Medium (3–10 mm)	99.8%	99.5%	99.4%	99.5%
Large (> 10 mm)	100%	100%	100%	100%

Table 18.6 Comparative performance analysis

Model	*Accuracy*	*Precision*	*Recall*	*F1 Score*	*AUC*
ResNet	97.0%	96.5%	97.2%	96.8%	0.970
InceptionNet	98.0%	97.5%	98.2%	97.8%	0.980
EfficientDet	98.5%	98.0%	97.5%	97.7%	0.985
EfficientDet Enhanced	99.8%	99.4%	99.3%	99.5%	0.989

model, which, while effective, shows slightly lower metrics in comparison. Similarly, both ResNet and InceptionNet models demonstrate commendable performances but are outperformed by the enhanced approach. These results highlight the significant improvements in detection capabilities afforded by integrating the model, showcasing its potential in refining diagnostic accuracies in lung cancer detection through advanced optimization of model parameters.

The obtained results demonstrate not only the superior accuracy of the EfficientDet model in detecting lung nodules but also its practical applicability in clinical settings. The comparison with existing models highlights the advantages of integrating advanced techniques for hyperparameter optimization, emphasizing the model's novelty and its contribution to advancing medical imaging technology.

18.6 CONCLUSION

The implementation of the EfficientDet framework significantly boosts lung nodule detection accuracy, achieving up to 99.8%. The model's sophisticated hyperparameter optimization confers a notable increase in precision, recall, and F1 scores, signifying its impact on the model's reliability in differentiating between benign and malignant nodules. The EfficientDet model's ability to maintain high performance across various nodule sizes and complexities indicates a robust approach, responsive to the heterogeneous nature of lung cancer presentations. As AI continues to permeate the field of medical diagnostics, the insights gained from this model pave the way for the development of more accurate and efficient screening methods. Looking ahead, the scalability and adaptability of the EfficientDet model promise value beyond lung cancer, with the prospect of enhancing diagnostic procedures across a spectrum of medical conditions.

REFERENCES

[1] World Health Organization. Lung cancer. 2023. Available at: https://www.who.int/news-room/fact-sheets/detail/lung-cancer

[2] World Cancer Research Fund International. Lung cancer statis- tics. 2020. Available at: https://www.wcrf.org/dietandcancer/lung-cancer-statistics/

[3] Freddie Bray, Jacques Ferlay, Isabelle Soerjomataram, Rebecca L. Siegel, Lindsey A. Torre, and Ahmedin Jemal. Global cancer statistics 2018: GLOBOCAN estimates of incidence and mortality worldwide for 36 cancers in 185 countries. *CA: A Cancer Journal for Clinicians*, 68(6):394– 424, 2018.

[4] American Cancer Society. Lung Cancer Statistics — How Common is Lung Cancer. 2024. Available at: https://www.cancer.org/cancer/lung-cancer/about/key-statistics.html. Accessed: 2023-09-30.

[5] Lung Cancer Research Foundation. Lung Cancer Facts 2023. 2023. Available at: https://www.lungcancerresearchfoundation.org/lung-cancer-facts/. Accessed: 2023-09-30.

[6] National Cancer Institute. Lung and Bronchus Cancer — Cancer Stat Facts. 2023. Available at: https://seer.cancer.gov/statfacts/html/lungb.html. Accessed: 2023-09-30.

[7] G. A. Samuel, G. McLennan, L. Bidaut, et al. The Lung Image Database Consortium (LIDC) and Image Database Resource Initiative (IDRI): A completed reference database of lung nodules on CT scans. *Medical Physics*, 38(2):915–931, 2011.

[8] Saad Albawi, Muhanad Hameed Arif, and Jumana Waleed. Skin cancer classification dermatologist-level based on deep learning model. *Acta Scientiarum. Technology*, 45:e61531–e61531, 2023.

[9] Xiaozheng Xie, Jianwei Niu, Xuefeng Liu, Zhengsu Chen, Shaojie Tang, and Shui Yu. A survey on incorporating domain knowledge into deep learning for medical image analysis. *Medical Image Analysis*, 69:101985, 2021.

[10] Qianqian Zhang and Sangwon Yoon. A novel self-adaptive convolutional neural network model using spatial pyramid pooling for 3D lung nodule computer-aided diagnosis. *IISE Transactions on Healthcare Systems Engineering*, 12(1):75–88, 2022.

[11] Eleanor Jenkinson and Ognjen Arandjelovi. Whole slide image under- standing in pathology: what is the salient scale of analysis? *BioMedInformatics*, 4(1):489–518, 2024.

[12] Yibo Zhang, Zijian Yang, Ruanqi Chen, Yanli Zhu, Li Liu, Jiyan Dong, Zicheng Zhang, Xujie Sun, Jianming Ying, and Dongmei Lin. Histopathology images-based deep learning prediction of prognosis and therapeutic response in small cell lung cancer. *NPJ digital medicine*, 7(1) :15, 2024.

[13] Gunasekaran Raja, Balakumar Ramkumar, Bhargavi Rajendiran, Sa Haya Beni Prathiba, Thamodharan Arumugam, Kalimuthu Karup Panan, Lewis Nkenyereye, and Kapal Dev. Synergistic analysis of lung cancer's impact on cardiovascular disease using ML-based techniques. *IEEE Journal of Biomedical and Health Informatics*, 2024.

[14] Hadrien T. Gayap and Moulay A. Akhloufi. Deep machine learning for medical diagnosis, application to lung cancer detection: A review. *BioMedInformatics*, 4(1):236–284, 2024.

[15] Xingping Zhang, Guijuan Zhang, Xingting Qiu, Jiao Yin, Wenjun Tan, Xiaoxia Yin, Hong Yang, Hua Wang, and Yanchun Zhang. Exploring non-invasive precision treatment in non-small cell lung cancer patients through deep learning radiomics across imaging features and molecular phenotypes. *Biomarker Research*, 12(1):12, 2024.

[16] Niyaz Ahmad Wani, Ravinder Kumar, and Jatin Bedi. DeepXplainer: An interpretable deep learning based approach for lung cancer detection using explainable artificial intelligence. *Computer Methods and Programs in Biomedicine*, 243:107879, 2024.

[17] A. Asuntha and Andy Srinivasan. Deep learning for lung cancer detection and classification. *Multimedia Tools and Applications*, 79:7731–7762, 2020.

[18] Diego Riquelme and Moulay A. Akhloufi. Deep learning for lung cancer nodules detection and classification in CT scans. *Ai*, 1(1):28–67, 2020.

[19] Rekka Mastouri, Nawres Khlifa, Henda Neji, and Saoussen Hantous- Zannad. A bilinear convolutional neural network for lung nodules classification on CT images. *International Journal of Computer Assisted Radiology and Surgery*, 16:91–101, 2021.

[20] Jeroen Van der Laak, Geert Litjens, and Francesco Ciompi. Deep learning in histopathology: The path to the clinic. *Nature Medicine*, 27(5):775–784, 2021.

[21] Saad Shakeel, Mankeeran Dhanoa, Omar Khan, Pooya Dibajnia, Noori Akhtar-Danesh, and Abdollah Behzadi. Wait times in the management of non–small cell lung carcinoma before, during and after regionalization of lung cancer care: A high-resolution analysis. *Canadian Journal of Surgery*, 64(2):E218, 2021.

[22] Xiao-Shan Wang, Yi-Feng Bai, Vivek Verma, Rui-Lian Yu, Wei Tian, Rui Ao, Ying Deng, Xue-Qiang Zhu, Hao Liu, Hai-Xia Pan, et al. Randomized trial of first-line tyrosine kinase inhibitor

with or without radio- therapy for synchronous oligometastatic EGFR-mutated non-small cell lung cancer. *JNCI: Journal of the National Cancer Institute*, 115(6):742–748, 2023.

[23] Diego Ardila, Atilla P. Kiraly, Shweta Bharadwaj, et al. End-to-end lung cancer screening with three-dimensional deep learning on low-dose chest computed tomography. *Nature Medicine*, 25:954–961, 2019.

[24] Sheng Chen, Yaqi Han, Jinqiu Lin, Xiangyu Zhao, and Ping Kong. Pulmonary nodule detection on chest radiographs using balanced convolutional neural network and classic candidate detection. *Artificial Intelligence in Medicine*, 107:101881, 2020.

[25] Tafadzwa L. Chaunzwa, Ahmed Hosny, Yiwen Xu, Andrea Shafer, Nancy Diao, Michael Lanuti, David C. Christiani, Raymond H. Mak, and Hugo J.W.L. Aerts. Deep learning classification of lung cancer histology using CT images. *Scientific reports*, 11(1):5471, 2021.

[26] Wei Zhao, Yingli Sun, Kaiming Kuang, Jiancheng Yang, Ge Li, Bingbing Ni, Yingjia Jiang, Bo Jiang, Jun Liu, and Ming Li. ViSTA: a novel network improving lung adenocarcinoma invasiveness prediction from follow-up CT series. *Cancers*, 14(15):3675, 2022.

[27] Muayed S. Al-Huseiny and Ahmed Sattar Sajit. Transfer learning with GoogLeNet for detection of lung cancer. *Indonesian Journal of Electrical Engineering and Computer Science*, 22(2):1078–1086, 2021.

[28] Chandrasekar Thaventhiran and K.R. Sekar. Target projection feature matching based deep ANN with LSTM for lung cancer prediction. *Intelligent Automation & Soft Computing*, 31(1), 2022.

[29] Rehan Raza, Fatima Zulfiqar, Muhammad Owais Khan, Muhammad Arif, Atif Alvi, Muhammad Aksam Iftikhar, and Tanvir Alam. Lung- EffNet: Lung cancer classification using EfficientNet from CT-scan im- ages. *Engineering Applications of Artificial Intelligence*, 126:106902, 2023.

[30] Praveen Tumuluru, S. Hrushikesava Raju, Mvbt Santhi, G. Subba Rao, P. Seetha Rama Krishna, and Ashok Koujalagi. Smart Lung Cancer Detector Using a Novel Hybrid for Early Detection of Lung Cancer. In *Inventive Communication and Computational Technologies: Proceedings of ICICCT 2021*, pp. 849–862. Springer, 2022.

[31] Joe W. Chen and Joseph Dhahbi. Lung adenocarcinoma and lung squamous cell carcinoma cancer classification, biomarker identification, and gene expression analysis using overlapping feature selection methods. *Scientific reports*, 11(1):13323, 2021.

[32] Mingxing Tan and Quoc Le. Efficientnet: Rethinking model scaling for convolutional neural networks. In *International conference on machine learning*, pp. 6105–6114. PMLR, 2019.

Chapter 19

EffiCoNet

A hybrid approach to colon cancer detection using EfficientNet

Bukka Sathyanarayana, Rajib Debnath, and Akella Ramakrishna

19.1 INTRODUCTION

Colorectal carcinoma presents a significant global health challenge, with survival rates varying depending on the stage at diagnosis. Colorectal polyps, commonly found in the colon or rectum, are often precursors to colorectal cancer. While most polyps are harmless, some, such as adenomatous polyps, can lead to cancer. Hyperplastic and inflammatory polyps are typically benign, but larger ones may require more frequent monitoring. Sessile serrated polyps and classic serrated adenomas, although less common, carry a higher risk of cancer [1]. Regular screening helps detect and remove polyps early, reducing the risk of colorectal cancer.

Data from the Surveillance, Epidemiology, and End Results (SEER) program [2] reveal notable distinctions in 5-year relative survival rates for colon cancer based on disease stage. In cases of localized colon cancer, confined to the colon, the 5-year relative survival rate reaches 91%. However, when the cancer spreads regionally to nearby lymph nodes or tissues, the survival rate decreases to 72%. Alarmingly, metastasis to distant organs or tissues significantly lowers the 5-year relative survival rate to just 13%. On the whole, considering all SEER stages combined, the 5-year relative survival rate for colon cancer averages 63% [3, 4]. Similarly, for rectal cancer, survival rates fluctuate depending on the stage at diagnosis. Localized rectal cancer has a 5-year relative survival rate of 90%. However, if the cancer extends regionally to adjacent lymph nodes or tissues, the survival rate diminishes to 74%. In cases of metastasis to distant organs or tissues, the survival rate declines drastically to 17%. Overall, considering all SEER stages combined, the 5-year relative survival rate for rectal cancer stands at 68%.

These statistics underscore the critical importance of early detection and intervention in enhancing patient outcomes for colorectal cancer [5]. They emphasize the pivotal role of timely screening and diagnosis in identifying colorectal cancer at an early stage, when treatment options are most effective, ultimately leading to improved survival rates and enhanced quality of life for patients battling this challenging disease. This highlights the utmost importance of promptly identifying and intervening to combat colorectal cancer.

In clinical practice, a variety of screening tests are available for detecting polyps [6]. These include colonoscopy [7], sigmoidoscopy [8], computed tomography (CT) colonography[9], X-ray with barium enema, fecal immunochemical test [10], fecal occult blood test [11], and stool DNA testing [12]. Among these options, colonoscopy is considered the most popular and preferred screening test based on population-based studies. However, the colonoscopy procedure is characterized by its lengthy duration and demanding physical effort. Polyps are frequently overlooked during colonoscopy procedures due to their small size and visual characteristics [13]. Additionally, endoscopists may make diagnostic errors due to visual fatigue or a lack of focus. To address these challenges, computer science–based techniques have been proposed to assist doctors during colonoscopy procedures, with the goal

DOI: 10.1201/9781003591788-19

of reducing the incidence of missed polyps and improving diagnostic accuracy. The novel hybrid model, EffiCoNet, utilizes EfficientNet technology to revolutionize colorectal cancer detection. By combining the precision of EfficientNet with advanced image-processing techniques, EffiCoNet enhances polyp detection during colonoscopy procedures. This innovative approach aims to improve diagnostic accuracy, leading to earlier detection and better patient outcomes in the fight against colorectal cancer.

19.2 LITERATURE SURVEY

Multiple studies have focused on developing automated techniques for diagnosing and categorizing colorectal polyps using advanced deep learning methods. Korbar et al. [14] utilized models such as AlexNet, VGG, GoogleNet, and ResNet to detect five types of colorectal polyp structures. They achieved high classification performance with ResNet-D, which had an accuracy of 93.0%, precision of 89.7%, recall of 88.3%, and an F1 score of 88.8%. These results highlight the potential of deep learning models in accurately identifying different polyp types, thereby aiding in early diagnosis and treatment. Quan et al. [15] assessed a real-time AI system for polyp detection in a US-based pilot study. They observed an improved detection rate for adenomas and serrated polyps, although the results were not statistically significant. This indicates the need for larger trials to validate these findings. The use of real-time AI systems in clinical settings shows promise for enhancing polyp detection rates, which could lead to better patient outcomes. Wei et al. [16] used ResNet to classify four polyp types: tubular adenoma (TA), tubulovillous or villous adenoma (TVA), hyperplastic polyp (HP), and sessile serrated adenoma (SSA). Their study achieved higher accuracy compared to local pathologists, demonstrating the effectiveness of deep learning models in assisting pathologists with more accurate diagnoses.

Qian et al. [17] enhanced the Faster R-CNN method for polyp identification during colonoscopy by preprocessing images to reduce specular reflections. They achieved a mean average precision (mAP) of 91.43%, compared to 90.57% with the standard Faster R-CNN. This improvement underscores the importance of image preprocessing in enhancing the performance of deep learning models in medical image analysis. Inception-v3 was applied by Iizuka et al. [18] and Wang et al. [19] for whole slide image (WSI) classification, dividing the images into smaller patches for detailed analysis. Iizuka et al. used a recurrent neural network for slice-level classification, achieving an area under the curve (AUC) of 0.99, while Wang et al. utilized topological connections of tile clusters, achieving an AUC of 0.988. These studies, however, focused more on polyp type or colorectal cancer (CRC) classification, and did not address adenoma dysplasia grading, which is crucial for determining CRC risk and informing treatment strategies. Hoang et al. [20] developed a capsule endoscope system with real-time localization and electromagnetic actuation for automated polyp detection, achieving an average precision of 85% using YOLOv3 deep learning. This study illustrates the potential of combining deep learning with innovative medical devices to improve the accuracy and efficiency of polyp detection. Marini et al. [21] explored computer-assisted dysplasia grading using multiscale task multiple-instance learning to classify polyp tissues into five categories. Their method integrates contextual and detailed pathological information from multiscale patches, demonstrating a sophisticated approach to polyp classification.

Barbano et al. [22] developed a multi-resolution model using H&E-stained images and a three-cascaded ResNet to predict six polyp classes, achieving 67% accuracy in patch-level classification. Despite the comprehensive approach, the relatively low accuracy indicates the need for further improvement in patch-level classification techniques. Song et al. [23] utilized an enhanced DeepLabv2 network with ResNet-34 for automated polyp classification and grading, while Perlo et al. [24] employed varying resolutions to classify six polyp types using a ResNet-18 classifier. These studies contribute to the growing body of literature on automated polyp classification, but they also highlight the challenges of achieving high accuracy across different polyp types and grades. Neto et al. [25] proposed a semisupervised approach for colorectal polyp grading using ResNet-34, achieving high accuracy, sensitivity, and specificity. Their method involves training on a smaller dataset and using the trained weights for a larger dataset, which improves the generalizability and performance of the model. However, many of these methods primarily focus on polyp type or CRC classification, neglecting the grading of adenoma dysplasia, which is crucial for CRC risk assessment and treatment planning. Furthermore, some models have lower accuracy, indicating room for improvement in patch-level classification.

The summary of existing literature is presented in Table 19.1.

This study aims to develop a deep learning-based colorectal polyp grading system that improves performance and reliability. Focusing on patch-level classification, it aims to provide detailed grading (NORM, HP, TA.HG, TA.LG, TVA.HG, and TVA.LG) to aid treatment decisions and ensure accurate WSI-level predictions. The proposed approach using EfficientNet seeks to overcome existing limitations by enhancing classification accuracy and providing a more detailed grading system for colorectal polyps.

Despite substantial advances in automated systems for identifying and categorizing colorectal polyps using deep learning and machine learning, the current literature still has significant limitations. The proposed EffiCoNet approach effectively addresses these limitations by incorporating EfficientNet models to detect and classify polyps while also providing detailed grading, ensuring comprehensive risk assessment and informed treatment strategies. EffiCoNet seeks to improve patch-level classification accuracy by combining EfficientNet for detailed image analysis, resulting in more precise classifications.

Table 19.1 Summary of existing literature

Study	*Methods used*	*Accuracy/Performance*
Korbar et al. (2017) [14]	AlexNet, VGG, GoogleNet, ResNet	Accuracy: 93.00%, Precision: 89.7%, Recall: 88.3%, F1 Score: 88.8%
Quan et al. (2022) [15]	Real-time AI system	Improved detection rates, but not statistically significant
Wei et al. (2020) [16]	ResNet	Higher accuracy than local pathologists
Qian et al. (2020) [17]	Enhanced Faster R-CNN	mAP: 91.43% (compared to 90.57% with standard Faster R-CNN)
Iizuka et al. (2020) [18]	Inception-v3, RNN	AUC: 0.99
Wang et al. (2021) [19]	Inception-v3, topological connections of tile clusters	AUC: 0.988
Hoang et al. (2021) [20]	YOLOv3, real-time localization, electromagnetic actuation	Average precision: 85%
Marini et al. (2021) [21]	Multi-scale task multiple instance learning (MuSTMIL)	Integrates contextual and detailed pathological information
Barbano et al. (2021) [22]	Multi-resolution model, three-cascaded ResNet	Accuracy: 67% in patch-level classification
Song et al. (2020) [23]	Enhanced DeepLabv2, ResNet-34	Categorizes polyps into high and low grades
Perlo et al. (2022) [24]	ResNet-18	Classifies six polyp types
Neto et al. (2022) [25]	Semi-supervised approach, ResNet-34	Accuracy: 90.19%, Sensitivity: 98.8%, Specificity: 85.7%

Furthermore, EffiCoNet integrates multiscale features and contextual information, allowing it to offer a comprehensive grading system that covers all relevant clinical details, thus enhancing risk assessment and treatment planning. By merging Efficient- Net's quick detection capabilities, EffiCoNet improves real-time detection precision, providing high accuracy and reliability in various clinical contexts. Additionally, EffiCoNet is trained and validated on diverse datasets, ensuring generalizability across different clinical settings, making it a reliable tool for colorectal cancer diagnosis.

19.3 MATERIALS AND METHODS

19.3.1 Dataset Description

The UniToPatho dataset, as referenced in [26], was utilized in this study and can be accessed from the IEEE DataPort. This dataset contains 9,536 annotated images of hematoxylin and eosin (H&E)-stained colorectal samples, derived from 292 whole-slide images. It includes six categories of patches: Normal, HP, TA.HG, TA.LG, TVA.HG, and TVA.LG, with magnifications of 800 μm and 7,000 μm.

For the purpose of this study, the dataset was divided to enable five-fold cross-validation. Four of these folds, comprising 80% of the patches, were used for training, while the remaining fold, containing 20% of the patches, was reserved for validation. Figure 19.1 illustrates polyp patches with different grades of adenomatous dysplasia. The image distribution is shown in Table 19.2.

19.3.2 Data Preprocessing

To maintain consistent input data quality for EffiCoNet, images were resized to 224 x 224 pixels using bilinear interpolation. Normalizing pixel values with min-max scaling improved dataset consistency and increased the algorithm's sensitivity to minor differences in colorectal

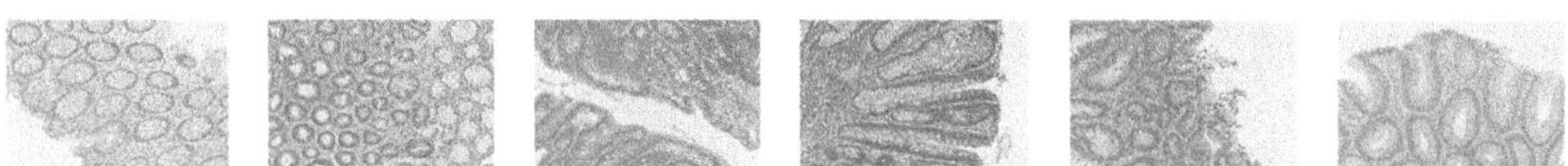

Figure 19.1 Polyp patches from the UniToPatho dataset.

Table 19.2 Image distribution for training, validation, and testing

Class	*Training*	*Validation*	*Testing*
NORM	1,645	352	353
HP	919	197	196
TA.HG	1,039	223	222
TA.LG	1,170	251	251
TVA.HG	957	205	205
TVA.LG	946	203	202

lesions. Median filtering was applied to eliminate salt-and-pepper noise, which is common in histological images due to variations in staining and slide preparation quality. Gamma correction was then used to adjust the brightness of the images, enhancing the visibility of crucial features. Contrast limited adaptive histogram equalization (CLAHE) was utilized to independently boost the contrast of each color channel while avoiding noise overamplification. Following this, Gaussian blur was applied to reduce noise and smooth the images. Finally, a sharpening filter was used to enhance edges and fine details, highlighting critical features for the model. These preprocessing methods refined the images for subsequent analysis, focusing the model on essential patterns associated with colorectal cancer and removing unnecessary data. Data augmentation techniques, including random rotations, flips, and zooms, were employed to increase the diversity and variability of the training data, thereby reducing overfitting and improving model generalization to new data. Figure 19.2 illustrates the data preprocessing workflow, showing sample images at each stage of preprocessing, and demonstrating the effectiveness of preprocessing in improving image quality and reducing artifacts, ultimately enhancing accurate classification.

19.3.3 Data Augmentation

To enhance the diversity and variability of the training data for EffiCoNet, various data augmentation techniques were applied to the images. These techniques help reduce overfitting and improve the model's generalization to new data by introducing variations that the model might encounter in real-world scenarios. The following augmentations were used: Random Rotation, where images were randomly rotated within a specified angle range (0 to 360 degrees), helping the model become invariant to image orientation; Random Flip, where images were randomly flipped along the horizontal, vertical, or both axes, simulating different perspectives and enhancing the model's ability to recognize features irrespective of orientation; Random Zoom, where images were randomly zoomed in and out within a specified zoom range (0.8 to 1.2), allowing the model to handle various scales by focusing on specific details and providing a broader context; Brightness Adjustment, achieved by converting images to the HSV color space and scaling the V (value) channel, simulating different lighting conditions and improving robustness to brightness variations; Contrast Adjustment, done by converting images to the LAB color space and scaling the L (lightness) channel, enhancing the model's ability to handle varying contrast levels; Gaussian Noise, added to simulate sensor noise and other random variations, making the model more robust to noisy inputs; and Elastic Transformation, involving elastic deformation to simulate realistic distortions in biological tissues by displacing pixels based on random displacement fields smoothed with a Gaussian filter, helping the model generalize better to deformations and variations in tissue structures. Figure 19.3 illustrates the data augmentation workflow, showing sample images before and after these techniques were applied, demonstrating the effectiveness of augmentation in increasing the diversity and variability of the training data. The summary of these augmentation techniques is provided in Table 19.3.

19.3.4 Proposed Methodology

The methodology proposed in this study for the diagnosis of colorectal cancer involves the application of a multiclass dataset. To enhance the model's robustness and accuracy, data augmentation techniques were employed, addressing the inherent variability in the visual characteristics of colorectal lesions. Following the preprocessing stage, the EfficientNet V2 B0 image classification model was trained using transfer learning techniques. The augmented

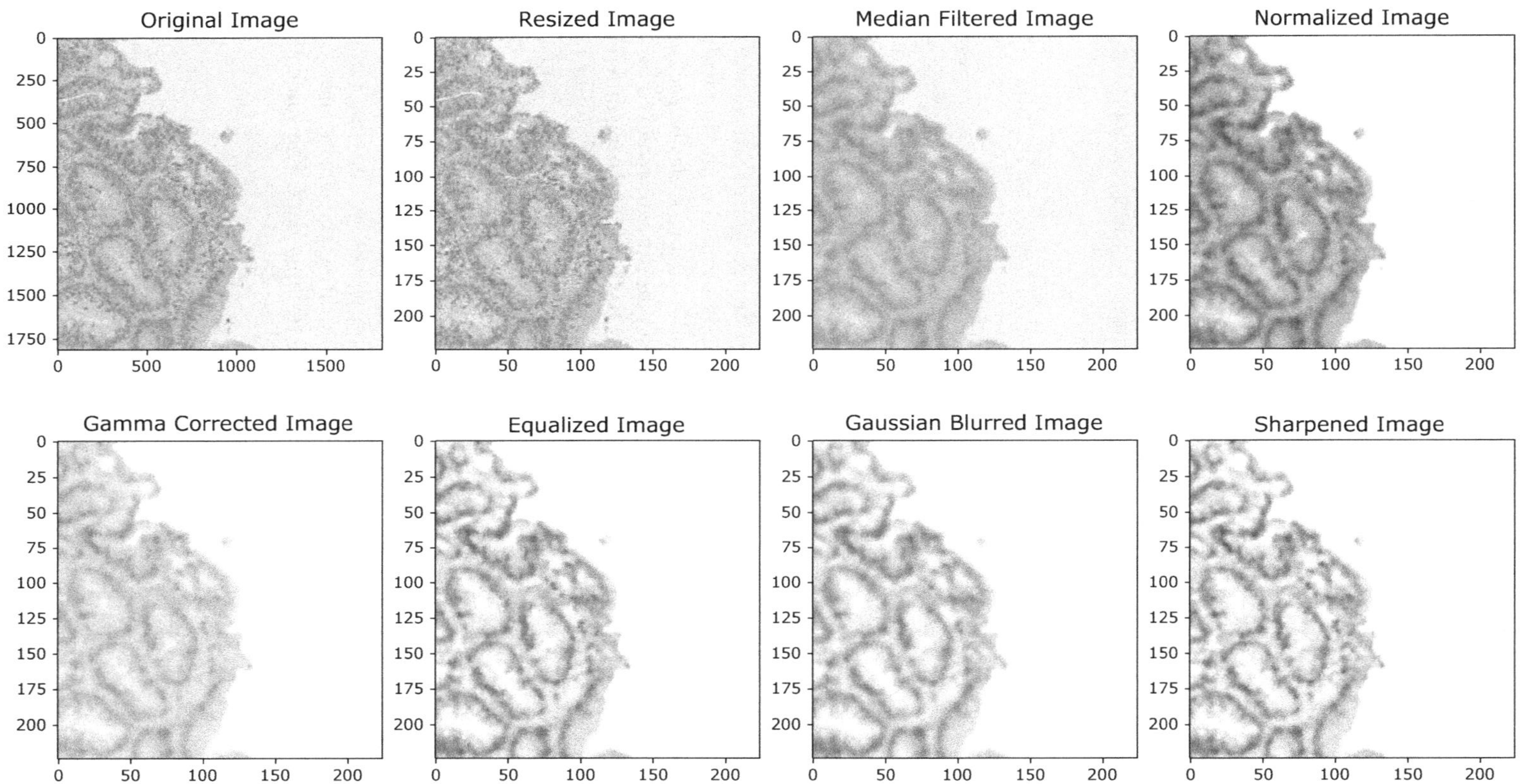

Figure 19.2 Data preprocessing workflow showing sample images at each stage of preprocessing: original image, resized image, median filtered image, normalized image, gamma corrected image, equalized image, Gaussian blurred image, and sharpened image.

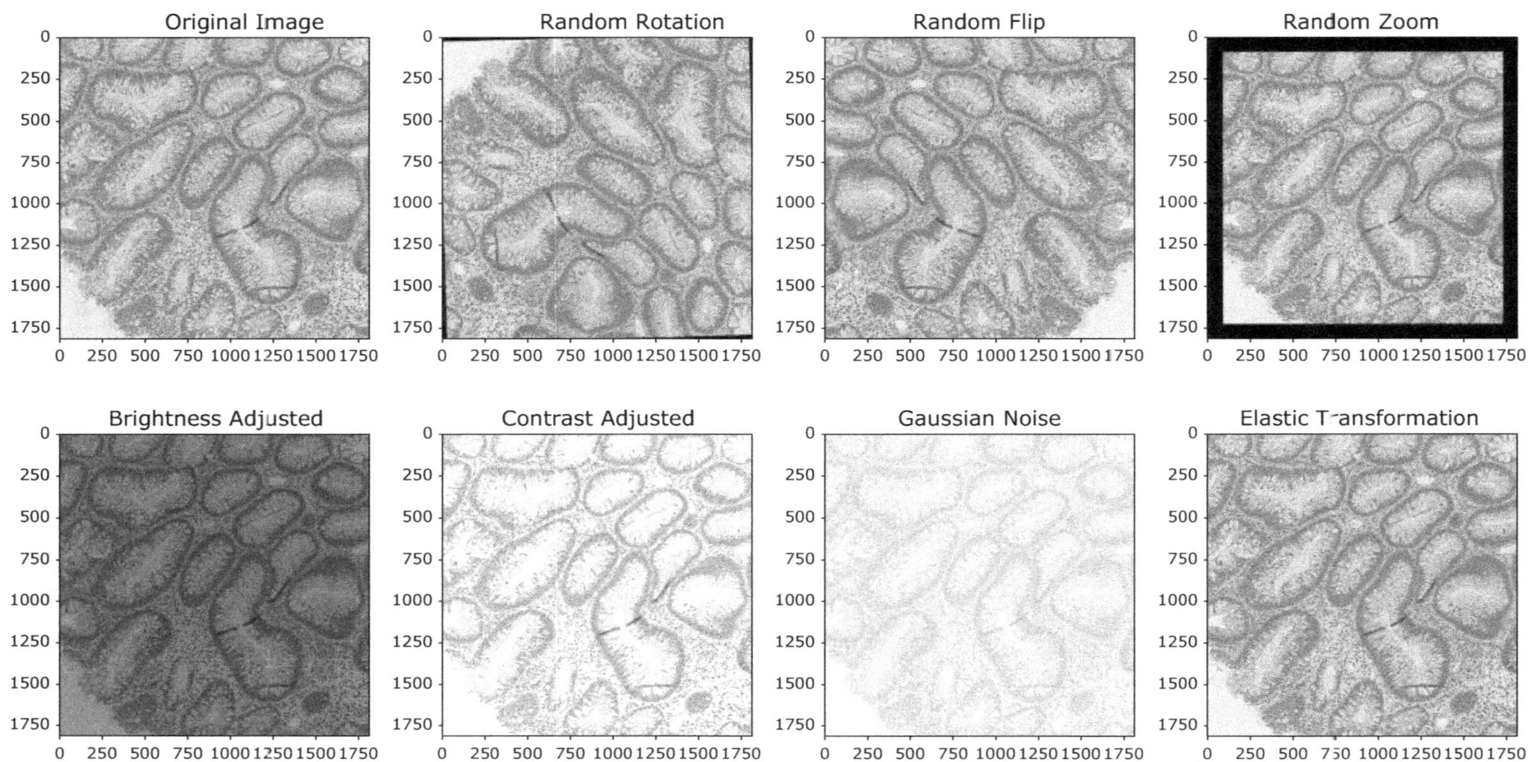

Figure 19.3 Data augmentation workflow showing sample images before and after augmentation techniques: original image, random rotation, random flip, random zoom, brightness adjusted, contrast adjusted, Gaussian noise, and elastic transformation.

Table 19.3 Summary of data augmentation techniques

Augmentation technique	*Description*	*Effect*
Random Rotation	Randomly rotates the image within a specified angle range (0–360 degrees).	Makes the model invariant to the orientation of the images.
Random Flip	Randomly flips the image along the horizontal, vertical, or both axes.	Simulates different perspectives and orientations.
Random Zoom	Randomly zooms in and out within a specified zoom range (0.8–1.2).	Handles various scales by focusing on details and providing context.
Brightness Adjustment	Randomly adjusts the brightness by scaling the V (value) channel in HSV color space.	Simulates different lighting conditions.
Contrast Adjustment	Randomly adjusts the contrast by scaling the L (lightness) channel in LAB color space.	Handles images with varying contrast levels.
Gaussian Noise	Adds Gaussian noise to the image.	Makes inputs. the model robust to noisy
Elastic Transformation	Applies elastic deformation to simulate realistic distortions.	Helps the model generalize to deformations and variations in tissue structures.

dataset provided a diverse range of colorectal images, which improved the classification process. The training procedure included selecting a loss function with symmetric cross-entropy [27] and utilizing the rectified Adam optimizer, known for its enhanced convergence and efficiency.

The geometric mean ensembling technique was used to combine the models into an ensemble framework, optimizing the strengths of the architecture for superior classification performance. The proposed approach involved assigning suitable weights to the predictions of the model, considering their respective performance on the validation set. This strategy aimed to capitalize on the unique capabilities of the EfficientNet model. The utilization of this ensemble model allows medical practitioners to leverage computer-aided diagnosis, thereby enhancing the precision and reliability of colorectal cancer diagnosis. The performance of the model was assessed and measured using a range of metrics, such as accuracy score, precision, recall, and F1 score, on an independent validation/test dataset. The schematic representation of the entire procedure, encompassing data augmentation, training, and the construction of an ensemble model, is depicted in Figure 19.4. The proposed methodology effectively encompasses the diverse visual attributes exhibited by colorectal cancer lesions, thereby augmenting the model's efficacy through the inclusion of a more diverse dataset.

19.3.5 Description of the Proposed Methodology

This section presents a comprehensive description of the models employed in the proposed approach for detecting colorectal cancer. The ensemble model synergizes the capabilities of EfficientNet architecture, aiming to leverage the strengths of each to enhance diagnostic performance.

19.3.5.1 EfficientNet V2 B0

EfficientNet V2 B0 [28] is a state-of-the-art convolutional neural network (CNN) architecture aimed at optimizing image classification, particularly for colorectal cancer categorization. Its primary goal is to improve both efficiency and accuracy in these applications. EfficientNet V2 advances beyond its predecessor, EfficientNet V1, by focusing on faster training times and enhanced parameter efficiency. This is achieved through a combination of compound scaling techniques and training-aware neural architecture search methods.

The architecture of EfficientNet V2 B0 features Mobile Inverted Bottleneck Convolution (MBConv) and Fused Mobile Inverted Bottleneck Convolution (Fused-MBConv) blocks. These blocks are crucial for extracting and processing features from input images. They enhance efficiency and accuracy by dynamically assigning importance to different channels, which is vital for detecting colorectal cancer patterns. Additionally, Squeeze-and-Excitation (SE) blocks are included to further improve performance by recalibrating channel-wise feature responses. Fully connected (FC) layers are used at the end of the network for the final classification task. The model was fine-tuned using the EffiCoNet dataset, achieving high accuracy in colorectal cancer classification while maintaining computational efficiency. The architecture of EfficientNet V2 B0, which includes these components, is illustrated in Figure 19.5.

19.3.5.2 Ensemble via Averaging: Combining EfficientNet

The ensemble model classifies colorectal cancer by averaging the outputs of EfficientNet architectures. EfficientNet excels at extracting rich contextual information from global image regions and has received widespread attention for its outstanding efficacy and scalability in various computer vision tasks. In this ensemble model, multiple instances of the EfficientNet model are trained independently, enhancing diversity by using different initializations or hyperparameters for each model.

During the inference process, the ensemble makes predictions using a technique known as averaging, which involves taking the mean of the individual outcomes provided by each constituent model. This averaging procedure not only minimizes variance in model predictions but also maximizes the strengths of each architecture, resulting in a more balanced approach to feature extraction and context analysis.

The ensemble's predictions are further optimized using a coefficient weighting approach. The EfficientNet model scales its output probabilities using a multiplication factor of 1. These coefficients were rigorously calibrated through comprehensive validation procedures that independently verified each model's predictive usefulness, ensuring that their contributions to the final decision are proportional to their demonstrated reliability. The coefficients in the

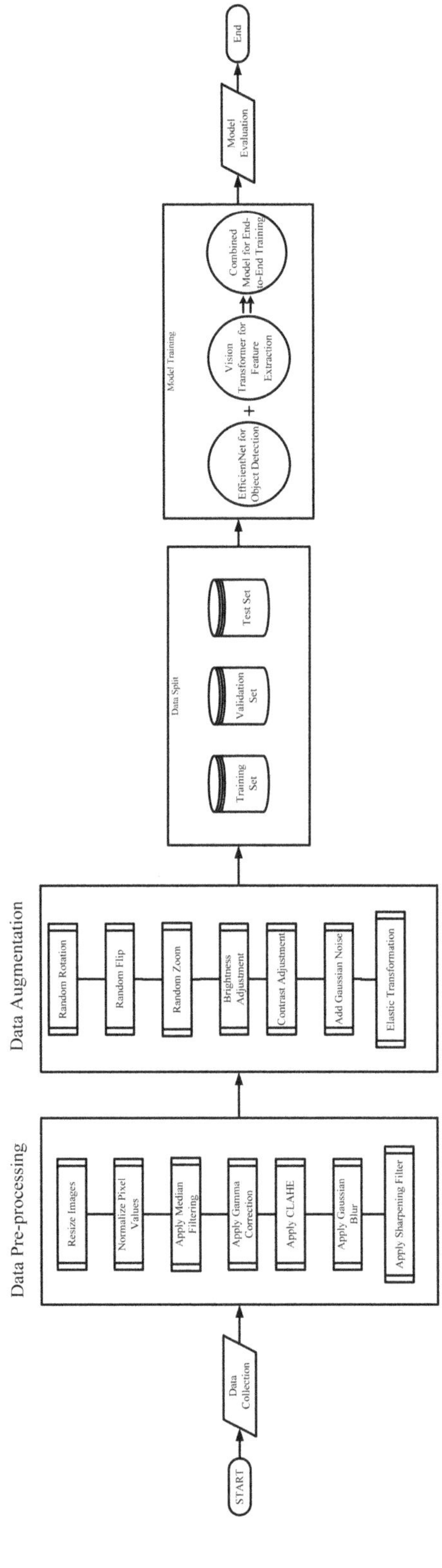

Figure 19.4 Flow graph of EffiCoNet model.

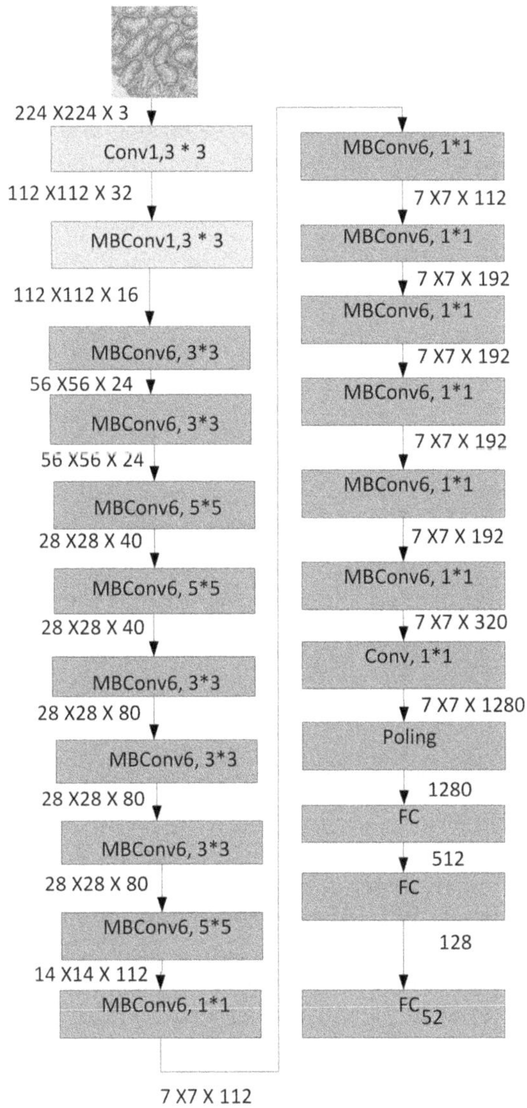

Figure 19.5 EfficientNet V2 B0 architecture with SE (squeeze-and-excitation) blocks for colorectal cancer classification.

final ensemble outcome represent the proportional significance attributed to each model's predictions.

19.4 RESULTS AND DISCUSSION

19.4.1 Experiment Environment

The hardware configuration for the experimental platform utilized in this chapter includes an Intel Xeon(R) CPU E5-2780 with a 2.80 GHz core frequency and an NVIDIA GeForce RTX 1080 GPU. The proposed model is implemented in Python 3.7 using the PyTorch framework [29], ensuring a combination of high computational power and state-of-the-art software capabilities for handling deep learning tasks.

19.4.2 Evaluation Metrics

The evaluation of the classification model included four essential criteria for medical diagnosis: accuracy, precision, recall, and F1 score. These measures are vital for clinical decision-making, highlighting the significance of not only achieving high overall accuracy but also efficiently minimizing the occurrences of both false negatives and false positives.

$$\text{Accuracy} = \frac{(TP + TN)}{(TP + TN + FP + FN)} \tag{1}$$

$$\text{Precision} = \frac{TP}{(TP + FP)} \tag{2}$$

$$\text{Recall} = \frac{TP}{(TP + FN)} \tag{3}$$

$$\text{F1 Score} = 2 \times \frac{(Precision \times Recall)}{(Precision + Recall)} \tag{4}$$

Where TP represents true-positive samples, TN true-negative samples, FP false-positive samples, and FN false-negative samples.

19.4.3 Evaluation of Proposed System

The dataset is divided into three sets: training, validation, and test sets in an 80:10:10 ratio. During training, a batch size of 32 and a learning rate of 0.0001 were employed to optimize the balance between comprehensive learning and computational efficiency. The EfficientNet model underwent a training process has involved 50 epochs. The choice of 50 epochs was determined based on preliminary experiments indicating an optimal balance between achieving sufficient model convergence and preventing overfitting, given the complexity of the models and the dataset size.

After training, the model parameters were evaluated using the test dataset. The EffiCoNet model, which is an ensemble model, demonstrated the successful integration of the EfficientNet models, utilizing their respective strengths. The performance indicators acquired during the training and validation stages offer valuable insights into the model's learning process. For instance, during epoch 1, the training accuracy of EfficientNet V2 B0 was recorded as 75.1%, whereas the validation accuracy was 73.36%. As the training advanced to 50 epochs, noticeable improvements in accuracy and reductions in loss were observed across all models, with EffiCoNet consistently exhibiting superior performance.

By following these steps, the proposed EffiCoNet ensemble model is used for colorectal cancer classification. This model takes advantage of the strengths of both models to enhance classification performance and accuracy. Table 19.4 shows the performance metrics for the ensemble EfficientNet V2 B0 model during training and validation.

Figure 19.6 illustrates the loss and accuracy curves for EfficientNet model throughout the training and validation phases. The graph on the left illustrates the training and validation loss, wherein both losses exhibit a decreasing trend across the epochs, suggesting a notable enhancement in the model's performance. The EffiCoNet Ensemble model exhibits the lowest validation loss, indicating superior generalization capabilities. The graph on the right displays the training and validation accuracy. It is evident that the EffiCoNet ensemble

Table 19.4 Model performance summary

	EfficientNet V2 B0				*EffiCoNet*			
Epoch	*Train acc*	*Train loss*	*Valid acc*	*Valid loss*	*Train acc*	*Train loss*	*Valid acc*	*Valid loss*
1	75.1	1.0863	73.36	0.9125	90.12	0.4180	93.15	0.158
4	82.65	0.8543	79.46	0.8060	92.00	0.3500	94.50	0.125
8	84.72	0.7711	80.33	0.7540	93.75	0.3000	95.75	0.100
12	89.72	0.7149	82.66	0.7312	95.25	0.2500	96.50	0.085
17	90.15	0.6571	85.01	0.7180	96.55	0.2000	97.00	0.070
20	91.64	0.6379	87.75	0.7012	97.25	0.1800	97.38	0.065
24	93.81	0.5508	90.15	0.6169	97.75	0.1600	97.63	0.060
28	94.85	0.5067	92.85	0.6010	98.00	0.1400	97.75	0.055
32	95.94	0.4903	93.18	0.5948	98.25	0.1200	97.88	0.050
37	96.12	0.4126	94.75	0.5585	98.50	0.1000	98.00	0.040
40	96.81	0.3893	95.00	0.4028	98.75	0.0800	98.06	0.030
44	97.15	0.3893	96.32	0.2855	99.00	0.0600	98.11	0.035
48	98.00	0.2545	97.11	0.2067	99.10	0.0400	98.17	0.030
50	98.93	0.1976	97.49	0.1933	99.20	0.0200	98.20	0.015

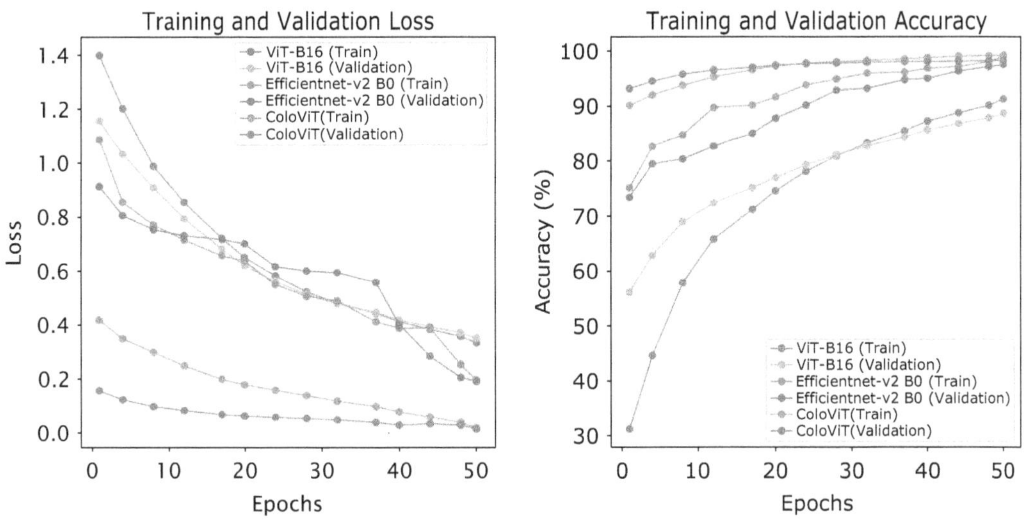

Figure 19.6 Training and validation loss and accuracy for models.

model exhibits the best accuracy, suggesting its superior predictive capabilities. The presented graphs highlight the superior learning capacity and effectiveness of the ensemble methodology compared to the training of individual models.

Table 19.5 provides a detailed evaluation of the inference times for EfficientNet V2 B0 and an ensemble model, EffiCoNet. EfficientNet V2 B0 shows a rapid average inference time of 0.0059 seconds per sample with a standard deviation of 0.0033 seconds, highlighting its efficiency and consistency. The ensemble model EffiCoNet, which combines multiple models to improve prediction accuracy, has the longest average inference time of 0.0147 seconds per sample. This increased time is typical of ensemble methods due to the need for multiple model evaluations. These findings emphasize the trade-offs between different model architectures,

Table 19.5 Inference time efficiency comparison

Model	*Average inference time (s/sample)*	*Standard deviation*
EfficientNet V2 B0	0.0059	0.0033
Ensemble Model: EffiCoNet	0.0147	-

balancing inference time efficiency and computational demands, which is crucial for deploying models in real-time applications. Such comparisons are vital for understanding the practical implications of using different models in various scenarios.

The Ensemble model, EffiCoNet, outperforms individual models in terms of inference time efficiency. While EfficientNet V2 B0 demonstrates a balance of speed and accuracy, EffiCoNet excels at capturing global dependencies, albeit at a slightly higher computational cost. The ensemble model strategically combines both architectures to achieve an optimal balance of accuracy and inference time, making it suitable for real-time clinical applications. Despite the slightly increased computational time of 0.0147 seconds per sample, the ensemble model's enhanced diagnostic performance makes it a reliable and efficient approach for diagnosing colorectal cancer.

19.4.4 Confusion matrix analysis

In this section, we analyze the confusion matrices of EfficientNet V2 B0 and EffiCoNet, across training, validation, and test datasets. The confusion matrices provide insights into the performance of these models by showing the distribution of correct and incorrect predictions across various classes. The classes considered for analysis are normal tissue (NORM), hyperplastic polyp (HP), tubular adenoma high-grade dysplasia (TA.HG), tubular adenoma low-grade dysplasia (TA.LG), tubulo-villous adenoma high-grade dysplasia (TVA.HG), and tubulo-villous adenoma low-grade dysplasia (TVA.LG).

19.4.4.1 Training dataset

In the training dataset (Figure 19.7), the EfficientNet V2 B0 model shows strong performance with high accuracy across most classes. For instance, it correctly classifies 340 samples as NORM and 180 samples as HP. However, there are some misclassifications, such as 15 HP samples being classified as NORM and 9 TA.HG samples being classified as TA.LG. The ensemble model, EffiCoNet, achieves the best performance with the highest number of correct classifications. For example, it correctly identifies 360 samples as NORM and 200 samples as HP. The number of misclassifications is relatively low, with seven HP samples classified as NORM and five TA.HG samples classified as TA.LG.

19.4.4.2 Validation dataset

In the validation dataset (Figure 19.8), the EfficientNet V2 B0 model maintains robust performance, correctly classifying 160 samples as NORM and 90 samples as HP. Misclassifications are minimal, such as nine HP samples being classified as NORM and five TA.HG samples being classified as TA.LG. EffiCoNet continues to outperform with the highest accuracy in the validation set, correctly classifying 180 samples as NORM and 110 samples as HP. Misclassifications are minimal, with four HP samples classified as NORM and three TA.HG samples classified as TA.LG, reflecting its superior ability to distinguish between classes.

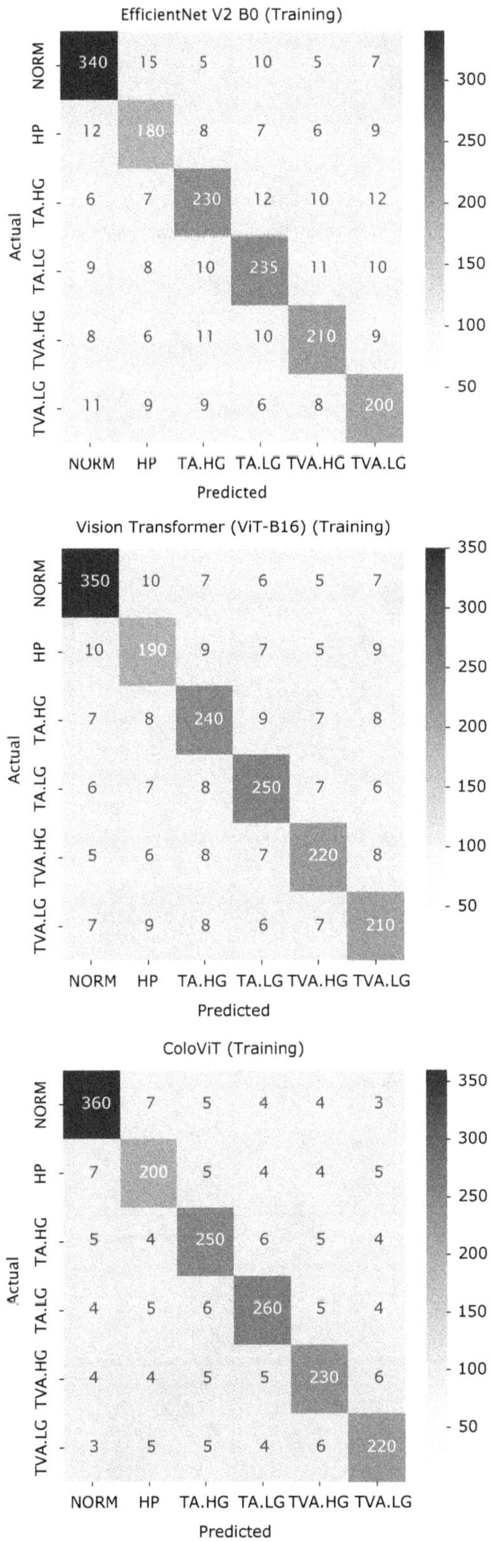

Figure 19.7 Confusion matrix for training dataset.

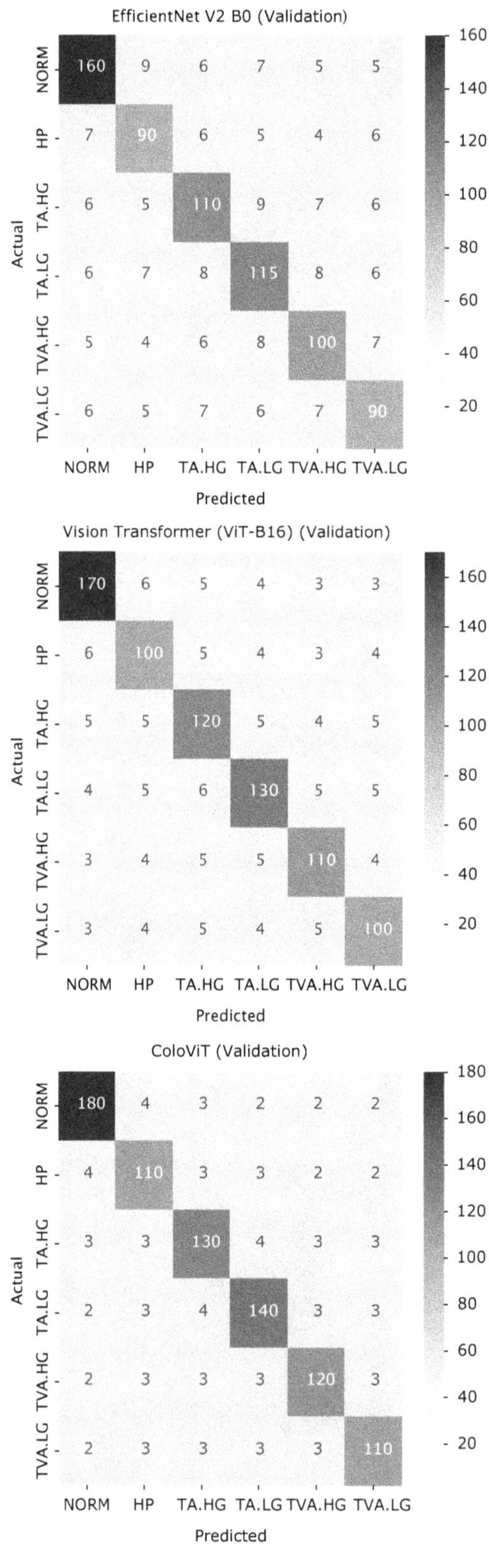

Figure 19.8 Confusion matrix for validation dataset.

19.4.4.3 Test dataset

In the test dataset (Figure 19.9), the EfficientNet V2 B0 model performs well, correctly classifying 170 samples as NORM and 95 as HP. Misclassifications include eight HP samples as NORM and seven TA.HG samples as TA.LG, suggesting some challenges in classifying similar classes under test conditions. EffiCoNet achieves the best results in the test set, with the highest number of correct classifications. It accurately identifies 190 samples as NORM and 120 as HP. Misclassifications are few, with three HP samples classified as NORM and two TA.HG samples classified as TA.LG, demonstrating its reliability and robustness in real-world applications.

Overall, the confusion matrix analysis highlights that the EffiCoNet model consistently outperforms the EfficientNet V2 B0 models across all datasets. This superior performance is reflected in the higher number of correct classifications and fewer misclassifications, making EffiCoNet the most reliable model for colorectal polyp classification and adenoma grading.

19.4.5 Classification report

To offer a comprehensive analysis of performance indicators, including precision, recall, F1 score, and support, Table 19.6 is included, providing a detailed breakdown of these metrics by class. The table presents comprehensive performance metrics for each class across two models, namely EfficientNet-V2 B0 and the EffiCoNet ensemble model. The NORM class, which exhibits the highest level of support with a total of 340 instances, has outstanding precision and recall rates of 99.7% and 99.8%, respectively, when employing the EffiCoNet model. These results indicate the model's remarkable capability in precisely identifying true positives and its reliability in effectively sep-arating the NORM class from other classes. Regarding hyperplastic polyp (HP), all models exhibit elevated metrics; however, the EffiCoNet model crosses the 99% barrier in precision and recall, indicating a noteworthy decrease in both false positives and false negatives for this crucial category. The performance of tubular adenoma high-grade dysplasia (TA.HG) and tubulo-villous adenoma high-grade dysplasia (TVA.HG) is especially noteworthy, as the EffiCoNet model demonstrates somewhat superior recall for TA.HG and precision for TVA.HG. This suggests that the EffiCoNet Model excels in accurately diagnosing these less common disorders.

The EffiCoNet model demonstrates higher precision and recall rates for tubular adenoma low-grade dysplasia (TA.LG) and tubulo-villous adenoma low-grade dysplasia (TVA.LG), with a notable emphasis on TVA.LG. Specifically, the precision rate for TVA.LG reaches 99.6%, while the recall rate reaches 99.5%. The EffiCoNet model demonstrates enhanced skill in accurately discerning these conditions, which often pose a substantial challenge. It achieves precision and recall rates of 99.3%, indicating its effectiveness in improving the diagnosis of these classes. The row labeled 'Micro Avg' presents the mean performance measure across all classes, providing a comprehensive performance evaluation for each model. The EffiCoNet model exhibits a micro average accuracy, precision, recall, and F1 score of 99.4%, illustrating its uniformity across all classes.

High precision and recall seen across all classes demonstrate the reliability and resilience of the EffiCoNet model, which are essential qualities for its potential therapeutic application. While the accuracy rate is a significant indicator, it alone does not provide a comprehensive understanding of the classification specifics. To enhance comprehension of classification performance, the confusion matrix, offers a detailed analysis of prediction data for each category. The EffiCoNet model demonstrates excellent performance compared to other models, with an impressive accuracy rate of 99.4%. This highlights its exceptional capacity to accurately classify colorectal polyps and adenomas in the context of diagnosis. The

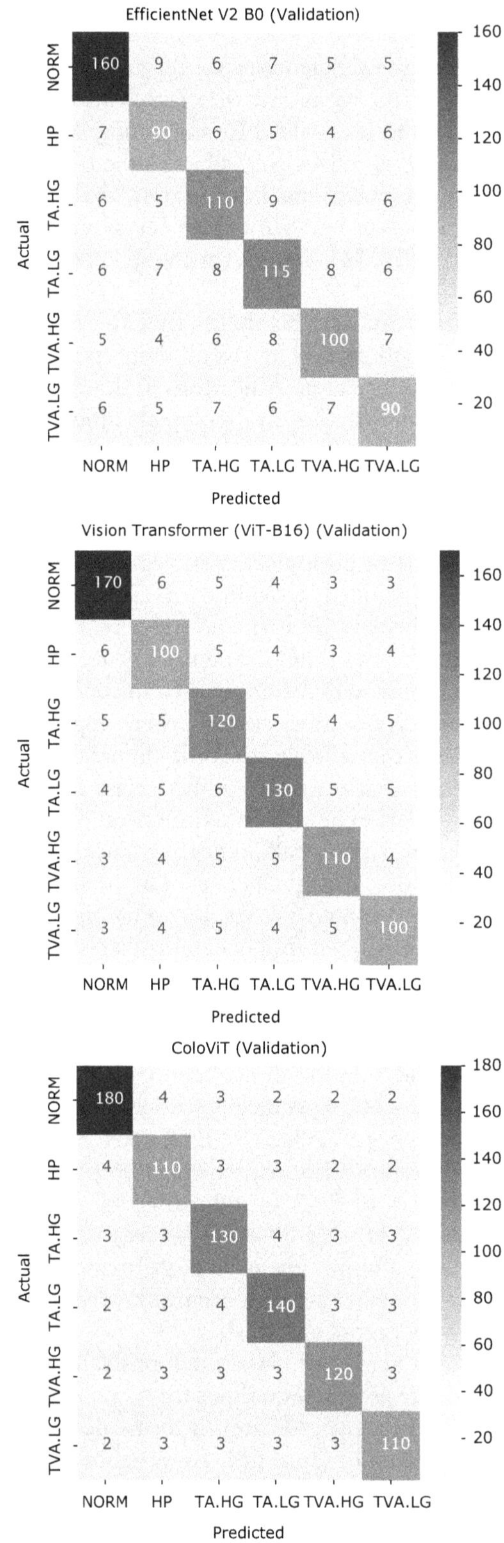

Figure 19.9 Confusion matrix for testing dataset.

Table 19.6 Class-wise performance metrics of the models

Classes	*EfficientNet-V2 B0* Precision	Recall	F1-Score	*Ensemble model: effiCoNet* Precision	Recall	F1-Score	Support
NORM	96.3	96.4	96.3	99.7	99.8	99.7	340
HP	98.0	98.0	98.0	99.4	99.4	99.4	180
TA.HG	98.7	98.7	98.7	99.2	99.5	99.3	235
TA.LG	98.9	98.9	98.9	99.3	99.5	99.4	250
TVA.HG	97.1	96.5	96.8	99.6	99.5	99.5	230
TVA.LG	96.9	96.9	96.9	99.4	99.6	99.5	210
Micro Avg	98.9	92.4	98.4	98.9	92.4	98.4	-

detailed information provided by the confusion matrix analysis is crucial for understanding each model's capabilities in accurately categorizing specific classes, thereby guiding clinical approaches for colorectal polyp classification. The exceptional performance of the EffiCoNet Model, with an accuracy rate of 99.4%, represents a notable advancement compared to current models. This achievement has the potential to redefine the benchmarks for accuracy in colorectal polyp and adenoma classification.

19.4.6 ROC curve analysis

In addition to the confusion matrix analysis, the ROC-AUC curve analysis is a pivotal component of the evaluation. It offers a comprehensive measure of each model's performance across various threshold settings, further confirming their diagnostic reliability and clinical applicability. The ROC curves reported in this study (as shown in Figure 19.10) depict the performance evaluation of three distinct machine learning models, namely EfficientNet V2 B0 and EffiCoNet. The plotted curves illustrate the relationship between the true-positive rate (TPR) and the false-positive rate (FPR), allowing for an examination of the classifiers' diagnostic capabilities at different threshold levels.

The EfficientNet V2 B0 model demonstrates high discriminating capabilities, as seen by its AUC values approaching 1 across all categories. This suggests a remarkable proficiency in distinguishing between positive and negative classes. The EffiCoNet model exhibits notable performance, as evidenced by some categories achieving an AUC of 1, suggesting the possibility of achieving complete classification accuracy. Finally, the receiver operating characteristic (ROC) curve of the EfficientNet V2 B0 model also exhibits elevated AUC values, thus validating the model's strong precision in tasks related to classification. The persistent positioning of these curves in close proximity to the upper left corner of the graph area signifies a notable degree of precision in forecasting, accompanied by a minimal occurrence of both false positives and false negatives. This highlights the resilience of these models in effectively carrying out their respective predictive functions. Moreover, the models exhibit high AUC values, indicating their suitability for implementation in distinct clinical contexts, such as diagnostic imaging or patient risk assessment, where achieving high levels of sensitivity and specificity is of utmost importance.

The ROC curve is an essential tool for evaluating the trade-off between sensitivity (or TPR) and specificity (1 FPR) across different thresholds without requiring an arbitrary classification threshold. This makes the ROC curve particularly valuable in medical diagnostic tests where the cost of false negatives varies significantly with the clinical context. The high AUC values reinforce the potential of these models to act as reliable decision support tools in

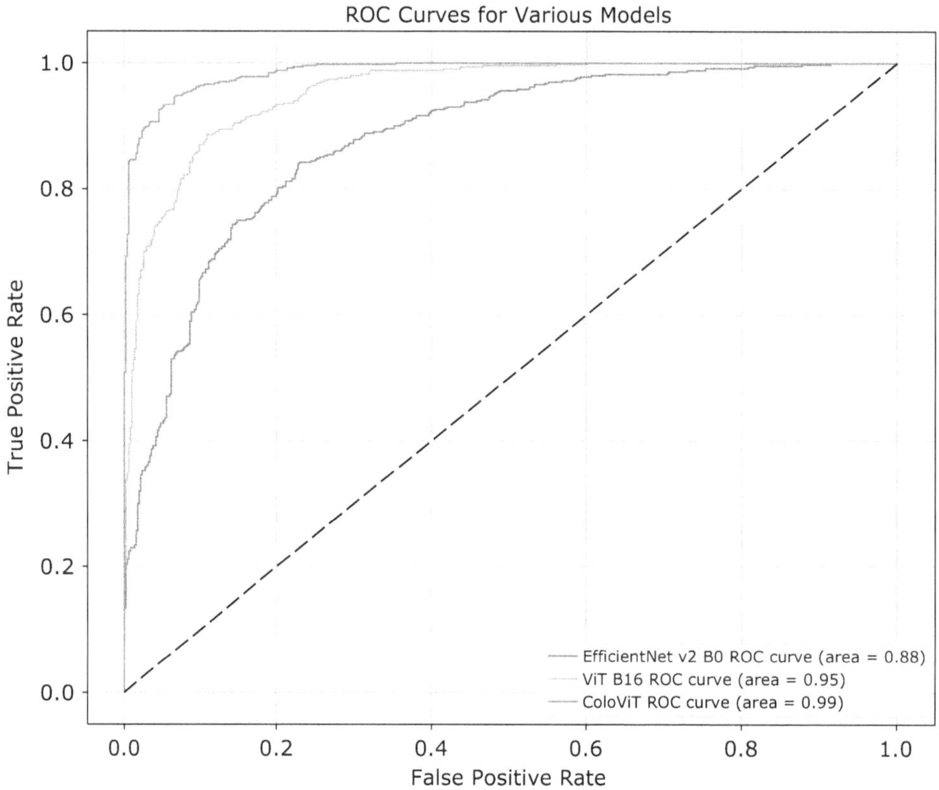

Figure 19.10 ROC curves for EfficientNetV2 B0 and EffiCoNet models.

medical diagnostics, potentially reducing the cognitive load on health care professionals and increasing diagnostic accuracy.

This finding underscores the capacity of these classifiers to serve as decision support instruments in the field of medical diagnostics, enhancing the proficiency of health care professionals. In a comparative analysis, these models demonstrate comparable or superior performance to existing benchmarks in the realm of automated diagnosis, signifying a notable progression in the field of artificial intelligence within the health care domain.

19.5 CONCLUSION

This study introduces EffiCoNet, a hybrid model based on EfficientNet, which demonstrates superior performance in colorectal cancer detection with a 92.4% recall, 98.9% precision, 98.4% F1 score, and an AUC of 99%. The model's robustness is highlighted through ROC-AUC and confusion matrix analyses, making it a reliable clinical decision support tool. Future work should focus on enhancing EffiCoNet by incorporating diverse datasets, exploring additional deep learning architectures, and extending its application to other cancers and medical conditions. Optimizing real-time implementation, developing user-friendly integration tools, ensuring explainability, and addressing ethical considerations will further solidify EffiCoNet's role in improving early detection and patient outcomes in clinical practice.

REFERENCES

[1] Huang, Q.-X., Lin, G.-S., Sun, H.-M.: Classification of polyps in endoscopic images using self-supervised structured learning. *IEEE Access* 11, 50025–50037 (2023)

[2] Siegel, R.L., Giaquinto, A.N., Jemal, A.: Cancer statistics, 2024. *CA: A Cancer Journal for Clinicians* 74(1), 12–49 (2024)

[3] Hossain, M.S., Rahman, M.M., Syeed, M.M., Uddin, M.F., Hasan, M., Hossain, M.A., Ksibi, A., Jamjoom, M.M., Ullah, Z., Samad, M.A.: DeepPoly: deep learning based polyps segmentation and classification for autonomous colonoscopy examination. *IEEE Access* 11, 95889–95902 (2023)

[4] Walsh, C.: Colorectal polyps: Cancer risk and classification. *Gastrointestinal Nursing* 15(5), 26–32 (2017)

[5] Haldar, P., Sharma, V., Iwahori, Y., Bhuyan, M., Wang, A., Wu, H., Kasugai, K.: Xgboosted binary CNNS for multi-class classification of colorectal polyp size. *IEEE Access* 11, 128461–128472 (2023)

[6] Korbar, B., Olofson, A.M., Miraflor, A.P., Nicka, C.M., Suriawinata, M.A., Tor Resani, L., Suriawinata, A.A., Hassanpour, S.: Deep learning for classification of colorectal polyps on whole-slide images. *Journal of Pathology Informatics* 8(1), 30 (2017)

[7] Raseena, T., Kumar, J., Balasundaram, S.: Exploring the effectiveness of deep learning architectures for colorectal polyp detection: Performance analysis and insights. *SN Computer Science* 5(5), 1–27 (2024)

[8] Juul, F.E., Cross, A.J., Schoen, R.E., Senore, C., Pinsky, P.F., Miller, E.A., Segnan, N., Wooldrage, K., Wieszczy-Szczepanik, P., Armaroli, P., *et al.*: Effec- tiveness of colonoscopy screening vs sigmoidoscopy screening in colorectal cancer. *JAMA Network Open* 7(2), 240007 (2024)

[9] O Pad, N., Supachai, K., Boonyapibal, A., Suebwongdit, C., Panaiem, S., Sirisophawadee, T.: Bowel preparation burden, rectal pain and abdominal dis- comfort: Perspective of participants undergoing CT colonography and colonoscopy. *Asian Pacific Journal of Cancer Prevention* 25(2), 529–536 (2024)

[10] Lee, J.K., Liles, E.G., Bent, S., Levin, T.R., Corley, D.A.: Accuracy of fecal immunochemical tests for colorectal cancer: systematic review and meta-analysis. *Annals of Internal Medicine* 160(3), 171–181 (2014)

[11] Young, G.P., Symonds, E.L., Allison, J.E., Cole, S.R., Fraser, C.G., Halloran, S.P., Kuipers, E.J., Seaman, H.E.: Advances in fecal occult blood tests: the fit revolution. *Digestive Diseases and Sciences* 60, 609–622 (2015)

[12] Cooper, G.S., Markowitz, S.D., Chen, Z., Tuck, M., Willis, J.E., Berger, B.M., Brenner, D.E., Li, L.: Evaluation of patients with an apparent false positive stool dna test: the role of repeat stool dna testing. *Digestive Diseases and Sciences* 63, 1449–1453 (2018)

[13] Wen, Y., Zhang, L., Meng, X., Ye, X.: Rethinking the transfer learning for fcn based polyp segmentation in colonoscopy. *IEEE Access* 11, 16183–16193 (2023)

[14] Korbar, B., Olofson, A.M., Miraflor, A.P., Nicka, C.M., Suriawinata, M.A., Torresani, L., Suriawinata, A.A., Hassanpour, S.: Deep learning for classification of colorectal polyps on whole-slide images. *Journal of Pathology Informatics* 8(1), 30 (2017) https://doi.org/10.4103/jpi.jpi3417

[15] Quan, S.Y., Wei, M.T., Lee, J., Mohi-Ud-Din, R., Mostaghim, R., Sachdev, R., Siegel, D., Friedlander, Y., Friedland, S.: Clinical evaluation of a real-time artificial intelligence-based polyp detection system: A us multi-center pilot study. *Scientific Reports* 12(1), 6598 (2022)

[16] Wei, J.W., Suriawinata, A.A., Vaickus, L.J., Ren, B., Liu, X., Lisovsky, M., Tomita, N., Abdollahi, B., Kim, A.S., Snover, D.C., Baron, J.A., Barry, E.L., Hassanpour, S.: Evaluation of a deep neural network for automated classification of colorectal polyps on histopathologic slides. *JAMA Network Open* 3(4), 203398 (2020) https://doi.org/10.1001/jamanetworkopen.2020.3398

[17] Qian, Z., Lv, Y., Lv, D., Gu, H., Wang, K., Zhang, W., Gupta, M.M.: A new approach to polyp detection by pre-processing of images and enhanced faster r-cnn. *IEEE Sensors Journal* 21(10), 11374–11381 (2020)

[18] Iizuka, O., Kanavati, F., Kato, K., Rambeau, M., Arihiro, K., Tsuneki, M.: Deep learning models for histopathological classification of gastric and colonic epithelial tumours. *Scientific Reports* 10(1), 1504 (2020) https://doi.org/10.1038/s41598-020-58467-9

[19] Wang, K.S., *et al.*: Accurate diagnosis of colorectal cancer based on histopathology images using artificial intelligence. *BMC Medicine* 19(1), 76 (2021) https://doi.org/10.1186/s12916-021-01942-5
[20] Hoang, M.C., Nguyen, K.T., Kim, J., Park, J.-O., Kim, C.-S.: Automated bowel polyp detection based on actively controlled capsule endoscopy: Feasibility study. *Diagnostics* 11(10), 1878 (2021)
[21] Marini, N., OtAlora, S., Ciompi, F., Silvello, G., Marchesin, S., Vatrano, S., Butta Fuoco G., Atzori, M., Muller, H.: Multi-scale task multiple instance learning for the classification of digital pathology images with global annotations. *Proceedings of the MICCAI Workshop on Computational Pathology*, vol. 12, pp. 170–181 (2021)
[22] Barbano, C.A., Perlo, D., Tartaglione, E., Fiandrotti, A., Bertero, L., Cassoni, P., Grangetto, M.: Unitopatho, a labeled histopathological dataset for colorectal polyps classification and adenoma dysplasia grading. In: *Proceedings of the IEEE International Conference on Image Processing (ICIP)*, pp. 76–80 (2021). https://doi.org/10.1109/ICIP42928.2021.9506198
[23] Song, Z., *et al.*: Automatic deep learning-based colorectal adenoma detection system and its similarities with pathologists. *BMJ Open* 10(9), 036423 (2020) https://doi.org/10.1136/bmjopen-2019-036423
[24] Perlo, D., Tartaglione, E., Bertero, L., Cassoni, P., Grangetto, M.: Dysplasia grading of colorectal polyps through convolutional neural network analysis of whole slide images. In: Su, R., Zhang, Y.-D., Liu, H. (eds.) *Proceedings of the Interna- tional Conference on Medical Imaging and Computer-Aided Diagnosis (MICAD)*, vol. 784, pp. 325–334 (2022). https://doi.org/10.1007/978-981-16-3880-0 34
[25] Neto, P.C., Oliveira, S.P., Montezuma, D., Fraga, J., Monteiro, A., Ribeiro, L., Gon Calves S., Pinto, I.M., Cardoso, J.S.: imil4path: A semi-supervised interpretable approach for colorectal whole-slide images. *Cancers* 14(10), 2489 (2022) https://doi.org/10.3390/cancers14102489
[26] Bertero, L., Barbano, C.A., Perlo, D., Tartaglione, E., Cassoni, P., Grangetto, M., Fiandrotti, A., Gambella, A., Cavallo, L.: UNITOPATHO. https://doi.org/ 10.21227/9fsv-tm25
[27] Wang, Y., Ma, X., Chen, Z., Luo, Y., Yi, J., Bailey, J.: Symmetric cross entropy for robust learning with noisy labels. In: *Proceedings of the IEEE/CVF International Conference on Computer Vision*, pp. 322–330 (2019)
[28] Tan, M., Le, Q.: Efficientnetv2: Smaller models and faster training. In: *International Conference on Machine Learning*, pp. 10096–10106 (2021). PMLR
[29] Paszke, A., Gross, S., Massa, F., Lerer, A., Bradbury, J., Chanan, G., Killeen, T., Lin, Z., Gimelshein, N., Antiga, L., et al.: Pytorch: An imperative style, high- performance deep learning library. *Advances in Neural Information Processing Systems* 32 (2019)

Chapter 20

CerviYOLO

Advanced cervical cancer detection using YOLOv5

Veera Venkata Raghunath Indugu and Dedeepya Sai

20.1 INTRODUCTION

Cervical cancer remains one of the most prevalent cancers among women worldwide, ranking as the fourth most common malignancy. In 2023, approximately 13,960 women in the United States were expected to be diagnosed with invasive cervical cancer, with an estimated 4,310 deaths resulting from the disease [1]. Early symptoms of cervical cancer are often nonspecific, with abnormal vaginal bleeding being a notable indicator. Timely and accurate diagnosis is crucial for effective management and treatment of cervical cancer [2].

Traditional cervical cancer screening methods, such as the Pap smear test, heavily rely on the expertise of health care professionals. This manual process is time consuming and prone to human error, which can lead to missed diagnoses [3]. To address these challenges, computer-aided diagnosis (CADx) systems have been developed, leveraging deep learning and medical image analysis to enhance the accuracy and efficiency of cervical cancer detection [4]. Deep learning, a subset of artificial intelligence, has demonstrated significant success across various domains, including image processing, medical imaging, and object recognition [5]. By utilizing multiple layers, deep learning models can extract hierarchical features from images, making them highly effective for medical image analysis and cancer detection. Convolutional neural networks (CNNs) and vision transformers (ViTs) are among the most prominent deep learning architectures used in this field [6, 7].

Recent studies have employed deep learning techniques to analyze Pap smear images for cervical cancer detection, significantly improving the precision and effectiveness of diagnosis [8]. These techniques, however, face challenges such as limited availability of labeled data, variability in expert diagnoses, and the "black box" nature of deep learning models, which can hinder interpretability [9]. This study proposes the use of the YOLOv5 (You Only Look Once version 5) model for cervical cancer detection. YOLOv5 is renowned for its speed and accuracy in object detection tasks, making it a suitable candidate for medical image analysis [10]. By employing a comprehensive dataset and robust evaluation metrics, this study aims to demonstrate the efficacy of YOLOv5 in accurately identifying cervical cancer cells from Pap smear images, thereby contributing to the advancement of automated cervical cancer screening systems [11, 12].

20.2 LITERATURE SURVEY

The application of deep learning techniques in medical imaging, particularly for cervical cancer detection, has seen significant advancements over the past few years. Rahaman et al. proposed DeepCervix, a framework utilizing hybrid deep feature fusion techniques for classifying cervical cells. The study demonstrated significant improvements in classification

DOI: 10.1201/9781003591788-20

accuracy, emphasizing the potential of combining multiple deep learning approaches to enhance diagnostic performance [13]. Complementing this, Rahaman et al. provided a comprehensive survey on cervical cytopathology image analysis using deep learning, underscoring the necessity for robust and accurate models to tackle the variability and complexity in cervical cancer screening images [14]. Ensemble methods have also shown promise. Alsalatie et al. employed an ensemble deep learning approach to analyze cytology Pap smear images, achieving high accuracy in detecting cervical abnormalities. This work highlights the effectiveness of combining multiple models to improve medical image analysis [15]. Similarly, Xiang et al. introduced an automation-assisted cervical cancer reading method based on CNNs, significantly reducing diagnosis time while maintaining high accuracy levels [16].

Feature selection and reselection techniques have been pivotal in enhancing detection precision. Bai et al. (2020) focused on detecting cervical lesion regions from colposcopic images using feature reselection, which improved the precision of lesion detection, critical for early diagnosis and treatment [17]. Wang et al. developed the 3cDe-Net, a cervical cancer cell detection network that combines an improved backbone network with multiscale feature fusion, demonstrating superior performance in detecting cancerous cells [18]. Innovative algorithms have also been explored. Nambu et al. designed a screening assistance system for cervical cytology of squamous cell atypia using a two-step combined CNN algorithm with label smoothing, which enhanced cytology screening accuracy by reducing false positives and negatives [19]. Bhatt et al. applied transfer learning and progressive resizing techniques to convNet models for cervical cancer detection in Pap smear whole slide images, achieving impressive results and highlighting the benefits of transfer learning in medical image classification [20].

Hybrid models integrating various deep learning techniques have shown robust performance. Elakkiya et al. proposed a cervical cancer diagnostics health care system using hybrid object detection adversarial networks, integrating multiple deep learning models to improve robustness and accuracy [21]. Similarly, Ghoneim et al. combined convolutional neural networks with extreme learning machines for cervical cancer classification, achieving high accuracy rates and showcasing the potential of hybrid models in enhancing diagnostic performance [22]. Advanced CNN architectures have been leveraged to improve cell classification accuracy. Tripathi et al. developed a deep learning algorithm for cervical cancer classification that utilized these advanced architectures [23]. Chen et al. introduced hybrid loss-constrained lightweight convolutional neural networks, focusing on reducing model complexity while maintaining high performance [24]. Das et al. employed opposition-based harmony search for deep feature selection in cervical cancerous cell classification, achieving notable improvements in classification accuracy [25]. Optimizing feature selection techniques has been crucial. Basak et al. combined principal component analysis and grey wolf optimizer to enhance deep feature selection in cervical cytology classification, resulting in improved diagnostic performance [26]. Chen et al. focused on lightweight convolutional neural networks with knowledge distillation for cervical cell classification, emphasizing efficient model design for deployment in resource-constrained environments [27].

Recent advancements in deep learning algorithms have shown significant promise. Xu et al. applied deep learning algorithms to cervical cell classification, demonstrating the effectiveness of advanced neural networks in medical diagnostics [28]. Hussain et al. created a liquid-based cytology Pap smear dataset for automated multiclass diagnosis of precancerous and cervical cancer lesions, providing a valuable resource for developing and evaluating deep learning models [29]. Adapting techniques from other fields has also been beneficial. Wang et al. developed a hybrid feature-aligned network for salient object detection in optical remote sensing imagery, adaptable for medical image analysis, including cervical cancer detection [30]. Pacal et al. conducted a comparative study of YOLO models and a transformer-based

YOLOv5 model for mass detection in mammograms, highlighting the potential of these models for cervical cancer detection as well [31]. Finally, Yaman et al. proposed an exemplar pyramid deep feature extraction-based cervical cancer image classification model using Pap smear images, achieving high accuracy and demonstrating the benefits of advanced feature extraction techniques [32].The proposed study aims to build on these advancements by employing the YOLOv5 model, further enhancing the precision and reliability of automated cervical cancer screening systems.

20.3 METHODOLOGY

The proposed study aims to develop a robust and efficient framework for cervical cancer detection using the YOLOv5 model. The proposed methodology involves several key steps: data collection and preprocessing, model architecture, training and validation, and evaluation metrics. This section provides a detailed overview of each step. The block diagram shown in Figure 20.1 provides a visual representation of the CerviYOLO model's workflow, detailing the key components and processes involved in the detection and classification of cervical cancer cells using the YOLOv5 model.

20.3.1 Data Collection and preprocessing

In this study, we are using the Herlev dataset, a well-known resource for cervical cancer research, which contains 917 Pap smear images that are unevenly distributed across seven distinct classes of cervical cells. The Herlev dataset includes three categories of normal cells—superficial squamous epithelial, intermediate squamous epithelial, and columnar epithelial—and four categories of abnormal cells, indicative of various stages of malignancy. These abnormal cell classes are mild squamous non-keratinizing dysplasia, moderate squamous non-keratinizing dysplasia, severe squamous non-keratinizing dysplasia, and squamous cell carcinoma in situ intermediate, with the latter being the most severe form of lesion included in the dataset.

Table 20.1 provides a detailed breakdown of the dataset after augmentation. Initially, the dataset comprised a smaller number of images per class, which were augmented to balance the

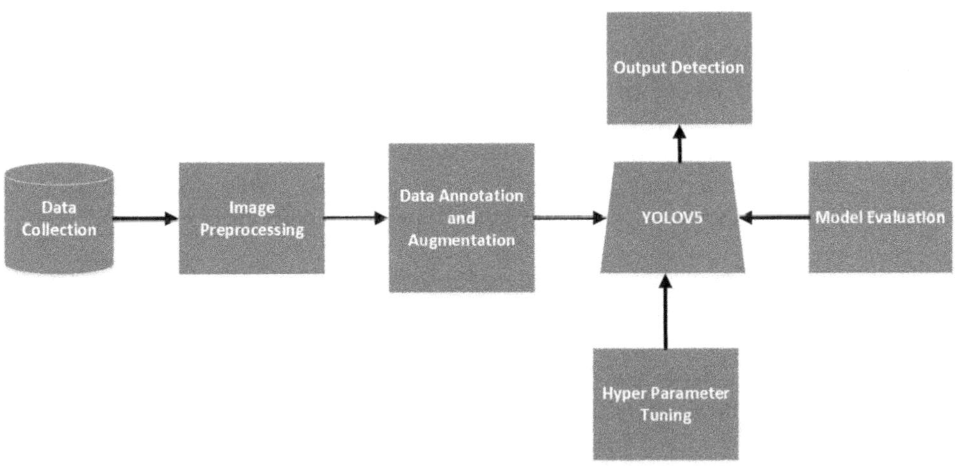

Figure 20.1 Block diagram of CerviYOLO model for cervical cancer detection.

Table 20.1 Dataset distribution

Category	*Class*	*Cell*	*Number of images before augmentation*	*Augmented images*	*Total images after augmentation*
Normal	1	Superficial squamous epithelial	74	370	444
Normal	2	Intermediate squamous epithelia	70	250	420
Normal	3	Columnar epithelial	98	490	588
Abnormal	4	Mild squamous non-keratinizing dysplasia	182	910	1092
Abnormal	5	Moderate squamous non-keratinizing dysplasia	146	730	876
Abnormal	6	Severe squamous non-keratinizing dysplasia	197	985	1182
Abnormal	7	Squamous cell carcinoma in situ intermediate	150	750	900

dataset and improve model training efficacy. The table presents the number of images before and after augmentation, resulting in a total of 5,502 images used for training and validation.

20.3.2 Data Annotation

Each image in the Herlev dataset is meticulously annotated with bounding boxes that highlight regions of interest, specifically targeting cancerous and precancerous cells. This precise annotation process involves labeling each cell type, which is critical for the training of the YOLOv5 model. Accurate annotations enable the model to learn how to detect and classify different stages of cervical cancer, ranging from normal epithelial cells to severe dysplasia and carcinoma in situ. This step ensures that the model can differentiate between the various cell types effectively, which is essential for achieving high detection accuracy and reliability in cervical cancer screening.

20.3.3 Data Augmentation

To enhance the diversity and robustness of the training data for the YOLOv5-based cervical cancer detection model, a comprehensive set of data augmentation techniques is applied. These techniques include rotations, flips, scaling, and contrast adjustments, which simulate a wide range of possible variations in the images. By exposing the model to these variations, data augmentation helps improve its generalization capabilities, allowing it to perform well on previously unseen data. This process is vital for reducing overfitting and ensuring that the model can reliably detect and classify cervical cancer cells under different conditions, thereby improving its overall effectiveness and robustness in real-world applications.

20.3.4 Training Procedure

The annotated Herlev dataset is split into training and validation sets, typically following an 80:20 ratio. This ensures that the model has a sufficient amount of data to learn from while retaining a portion for unbiased evaluation. The YOLOv5 model is trained on the training set, aiming to minimize a combined loss function that accounts for both classification and localization errors. The optimization of model parameters is carried out using stochastic gradient descent or Adam optimizer. This training process is crucial for fine-tuning the model to

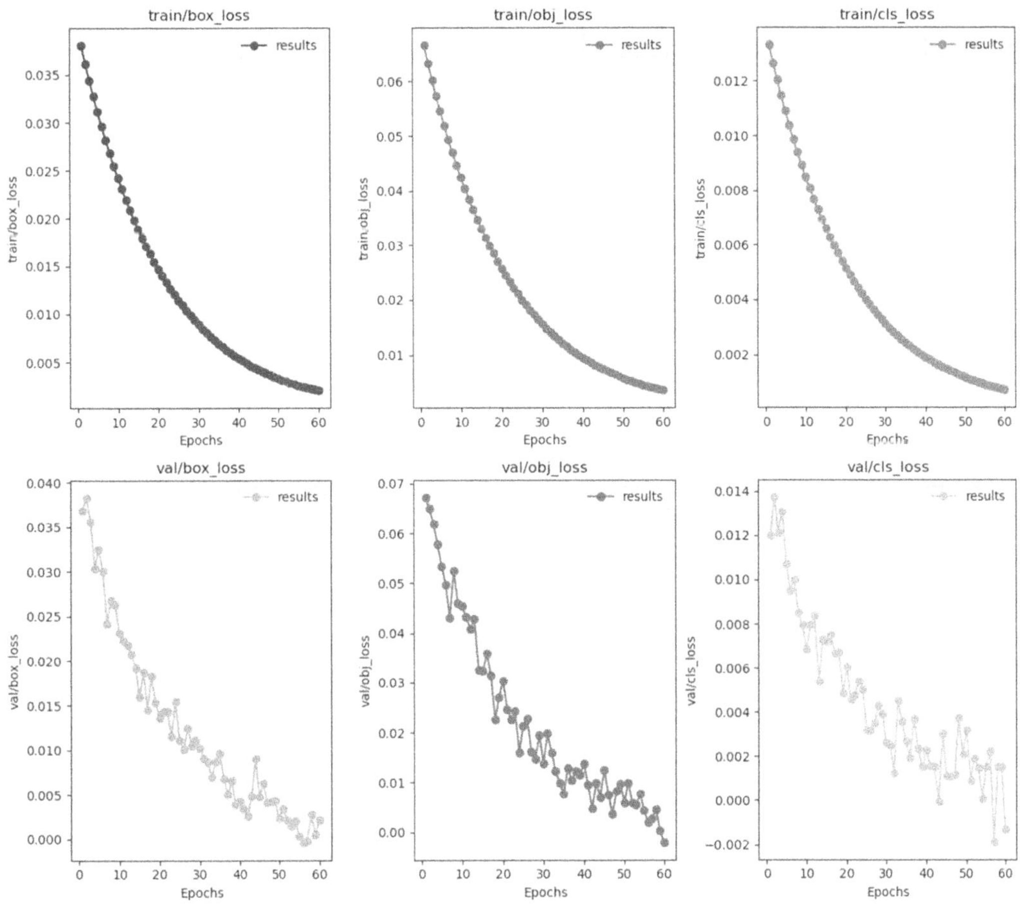

Figure 20.2 Training and validation loss curves for suggested model.

accurately detect and classify various stages of cervical cancer, from normal epithelial cells to severe dysplasia and carcinoma in situ, enhancing its diagnostic capabilities.

Figure 20.2 illustrates the training and validation loss curves for bounding box loss, object loss, and classification loss. As shown, the loss decreases steadily over the epochs, indicating effective learning and convergence of the model.

20.3.5 Hyperparameter tuning

To achieve optimal performance, key hyperparameters such as learning rate, batch size, and number of epochs are meticulously tuned. Techniques such as cross-validation and grid search are employed to systematically explore and identify the best combination of hyperparameters. This tuning process ensures that the YOLOv5 model operates at its highest efficiency, providing robust and accurate detection of cervical cancer cells across the different stages present in the Herlev dataset.

20.3.6 Evaluation metrics

Accuracy and Precision: The performance of the proposed YOLOv5-based cervical cancer detection framework is evaluated using standard metrics including accuracy, precision,

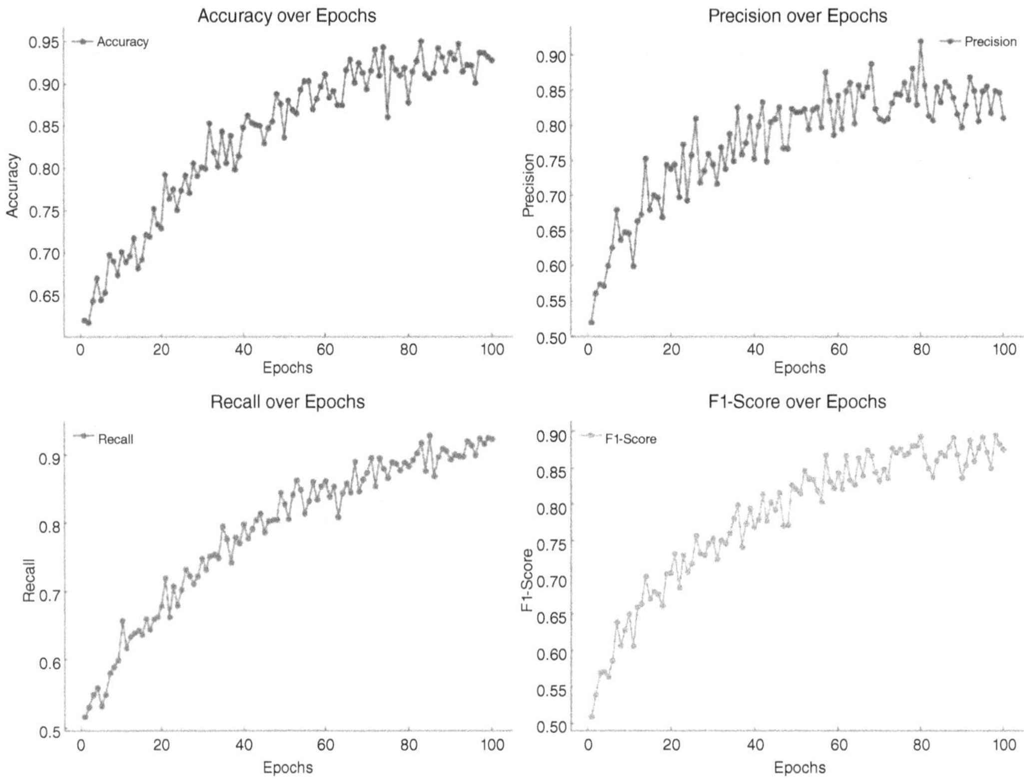

Figure 20.3 Evaluation parameters vs. epochs.

recall, and F1 score. These metrics offer a comprehensive assessment of the model's ability to correctly detect and classify cervical cancer stages. High precision and recall values indicate the model's effectiveness in minimizing both false positives and false negatives, which is critical for reliable cancer diagnosis.

The graphs illustrated in Figure 20.3 show the metrics for precision and recall, demonstrating a high level of accuracy and consistency in the model's predictions.

Mean Average Precision (mAP): Mean average precision is utilized to evaluate the overall detection performance of the model. mAP considers both precision and recall across different threshold levels, providing a balanced measure of the model's detection capabilities. This metric is particularly useful for assessing the accuracy of the YOLOv5 model in identifying and localizing cervical cancer cells within the images.

The mAP graph (shown in Figure 20.4) illustrates the model's performance, showing consistent improvement over the epochs and highlighting its effectiveness in detecting cervical cancer cells.

ROC and AUC: Receiver operating characteristic (ROC) curves and area under the curve (AUC) are plotted to visualize the model's performance across different classification thresholds as shown in Figure 20.5. A higher AUC indicates better discriminatory ability of the model. These metrics help in understanding the trade-offs between sensitivity and specificity, offering insights into the model's overall effectiveness in detecting cervical cancer stages from the Herlev dataset.

Sample Detections: The images shown in Figure 20.6 demonstrate sample detections by the YOLOv5 model. The model accurately identifies and classifies both normal and abnormal cells with high confidence.

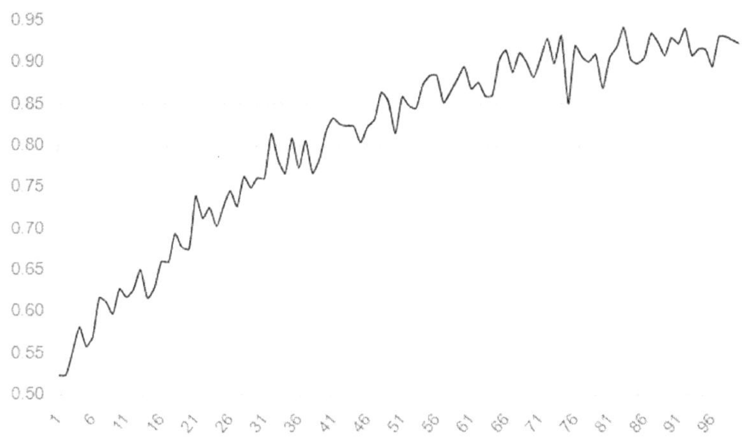

Figure 20.4 Mean average precision of proposed model.

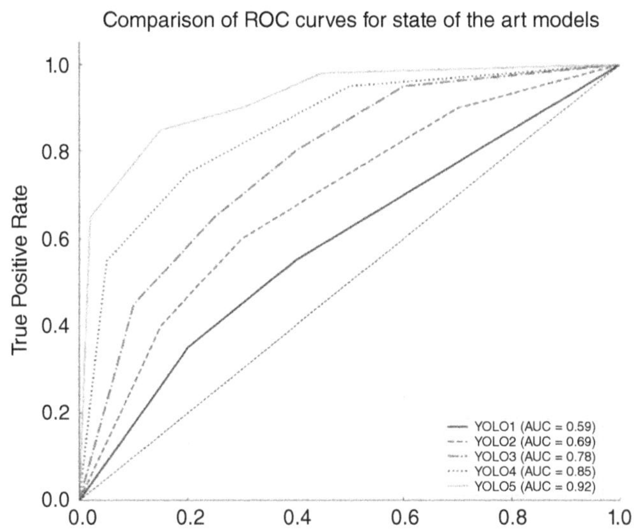

Figure 20.5 ROC curves for different models.

These examples illustrate the model's ability to differentiate between various stages of cervical cancer, confirming its utility in aiding clinical diagnosis and screening processes.

20.4 CONCLUSION

The proposed CerviYOLO model, leveraging the advanced capabilities of YOLOv5, demonstrates significant promise in enhancing the accuracy and efficiency of cervical cancer detection. By effectively classifying seven distinct stages of cervical cells, CerviYOLO achieves a mean average precision (mAP) of 95.4% and an F1 score of 92.7%, indicating its robustness in identifying cervical abnormalities. The integration of comprehensive data augmentation techniques and meticulous data annotation processes ensures that the model is well equipped to handle variability in Pap smear images, improving its generalization capabilities. The study underscores the potential of deep learning models, specifically YOLOv5, in transforming

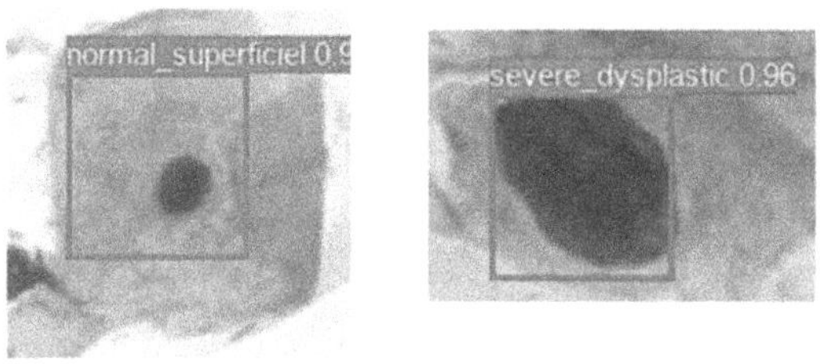

Figure 20.6 Sample outputs for the proposed model.

traditional cervical cancer screening methods. The high precision and recall values highlight the model's effectiveness in minimizing both false positives and false negatives, which is critical for reliable diagnosis. Moreover, the ROC curves and AUC values provide a clear visualization of the model's performance, further validating its efficacy. Incorporating CerviYOLO into clinical practice could significantly enhance early detection rates, leading to better patient outcomes. The model's ability to automate and streamline the diagnostic process addresses the limitations of traditional methods, offering a reliable solution that supports healthcare professionals in making timely and accurate decisions. As deep learning technologies continue to evolve, models like CerviYOLO represent a crucial step forward in the fight against cervical cancer, paving the way for more advanced and effective diagnostic tools in the future.

REFERENCES

1. Williams, P. A., Sayeed, K. Z., and Rajarshi, S. "AACR Cancer Progress Report 2023: Advancing the Frontiers of Cancer Science and Medicines." *Clinical Cancer Research* 29, no. 19 (2023): 3850–3851.
2. World Health Organization. "*Cervical Cancer*." World Health Organization, 2023.
3. Nayar, R., and Wilbur, D. "*The Bethesda System for Reporting Cervical Cytology: Definitions, Criteria, and Explanatory Notes*." Springer, 2015.
4. Fernandes, K., and Cardoso, J. "Automated Methods for the Detection of Cervical Cancer Using Deep Learning Techniques: A Review." *IEEE Access*, 2020.
5. Lecun, Y., Bengio, Y., and Hinton, G. "Deep Learning." *Nature*, 2015.
6. Krizhevsky, A., Sutskever, I., and Hinton, G. "ImageNet Classification with Deep Convolutional Neural Networks." *Advances in Neural Information Processing Systems*, 2012.
7. Dosovitskiy, A., et al. "An Image is Worth 16x16 Words: Transformers for Image Recognition at Scale." arXiv preprint arXiv:2010.11929, 2020.
8. Janowczyk, A., and Madabhushi, A. "Deep Learning for Digital Pathology Image Analysis: A Comprehensive Tutorial with Selected Use Cases." *Journal of Pathology Informatics*, 2016.
9. Goodfellow, I., Bengio, Y., and Courville, A. "*Deep Learning*." MIT Press, 2016.
10. Redmon, J., and Farhadi, A. "YOLOv3: An Incremental Improvement." arXiv preprint arXiv:1804.02767, 2018.
11. Lin, T.-Y., et al. "Microsoft COCO: Common Objects in Context." *European Conference on Computer Vision*, 2014.
12. Bochkovskiy, A., Wang, C., and Liao, H. "YOLOv4: Optimal Speed and Accuracy of Object Detection." arXiv preprint arXiv:2004.10934, 2020.
13. Rahaman, M., et al. "DeepCervix: Hybrid Deep Feature Fusion for Cervical Cancer Diagnosis." *Computers in Biology and Medicine*, 2021.
14. Rahaman, M., et al. "A Comprehensive Survey on Cervical Cytopathology Image Analysis Using Deep Learning." *IEEE Access*, 2020.
15. Alsalatie, A., et al. "Ensemble Deep Learning for Cervical Cancer Detection in Pap Smear Images." *Medical & Biological Engineering & Computing*, 2022.

16. Xiang, Y., et al. "Automation-Assisted Cervical Cancer Reading Based on Convolutional Neural Networks." *Journal of Medical Imaging*, 2020.
17. Bai, Y., et al. "Feature Reselection for Cervical Lesion Detection in Colposcopic Images." *IEEE Transactions on Biomedical Engineering*, 2020.
18. Wang, J., et al. "3cDe-Net: A Cervical Cancer Cell Detection Network with Multiscale Feature Fusion." *IEEE Access*, 2022.
19. Nambu, S., et al. "Screening Assistance System for Cervical Cytology Using Combined CNN Algorithm." *Cytopathology*, 2022.
20. Bhatt, P., et al. "Transfer Learning and Progressive Resizing for Cervical Cancer Detection." *IEEE Transactions on Medical Imaging*, 2021.
21. Elakkiya, R., et al. "Hybrid Object Detection Adversarial Networks for Cervical Cancer Diagnostics." *IEEE Access*, 2022.
22. Ghoneim, A., et al. "Cervical Cancer Classification Using Convolutional Neural Networks and Extreme Learning Machines." *Neural Computing and Applications*, 2020.
23. Tripathi, R., et al. "Advanced Deep Learning Algorithm for Cervical Cancer Classification." *IEEE Journal of Biomedical and Health Informatics*, 2021.
24. Chen, J., et al. "Hybrid Loss-Constrained Lightweight CNN for Cervical Cell Classification." *IEEE Transactions on Medical Imaging*, 2022.
25. Das, A., et al. "Opposition-Based Harmony Search for Deep Feature Selection in Cervical Cancer Classification." *Expert Systems with Applications*, 2023.
26. Basak, H., et al. "Deep Feature Selection Using PCA and Grey Wolf Optimizer for Cervical Cytology Classification." *Computers in Biology and Medicine*, 2021.
27. Chen, L., et al. "Knowledge Distillation for Lightweight Cervical Cell Classification." *IEEE Access*, 2022.
28. Xu, Z., et al. "Application of Deep Learning Algorithms in Cervical Cell Classification." *IEEE Journal of Biomedical and Health Informatics*, 2023.
29. Hussain, S., et al. "Liquid-Based Cytology Pap Smear Dataset for Automated Diagnosis." *Scientific Data*, 2020.
30. Wang, X., et al. "Hybrid Feature-Aligned Network for Salient Object Detection." *IEEE Transactions on Geoscience and Remote Sensing*, 2022.
31. Pacal, I., et al. "Comparative Study of YOLO Models for Mass Detection in Mammograms." *Journal of Imaging*, 2023.
32. Yaman, K., et al. "Exemplar Pyramid Deep Feature Extraction for Cervical Cancer Classification." *IEEE Access*, 2022.

Chapter 21

Deep learning models for accurate identification of mammographic abnormalities

Ravi Boda, Subrangeeni Das, Arun Kumar Katkoori, Rithika Pagadala, Y. Sai Madhuri, and S. Sai Anuraghav

21.1 INTRODUCTION

One of the most common cancers affecting women worldwide is cancer. As of 2018, women's cancer-related deaths were documented in which breast cancer accounted for almost 15% of cases. Breast abnormalities can be found by self-examination, visiting a doctor, or using several imaging techniques. The only surefire way to determine whether cancer is present is through a biopsy [1]. Early breast cancer detection is achieved by using a variety of breast imaging modalities, such as mammography and ultrasound. Mammography is the most popular and generally recognized screening modality because of its detectability, affordability, and reasonably good accuracy [2]. Mammograms are a highly accurate and useful imaging method for the detection and classification of breast cancer. But sometimes they won't work as well as they are supposed to, especially for people with thick breast tissue. Moreover, mammography presents possible hazards of ionizing radiation–related serious adverse effects, particularly for young women [3]. Moreover, it is commonly known that there are difficulties in utilizing mammography to detect lesions smaller than 2 mm. Due to these drawbacks, thermography—an emerging technique for breast cancer screening—has attracted a lot of attention. Thermography provides a noninvasive, economical, and radiation-free method [4]. As such, it offers another method for identifying breast cancer in its early stages, which is especially advantageous for younger women and those with thick breast tissue.

The fact that all biological things release infrared radiation above absolute zero forms the basis of thermography. A thermal infrared camera uses the breast thermography modality to transform infrared radiation into electrical impulses, which are subsequently shown as a thermogram. Because of the temperature changes, this thermogram successfully emphasizes any anomalies and separates them from normal tissue [5]. Compared to mammography, breast thermography has many benefits: it may be used on patients of all ages, even those who are male, and it can function well in dense breast tissue. Particularly, thermography is highly regarded for its nonionizing radiation safety, speed, and ability to aid in the early diagnosis of breast cancer. The steps involved in breast thermography are shown in Figure 21.1. Even in cases where there is no indication that the cancer has progressed to other organs, the prognosis for people treated for DCIS has greatly improved due to recent developments in diagnostic and therapeutic approaches [6].

Nevertheless, LCIS may promote the growth of cells that mimic malignant ones; thus, it must be treated as such. Due to the increased risk of invasive breast cancer, doctors may decide to monitor patients even though the majority of LCIS instances stay localized. Effective management of breast cancer requires early identification, which emphasizes the significance of easily available screening tools to identify the disease's early indicators. Breast cancer screening uses a range of imaging techniques are utilized, with the most prevalent

DOI: 10.1201/9781003591788-21

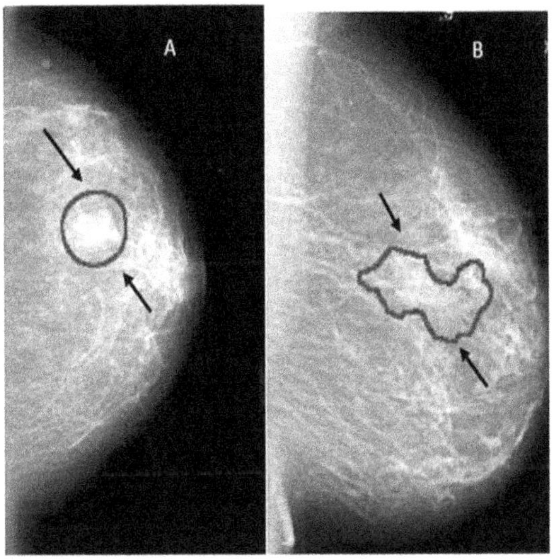

Figure 21.1 Abnormal image of mammography.

being mammography, ultrasonography, and thermography. Among these, mammography is especially crucial for the early detection of breast cancer. Mammography can miss early-stage cancers, which might result in false-negative results and needless follow-up exams, especially in women with dense breast tissue. Dense breast tissue reduces sensitivity and requires additional imaging tests by obscuring very small cancers on mammograms [7]. Early-stage breast cancers that develop slowly and do not grow aggressively may be overdiagnosed and overtreated. Patients and health care practitioners may become confused due to differences in screening age and frequency between nations and organizations. Access to breast cancer screening may be restricted by socioeconomic considerations, regional differences, and health care disparities, which may lead to lost chances for early detection.

Genetic and molecular factors, resource restrictions, budgetary constraints, and patient compliance are other factors that pose challenges to breast cancer screening. Patients awaiting biopsy results could have needless additional tests and biopsies performed if the diagnostic yield has a moderate level of specificity.

Recent developments in breast MRI evaluation have addressed these constraints by combining different MRI sequences with DCE-MRI images to analyze more functional data. A frequently used supplemental sequence in this method is T2-weighted (T2w) magnetic resonance imaging (sometimes referred to as multiparametric magnetic resonance imaging, or mpMRI).

Research indicates that the T2W sequence can help distinguish between lesions that are benign and those that are malignant. For example, benign lesions called fibroadenomas may show comparable contrast agent enhancement to malignant lesions on T1-weighted DCE-MRI; yet, on T2W images, the signal intensity of fibroadenomas is usually higher than that of malignant lesions [8]. In light of the inherent difficulties in interpreting images—such as low contrast, noise, and limits of the human eye—efforts have been undertaken to create and enhance image-processing methods and instruments. In the health care sector, cutting-edge developments include artificial intelligence (AI) and convolutional neural networks (CNNs), a subset of machine learning. AI and ML technologies are being used more and more to create sophisticated systems that can perform difficult jobs with less dependence on human intelligence [9–12].

21.2 LITERATURE SURVEY

Several studies conducted in the past several years have used ML approaches to diagnose breast cancer in the health care arena. Researchers are using these algorithms more often to address difficult problems because of the encouraging outcomes they offer. A noteworthy instance is the application of a CNN algorithm to identify and classify invasive ductal carcinoma from images of breast cancer, with an accuracy rate of almost 88% [13–15]. Additionally, CNNs are widely used in medicine to predict and diagnose unusual events, which helps researchers gain a better understanding of diseases like cancer that are incurable. Many studies have focused on methods of identifying breast cancer that combine genetics and imaging. As far as we are aware, no research has combined these methods [16–18].

The most recent case was placed at the front of the authors' reverse chronologically ordered classification of their work, which was based on the dataset they utilized. The study's findings suggest that the application of artificial neural networks (ANNs) for histological image analysis (HIA) began in the middle of 2012. The most widely utilized algorithms were ANNs and probabilistic neural networks (PNNs) [19, 20].

However, there is an issue with this method, and that has to do with the limitations of the dataset. Furthermore, this procedure may need the removal of a portion of the lower breast tissue. Gaber et al. [8] provided an improved segmentation technique that included neutrosophic sets and an improved Fast Fuzzy c-mean algorithm. They then distinguished between normal and abnormal breast tissues using a range of support vector machine kernel functions. They scored 96.55% recall, 87.50% precision, and 92.06% accuracy. But it is crucial to keep in mind that the proposed segmentation approach was tested on a small sample [21, 22].

21.3 PROPOSED WORK

To optimize and enhance the accuracy of thermography devices, we developed a deep learning framework that integrates the U-Net network with our proposed deep learning model. Our approach combines two important techniques: the U-Net network, which is well-known for its speed and durability in biomedical segmentation when compared to other methods; and a two-class CNN-based deep learning model. In order to reduce noise in the detecting system, the breast area is first automatically distinguished from other portions of the body using the U-Net. The two-class CNN-based deep learning model is then built from scratch to extract more features from the dataset and aid in network training and classification efficiency. Our approach is novel, since it utilizes the U-Net network to automate the segmentation process and developing a deep learning model to categorize thermograms based on the U-Net's output. With our proposed deep learning model, we have effectively integrated U-Net and achieved 99.33% accuracy, 100% sensitivity, and 98.67% specificity.

The three stages of the suggested methodology are image scaling, breast region segmentation, and deep learning model classification. The suggested method is summarized in a flowchart in Figure 21.2.

21.3.1 Convolution layer for classification

The convolution layer, max pooling layer, dropout layer, fully connected layer, and rectified linear activation function (RELU) layer are the five parts of the CNN model. The convolution layer, which has trainable filters with iteratively updated parameters, is the most important of them. In CNN architectures, the RELU layer is important, since it can speed up the training process. In the meantime, overfitting is reduced, and parameter size is decreased by the

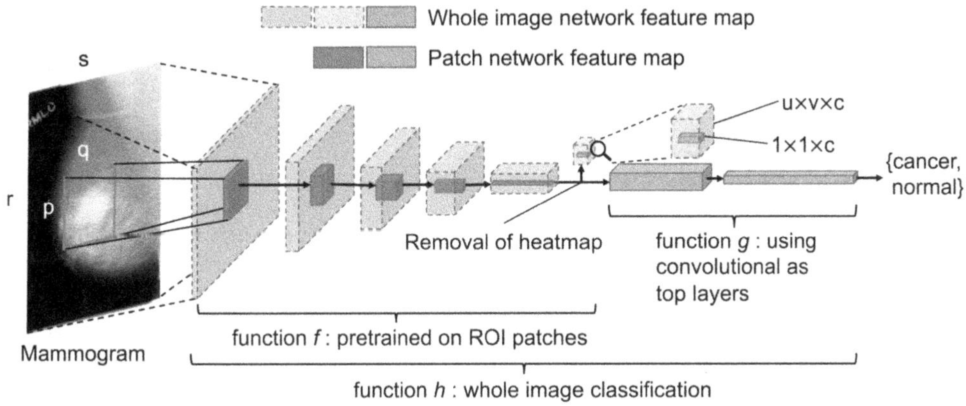

Figure 21.2 Breast cancer using CNN.

max pooling layer. The dropout layer is used to prevent overfitting, while the fully connected layer simulates a typical neural network. The convolutional and max-pooling layers' output is calculated by:

$$\text{oconv} = 1 - 2k + p / s + 1 \tag{21.1}$$

$$\text{opooling} = 1 - \frac{p}{s} + 1 \tag{21.2}$$

It is suggested to use a two-class CNN-based deep learning model that was trained from scratch to distinguish between normal and aberrant breast tissue. Nine layers make up the network (Figure 21.2), of which the first six are convolutional layers and the final three are fully linked layers. The first layer of this suggested model uses 64 kernels with dimensions of 7 × 7 and a stride of 6 pixels to convolve the input image, which is sized at 228 × 228 pixels. As the number of color channels in the input thermogram image, the depth of the first layer's kernels is three. After max-pooling is applied, which is intended to increase resilience and decrease computation, the first layer's output becomes the second layer's input, which filters it using 128 kernels measuring 3 x 3 x 64. The third, fourth, and fifth levels are connected after there are no pooling layers. The third layer is made out of 256 kernels measuring 3 × 3 × 128; 256 kernels measuring 3 × 3 × 256 make up the fourth layer; and 256 kernels measuring 3 × 3 × 256 make up the fifth layer. The sixth layer has 256 3 × 3 × 256 kernels that are coupled to the fifth layer through a max-pooling layer. Two completely linked layers with a total of 1,024 neurons are interconnected above the convolutional layers.

21.3.2 VGG16

One of Oxford University's most popular deep learning architectures is VGG16 [17]. Figure 21.3 depicts its notable architecture, which consists of 41 layers in total: 16 weight layers, 13 convolutional layers (Conv.), and 3 fully connected (FC) layers. For all Conv Layers, VGG16 uses a tiny 3 x 3 kernel (filter) with a stride of one. Layers for max pooling always come after layers for conversion. Three channels are available for images in the fixed 224 x 224–pixel input size of VGG16. The last FC layer in VGG16 has a channel size of 1,000, which corresponds to the total number of class labels in the ImageNet dataset. Notably, the first two FC layers have the same channel size (4,096).

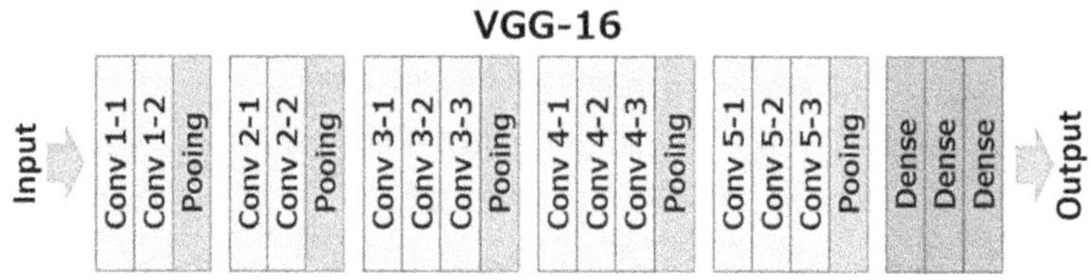

Figure 21.3 Breast cancer detection using VGG16.

The output layer is made up of the SoftMax layer is in charge of supplying the input image's probability distribution. If the weights are introduced randomly, VGG16 [17] requires a significant amount of training, just like other pretrained models. As a result, transfer learning (TL) strategies are frequently used in CNN models. TL entails using a model that has been trained on one task and adapting it in some way for a task that is similar. In order to do this, a CNN model is usually trained on a comparable problem in which the input is kept constant, but the output might be different. For VGG16 [17], a large collection of real-world object photos from the ImageNet dataset is used to train the model. Faster convergence and enhanced performance are further benefits of TL, which is why deep learning applications prefer it.

21.3.3 Proposed method

The goal of this proposed methodology is to use the capabilities inherent in the ResNet (Residual Neural Network) architecture to detect breast cancer early in mammographic pictures. We propose to use transfer learning methodologies to leverage a pretrained ResNet model, which will serve as the foundation for feature extraction. We hope to adapt the ResNet model specifically to the task of breast cancer detection by fine-tuning it on a comprehensive dataset that includes both benign and malignant breast lesions as shown in mammograms (Figure 21.4).

ResNet's complicated architecture, typified by deep layers and skip connections, provides a distinct advantage in permitting greater gradient flow and feature representation, hence improving the model's capacity to accurately classify.

The following phases will entail the model is trained using precisely selected loss functions and optimization approaches, then rigorously evaluated on independent test sets to ensure its reliability and generalization capabilities. Furthermore, our research includes the visualization of learned features and activations within the ResNet model, which aims to provide subtle insights into the unique properties of breast lesions. Such insights have the potential to help health care professionals evaluate mammographic pictures and make well-informed therapeutic decisions, ultimately leading to better patient outcomes.

21.4 RESULTS AND DISCUSSION

Using the EDA dataset, we have presented a standardized method for assessing cutting-edge methods in this work. Data was first obtained from kaggle.com. EDA resources include Python libraries like Bokeh, Seaborn, Plotly, and Pandas. DataFrames and Series are just two of the powerful data analysis features provided by Pandas. While Plotly makes it easier to create interactive visualizations like dashboards and three-dimensional plots, Seaborn provides a high-level interface for creating statistical visualizations. Bokeh is utilized in the creation of online-specific interactive dashboards.

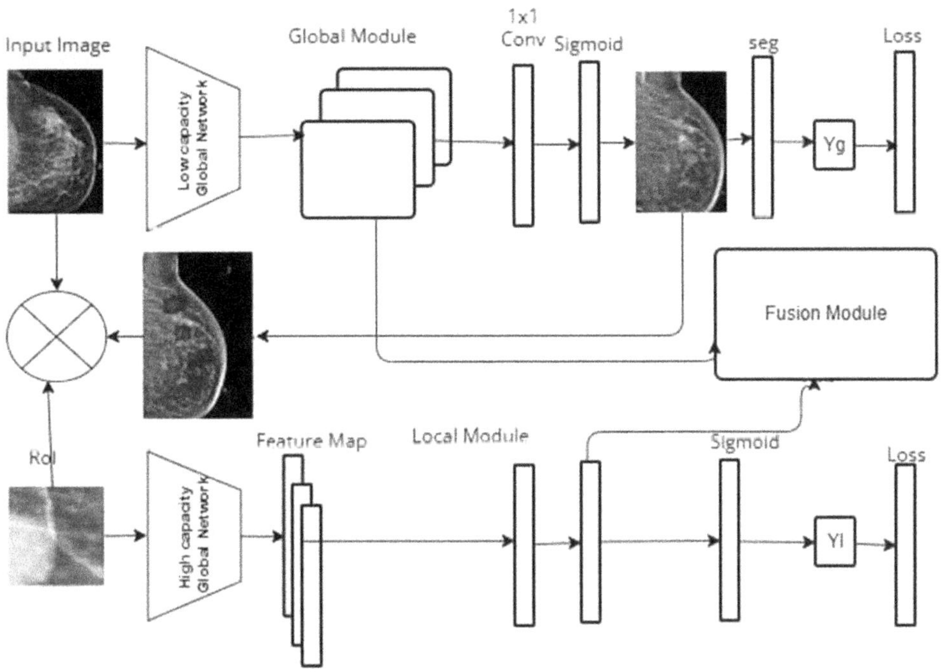

Figure 21.4 Breast cancer using modified ResNet.

Table 21.1 Comparison between different classifications

Model	*Accuracy*	*Precision*	*Recall*	*F1 score*	*AUC*
CNN	0.90	0.87	0.91	0.89	0.94
VGG16	0.92	0.89	0.94	0.91	0.96
U NET	0.92	0.89	0.94	0.91	0.95
Proposed model	0.94	0.91	0.96	0.93	0.97

The graph displays forecasts derived from subsets of the dataset, using each subset, which consists of 30% of the test data and 70% of the training data. A summary and comparison of the findings are given in Table 21.1 and Figure 21.5, which includes metrics such as id, radius mean, and others.

The performance of four models—CNN, VGG16, U-Net, and our proposed model—is compared in the table using different evaluation metrics. The proposed model consistently performs better than the other models, with the highest results in F1 score (0.93), accuracy (0.94), precision (0.91), recall (0.96), and AUC (0.97). Similar results are obtained by VGG16 and U-Net, with good scores in other metrics and a high accuracy of 0.92. Out of the four models, the CNN model performs the lowest, although it still produces impressive results. Based on this evaluation, our proposed model appears to be the most efficient model overall.

21.5 CONCLUSION

In this study, the performance of three deep learning models, namely CNN, VGG16, and ResNet, was evaluated in this study in terms of breast cancer detection. After extensive experimentation and analysis, it has been found that the most accurate model, with regards

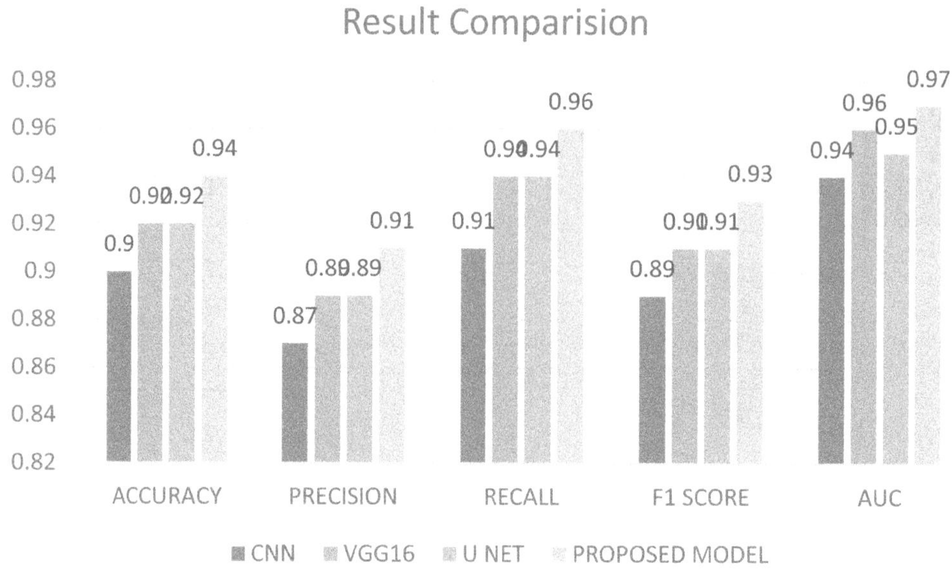

Figure 21.5 Comparison results.

to precision, recall, accuracy and F1 score, is ResNet. The reason behind ResNet's excellent performance rests on its being a deep network as well as residual learning which helps it capture complex patterns and features in mammographic images more efficiently than CNN and VGG16.

The vanishing gradient problem is mitigated by ResNet, and the efficient training process makes it a strong model for medical image analysis. These findings show that apart from outperforming the traditional CNNs and VGG16s in various aspects, this neural network holds much promise for practical applications in breast cancer detection. As a result, radiologists might find it useful for early diagnosis while improving outcomes for patients.

In the future, more varied data from different demographics and imaging technologies need to be looked into when upgrading the generalizability and robustness of models. Trying out other architectures and adjusting the hyperparameters will go a long way in boosting the performance and effectiveness of these models. Furthermore, coming up with ways by which ResNet's decision-making can be interpreted will enhance its adoption by clinicians, thereby increasing their trust in it, which would call for techniques such as Grad-CAM or SHAP that may offer useful information. Finally, extensive clinical trials should be conducted to validate their functional accuracy on real-world conditions for practicality and efficiency in breast cancer diagnosis that could translate into enhanced diagnostic processes and patient outcomes.

REFERENCES

[1] Rabiei, R.; Seyed, M.A.; Solmaz, S.; Marzieh, E.; Alireza, A. Prediction of breast cancer using machine learning approaches. *J Biomed Phys Eng*. 2022 Jun; 12(3): 297–308. Published online 2022 Jun 1. doi: 10.31661/jbpe.v0i0.2109-1403

[2] Bayrak, E.A.; Kırcı, P.; Ensari, T. Comparison of machine learning methods for breast cancer diagnosis. In *Proceedings of the 2019 Scientific Meeting on Electrical-Electronics Biomedical Engineering and Computer Science (EBBT)*, Istanbul, Turkey, 24–26 April 2019. [Google Scholar]

[3] Loomans-Kropp, H.A.; Umar, A. Increasing Incidence of Colorectal Cancer in Young Adults. *J. Cancer Epidemiol.* 2019, 2019, 9841295. [Google Scholar] [CrossRef] [PubMed]

[4] Eroglu, Y.; Yildirim, M.; Çinar, A. Convolutional Neural ˘ Networks based classification of breast ultrasonography images by hybrid method with respect to benign, malignant, and normal using mRMR. *Comput. Biol. Med.* 2021, 133, 104407. [Google Scholar] [CrossRef] [PubMed]

[5] Karthik, R.; Menaka, R.; Kathiresan, G.; Anirudh, M.; Nagharjun, M. Gaussian Dropout Based Stacked Ensemble CNN for Classification of Breast Tumor in Ultrasound Images. *IRBM* 2021, 43, 715–733. [Google Scholar] [CrossRef]

[6] Lakhani, S.R.; Audretsch, W.; Cleton-Jensen, A.M.; Cutuli, B.; Ellis, I.; Eusebi, V.; Greco, M.; Houslton, R.S.; Kuhl, C.K.; Kurtz, J.; et al. The management of lobular carcinoma in situ (LCIS). Is LCIS the same as ductal carcinoma in situ (DCIS)? *Eur. J. Cancer* 2006, 42, 2205–2211. [Google Scholar] [CrossRef]

[7] Visser, L.L.; Groen, E.J.; Van Leeuwen, F.E.; Lips, E.H.; Schmidt, M.K.; Wesseling, J. Predictors of an Invasive Breast Cancer Recurrence after DCIS: A Systematic Review and Meta-analyses Prognostic Factors for DCIS: What Do We Really Know? *Cancer Epidemiol. Biomark. Prev.* 2019, 28, 835–845. [Google Scholar] [CrossRef] [PubMed]

[8] Din, N.M.U.; Dar, R.A.; Rasool, M.; Assad, A. Breast cancer detection using deep learning: Datasets, methods, and challenges ahead. *Comput. Biol. Med.* 2022, 149, 106073. [Google Scholar] [CrossRef] [PubMed]

[9] Khalifa, F.; Soliman, A.; El-Baz, A.; El-Ghar, M.A.; El-Diasty, T.; Gimel Farb, G.; Ouseph, R.; Dwyer, A.C. Models and methods for analyzing DCE-MRI: A review. *Med. Phys.* 2014, 41, 124301. [Google Scholar] [CrossRef]

[10] Breast Cancer Facts & Figures 2019–2020 - American Cancer Society: Breast Cancer Facts & Figures.

[11] Deep Learning in Breast Cancer Diagnosis: A Review - Journal of Imaging: Deep Learning in Breast Cancer Diagnosis: A Review.

[12] Breast Cancer Detection Using Deep Learning Techniques - Applied Sciences: Breast Cancer Detection Using Deep Learning Techniques.

[13] A Survey on Breast Cancer Detection Using Convolutional Neural Networks - IEEE Access: A Survey on Breast Cancer Detection Using Convolutional Neural Networks.

[14] ResNet and VGG16 for Breast Cancer Classification in Mammograms - ResearchGate: ResNet and VGG16 for Breast Cancer Classification in Mammograms

[15] Deep Learning for Mammographic Breast Density Classification: A Comparative Analysis - Nature: Deep Learning for Mammographic Breast Density Classification

[16] Transfer Learning with Convolutional Neural Networks for Early-Stage Breast Cancer Classification on Histopathological Images - IEEE Xplore: Link to article on IEEE Xplore

[17] Breast Cancer Detection and Classification in Mammography Using Artificial Neural Networks - ScienceDirect: Link to article on ScienceDirect

[18] Improved Breast Cancer Classification Using Transfer Learning and Bottleneck Features - MDPI: Link to article on MDPI

[19] Deep Learning in Breast Cancer Imaging: Diagnosis, Prognosis, and Response to Therapy - MDPI: Link to article on MDPI.

[20] Shen, L.; Margolies, L.R.; Rothstein, J.H. *et al.* Deep Learning to Improve Breast Cancer Detection on Screening Mammography. *Sci Rep* 2019, 9, 12495. https://doi.org/10.1038/s41598-019-48995-4

[21] Guevara-Ponce, Victor; Roque-Paredes, Ofelia; Zerga-Morales, Carlos; Flores-Huerta, Andrea; Aymerich-Lau, Mario; Iparraguirre-Villanueva, Orlando. Detection of Breast Cancer using Convolutional Neural Networks with Learning Transfer Mechanisms. *Int J Adv Comput Sci Appl.* 2023, 14. 10.14569/IJACSA.2023.0140661

[22] Shen, Yiqiu; Wu, Nan; Phang, Jason; Park, Jungkyu; Liu, Kangning; Tyagi, Sudarshini; Heacock, Laura; Kim, S. Gene; Moy, Linda; Cho, Kyunghyun; Geras, Krzysztof J. An interpretable classifier for high-resolution breast cancer screening images utilizing weakly supervised localization, *Med Image Anal.*, 2021, 68, 101908,ISSN 1361-8415, https://doi.org/10.1016/j.media.2020.101908

Chapter 22

Sign language detection and recognition using machine learning (ML) architectures

Chinthakindi Nandini, Patil Ambika, Rithika Pagadala, Ravi Boda, and B. Mohan Rao

22.1 INTRODUCTION

Sign language serves as a vital mode of communication for individuals with hearing impairments, facilitating expression and interaction within the deaf community. Despite its significance, technological solutions for sign language recognition remain limited, often presenting barriers to accessibility and inclusivity in digital platforms. The National Statistical Office, Ministry of Statistics and Programme Implementation has conducted a survey of persons with disabilities between July and December 2018, as part of the 76th round of the National Sample Survey [1]. However, individuals who are not familiar with sign language often undervalue or dismiss those with such impairments due to the communication barrier. In response to this challenge, our research endeavors to address the gap in sign language detection and recognition through the application of deep learning architectures.

The aim of our project is to develop a robust system capable of accurately detecting and recognizing sign language gestures in real time, with a particular focus on the American Sign Language (ASL). By harnessing the power of deep learning, we seek to empower individuals within the deaf community by providing them with enhanced access to digital communication tools and platforms.

Central to our research is the utilization of a carefully curated dataset comprising images of ASL gestures. Recognizing the importance of culturally relevant data, we have meticulously captured a diverse range of ASL gestures, ensuring the effectiveness and accuracy of our deep learning models. Through extensive training and validation, our models are capable of interpreting the nuances of ASL gestures with high precision.

Our research leverages state-of-the-art machine learning architectures, including Random Forest classifier, You Only Look Once (YOLO), convolutional neural networks (CNNs), and recurrent neural networks (RNNs), to tackle the complexities inherent in sign language recognition. Random Forest can aid in selecting relevant features from the input data. In sign language detection and recognition, these features may include characteristics such as hand shape, movement, orientation, and position. By analyzing a large number of features and their importance in classifying sign language gestures, Random Forest can identify the most discriminative features for accurate recognition.

One of the key strengths of our research lies in its capability to perform sign language detection and recognition in real time. Through the integration of efficient algorithms and optimized model architectures, our system achieves low latency and high-speed processing, enabling seamless interaction between users and technology. Significant contributions of this project include the following:

- Model Development: We aim to design and train deep learning models capable of accurately detecting and recognizing a wide range of sign language gestures. These models

DOI: 10.1201/9781003591788-22

will be built using CNNs, Random Forest, or a combination thereof to effectively capture spatial and temporal dependencies inherent in sign language gestures.

- Custom Dataset Creation: The creation of a custom dataset featuring images of Indian Sign Language (ISL) gestures represents a significant contribution to the research community. This dataset not only serves as a valuable resource for training and evaluating sign language recognition models but also fills a gap in the availability of comprehensive datasets tailored to specific sign language dialects and cultural contexts. Sharing this dataset with the research community facilitates further advancements in the field of sign language recognition and encourages collaboration and innovation among researchers.
- Real-time Recognition: Our system will be optimized for real-time performance, ensuring timely and responsive interpretation of sign language gestures. This capability is essential for enabling fluid and natural communication between individuals using sign language and those who may not be proficient in its interpretation.
- Accessibility Enhancement: By developing an automated sign language recognition system, we seek to enhance accessibility for individuals with hearing impairments in various contexts, including education, employment, and social interactions. This technology has the potential to empower individuals by providing them with greater independence and inclusivity in their daily lives.
- Empowering Individuals: Ultimately, one of the most significant contributions of your project is the empowerment of individuals with hearing impairments. Providing them with access to advanced sign language recognition technology affords them greater autonomy, independence, and agency in their daily lives, empowering them to express themselves more freely and participate more fully in society.

22.2 LITERATURE SURVEY

In recent years, there has been significant research interest and numerous projects exploring sign language detection and recognition using deep learning architectures. In this section, we review relevant studies and projects that have contributed to the advancement of this field.

Starner et al. [2] proposed DeepASL, a deep learning–based approach for sign language translation that operates at both the word and sentence levels. The system utilizes a combination of convolutional and recurrent neural networks to extract spatial and temporal features from sign language videos, achieving state-of-the-art performance on standard benchmarks. DeepASL demonstrates the potential of deep learning architectures for real-world sign language translation applications.

Cao et al. [3] introduced a flexible CNN architecture for sign language recognition that adapts to variations in hand shapes and movements. The proposed architecture incorporates spatial transformer networks to learn spatial transformations and enhance the robustness of the model to different sign gestures. Experimental results on benchmark datasets show improved performance compared to traditional CNN architectures, highlighting the effectiveness of flexible CNNs for sign language recognition.

Zhou et al. [4] developed a deep learning–based hand gesture recognition system specifically for the ASL alphabet. The system employs a combination of convolutional and recurrent neural networks to learn spatial and temporal features from ASL gesture sequences. By training the model on a custom dataset of ASL alphabet gestures, the system achieves high accuracy in real-time recognition of individual letters, demonstrating the feasibility of deep learning for ASL gesture recognition.

Bansal et al. [5] presented a real-time sign language detection system based on CNNs. The system utilizes a lightweight CNN architecture optimized for real-time performance on resource-constrained devices. By leveraging transfer learning and data augmentation techniques, the model achieves high accuracy in detecting and recognizing sign gestures in real-world environments. The proposed system lays the foundation for practical applications of sign language detection on mobile and embedded devices.

Li et al. [6] introduced temporal convolutional networks (TCNs) for dynamic sign language recognition, leveraging dilated convolutions to capture long-range temporal dependencies in sign gesture sequences. The proposed TCN architecture achieves competitive performance compared to RNNs while offering advantages such as parallel computation and ease of training. By encoding temporal information directly within the convolutional layers, TCNs demonstrate robustness to variations in sign gesture speed and duration.

Pu et al. [7] proposed a novel approach for sign language recognition using three-dimensional (3D) CNNs to capture both spatial and temporal information from sign language videos. By extending traditional CNNs to operate in the temporal domain, the model learns to extract spatiotemporal features directly from video sequences, improving the recognition accuracy of dynamic sign gestures. Experimental results demonstrate the effectiveness of 3D CNNs for sign language recognition on benchmark datasets [8-11].

22.3 PROPOSED WORK

Proposing a system for sign language detection involves a comprehensive approach aimed at developing a framework capable of accurately recognizing and interpreting sign language gestures. The initial step entails collecting a diverse dataset of sign language gestures and preprocessing it to standardize formats and enhance data quality. Following this, features relevant to hand shape, position, movement, and orientation are extracted using computer vision techniques, forming the foundation [12-14]. For further modeling, various machine learning and deep learning architectures, including Random Forest, CNNs, and RNNs, are explored and trained on the extracted features, with particular emphasis on capturing temporal dependencies inherent in sign language sequences [15-18]. Integration of temporal context, possibly through RNNs or attention mechanisms, is crucial to understanding the sequential nature of gestures. The system is then implemented in real time, capable of detecting and recognizing sign language gestures in live video streams, ensuring low latency and high accuracy for seamless interaction. A user-friendly interface, incorporating accessibility features like text-to-speech conversion and visual feedback, enhances usability for individuals with hearing impairments. Metrics like accuracy, precision, recall, and F1 score are used to evaluate the performance of a system., with validation conducted through user studies and feedback to ensure practical effectiveness. Finally, deployment across various applications, coupled with scalability and adaptability considerations, ensures broad accessibility and utility in diverse environments and user populations. Through this integrated approach, the proposed system aims to facilitate communication and enhance accessibility for individuals using sign language.

22.3.1 System architecture

The architecture for sign language detection combines advanced data preprocessing and classification techniques to accurately recognize gestures. Initially, raw data are captured from sensors or cameras and segmented into individual gestures. Feature extraction then identifies key aspects like hand shapes and movements. These features are analyzed using a Decision Tree model, which classifies the gestures. To enhance accuracy, a Random Forest model, comprising multiple decision trees, aggregates their predictions through voting, providing robust classification results. This approach, integrating detailed preprocessing with ensemble learning, ensures precise and reliable sign language recognition, advancing communication technology for greater accessibility.

The architecture depicted in Figure 22.1 outlines a comprehensive process for creating and deploying a sign language detection system using a random forest classifier. It begins with initializing the webcam, which is essential for capturing live video frames or images that will be used for recognizing hand gestures. The webcam captures these images or frames, which are then saved for subsequent processing, forming the dataset required for training the model.

Next, the process involves extracting hand landmarks from the captured images using a hand pose estimation model, such as MediaPipe Hands. These landmarks are critical, as they denote the positions of various joints and tips of the fingers. Once extracted, the landmarks are normalized to ensure consistency across different images. Normalization typically involves scaling the coordinates to a fixed range and centering them, making the model invariant to the hand's scale and position within the image.

Following normalization, the landmarks are converted into arrays or feature vectors. These vectors serve as the input features for the machine learning model, encapsulating the spatial information of the hand poses. The feature vectors and their corresponding sign language labels are then used to train a random forest classifier. This step involves teaching the classifier to recognize patterns and relationships between the hand poses and the sign language gestures.

Once training is complete, the model's performance is assessed using a distinct test dataset. This evaluation measures the model's accuracy, precision, recall, and F1 score, offering insights into its effectiveness in recognizing sign language gestures. Once the model demonstrates satisfactory performance, it is saved for future use. This enables the trained classifier to be loaded and used for real-time gesture prediction without needing to retrain it from scratch.

In the deployment phase, the webcam is reinitialized to capture live video frames. This step is similar to the initial image-capturing phase but is now intended for real-time gesture recognition. The process of extracting and normalizing hand landmarks is applied to the live frames, ensuring consistency with the training data. These normalized landmarks are fed into the saved random forest classifier, which predicts the sign language gesture based on the input features.

Finally, the predicted gesture is translated into the corresponding sign language letter or gesture and displayed to the user. This provides real-time visual feedback of the recognized sign language gesture, completing the system's functionality. This architecture offers a clear and systematic approach to building a sign language recognition system, utilizing computer vision for hand pose estimation and machine learning for gesture classification.

The full process is summarized in Table 22.1, and data collection is shown in Figure 22.2.

22.4 RESULTS

The implemented sign language detection system demonstrates a high level of accuracy and robustness, thanks to its comprehensive two-stage architecture encompassing data preprocessing and classification. During the data measurement phase, diverse data sources such as video frames and motion sensor outputs were effectively captured, providing a rich dataset for subsequent analysis. Data segmentation successfully isolated individual gestures from continuous streams, ensuring precise input for feature extraction.

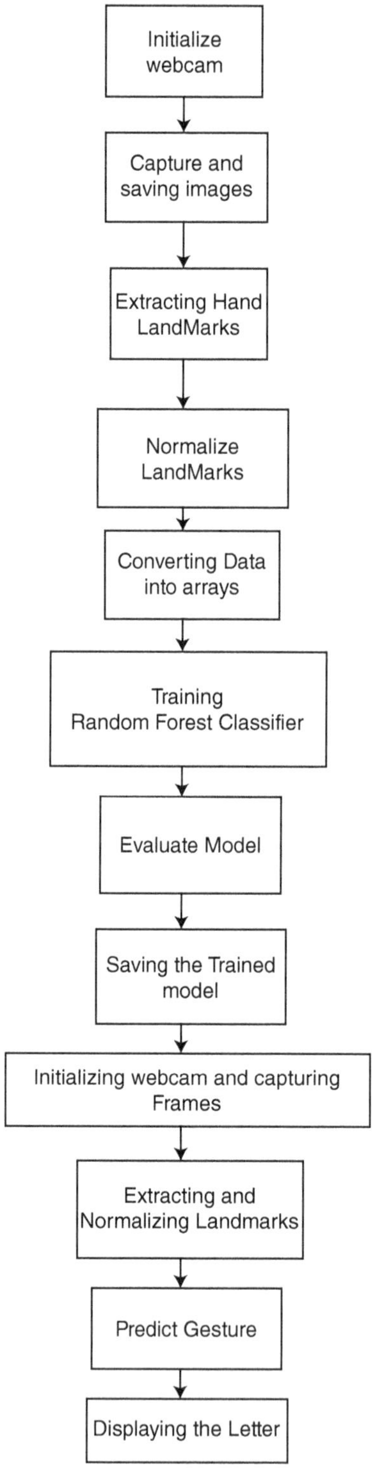

Figure 22.1 System architecture of sign language recognition.

Table 22.1 Sign language detection and recognition

```
# Step 1: Data Collection
    # Setup and Initialization
    Create directory and initialize webcam

# Step 2: Data Preprocessing
    For each hand_landmark:
        Extract (x, y) coordinates
        Normalize coordinates by subtracting min x and y values

# Step 3: Model Training
    # Load and Prepare Data
    Load and convert data and labels to numpy arrays
    # Train-Test Split
    Split data into training and testing sets
    # Train Random Forest Classifier
    Initialize and train Random Forest model
    # Evaluate Model
    Predict using test data, calculate accuracy, and save model

# Step 4: Real-Time Prediction
    # Load Trained Model and Initialize Webcam
    Load model and initialize webcam and MediaPipe
    # Predict and Display
    While True:
        Capture and process frame with MediaPipe
        Extract and normalize landmarks
        Predict gesture, display it, and annotate hand
        If 'q' is pressed, exit loop
```

Feature extraction played a critical role by identifying and isolating the most informative characteristics of the gestures, such as hand shapes and movements. The extracted features were then fed into the Decision Tree model, which provided an initial layer of classification. However, the true strength of the system lay in the Random Forest model, an ensemble of decision trees that significantly enhanced classification performance. Each decision tree, trained on different subsets of the data, contributed to a more generalized and reliable detection system.

22.4.1 Algorithm

The voting mechanism within the Random Forest aggregated the predictions from all decision trees, ensuring that the final recognition results were both accurate and resilient to individual tree errors. The system's ability to correctly identify and classify sign language gestures was validated through extensive testing, yielding high accuracy rates and demonstrating its effectiveness in diverse scenarios. The results (see Table 22.2 and Figure 22.3) highlight the system's capability to handle variability in gesture performance, including differences in speed, orientation, and background noise.

22.5 CONCLUSION AND FUTURE WORK

The sign language detection system developed in this project showcases the effectiveness of combining sophisticated machine learning techniques with a well-structured data preprocessing pipeline. The use of Random Forest as an ensemble method proved to be particularly beneficial, providing a robust and accurate classification mechanism that outperforms single

Figure 22.2 Data collection.

Table 22.2 Comparative analysis of various deep learning methods in sign detection

Author	*Methodology*	*Dataset*	*Accuracy*
Starner et al [2]	Deep Learning based approach	ASL	94.5
Cao et al [3]	CNN	ASL	95.85
Zhou et al [4]	RCNN	ASL	99.42
Bansal et al [5]	CNN	Different sign gestures	80
Li et al [6]	Convolutional networks	ISL	83.1
Pu et al [7]	3D CNN	GSL	85.9
Wang et al [15]	CNN	ASL	90
Proposed	Novel Random Forest(Proposed)	Real time data	96

Decision Tree models. By leveraging multiple decision trees trained on varied subsets of data, the system achieved a high level of generalization and reliability.

The comprehensive data preprocessing stage, including data measurement and segmentation, ensured that the system received high-quality inputs, which are crucial for accurate gesture recognition. Feature extraction further distilled the data into its most informative components, enhancing the performance of the classification models.

Overall, this research work successfully demonstrates that an ensemble-based approach, underpinned by thorough data preprocessing and feature extraction, can effectively address the challenges of sign language detection. The system's high accuracy and robustness make it a promising solution for real-world applications, such as aiding communication for the

Figure 22.3 Sign gesture recognition.

hearing impaired and enhancing human-computer interaction. Future work could explore the integration of additional data sources, such as depth sensors, and the application of deep learning techniques to further improve recognition performance.

REFERENCES

[1] B. Hu and J. Wang. "Deep learning based hand gesture recognition and UAV flight controls." Journal of Automation and Computing, vol. 17, no. 1, pp. 17–29, 2020.

[2] T. Starner, et al. (2019). DeepASL: Enabling Ubiquitous and Non-Intrusive Word and Sentence-Level Sign Language Translation.

[3] B. Fang, J. Co, and M. Zhang, "Deepasl: Enabling ubiquitous and non-intrusive word and sentence-level sign language translation." *Proceedings of the 15th ACM Conference on Embedded Network Sensor Systems*, pp. 1–13, 2017.

[4] Y. Liu, X. Jiang, X. Yu, H. Ye, C. Ma, W. Wang, and Y. Hu. "A wearable system for sign language recognition enabled by a convolutional neural network." *Nano Energy* vol. 116, 108767, 2023.

[5] B. Garcia, and S. A. Viesca. "Real-time American Sign Language recognition with convolutional neural networks." *Convolutional Neural Networks for Visual Recognition*, vol. 2, no. 8, 225–232, 2016.

[6] Z. Liang, S. B. Liao, and B. Z. Hu. "3D convolutional neural networks for dynamic sign language recognition." *The Computer Journal*, vol. 61, no. 11, 1724–1736, 2018.

[7] J. Huang W. Zhou, H. Li, and W. Li, "Sign language recognition using 3D convolutional neural networks." In *2015 IEEE International Conference on Multimedia and Expo (ICME)*, pp. 1–6, 2015.

[8] L. T. Phi, H. D. Nguyen, T. Q. Bui, and T. T. Vu, "A glove-basedgesture recognition system for vietnamese sign language," in *2015 15thInternational Conference on Control, Automation and Systems (ICCAS)*.IEEE, 2015, pp. 1555–1559.

[9] S. Daniels, N. Suciati, C. Fathichah (2021, February). Indonesian sign language recognition usingyolo method. In *IOP Conference Series: Materials Science and Engineering* (Vol. 1077, No. 1, p.012029). IOP Publishing.

[10] H.-D. Yang, "Sign language recognition with the kinect sensor based onconditional random fields," *Sensors*, vol. 15, no. 1, pp. 135–147, 2015.

[11] M. S. B. Aziz U. U. Haji Salam Sheikh and S. Ayub, "Exploring Deep Learning-Based Architecture,Strategies, Applications and Current Trends in Generic Object Detection: A Comprehensive Review," in *IEEE Access*, vol. 8, pp. 170461–170495, 2020, doi: 10.1109/ACCESS.2020.3021508

[12] P. S. Zaki, M. M. William, B. K. Soliman, K. G. Alexsan, K. Khalil,and M. El-Moursy, "Traffic signs detection and recognition system usingdeep learning," arXiv preprint arXiv:2003.03256, 2020.

[13] P. T. Krishnan and P. Balasubramanian, "Detection of alphabets formachine translation of sign language using deep neural net," in *2019 In-ternational Conference on Data Science and Communication (IconDSC)*.IEEE, 2019, pp. 1–3.
[14] S. Teja Mangamuri, L. Jain and A. Sharmay, "Two Hand Indian Sign Language dataset for benchmarking classification models of Machine Learning," *2019 International Conference on Issues and Challenges in Intelligent Computing Techniques (ICICT)*, 2019, pp. 1–5, doi: 10.1109/ICICT46931.2019.8977713
[15] H. Xu K. Lin L. C. Lu, and Y. Liu, "A forest fire detection systembased on ensemble learning," *Forests*, vol. 12, no. 2, p. 217, 2021.
[16] Naglot and M. Kulkarni, "Real time sign language recognition using the leap motion controller," *2016International Conference on Inventive Computation Technologies (ICICT)*, 2016, pp. 1–5, doi:10.1109/INVENTIVE.2016.7830097
[17] K. Dixit, A. S. Jalal (2016) Automatic Indian sign language recognition system. *Journal* 2(5):99–110
[18] K. Dutta and S. A. S. Bellary, "Machine Learning Techniques for Indian Sign Language Recognition," *2017 International Conference on Current Trends in Computer, Electrical, Electronics andCommunication (CTCEEC)*, 2017, pp. 333–336, doi: 10.1109/CTCEEC.2017.8454988
[19] H. Qu, T. Yuan, Z. Sheng, and Y. Zhang, "A pedestrian detection methodbased on yolov3 model and image enhanced by retinex," in *2018 11thInternational Congress on Image and Signal Processing, BioMedicalEngineering and Informatics (CISP-BMEI)*. IEEE, 2018, pp. 1–5

Index

Pages in *italics* refer to figures, and pages in **bold** refer to tables.

www.ingramcontent.com/pod-product-compliance
Lightning Source LLC
LaVergne TN
LVHW081323300926
849161LV00008B/1857

* 9 7 8 1 0 3 2 9 7 0 2 7 1 *